There would be little tourism, if any at all, without collective subjective experiences of feelings and affective atmospheres and intensities. Taking the constitutive nature of embodied emotion and affect in tourism as a starting point, this thought-provoking edited volume disentangles in great detail, and through different analytical lenses, what affects and emotions actually *do* in tourism, tourism practice, and also tourism studies. In formulating their answers to this key question, the various contributors propose novel theoretical ideas and epistemologies as well as innovative methodologies. As such, this illuminating book takes our holistic understanding of the complexities of tourism, always relational and always political, to the next level.

Noel B. Salazar, Cultural Mobilities Research (CuMoRe), KU Leuven, Belgium

A new thematic revolution beckons tourism analysis in critical interrogations of the ways embodied sensations, feelings and affects become interlaced in the tourist experience. Bringing centre-stage questions of mobility and embodiment, Buda and Germann Molz produce an intellectual collective that masterfully deliberates on entanglements of affect with space/place, asserting the immanence of atmospheres in the world. Individual contributors to this collective volume explore the importance of such entanglements to situate subjective and material presence, agency, power and precognition in tourism as an activity and an industry. This book is as delightful to read as it is to 'travel with' intellectually.

Rodanthi Tzanelli, University of Leeds, UK

This is an important book which opens up the rich complexities of thinking with and through affect and emotion in tourism. Going beyond accounts of what affect and emotion are, this is a must-read for anybody interested in what affect and emotion do. Individually and collectively, the chapters make a thought-provoking case for why matters of affect and emotion deserve to be at the top of the tourism research agenda.

Professor Hazel Tucker, University of Otago, New Zealand

T0291247

Affect and Emotion in Tourism

Bringing affect and emotion to the forefront of tourism studies, this book presents a new generation of scholars who consolidate emerging affective approaches and establish a route for scholarship that examines the roles of emotion and affect in tourism.

Attuning to affect and emotion, this book steers the affective turn to encompass touring bodies and tourism places. Engaging the concept of affect as a constitutive element of social life often leaves academics grasping for terminology to describe something that is, by its very nature, beyond words. For this reason, as evident in the four interconnected sections of this volume, studying affect poses a significant and fruitful challenge to the status-quo of social scientific method and analysis. From African-American emotional labour while travelling, to visiting Banksy's Dismaland park, to affective heritagescapes, self-love, and travelling mittens, and across socio-spatial theories of emotions, decolonial feminist theory, and atmospheric politics, this book demonstrates the epistemic and empirical richness of affective tourism.

Along with the contributors to this volume, the editors make a case for thinking about emotions and affects through collective and individual practices as interrelated shaping tourism encounters *in* and *with* places. That is, to break it down as *doing* and as *shared* between bodies and places through the *doing*. The chapters in this book were originally published as a special issue of *Tourism Geographies*.

Dorina-Maria Buda conducts interdisciplinary research focusing on the interconnections between tourist spaces, people and emotions in times and places of socio-political conflicts. She conducts ethnographic work in such places of on-going turmoil like Jordan, Israel, and Palestine. She is the author of *Affective Tourism: Dark Routes in Conflict*.

Jennie Germann Molz teaches courses on emotion, social theory, travel and tourism, and family life at the College of the Holy Cross. She is the author of *The World is Our Classroom: Extreme Parenting and the Rise of Worldschooling* and *Travel Connections: Tourism, Technology and Togetherness in a Mobile World*.

Affect and Emotion in Tourism

Edited by
Dorina-Maria Buda and Jennie Germann Molz

Routledge
Taylor & Francis Group

LONDON AND NEW YORK

First published 2023
by Routledge
4 Park Square, Milton Park, Abingdon, Oxon, OX14 4RN

and by Routledge
605 Third Avenue, New York, NY 10158

Routledge is an imprint of the Taylor & Francis Group, an informa business

Foreword © 2023 Mike Robinson
Chapters 1–3, 5, 8–13 © 2023 Taylor & Francis
Conclusion © 2023 Matilde Córdoba Azcárate
Introduction © 2021 Jennie Germann Molz and Dorina-Maria Buda. Originally published as Open Access.
Chapter 4 © 2019 Katherine Burlingame. Originally published as Open Access.
Chapter 6 © 2020 Maria Sofia Pimentel Biscaia and Lénia Marques. Originally published as Open Access.
Chapter 7 © 2020 Siri Driessen. Originally published as Open Access.
Chapter 14 © 2020 Outi Kugapi and Emily Höckert. Originally published as Open Access.

British Library Cataloguing in Publication Data
A catalogue record for this book is available from the British Library

ISBN13: 978-1-032-27313-6 (hbk)
ISBN13: 978-1-032-27314-3 (pbk)
ISBN13: 978-1-003-29224-1 (ebk)

DOI: 10.4324/9781003292241

Typeset in Myriad Pro
by codeMantra

Publisher's Note
The publisher accepts responsibility for any inconsistencies that may have arisen during the conversion of this book from journal articles to book chapters, namely the inclusion of journal terminology.

Disclaimer
Every effort has been made to contact copyright holders for their permission to reprint material in this book. The publishers would be grateful to hear from any copyright holder who is not here acknowledged and will undertake to rectify any errors or omissions in future editions of this book.

Contents

     Siri Driessen

8   Traveler sensoryscape experiences and the formation of destination identity   166
     Junghye Angela Kah, Hye Jin Shin and Seong-Hoon Lee

PART III
Symbolic sentiments   187

9   Feeling opulent: Adding an affective dimension to symbolic
     consumption of themes   189
     Namita Roy and Ulrike Gretzel

10   Tourists' savoring of positive emotions and place attachment formation:
     A conceptual paper   212
     Nanxi Yan and Elizabeth A. Halpenny

11   Self-love emotion as a novel type of love for tourism destinations   233
     Dimitra Margieta Lykoudi, Georgia Zouni and Markos Marios Tsogas

PART IV
Affective epistemologies   255

12   The 'MeBox' method and the emotional effects of chronic illness on travel   257
     Uditha Ramanayake, Cheryl Cockburn-Wootten and Alison J. McIntosh

13   Attuning to the affective in literary tourism: Emotional states in
     Aberystwyth, Mon Amour.   280
     Jon Anderson and Kieron Smith

14   Affective entanglements with travelling mittens   302
     Outi Kugapi and Emily Höckert

     Conclusion: Affective railway journeys in an age of extremes   320
     Matilde Córdoba Azcárate

     Index   325

Citation information

The chapters in this book were originally published in the journal *Tourism Geographies*, volume 24, issue 2–3 (2022). When citing this material, please use the original page numbering for each article, as follows:

For any permission-related enquiries please visit:
http://www.tandfonline.com/page/help/permissions

Notes on Contributors

Derek H. Alderman is Professor of Geography at the University of Tennessee, Knoxville, USA. He is Founder and Co-Coordinator of the RESET (Race, Ethnicity, and Social Equity in Tourism) Initiative. His interests are in the racial politics of geographic mobility and tourism in the context of the African-American freedom struggle.

Jon Anderson is Professor of Human Geography at the School of Geography and Planning at Cardiff University, UK. His research interests focus on the relations between culture, place, and identity, particularly the geographies, politics, and practices that emerge from these. His key publications include *Understanding Cultural Geography: Places and Traces* (2010, 2015 Second Edition), *Water Worlds: Human Geographies of the Ocean* (edited with Peters, K, 2014), and *Page and Place: Ongoing Compositions of Plot* (2014).

Matilde Córdoba Azcárate is Associate Professor in the Communication Department at the University of California, San Diego, USA. Her research examines tourism, capitalism, and crisis. Among other publications, she is the author of *Stuck with Tourism: Space, Power and Labor in Contemporary Yucatán* (2020) and co-editor of *Tourism Geopolitics: Assemblages of Infrastructure, Affect, and Imagination* (2021).

Ethan Bottone is Doctoral Candidate in the Department of Geography at the University of Tennessee, Knoxville, USA, where he studies intersections of race, disabilities, inequality, and critical tourism.

Dorina-Maria Buda conducts interdisciplinary research focusing on the interconnections between tourist spaces, people, and emotions in times and places of socio-political conflicts. She conducts ethnographic work in such places of on-going turmoil like Jordan, Israel, and Palestine. She is the author of *Affective Tourism: Dark Routes in Conflict*.

Katherine Burlingame is Postdoctoral Fellow at the Department of Archaeology, Conservation and History at the University of Oslo, Norway.

Cheryl Cockburn-Wootten is Senior Lecturer at the University of Waikato, Hamilton, New Zealand. Her work adopts an interdisciplinary approach but mainly draws on organizational communication theories to apply to tourism, hospitality, and contexts involving social issues. She is also, along with Professor Alison McIntosh, Co-Founder and Co-Facilitator of the Network for Community Hospitality, which bridges teaching and research expertise with external stakeholders and organizations to make a difference to issues facing New Zealand society.

Isis Arlene Díaz-Carrión is Associate Professor of Tourism Geography and Sustainable Development in the Facultad de Turismo y Mercadotecnia at the Universidad Autonoma de Baja California, Mexicali, Mexico. She is interested in tourism, sustainability, and gender.

Siri Driessen is PhD Candidate at the Erasmus School of History, Culture and Communication at Erasmus University Rotterdam, The Netherlands.

Phoebe Everingham is multidisciplinary/interdisciplinary ECR working across several departments, including Human Geography, Sociology/Anthropology, Education, and Business at the University of Newcastle, Australia.

Ulrike Gretzel is Senior Fellow at the Centre of Public Relations at the University of Southern California, Los Angeles, USA, and Director of Research at Netnografica. Her research focuses on persuasion in human-technology interactions, smart technologies and intelligent systems, tourism experiences, online and social media marketing, adoption, and use of technologies, as well as non-adoption and digital detox.

Elizabeth A. Halpenny, PhD, is Associate Professor at the Faculty of Kinesiology, Sport, and Recreation at the University of Alberta, Edmonton, Canada. She teaches and conducts research in the areas of tourism, marketing, environmental psychology, and protected area management. Elizabeth's research focuses on individual's interactions with nature environments, tourism experience, and environmental stewardship.

Emily Höckert is Post-Doctoral Fellow in Tourism Studies at the University of Lapland, Multidimensional Tourism institute, Rovaniemi, Finland. She is a member of a project on culturally sensitive tourism in the Arctic (ARCTISEN, NPA) and research group Intra-Living in the Anthropocene (ILA). Emily is the author of *Negotiating Hospitality* (2018) and co-author of *Disruptive Tourism and Its Untidy Guests* (2014).

Junghye Angela Kah is in Tourism Management at Kyonggi University, Suwon, Korea. Her research interest includes touristic information search using information technology and tourists' behaviors.

Catherine Kelly is Senior Lecturer in Heritage and Tourism Management at the University of Greenwich, UK. She teaches and researches in a range of fields including tourism, well-being, sustainability, and heritage studies. In addition, she is Pactitioner in coastal and education sector well-being, based in Brighton, South-East England.

Outi Kugapi is Doctoral Candidate in Tourism Research at the University of Lapland, Multidimensional Tourism institute, Rovaniemi, Finland. She knits and purls together her PhD, warm mittens, and two projects concerning cultural sensitivity (ARCTISEN, NPA) and handicraft tourism (Handmade in Lapland, ESF). She has co-authored chapters on Indigenous tourism in *Tourism and ethnodevelopment, Inclusion, Empowerment and Self-Determination* (2018) and *Key Concepts in Tourism/Matkailututkimuksen avaink€asitteet* (LUP, 2017).

Seong-Hoon Lee is in Economic Policy at Korea University, Seoul, South Korea. His research includes analysis of information and knowledge in tourism and economics.

Dimitra Margieta Lykoudi is PhD Candidate in Tourism Marketing at the University of Piraeus, Greece. Her research interests pertain to Services & Tourism Marketing, Emotions in Tourism, Consumer Behavior, and Business Research Methods.

Lénia Marques is Assistant Professor of Cultural Organizations and Management at the Erasmus University Rotterdam, The Netherlands. She is a member of the Board of Directors of the World Leisure Organization and the author of several publications in comparative literature, event studies, creative tourism, and creative industries.

Alison J. McIntosh is Professor of Tourism and Hospitality at Auckland University of Technology, New Zealand. As a critical scholar, her main research interests are in social justice, inclusion, and advocacy through tourism and hospitality; accessible tourism, community hospitality, and volunteering; and reflexivity, creative and participative research approaches, and community engagement methods. She has published widely in leading international journals and is Founding Co-Editor of the interdisciplinary journal *Hospitality & Society* and the open access journal *Hospitality Insights*.

Jennie Germann Molz teaches courses on emotion, social theory, travel and tourism, and family life at the College of the Holy Cross, USA. She is the author of *The World is Our Classroom: Extreme Parenting and the Rise of Worldschooling* and *Travel Connections: Tourism, Technology and Togetherness in a Mobile World*.

Sara C. Motta is a mother, critical theorist, poet, and popular educator and is A/Prof in Politics and Political Economy at the Discipline of Politics at the University of Newcastle, Australia.

Maria Sofia Pimentel Biscaia is Researcher at Centre for Languages and Cultures at the University of Aveiro, Portugal. With a PhD on Postcolonialism, she has recently been working on dark tourism and affects. She currently teaches at the Universities of Beira Interior and Trás-os-Montes e Alto Douro, Portugal.

Uditha Ramanayake is Doctoral Candidate at the University of Waikato, Hamilton, New Zealand. His current research focuses on senior tourism.

Mike Robinson is Professor of Cultural Heritage at Nottingham Trent University, UK. He has worked on heritage- and tourism-related projects in over 40 countries and has set new agendas through his publications, creative partnerships, his supervision of more than 30 PhDs, and his design and organization of 35 international academic and practitioner conferences.

Namita Roy is Researcher at the School of Management, Operations and Marketing at the University of Wollongong, Australia. She is Interdisciplinary Researcher and studies tourism experiences using post-humanist ontologies. Her interests include studying the role of emotions, space, and culture on consumption.

Hye Jin Shin is in the Graduate program at Kyonggi University, Suwon, Korea. Her research interests Include psychology and behavior of tourists including destination branding and marketing, sensory marketing, destination identity, and tourist behavior.

Kieron Smith is Researcher working in the field of Welsh Writing in English. He has written on a range of topics connected with this field, including literary geography, media and television, and cultural policy. He is currently Research Associate at Cardiff University, UK.

Markos Marios Tsogas is Associate Professor of International Marketing at the University of Piraeus, Greece. His research interests are evolving around international market selection and segmentation, international marketing research, tourism marketing, and value creation.

Paola Vizcaino is Lecturer in the Faculty of Management at Bournemouth University, UK. Her research focuses on the gender dimensions of tourism, hospitality, and events, with a particular interest in the Latin American context.

Kortney Williams is Doctoral Candidate in the Department of Anthropology at Binghamton University, USA. Previously, while attending the University of Tennessee, Knoxville, USA, she held an internship at the Beck Cultural Exchange Center, where she led the collection of oral histories related to African-American automobile travel.

Nanxi Yan is PhD Student at the Faculty of Kinesiology, Sport, and Recreation at the University of Alberta, Edmonton, Canada. She studies tourism and positive psychology. Specifically, she is interested in how to make people obtain more health and wellness benefits from their tourism experiences.

Georgia Zouni is Lecturer in Tourism Marketing at the University of Piraeus, Greece. Her research interests focus on destination marketing, destination experience, tourism satisfaction, and digital marketing.

Foreword

In some recent work I have been conducting on tourism to the now almost dried-up Aral Sea in Uzbekistan, I have been closely following the on-line documented 'feelings' of international tourists on encountering this human-made ecological disaster, accentuated by climate change. These post-trip recordings of the experiences, predominantly, though not exclusively, of 'western', young, travellers are infused with attempts to convey their emotions on seeing – or rather not seeing – the former Sea that is likely never to return and whose legacy is a recently created desert and a series of stranded communities. While post-event written language is far from being a perfect way of attempting to assess emotional states, it is nevertheless evident that the tourists visiting this desolate place were moved to express several of what Izard (2007) has termed the 'discrete emotions', that is, the core emotional states that appear to transcend cultural differences. In reading through the various tourist accounts I could discern expressions of interest, surprise, sadness, anger and shame. The imprecision of these TripAdvisor entries and travelblog accounts did not detract from the fact that the experience of place had apparently induced the tourists to communicate their emotions.

Notwithstanding some prickly methodological matters, three interwoven reflections emerge from my initial observations which serve to problematise the ways in which we now focus upon the emotions in tourism studies. First, we all too readily assume that there is some causal relationship at work, so that seeing that there is no Aral Sea affects us and induces an emotion such as sadness. This implies that it is the actual 'being there' that matters; the place itself acting akin to Bourdieu's 'punctum' of the photograph. The drama of the desert that now exists in place of the Sea is certainly powerful, but is it enough to pull so strongly on the emotions? It is the case that emotions arise in *relation to* things, objects, places and events but when and how do we form such relationships? As I have argued elsewhere (Robinson, 2005), in the age of the seasoned traveller, we seldom experience our destinations as epistemic virgins. Rather, we are "trans-textured tourists", already laden with the news reports, documentaries, fictional texts, popular cultural circulations and worldly discourse so that we already know the Aral Sea has all but disappeared and that climate change is an existential threat. The visit may confirm or heighten our awareness, but the emotional response may have been constructed well before, prompted by an encounter far removed from the destination. Indeed, if we can 'self-regulate' our emotions (Gross, 2014), then we visit such a place as the Aral Sea, specifically because it will accentuate and validate a particular emotional state we have already encountered. This accords with the notion that as tourists we are not only seeking experiences but also trying to access the emotions that we have learned usually accompany these experiences.

Second, knowing the emotions that a site, a destination, or an event invokes tells us little about the 'after-life' of the tourist and degree of agency that he or she may have. It would be encouraging to think that having witnessed the devastated landscape of the former Aral Sea, affected tourists would then operationalise some degree of positive action to eliminate global warming or offer assistance to the local communities that have been impacted by the disaster. This would fit with ideas, as explored by Berridge (2018), that emotions, though with a distinction between more immediate feelings that are subjective and emotional reactions that are objective, can provide incentives for motivation, with different parameters of saliency. Researching this is problematic, with issues of memory and culture apparent, but in the case of the short-term, surface encounters of the tourist, is highly likely that the very recounting/documenting of emotions felt is, of itself, an end state and a mere reflection of our own 'narrative self' (Ricouer, 1984), where we have positioned ourselves at a point where 'doing' the tourism we choose to do rubs up against our identity. We momentarily feel sadness, we test it against our authentic self and we move on – geographically and emotionally. This admittedly pessimistic view at least opens up discussion as to the authenticity of emotions or at least their comparative value with the notion that some emotions are more deeply felt and lasting than others and thus are capable of stimulating further action. With the tourism studies literature, there is a subtext that emotions such as shame, guilt, regret, sadness, sorrow and disdain are somehow more authentic and worthy of study than enjoyment, delight, and pride. Examining what we may term the more positive end of the emotional spectrum and how this relates to tourist behaviour and motivation may risk the label of 'not being serious', which has dogged tourism studies since its inception. Of course, the majority of studies are directed more by the choice and nature of the site or destination rather than by an *a priori* investigation of a particular type of emotion. In my reviews of tourist accounts of the Aral Sea, I would not have expected expressions of joy to come before those of sadness, though it is clear that visitors do express states of awe, inspiration and gratitude.

Third, for every visitor record of their emotional state there are thousands that did not reflect any sense of emotional engagement, and many more thousands of visitors that do not bother to leave any trace of their experience, at least publicly. In the case of the Aral Sea, as with many other sites and destinations reflecting some historical or contemporary rupture, or indeed any site that is associated with awe and the sublime, a widely held assumption is that even without any form of assessment, the visitor experience will be an emotional one. This is certainly played upon in the promotional narratives associated with such sites which, in theatrical vein, have learned to prompt the visitor to experience various emotional states. This directed discourse, whether originating from marketing or more robust guide books, suggests that certain tourist experiences/visits are invariably aligned with particular emotions. Elsewhere I have suggested (Robinson, 2012) that the tourist experience is arguably more likely to be fleeting, neutral and largely unemotional or at least conforming to pre-learned affective states and constrained more by socio-cultural expectation than by immediate and novel stimulus. This is a hard lesson for those who oversee sites of dissonant or traumatic heritage. There may well be a reality of emotional indifference, however advanced and attuned the interpretation. Cognitive disconnection across cultures and generations is not something that can be readily fixed by emotionally laden narratives; it may well be that the audience is just not that bothered and is not collapsing into anticipated emotional moulds. Does this matter? Well, not really. In my Aral Sea work, I can see that it makes more sense to speak of the emotions felt and lived in by the impacted communities, rather than those occasionally claimed by the largely disconnected and transient tourists.

The above reflections raise a series of questions that are all foundational to this well-curated collection of papers which consider the varying roles that the emotions play in the 'doing' of tourism. The complexities of places, pasts and peoples come together through differing disciplinary lenses, all enlightening, all partial, all problematic and all creating spaces for further work. The editors rightly suggest that the so-called emotional or affective turn is no longer novel, nor is it restricted to tourism studies but is well established in sociology, geography and cultural studies. Certainly, over fifty years or so, tourism studies has shifted in its concerns from systems, flows, spaces and impacts to that of subjectivities; a move broadly defined as being from tourism to the tourist. Across many cultures, it reflects a more open acceptance that emotional states matter and that the 'passions' are integral to daily life. We move closer to neurobiological approaches of what tourism does to 'us', though there remains deeply contested ground regarding the ways that the emotions are and can be, used, strategically and instrumentally. We need to remind ourselves that, as with any 'turn', it should not be seen as a discrete break but as just another layer of understanding that can enrich when situated amongst others.

Mike Robinson

Professor of Cultural Heritage, Nottingham Trent University, UK.

References

Berridge, K. C. (2018) Evolving Concepts of Emotion and Motivation. *Frontiers of Psychology*, Vol. 9, No. 1647, pp. 1–20.

Gross, J. J. (2014) Emotion Regulation: Conceptual and Empirical Foundations. In J. J. Gross (Ed.), *Handbook of Emotion Regulation* (pp. 3–20). New York: The Guilford Press.

Izard, C. E. (2007) Basic Emotions, Natural Kinds, Emotion Schemas, and a New Paradigm. *Perspectives on Psychological Science*, Vol. 2, No. 3, pp. 260–280.

Ricoeur, P. (1984) *Time and Narrative:* Volume 1, trans. K. McLaughlin and D. Pellauer. Chicago: University of Chicago Press.

Robinson, M. (2005) The Trans-textured Tourist: Literature as Knowledge in the Making of Tourists. *Tourism Recreation, Research*, Vol. 30, 1, pp. 73–81.

Robinson, M. (2012) Beyond Stendhal: Emotional Worlds or Emotional Tourists? *Literature and Aesthetics*, Vol. 22, No. 1, pp. 1–19.

Introduction: Attuning to affect and emotion in tourism studies

Jennie Germann Molz Ⓡ and Dorina-Maria Buda Ⓡ

ABSTRACT

Affect and emotion permeate all levels of the everyday and extra-ordinary entanglements of travel and tourism with personal, collective and political life. With this Special Issue, we consolidate an emerging approach and establish a route for scholarship that explores these entanglements. Through a range of theoretical and empirical lenses, the contributors reveal what emotion does in tourism, tourism practices, and tourism studies. Attuning to affect and emotion in tourism studies we steer the affective turn already underway in cultural studies and geography so as to encompass touring bodies and tourism places. Engaging the concept of affect as a constitutive element of social life often leaves us grasping for terminology to describe something that is, by its very nature, beyond words. For this reason, as we see in some of the papers in this collection, studying affect poses a significant and fruitful challenge to the status quo of social scientific method and analysis. Along with the contributors to this Special Issue, we make a case for thinking about emotions and affects through 'collective practice' as interrelated shaping tourism encounters *in* and *with* places. That is, to break it down as *doing* and as *shared between bodies (and places) through the doing*.

摘 要

情感和情绪遍布于旅行游览与个人、集体的政治生活日常性和临时性的相互影响的方方面面。通过本期特刊，我们着力推出了一种新兴的学术路径，并建立了研究旅行游览与政治生活复杂影响的研究路线 。通过一系列的理论和经验成果，作者们揭示了情感情绪在旅游，旅游实践和旅游研究中的影响。为了探索旅游研究中的情感和情绪，我们承袭文化研究和地理研究中的情感转向以涵盖各种旅行的主体和旅游场所。

将情感概念作为社会生活的组成部分，常常会让我们运用术语来捕捉一些本质上无法用语言表达的东西。因此，正如我们在本期一些论文中所看到的，研究情感对社会科学分析方法的现状提出了重大而富有成效的挑战。我们与本期的作者们一起，通过"集体性的实践"充分地探索了情感和情绪在人们旅行生活中的复杂影响，因为它们相互关联地塑造了旅游地内部和旅游地之间的各种旅游邂逅。也就是说，在旅行游览中解构情感情绪，通过旅游实践在旅游者与旅游场所中共享情感与情绪。

Introduction

This editorial began to take shape several months before the COVID-19 pandemic brought travel to a standstill. The two of us were travelling together from Leeds to visit a mutual colleague in Edinburgh and the train journey seemed like a good opportunity to work on this piece. We sat across from each other, laptop open on the small table between us, and talked about emotion, affect, and tourism as the train shifted our bodies side-to-side, forward and backward, accelerating ahead and then settling to a stop as we pulled into a station. The urban landscape outside melted into rural pastures, first green and brown then white with snow. At times the movement of the train seemed to jog ideas; at others, it lulled and distracted us. Inside the carriage, passengers dozed or chatted or, like us, tapped away at laptop keyboards. We made a note of the atmosphere on the train:

> This is not a quiet carriage. Someone plays a video game on their phone and the game's digital music becomes part of the soundscape. A nervous terrier parks himself under one of our seats and keeps watch. The atmosphere shifts like different acts in a play as passengers file off and on at each stop. At one station, a little girl boards with her family. She chats animatedly – first about drawing a picture and then about seeing her grandmother – until the family disembarks at the next station.

> There, a group of mothers and their adolescent daughters board, apparently on their way to an event. There aren't enough open seats for them to sit together, so the girls sit near the back of the train carriage while their mothers find seats elsewhere. The girls talk to each other and their mothers call back to them as they pass packed snacks up and down the aisle to one another. One of the women opens a bottle of sparkling wine with a loud 'pop' that sets the rest of her group into giggles. Other passengers glance up from their books or phones. Some seem amused, some seem annoyed.

> More people get on at the next stop and the next and soon the crush of bodies creates a heat and vibrancy that is at once exhilarating and suffocating. People brush past in the aisle, knocking our elbows as we try to type. And then the train slows to a stop. A clutch of passengers disembarks at Berwick upon Tweed. The girls and their mothers stay on, but their excitement settles. They stare quietly out of the window. As space frees up and silence sets in for a moment, the atmosphere shifts. A sense of relief. An arc of anxiety, claustrophobia, tension, and release.

Revisiting our observations now, more than a year into a global pandemic that has taken us on an emotional journey even while many of us were stuck at home, invokes nostalgia for a less-than-perfect pre-COVID world and a sense of anticipation for what might come next for tourism. These notes from our journey also recall geographer David Bissell's (2010, p.270) ethnographic observations of passenger mobilities and the way 'different affective atmospheres erupt and decay in the space of the train carriage' as passengers board and alight, as the train accelerates, slows, or halts, and as bodies avoid each other or come together. According to Bissell, these atmospheres emerge from something other than conversational interaction among passengers and they register at something other than a conscious level (p. 276). He takes care to distinguish these 'precognitive, prediscursive affective registers of communication' from the more subjective sense-making and reflexive interpretation of the 'emotional dimensions of experience' (p. 271). Bissell reminds us of the intensities that swell and flow through embodied proximities in places and on the move. Some of those intensities sediment into emotions we can name and manage, like irritation or relief, while others circulate beyond individual consciousness and between bodies.

We start with this moment from our train journey not because it breaks new ethnographic ground, but because it orients us to the way travel and tourism are entangled with embodied sensations, subjective emotions, and affective atmospheres. These are the entanglements we invited contributors to explore in this Special Issue. The response to our call affirmed that tourism scholars are eager to examine these concepts and that they are already doing so across a wide range of empirical venues and theoretical perspectives. In the articles included here, readers will not find one settled definition or established framework of emotion and affect. Some of the contributors make a clear distinction between these two terms while others argue that we must interweave concepts of emotion, feeling, embodiment, attachment, and affect.

David Bissell's description of emotion and affect is a helpful starting point for teasing out these different approaches. On the one hand, he refers to emotion as a subjective experience of feelings that we can think about, name, and manage. Emotions are the feelings that come into consciousness, straddling the biological aspects of embodied experience, such as a sensation in the heart or gut, and the social structures of race, class, and gender that discipline both the feeling of those feelings and the way we express them. This brings to mind the work of sociologist Arlie Hochschild (1983), who argues that emotions are governed by socially constructed 'feeling rules' that compel us to induce or suppress the proper emotions for a given situation. They are also subject to being compartmentalized and commodified as 'emotional labor'.

Affect, on the other hand, refers to the intensities and atmospheres that exist beyond conscious representation or discursive structures. Following theorists like Massumi (1995, 2015) and Clough (2007), several of the contributors in this issue describe affect as the ineffable moods or sensations that well up before we are aware of them, if we ever are. Like emotion, affect is corporeal, but in the sense that it circulates in between rather than residing within individual bodies. Engaging the concept of affect as a constitutive element of social life often leaves us grasping for terminology to describe something that is, by its very nature, beyond words. For this reason, as we see in some of the papers in this collection, studying affect poses a significant and fruitful challenge to the status quo of social scientific method and analysis.

The thirteen papers included here expand on the critical and multilayered insights that tourism scholars, many inspired by the turn toward emotion and affect in cultural studies, have brought to the field in recent years. This is not to suggest that emotion or multisensory experiences were previously absent from tourism studies. Thanks to the increasing popularity of various forms of experiential tourism over the past two decades, tourists' emotions have long been a part of business and management accounts of the industry. A relatively large body of research has developed out of this perspective, much of it focused on measuring customer satisfaction, commodifying and marketing experiences, designing emotional outcomes, and even using virtual reality to simulate tourists' good feelings (Nawijn & Fricke, 2015; Pestek & Sarvan, 2021; Pine & Gilmore, 1999; Volo, 2017).

We argue that thinking about emotion not just as a subjective outcome but as constitutive of tourism worlds leads down a somewhat different theoretical path than the impulse to measure, market, and manage tourists' emotional experiences. For this reason, we invited contributors to consider what embodied emotions, feelings, senses, and affects *do* in tourism. Inspired by Ahmed's (2014) work on the cultural politics of emotion, this question moves us beyond the realm of tourists' individual or interior feelings and opens onto emotion and affect as relational and political practices. Rather than asking how tourists feel, then, this approach explores the kinds of togetherness and tensions, privileges and hierarchies, places and relations, or presence and futures that emotion and affect make possible within the context of tourism.

The aim of this Special Issue is to create a space for scholars to explore and debate the insights such an approach can yield. In this sense, we are building on existing layers of critical thinking in tourism studies. Energized initially by a desire to shift the focus in tourism studies away from a disembodied 'tourist gaze' (Urry, 1990), critical and feminist theorists turned our attention toward the differentiated and multisensory experiences of embodied tourists (Veijola & Jokinen, 1994). Since then, tourism scholars have traced the emotional geographies and multisensuous performances of tourism (Crouch & Desforges, 2003; Edensor & Falconer, 2011; Everett, 2008; Saul & Waterton, 2019). Feminist scholars have revealed how emotions like pride and shame are intertwined with gendered and sexualized tourism spheres and tourism work (Johnston, 2007; Veijola, 2009). They have interrogated the emotional labor of tourism work (Heimtun, 2016; Veijola & Jokinen, 2008), including the intimate labor of sex tourism (Pritchard & Morgan, 2000; Williams, 2013). They have highlighted the interplay between motion and emotion in the realm of tourism (Picard & Robinson, 2012), and examined the politics of feeling in tourism (Buda et al., 2014). Meanwhile, the affective dimension of doing fieldwork (Pocock, 2015) sensitized tourism scholars to the significance of emotion in understanding tourism and tourism research in all its complexity.

Building on the rich insights into the ambivalent desires, affective flows, and emotional geographies that shape and are shaped by tourism, our intention here is to provide a foundation for further advancement into this emerging theoretical and empirical terrain. If we follow Ahmed's (2004) question about the way emotions work to align some bodies into collectives, we can move beyond individual feelings to better understand how tourists come together, with each other or with 'other others', as Ahmed puts it, and how they move apart. Sociologist Bialski's (2012) concept of 'intimate tourism', for example, captures tourists' desires not just to gaze at places but to have meaningful embodied and emotional encounters with strangers in their private lives and domestic spaces. Research on voluntourism similarly reveals how emotions such as intimacy or care, can align bodies into familiar relations but also differentiate 'helpers' from 'those in need' (Everingham & Motta, this issue; Germann Molz, 2017; Mostafanezhad, 2016; Sin, 2010).

The affective qualities of tourism are also apparent in the 'emotional risk-taking' and existential edgework of dark tourism (Buda, 2015; Tzanelli, 2021). As Tzanelli points out, COVID-19 now presents a set of timely questions about emotions and biopolitics; the papers in this issue were researched and submitted pre-COVID and so the pandemic is not a visible protagonist in the issue, but the questions, theories, frameworks, and approaches offered here may shed light on how tourist scholars might make sense of the affective contours of the 'post-viral' tourism world Tzanelli describes.

We have organized the articles around four central themes: emotion, labor, and power; feeling places; symbolic sentiments; and affective epistemologies. As readers will quickly realize, however, the articles included here overlap and inform one another in multiple ways that spill across these thematic categories.

Emotion, work, and power

The emotional geographies and affective mobilities of tourism are often entangled with histories of violence and hierarchies of power, as the articles in the first section illustrate. In this section we discuss the 'workings' of emotions and power – *emotional work, the work of emotion,* and *emotions at work* – to show how these unequal hierarchies of power work through specific articulations of emotion.

In their historical analysis of automobile tourism during the Jim Crow era in the United States, Alderman, Williams, and Bottone examine how the 'atmospheric politics' of white supremacy created an emotional geography of fear and intimidation for Black tourists. At the same time, however, automobility represented an avenue of freedom and defiance for African American motorists. With poignant details of the emotion work African American tourists did not just to navigate but to survive this fraught landscape, the article sheds light on the violent histories that echo in the present-day policing of Black mobilities. Atmospheres of fear, anxiety, harassment and intimidation can generate anger, which in turn can challenge the status quo and generate pro-social action. Fear can awaken anger and shame, but as in the case of Black motorists during the Jim Crow era help build resilience and resistance in the face of white supremacy.

Everingham and Motta's article also brings attention to enduring legacies of power inequalities, this time in relation to the emotional and affective work of volunteer tourism. They observe that the critical scholarship on voluntourism has tended to either frame its emotional appeal as symptomatic of colonial and neoliberal geopolitics or emphasize the ability of affective voluntourism encounters to transcend such power dynamics. To unsettle this binary, Everingham and Motta engage with decolonial feminist theory. From this perspective, they uncover the nuanced moments of vulnerability and critical intimacy that temporarily subvert the power relations that voluntourism also reproduces. This resonates with Burrai et al.'s work (2015, 2017, 2019) and the calls to re-think the ideology of volunteer tourism, and indeed decolonize all claims of 'sustainability' and 'responsibility' in travel and tourism. The current flawed moral and ideological character of volunteer and responsible tourism continue to sustain a replicating neoliberal mechanism of modern global capitalism.

The final article in this section is Díaz-Carrión and Vizcaino's study of rural tourism in Mexico in which they detail the emotional work Mexican women use to navigate the social and spatial restrictions placed on them. In this analysis, we again see how emotions work both as a mechanism of social control and as a site of resistance to traditional gender stereotypes. The women they interviewed expressed ambivalent emotional responses of anger, shame, happiness, and joy as they negotiated gender roles. Here, tourism work intersects with gender and power through contradictory emotions. Shame as a barrier to engage in the tourism sector is one of the most important findings, according to Díaz-Carrión and Vizcaino. The authors' treatment of shame as 'core affective or emotional responses by women in relation to their work in tourism' echoes Elspeth Probyn's argument that shame is productive both 'politically and conceptually in advancing a project of everyday ethics' (2004, p. 329). Indeed, shame as affect explains what 'the feeling body does in shame' (p. 330), whereas shame as emotion, privileges cognition. Negotiating these blurred boundaries between shame as visceral affect and cognitive emotion, Mexican women are able to reclaim tourism work for themselves with joy and happiness.

Feeling places

The articles in this section explore the emotional relationship between humans, places, and nature in the context of heritagescapes, family holidays, and dark tourism sites. In these accounts, emotions do not reside in the tourist or in the destination. Instead, inter-actions between people and places afford the emergence of certain emotional experiences or affective atmospheres. For example, Burlingame's phenomenological account of a Viking heritage site in Sweden uses the concept of 'presence' to highlight the affective and emotional potential of landscape. Acknowledging a growing sense of 'emotional curiosity' among tourists, Burlingame suggests that site managers collaborate with tourists' desires to have multisensory experiences of presence within the heritage landscape.

Kelly's case study of family holidays in Brighton, UK similarly focuses on the emotional affordances of place. This study describes how coastal spaces allow certain emotions to 'flow', with families imagining and performing themselves *as* families through their emotional connections with one another and with the seascape.

The last two articles in this theme, Biscaia and Marques, as well as Driessen deploy the concept of dark tourism. They address a long-standing critique levelled at dark tourism studies, that death, disaster and atrocities are analysed as commoditised products, and experiences at dark sites being devoid of emotions, feelings and affects (Buda et al., 2014; Buda, 2015; Lisle, 2000).

Biscaia and Marques analyze Dismaland: the Bemusement Park built in Weston-Super-Mare, North Somerset, a seaside destination in England by the elusive English artist Banksy. Their description of the seaside park's affective atmosphere as dystopic and dismal reminds us that the emotional affordances of place are relational, contextual, and contradictory. Dark tourism experiences in this park challenge the pervasive industry-based commodifications, and bring forth socio-affective encounters immensely productive to empathise, and affectually connect with the human tragedies of the Mediterranean refugee crisis, for example.

A similar theme emerges in the final article in this section, an analysis of immersive tourism at former war sites in Europe. Drawing on interview data with volunteers, Driessen describes the affects that circulate between volunteers and these sites of war and conflict as complex and highlights the contradictory feelings of purpose and powerlessness, sympathy and connection, guilt and disappointment that emerge in these settings. Like the other articles in this section, the focus here is on tourists' desires to be affected, but also on what emotions 'do' and how they shape and are shaped by tourists' performances in and with places.

Driessen, and Biscaia and Marques anchor their forays into emotions and affects in dark tourism in the affective tourism framework which contextualizes affects as transactions between touring bodies and tourist places (Buda, 2015). Their work expands the concept of affective tourism with due attention to the ways affects, emotions, and feelings are accessed, felt, experienced and performed in encounters with places of 'present dystopian darkness', or 'darkness' of past wars.

Symbolic sentiments

The articles in this section expand on the idea that tourists travel not just to experience certain places, but to feel certain feelings. Particular emotions may be symbolically attributed to a place, but as the contributors in this section illustrate, these affective experiences emerge in complex webs of human and non-human interactions and in-between cognitive meaning-making and pre-cognitive impressions. In their study of a gastronomic tourist route through Hunter Valley, Australia, Roy and Gretzel describe how tourists engage cognitively as well as bodily as they travel to the valley and move through the themed trail. In this case, the socio-material interactions between tourists and the food and wine, stories of authenticity, and services and scenery allow tourists to express and embody opulence, exclusivity, and indulgence.

The article that follows similarly focuses on tourists' desires to experience symbolically 'positive' emotions. In this conceptual paper, Yan and Halpenny introduce 'savoring' as one of the mechanisms through which tourists become positively attached to places. Like gazing, interpreting, or evaluating, savoring is a way of interacting with and making meaning of a destination. Savoring is not just an orientation to a place, however, but to the tourist's own emotional state; a mode of attuning to, regulating, or prolonging pleasurable feelings. In this sense, we might consider savoring as part of the emotion work tourists do.

Another dimension of emotion work involves what the authors of the last article in this section refer to as 'self-love'. In this exploratory study, Lykoudi, Zouni and Tsogas propose the framework of self-love in relation to symbolic consumption and destination branding. Highlighting survey results in which tourists associated a particular place with self-focused sentiments like actualization, confidence, discovery or fulfillment, the authors draw a parallel between tourists' love for a destination and their desire to experience self-love.

Affective epistemologies

The articles in this final section illustrate the way tourism researchers feel their way in the field. They engage with theories of knowledge that foreground our embodied being, and being with others, in the world as both an object of knowledge and a way of knowing. Feminist epistemology, in particular, recuperates the forms of embodied knowledge and ways of knowing through feeling and affect that have historically been discounted (Berlant, 2011; Collins, 1990; Stewart, 2007). These theories take seriously the idea that feelings are 'clues' to some kind of truth, as Hochschild (1983) puts it, while acknowledging the power relations that have made certain questions worth asking, certain sources of knowledge more reliable, or certain truths more true.

While embodied or expressed emotions appear to be more available to the researcher's eye, the more-than-representational qualities of affect pose a methodological challenge. How can we know, let alone represent in some recognizable form of scholarship, something that is by definition, beyond cognition or representation? Each of these articles situates its epistemological approach as a bridge between emotion and affect, focusing on the *relationality* of bodies, places, and things as a site of knowledge.

Ramanayake, Cockburn-Wootten, and McIntosh recognize that conventional social scientific techniques are limited in their ability to uncover the often invisible or unspoken aspects of people's affective experiences of traveling with a chronic illness. To address these limitations, the researchers employed a creative visual technique called the 'MeBox' method to make room for respondents to share a sense of intensity, loss, grief, or pain that might otherwise be 'unshareable'. Anderson and Smith similarly explore methodological techniques that span the conscious feeling of emotions and the unconscious realm of affect, in this case in between the real and imagined worlds of places featured in literature. To study the emotional dimensions of literary walking tours, they engaged a 'relational methodology' with small groups of tourists, an approach that combined the embodied practice of 'walking whilst talking', cues from the book and the place, and interactions within the group to create a literary map that merges both affective and cognitive elements.

Paying careful attention to the way people, places, and objects affect one another, Kugapi and Höckert use craft tourism as a method for exploring embodied encounters with material souvenirs. In this concluding article, their autoethnographic account of crafting, gifting, and touching a pair of green-and-white mittens traces the multisensory tourism geographies in which, as Kugapi and Höckert write, 'non-human actors … entangle us with places and to other members of the Earth'.

Conclusion

The intention in this Special Issue is not to add yet another turn to the research agenda in tourism studies, but rather to steer one that is already underway in cultural studies and geography so as to encompass touring bodies and tourism places. Where has it led us so far and what new directions it might yet yield. We aim to establish a route; consolidate an approach; make explicit what emotion does in tourism, tourism practice, tourism studies. What this Special Issue demonstrates is that emotions and affects are the drivers behind travel and tourism. We make a case for thinking about emotions and affects through 'collective practice' as interrelated shaping tourism encounters *in* and *with* places. That is, to break it down as *doing* and as *shared between bodies (and places) through the doing*.

One thing that all of the articles in this issue have in common is that they illustrate how tourism geographies register as emotional and affectual geographies (Anderson & Smith, 2001; Davidson et al., 2007; Pile, 2010). This goes some way to addressing a longstanding critique levelled at tourism studies – that an intimate language of emotions, feelings, affective style, moods, sentiments, passions is not pervasive in our vocabulary. Moreover, it has been lamented that *the tourist* as the central tenet in tourism studies, has been historically portrayed as passively consuming commoditized products, largely, devoid of emotions, feelings and affects. Earlier engagements with a commoditised tourism phenomenon have thus far obfuscated feelings, emotions, moods and affects that circulate in tourism places amongst tourists, locals, and everyone else in between.

Our re-routing of tourism studies more steadily towards emotional and affectual geographies can be considered within the wider turn to affect in the social sciences and humanities. Indeed, a re/turn to affect was registered in cultural studies and geography starting in the early 1990s (Clough, 2007; Harding & Pribram, 2002; Stewart, 2007). That call to re-turn to affect, was, at the time, largely ignored in tourism, surprisingly so, since tourism is about movement *to*, *in* and *between* places whereby social practices relating to physical motions of touring bodies are experienced *in* and *through* affects and emotions. The subjective experience of emotions becomes most obvious in tourism since tourism moves people (Picard & Robinson, 2012), in a physical sense, emotionally and affectively.

The affective turn occurs at a time when critical cultural theories face challenges to analyse, interpret and understand terrorism, on-going conflicts, pandemics, tortures and massacres. Considering such events as mirroring deep cultural, socio-political, economic and spatial transformations, the affective turn can be argued to be symptomatic of the changes in the cultural, political and economic co-functioning. Within the affective turn, the focus of critical cultural, social and spatial theories has been on dis/connections and circuits between affect and emotion and a re-consideration of the subject as 'subject of emotion' (Clough, 2007).

The affective turn in its twists, turns, and meanderings has detoured the life sciences, neurosciences, and biology's dealings with emotions and affects. John Cromby reminds us that 'between neuroscience and social science there has been something of a history of mutual distrust' (2007, p. 149). In a cautiously hopeful account Cromby details the potentials for biology, psychology and neurosciences together with increasing attention in the social sciences on the body, embodiment and affect, to produce more systematic collaborations. From its beginning the affective turn has invited 'a transdisciplinary approach to theory and method' (Clough, 2007, p. 3). Yet, there seem to have been 'some fascinating missteps characterizing the taking up of scientific literature' (Papoulias & Callard, 2010, p. 29). As affective meanderings seep into our worlds attuning them to the mind, brain, body and soul, for the next affective journey we invite colleagues to head these calls for transdisciplinarity and interrogate Spinozan cultural theories on emotion and affect in connection with biology's gift, or neurosciences' theory of mind.

In the meantime, investigations of affect and emotion permeating all levels of the everyday, the extra-ordinary of travel, personal, collective and political life and, thus undermining entrenched hierarchies of power – need to further make their way to the top of the tourism research agenda.

Disclosure statement

No potential conflict of interest was reported by the authors.

Funding

Nederlandse Organisatie voor Wetenschappelijk Onderzoek

ORCID

Jennie Germann Molz ⓘ http://orcid.org/0000-0001-6858-8144
Dorina-Maria Buda ⓘ http://orcid.org/0000-0003-1368-0562

References

Ahmed, S. (2004). Collective feelings: Or, the impressions left by others. *Theory, Culture and Society, 21*(2), 25–42. https://doi.org/10.1177/0263276404042133

Ahmed, S. (2014). *The cultural politics of emotion* (2nd ed.). Edinburgh University Press.

Anderson, K., & Smith, S. J. (2001). Emotional geographies. *Transactions of the Institute of British Geographers, 27*, 7–10.

Berlant, L. (2011). *Cruel optimism*. Duke University Press.

Bialski, P. (2012). *Becoming intimately mobile*. Peter Lang.

Bissell, D. (2010). Passenger mobilities: Affective atmospheres and the sociality of public transport. *Environment and Planning D: Society and Space, 28*(2), 270–289. https://doi.org/10.1068/d3909

Buda, D. (2015). *Affective tourism: Dark routes in conflict*. Routledge.

Buda, D., d'Hauteserre, A.-M., & Johnston, L. (2014). Feeling and tourism studies. *Annals of Tourism Research, 46*, 102–114. https://doi.org/10.1016/j.annals.2014.03.005

Burrai, E., Buda, D. M., & Stanford, D. (2019). Rethinking the ideology of responsible tourism. *Journal of Sustainable Tourism, 27*(7), 992–1007. https://doi.org/10.1080/09669582.2019.1578365

Burrai, E., Font, X., & Cochrane, J. (2015). Destinations stakeholders' perceptions of volunteer tourism: An equity theory approach. *International Journal of Tourism Research, 17*(5), 451–459. https://doi.org/10.1002/jtr.2012

Burrai, E., Mostafanezhad, M., & Hannam, K. (2017). Moral assemblages of volunteer tourism development in Cusco. *Tourism Geographies, 19*(3), 362–377. https://doi.org/10.1080/14616688.2016.1236145

Clough, P. T. (2007). Introduction. In P. T. Clough & J. Halley (Eds.), *The affective turn: Theorising the social* (pp. 1–34). Duke University Press.

Collins, P. H. (1990). *Black feminist thought: Knowledge, consciousness, and the politics of empowerment*. Routledge.

Cromby, J. (2007). Integrating social science with neuroscience: Potentials and problems. *BioSocieties, 2*(2), 149–169. https://doi.org/10.1017/S1745855207005224

Crouch, D., & Desforges, L. (2003). The sensuous in the tourist encounter. *Tourist Studies, 3*(1), 5–22. https://doi.org/10.1177/1468797603040528

Davidson, J., Bondi, L. & Smith, M. (Eds.) (2007). *Emotional geographies*. Ashgate.

Edensor, T., & Falconer, E. (2011). The sensuous geography of tourism. In J. Wilson (Ed.), *The Routledge handbook of tourism geographies* (pp. 73–112). Routledge.

Everett, S. (2008). Beyond the visual gaze? The pursuit of an embodied experience through food tourism. *Tourist Studies, 8*(3), 337–358. https://doi.org/10.1177/1468797608100594

Germann Molz, J. (2017). Giving back, doing good, feeling global: The affective flows of family voluntourism. *Journal of Contemporary Ethnography, 46*(3), 334–360. https://doi.org/10.1177/0891241615610382

Harding, J., & Pribram, E. D. (2002). The power of feeling: Locating emotions in culture. *European Journal of Cultural Studies, 5*(4), 407–426. https://doi.org/10.1177/1364942002005004294

Heimtun, B. (2016). Emotions and affects at work on Northern Lights tours. *Hospitality & Society*, *6*(3), 223–241. https://doi.org/10.1386/hosp.6.3.223_1

Hochschild, A. R. (1983). *The managed heart: Commercialization of human feeling.* University of California Press.

Johnston, L. (2007). Mobilizing pride/shame: Lesbians, tourism and parades. *Social & Cultural Geography*, *8*(1), 29–45. https://doi.org/10.1080/14649360701251528

Lisle, D. (2000). Consuming danger: Reimagining the war/tourism divide. *Alternatives: Global, Local, Political*, *25*(1), 91–116. https://doi.org/10.1177/030437540002500106

Massumi, B. (1995). The autonomy of affect. *Cultural Critique*, (31), 83–109. https://doi.org/10.2307/1354446

Massumi, B. (2015). *Politics of affect.* Polity.

Mostafanezhad, M. (2016). *Volunteer tourism: Popular humanitarianism in neoliberal times.* Routledge.

Nawijn, J., & Fricke, M. C. (2015). Visitor emotions and behavioral intentions: The case of concentration camp memorial Neuengamme. *International Journal of Tourism Research*, *17*(3), 221–228. https://doi.org/10.1002/jtr.1977

Pestek, A., & Sarvan, M. (2021). Virtual reality and modern tourism. *Journal of Tourism Futures*, *7*(2), 245–250. https://doi.org/10.1108/JTF-01-2020-0004

Picard, D. & Robinson, M. (Eds.) (2012). *Emotion in motion: Tourism, affect and transformation.* Ashgate.

Pile, S. (2010). Emotions and affect in recent human geography. *Transactions of the Institute of British Geographers*, *35*(1), 5–20. https://doi.org/10.1111/j.1475-5661.2009.00368.x

Pine, B. J., & Gilmore, J. H. (1999). *The experience economy.* Harvard Business Press.

Pocock, N. (2015). Emotional entanglements in tourism research. *Annals of Tourism Research*, *53*(2015), 31–45. https://doi.org/10.1016/j.annals.2015.04.005

Papoulias, C., & Callard, F. (2010). Biology's gift: Interrogating the turn to affect. *Body & Society*, *16*(1), 29–56. https://doi.org/10.1177/1357034X09355231

Pritchard, A., & Morgan, N. J. (2000). Privileging the male gaze: Gendered tourism landscapes. *Annals of Tourism Research*, *27*(4), 884–905. https://doi.org/10.1016/S0160-7383(99)00113-9

Probyn, E. (2004). Everyday shame. *Cultural Studies*, *18*(2-3), 328–349. https://doi.org/10.1080/0950238042000201545

Saul, H. & Waterton, E. (Eds.) (2019). *Affective geographies of transformation, exploration and adventure.* Routledge.

Sin, H. L. (2010). Who are we responsible to? Locals' tales of volunteer tourism. *Geoforum*, *41*(6), 983–992. https://doi.org/10.1016/j.geoforum.2010.08.007

Stewart, K. (2007). *Ordinary affects.* Duke University Press.

Tzanelli, R. (2021). Post-viral tourism's antagonistic tourist imaginaries. *Journal of Tourism Futures*, *7*(3), 377–389. (ahead of print). https://doi.org/10.1108/JTF-07-2020-0105

Urry, J. (1990). *The tourist gaze.* Sage.

Veijola, S. (2009). Gender as work in the tourism industry. *Tourist Studies*, *9*(2), 109–126. https://doi.org/10.1177/1468797609360601

Veijola, S., & Jokinen, E. (1994). The body in tourism. *Theory, Culture & Society*, *11*(3), 125–151. https://doi.org/10.1177/026327694011003006

Veijola, S., & Jokinen, E. (2008). Towards a hostessing society? Mobile arrangements of gender and labour. *Nora - Nordic Journal of Feminist and Gender Research*, *16*(3), 166–181. https://doi.org/10.1080/08038740802279901

Volo, S. (2017). Emotions in tourism: From exploration to design. In D. Fesenmaier & Z. Xiang (Eds.), *Design science in tourism* (pp. 31–40). Springer.

Williams, E. L. (2013). *Sex tourism in Bahia: Ambiguous entanglements.* University of Illinois Press.

Part I

Emotion, work and power

Jim Crow journey stories: African American driving as emotional labor

Derek H. Alderman (iD), Kortney Williams and Ethan Bottone

ABSTRACT

Automobile-based tourism during the USA Jim Crow era, while providing a mechanism for African Americans to circumvent institutionalized discrimination and segregation, was nonetheless fraught with anti-black harassment and denied accommodations, and even violence. The emotional geographies that undergirded this Jim Crow travel have traditionally not attracted significant attention from tourism scholars despite the foundational role they play in shaping current travel patterns, preferences, and anxieties among African Americans. We interpret Jim Crow travel in the context of the atmospheric politics of White supremacy that negatively affected Black motorists on the road and the counter mobility-work of African Americans using the automobile to survive, negotiate, defy, and redefine these atmospheres of uncertainty, fear, and intimidation. In particular, our paper focuses on the emotional labor behind Jim Crow automobile travel, using oral histories collected through a partnership with the Beck Cultural Exchange Center, a Knoxville, Tennessee Black heritage site, to highlight the travel experiences of people of color. Results suggest that seemingly practical and mundane driving practices, decisions, and preparations were always deeply informed by the emotion-laden work of African Americans controlling the degree to which racism might affect them and their children, both physically and psychologically, as well as controlling the extent to which their presence on the road might affect and inflame a hostile White public.

摘要

在美国种族隔离时期, 汽车旅游虽然为非裔美国人提供了一种规避制度化歧视和种族隔离的机制, 但仍然充满了反黑人骚扰、拒绝住宿, 甚至暴力。尽管情绪地理学在塑造当前非裔美国人的旅游模式、偏好和焦虑方面发挥着基础性作用, 但传统上强化这种"种族歧视"旅游的情绪地理学并没有引起旅游学者的明显关注。我们在白人至上的政治氛围的背景下阐释了黑人旅行, 这种氛围对旅途中的黑人司机产生了负面影响, 也影响了非裔美国人的反移动动员, 这些非裔美国人利用汽车生存、谈判、反抗, 并重新定义了这些充满不确定性、恐惧和恐吓的氛围。我们的论文特别关注黑人汽车旅行背后的情绪劳动, 通过与田纳西州诺克斯维尔贝克黑人文化遗产文化交流中心(Beck Cultural Exchange Center)合作收集的口述历史, 突出有色人种的旅行体验。结果表明, 看似实用和平凡的驾驶实践,驾驶决策和准备工作总是深深充满非裔美国

人的感情劳动工作，这种情绪劳动掌控着种族歧视从身体和心理
上可能会影响他们和他们的孩子的程度，掌控着他们在路上旅行可
能会影响和激怒一个充满敌意的白人公民的程度。

Introduction

Travel has, and still remains, fraught with emotions, ranging from the anxiety of making arrangements to the excitation of arriving at a destination. The affective aspect of travel extends to all corners of the tourism industry, yet not everyone experiences the same emotions while traveling. On this point, Williams (2018, p. 33) notes that the emotions that people carry with them as they move—while certainly felt individually—are social and political and for travelers of color, 'embedded in histories of racism and survival'. This paper advances the study of the affective politics of tourism by applying, theoretically and empirically, the concepts of emotional labor and atmospheric politics to understand the historical racialized experiences and inequalities of travel in the United States. Specifically, we explore the constitutive role that the management of feelings and affects played among African Americans who drove automobiles during the Jim Crow era that preceded and accompanied the USA Civil Rights Movement. As the 'nadir' of American race relations (Logan, 1965), this historical period was characterized by institutionalized discrimination, dispossession, and segregation and represented important moments of police harassment, denied accommodations, and even death for mobile people of color.

We interpret Jim Crow travel in the context of the atmospheric politics of White supremacy that negatively affected Black motorists socially, physically, and psychologically. 'The affective power of this atmosphere has roots in a wider historical geography of racialized violence, inequality, and debasement that African Americans experienced generationally and came to anticipate as a fact of life' (Inwood & Alderman, 2018, p. 363). Importantly, the dominance of state-sanctioned racism was open to contest, and African Americans sought to mitigate and defy this atmosphere of White hostility and Black subjugation through both overt protests and, important to this paper, the embodied practices of traveling (Alderman & Inwood, 2016). We argue in this paper that these Jim Crow journeys, while poorly studied by tourism scholars until now, constitute a creative, everyday activism in which ordinary people of color appropriated and reworked the act of traveling, specifically driving practices, into a counter-mobility that subverted, negotiated, and survived racial apartheid.

At the same time that our paper offers a macro-level analysis of racialized travel in terms of the 'atmospheric politics of White supremacy', we also develop and employ a micro-level analysis of Jim Crow tourism in terms of the emotional labor of fearful but resilient drivers and their families. By moving back and forth between these different scales of analysis, we advance beyond many existing studies by capturing both the structural constraints and the socio-spatial agency that shape the affective politics of the travel experience. We theorize that African American motorists worked emotionally as well as physically, socially, and logistically to circumvent, resist and, to some extent, redefine the atmosphere of fear, intimidation, and uncertainty that White supremacy deployed against people of color. Conventionally, hospitality and tourism scholars use emotional labor to discuss the regulation and suppression of publicly expressed feelings among paid service workers. However, recent research seeks to broaden what counts as emotional labor, who engages in such work, and when and for what purpose this emotional labor is carried out (e.g. Maruyama, 2017; Taylor, Levi, & Dinovitzer, 2012; Williams, 2018). We conceptualize emotional labor to include a wider and deeper management of feelings, embodied performances, and affects among tourists at destinations and along travel routes as they navigate and negotiate a broader politics of identity and belonging within society.

The concept of emotional labor allows us to answer recent calls for a greater scholarly focus on the politics of feelings and how '[e]motions are crucial to the way in which touring bodies relate to others and to places' (Buda, d'Hauteserre, & Johnston, 2014, p. 112). Racialized differences and inequalities in travel are reinforced but also challenged through emotion-laden relations that have received scant attention within tourism studies. The emotional labor of African American automobile tourism offers us a needed opportunity to reassess everyday driving strategies and travel decisions undertaken by African Americans as acts of resourcefulness and resistance and to interpret the affective significance of these practices in terms of creating a sense of place, resilience, and self-determination amid the alienating and oppressive realities of Jim Crow.

As an empirical exploration of the resistant emotional labor of Black motorists, we draw from in-depth oral history interviews with several older African Americans living in Knoxville, Tennessee (USA) who engaged in tourism during the Jim Crow era. The interviews resulted from a partnership between Tourism RESET and an African American museum and cultural center devoted to remembering and preserving marginalized, and in many instances, destroyed Black heritage. RESET (Race, Ethnicity, and Social Equity in Tourism) is a multidisciplinary and multi-university initiative that studies and challenges the role of racial inequality in the historical and contemporary development of tourism and, in particular, the emotionally and politically charged place of travel within the civil rights experiences of African Americans. The partnership resulted in the collection of 'Jim Crow Journey Stories' that cast light onto how Black motorists felt about traveling amid intense discrimination and segregation and how their travel tactics were shaped by an embodied and emotive management of their vulnerability and exposure to racial discrimination on the road. Informing and shaping Jim Crow driving practices—from issues of timing and choice of route to pace of trip and travel preparations—were efforts on the part of African Americans to manage their feelings about the potential dangers of racial victimization. Rather than just the technological and physical work of getting around, automobility was deeply embedded in the emotional work of African Americans controlling the degree to which racism might affect them and their children, both physically and psychologically, as well as controlling the extent to which their presence on the road might affect and inflame a hostile White public.

Our study contributes to growing scholarly interest in tourism and travel as sites of racism and anti-racist resistance and the larger project of moving toward an understanding of the foundational role that racial inequality, White privilege, and social othering have long played in shaping spatial mobility and tourism in particular

(Henry 2018; Torabian & Miller, 2017). The value of (re)discovering the emotional geography of tourism during racial segregation goes beyond historical analysis since these histories have a legacy within the present. Some destinations continue to employ White-centric marketing that makes African Americans invisible and arguably unwelcome (Alderman & Modlin, 2013; Butler, 2001). Social media analysis and market surveys of African Americans show that concerns over racial profiling remain strong (Mandala Research, 2017), even as Black travelers have 'shown resistance and resilience to the racism and discrimination by continuing to travel' and creating spaces and communities for themselves through their own travel agents, tours, organizations, and publications (Dillette, Benjamin, & Carpenter, 2018, p. 2).

By acknowledging the emotional labor that undergirded Black travel in the United States historically, we can gain a better analytical and empathetic perspective on affective politics of contemporary tourism for African Americans and other marginalized groups. Interestingly, while scholars increasingly write about the racialized experiences and difficulties of 'Traveling While Black', few studies have sought to go back in time to understand the genealogy of these inequalities and even fewer have addressed in a systematic way the emotional reactions of individual African American travelers in the past. We suggest that any meaningful attempt to come to terms with current tourism injustice must recognize how White supremacy has long structured not just access to material opportunities but also the broader atmospheric politics of traveling.

Finally, by foregrounding the voices of African American travelers, our study recognizes and contends with the ethical complications of scholars speaking about (and not for) discriminated communities. We demonstrate the methodological value of collecting and analyzing oral histories to delve into the power of affects and emotions as forces in constituting and shaping the touristic experience and, in particular, social inequality in tourism.

Background

Toward a genealogy of African American tourism

A growing number of scholars focus on the historical and contemporary role of social exclusion, inequality, and discrimination in structuring the experiences of tourists (Barton & Leonard, 2010; Cole & Morgan, 2010; Jamal & Camargo, 2014; Pritchard & Morgan, 2000; Ruhanen & Whitford, 2018). Among these efforts to explore the social justice implications of travel, a literature has emerged that addresses the marginal and often contested place that African Americans have long held and, to some degree, still hold within travel and tourism (Alderman, 2013; 2018; Alderman & Modlin, 2013; Butler, Carter, & Brunn, 2002; Gordon, 2015; Lee & Scott, 2016; Pryor, 2016; Tucker & Deale, 2018). This literature makes important inroads into documenting the under-representation of African Americans (and other people of color) at certain destinations, particularly state and national parks, while also theorizing reasons to explain these patterns of uneven participation (Finney, 2014; Jackson, 2018; O'Brien, 2015; Weber & Sultana, 2013a, 2013b). Moving beyond traditional theoretical models that tend to minimize discrimination or consider it as just one of many possible ways of understanding the travel behavior of African American tourists, this newer work more directly exposes the role of racism—both expected and experienced—in shaping their destination-related decisions and the degree of anxiety or welcome they feel in traveling (Alderman & Modlin, 2013; Lee & Scott, 2017; Philipp, 1994). Carter (2008, p. 268), in particular, addresses explicitly how people of color view tourism decisions, how African Americans experience travel spaces in racialized ways, and how they perceive most tourism landscapes as 'White, spaces in which to be on guard'.

To understand the contemporary travel behavior of African Americans, their apprehension about certain tourist destinations, and the way in which they see their travel to these destinations in racially charged ways, one must acknowledge that 'the ability to be mobile in the United States has been fundamentally intertwined with the construction of racial identities' (Hague, 2010, p. 331). Past eras of discrimination—particularly Jim Crow—continue to influence contemporary travel patterns, preferences, and anxieties (Carter, 2008; Johnson, 1998; Lee & Scott, 2017; Nicholson, 2016). How African Americans feel about where and how to travel are not just influenced by their own direct experiences of discrimination but also social or collective memories of institutionalized racist violence, brutality, and humiliation passed down from generation to generation, as recently demonstrated by Dillette et al. (2018) in their analysis of Black tourists using the social media hashtag #TravelingWhileBlack to draw pubic attention to still finding discriminatory situations and destinations. A group's memories are formed, shared, and shaped within certain social milieus. Collective memories of past racism, according to Johnson and Bowker (2004), shape Black interaction with and movement through places.

A critical and impactful study of African American travel must be done with an understanding of the 'violent biopolitics of mobility' that has long surrounded not just tourism but almost every facet of moving through and against White supremacist societies and spaces intent upon controlling Black bodies, spirits, and access to resources (Alderman, 2018). According to Nicholson (2016, p. 553), there is a long history of violently criminalizing freely mobile Black bodies and the 'intersections of mobilities and race in North America are frequently interpreted through automobilities and blackness'. Interestingly, given this growing recognition of the importance of mapping the genealogy of African American touristic mobilities back to earlier eras, we have seen very few studies of travel during the Jim Crow era of segregation and discrimination (but see Gordon, 2015; Jackson, 2018; Seiler, 2006). This paper adds valuable insights that contribute to the growing understanding of historical and contemporary Black travel.

An atmospheric approach to Jim Crow travel

There has never been an historical period in which the movements of African Americans were not the subject of White control; it is a fact of life that began with forced migration during enslavement and continues to be seen now with the hyperpolicing of 'Driving While Black' (Finney & Potter, 2018; Nicholson, 2016). However, the Jim Crow era that followed Reconstruction in the 1870 s and presumably ended with the de-segregation victories of the mid 1960s Civil Rights Movement was a time when

the apartheid politics of mobility were especially intense. African Americans confronted considerable humiliation, racial profiling, threats of violence, and uncertainty
of finding welcoming accommodations when traveling. When they could find places
that would serve them, African Americans were restricted to a limited number of segregated parks, beaches, hotels, restaurants, restrooms, and other accommodations
(Algeo, 2013; Jackson, 2018; O'Brien, 2015), and, in some instances, there were entire
towns in which their presence was not allowed after sundown (Loewen, 2018).

While Jim Crow presented numerous logistical, physical, and social-economic barriers that communicated the second-class citizenship afforded travelers of color, its
power came not only from its unjust material distribution of resources and spaces but
also from the atmosphere of fear and anxiety that African Americans were made to
feel when traveling. Studies of atmosphere have gained traction in the social science
and geography literatures (e.g. Sumartojo & Pink, 2018; Waterton & Dittmer, 2014) as
scholars theorize 'the "feel" that emanates from a dynamic combination of built environment, place and people' and how these atmospheres—which can be engineered
and controlled through law and informal social practice—influence human sensory
experience, identity, and the affective power of one's social-spatial order (Sumartojo,
2016, p. 544). Recent research argues, in particular, for examining race and racism as
'technologies of affect': how emotions, feelings, and affects are mobilized to breathe
life into racialized identities and hence shape social power relations and what a body
can do and be racially speaking (Zembylas, 2015).

Inwood and Alderman (2018, p. 363) also note the affective politics underlying
racism: 'The political potency of White supremacy, while certainly supported by de
jure discrimination and violence, also relies upon the active creation of an atmosphere
to affect negatively and often brutally the psychological well-being, sense of dignity,
and sense of belonging of people of color'. The intense atmospheric politics of racialized travel and African American anxieties about encountering threats to their well-
being on the road is captured quite well in a story published in *Smithsonian*
(Townsend, 2016). In the account, Paula Wynter described the visceral reaction of her
family on a road trip upon being followed by police; fear of harassment if not arrest
and abuse by law enforcement was a common fear among Black motorists during
Jim Crow.

> In North Carolina, Paula Wynter's family hid in their Buick after a local sheriff passed
> them, made a U-turn and gave chase. Wynter's father, Richard Irby, switched off his
> headlights and parked under a tree. 'We sat until the sun came up. "She says". We saw
> his lights pass back and forth. My sister was crying; my mother was hysterical'.
> (Townsend, 2016, para 2)

Importantly, while atmosphere can be controlled (and controlling) when put in the
service of power, we must recognize that 'people [can] modify and co-create ... atmosphere, rather than merely considering them as passive figures with little agency to
constitute their own sensory experience' (Edensor & Sumartojo, 2015, p. 253). Indeed,
at the same time that the story of African American car travel during Jim Crow was
one of control and oppression, it also was a story of African American tourists using
the automobile to at least mitigate the atmosphere of fear and intimidation that
would otherwise surround travel. On a macro, symbolic level, as Franz (2008) notes,

the automobile was a symbol of respectability and racial uplift for some middle class African Americans. At the practical, micro level, purchase and use of cars allowed these same African Americans to avoid physically and socially some of the denigration and lack of freedom found within segregated railroad cars, buses, and even airport terminals (Ortlepp, 2017). African American tourists sought to use their newly found automobility to negotiate, if not overcome, a hostile social landscape with the help of Black tourism operators, special guidebooks to safe places, the advice of other travelers, and a strategic reading of racial boundaries at destinations. Thus the automobile was simultaneously enveloped within an affective atmosphere of racism while also being a tool for challenging the political-emotive control of White supremacy, if only temporarily, through the creation of a subaltern atmosphere of Black defiance, hope and self-determination.

Driving as creative resilience and resistance

There is a growing public awareness of the great difficulties which faced Black motorists during Jim Crow, spurred in part by the rediscovery of *The Green Book*, a travel guide published by and for African Americans from 1936 to 1966 (Kahn, 2015; Townsend, 2016). The guide was one of several produced during segregation to assist motoring tourists and travelers in navigating and negotiating racial discrimination and locating commercial establishments—from hotels, motels, and tourist homes to restaurants, gas stations, and beauty parlors—that would welcome travelers of color. Listing these accommodations by state, city, and street address, the guide has become a powerful reminder of the national pervasiveness of White control over Black movement. According to Pesses (2017, p. 679), the *Green Book* exposes the racialized origins of American automobility and 'challenge[s] prevailing notions of freedom and the road in twentieth century America'. But the travel guide also demonstrates the capacity of African Americans to offer an alternative mapping of travel routes, public spaces, and spaces of consumption that tried to avoid and subvert the harmful material and psychological effects of racism (Alderman & Inwood, 2014; Mitchell & Collins, 2014).

The Green Book, now the title of an award-winning feature film, has been helpful in casting light on the foundational role of racism within the history of American tourism as well as the resourcefulness and resilience of Black motorists. However, we still lack a full understanding of the difficulties faced by travelers of color during Jim Crow and the creative strategies they developed and carried out to survive and resist those injustices. In particular, it is important to explore these questions among Black motorists who did not have access to or did not use the *Green Book*. One of the unintended possible consequences of the intense discussion of the *Green Book* is the impression that circumventing and contesting racial hostility could be reduced to following the directions of a travel guide, however important it may have been. In reality, even with the help of segregation era travel guides, African American tourism was a much more complex process of spatial, bodily, and emotional navigation and social negotiation. Thus, one of the primary objectives of this paper is to offer a theoretical and empirical exploration of car travel during Jim Crow by African Americans that recognizes their wider agency in moving in resilient and strategic ways that attempted to mitigate and redefine the atmospheric politics of driving amidst and against White supremacy.

To facilitate a conceptual and empirical understanding of the touristic agency and creative resilience of African American motorists in the face of Jim Crow racism, we cast driving as 'counter-mobility work' (see Alderman & Inwood, 2016). Counter-mobility work captures the bodily, technological, social, and particularly emotional practices that not only facilitated physical movement, but which also constituted the racialized labor and resourcefulness of resisting and surviving White supremacy. While automobility was not the same kind of activism as overt civil rights protests, driving could take on anti-racist intent, meaning, and consequences and thus allow Black motorists to claim a certain measure of place and self-determination within a disenfranchizing social and spatial order. Alderman and Inwood (2016) argue for a broader consideration of the resistant work of mobility that undergirded the African American experience, not only in spectacular, highly publicized moments but especially through everyday movements and practices. They encourage scholars to cast political and emotional significance upon even the most seemingly quotidian and ordinary of driving practices; for living within and resisting racism is inherently a political project while also a matter of practicality.

Broadening the idea of emotional labor

The idea of counter-mobility can cover a wide range of practices and tactics of resistant survival employed by African American tourists on the road, but our focus here is on the emotional labor that undergirded their car travel as they reacted to and sought to reclaim the atmospheric politics of racial inequality on the road. Since the seminal work by Hochschild (1983), emotional labor has become an important concept applied by scholars to understand the strategies of employees to regulate or manage their public affect or displayed feelings, to 'act' in a certain way in order to produce a desired emotional state in another person, particularly customers and supervisors. This type of emotional labor can include the superficial hiding or suppressing of felt emotions to show what is required as part of one's work as well as deeper changes in one's internal feelings to align with employer rules and customer normative expectations (Veijola, 2009; Gabriel, Daniels, Diefendorff, & Greguras, 2015). The amount of effort workers devote to expressing organizationally desired emotion during interpersonal transactions and the degree of dissonance between felt and feigned emotions have an impact on the well-being of the person who must engage in this affective regulation as well the organization profiting from the public display or suppression of certain emotions (Kruml & Geddes, 2000).

The tourism literature has also found the idea of emotional labor helpful in understanding the full range of work involved in serving tourists, and how this 'emotional labor is so embedded in service work that it goes unseen, unrewarded and even exploited' (Salman & Uygur, 2010, 194). For example, tourism scholars note the emotional labor of guiding tours and the significant burden tour leaders carry in determining which publicly expressed emotions and affects are appropriate in given situations as they manage touristic experiences and expectations (Wong & Wang, 2009). More broadly, there is an ongoing shift toward analyzing tourism in terms of work and the practices and lived encounters of tourism workers. The focus on work has brought needed attention to the challenges faced by tourism industry laborers, particularly those marginalized on the basis of race, gender, and nationality (Veijola, 2009). However, the ideas of tourism work and emotional labor are not restricted to the commercial responsibilities of hospitality workers, guides, and other staff members serving visitors.

We contribute needed attention to the possibility that travelers, especially those from marginalized communities, also engage in emotional labor as they struggle to move freely, find a place of belonging within a destination and make sense of differences and boundaries between them, locals, and other tourists (Maruyama, 2017). Emotional labor encompasses wider cultural situations and encounters in which people work to regulate their emotional state and that of others, not simply to satisfy a consuming public but also for achieving larger sets of social, psychological, and political needs and goals as part of the travel experience. Taylor et al. (2012) point to the important emotional work that underlie identity formation among travelers, especially those from stigmatized ethnic minority groups, as they participate in organized tours. Taylor et al. (2012, p. 83) use the term 'identity labor' to refer to the 'complex set of psychological, emotional, and social processes that allow people to determine a place for themselves and a method for enacting it' within their social groups and at affectively-charged touristic destinations. In studying African American women traveling to Jamaica, Williams (2018) examines how tourists 'carry emotion with them as they move', how those emotions are linked to racialized and gendered experiences, and the considerable emotional labor required to pursue happiness, a sense of belonging, and safe spaces (p. 6).

Although not in the context of tourism, Evans and Moore (2015, p. 439) argue that because of the tough identity work undertaken in negotiating and resisting racial aggression, 'people of color experience [in institutional White spaces] an unequal distribution of emotional labor'. The emotional labor of anti-racist resistance is especially burdensome because it requires oppressed people to 'protect themselves from denigration while minimizing the risk of severe consequence' (Evans & Moore, 2015, p. 439). Similarly, Smith, Hung, and Franklin (2011, p. 64) find evidence that fending off racial aggressions in White-dominated environments produces psychological and physiological stress, or 'racial battle fatigue', among African Americans. They expend considerable emotional energy predicting and managing the reactions of Whites and developing counter-strategies for coping with and fighting against racism, while also pursuing their own personal goals.

Our efforts to understand the history of African American tourism recognizes the emotional labor that tourists take on not only at destinations and on tours but also on the road as they travel and negotiate the racialized politics of their mobility. To Evan and Moore's point, driving during Jim Crow was very much about African Americans navigating the identity-related obstacles and inequalities embedded within American travel in ways that avoided and subverted racial aggressions while also maintaining their safety and that of their families. The emotional labor of African

American automobile tourism during Jim Crow was simultaneously about driving *within* but also *against* an atmosphere of White supremacy, blurring the hard lines we often fix between accommodation and resistance (Alderman & Inwood, 2016). To be sure, even when Black motorists sought to drive undetected and unmolested by White authorities, they were engaged in the consequential work of fashioning a touristic social identity that countered dominant racist efforts to control Black opportunity and mobility, as well as finding spaces where people of color might be safe, exercise their consumer power, and realize some limited sense of belonging and expression.

Practical driving as political practice

For African Americans, driving was and remains about more than simply transport. The automobile is also part of the emotion-laden identity work of carving out places—literally and figuratively—where Black tourists might contest and survive racism and make an intervention in the embodied relations and atmospheres of White supremacy that so negatively affect them. As Sheller (2004) argues, cars are about moving people, not only in a physical sense but also emotionally as we recognize the intimate relationship between automobiles and travelers and take 'seriously how people feel *about* and *in* cars, and how the feel of different car cultures elicits specific dispositions and ways of life'. Like Sheller, we recognize that these automotive feelings cannot be separated from the material practices, physical and mechanical movements, and the spaces and places of driving.

The emotional labor and affective politics of driving, rather than simply being felt or expressed, 'arises out of particular material relations and sensations, and at the same time organizes material relations and sensations into wider esthetic and kinesthetic cultures' (Sheller 2004, p. 223). The close connection between the emotional and kinesthetic (tactile) dimensions of traveling is ever-present among all drivers, but especially so for African Americans. Bodily driving practices and how drivers interact with the material world and with the automobile as a machine might appear to be ordinary or practical decisions, but they were always (and still are) informed by the labor of managing the effect of racism on the driver, and particularly his/her children, as well as the work of controlling the potential for White feelings of hostility toward African American mobility. It is the purpose of this study to examine the remembered 'Jim Crow Journey Stories' of older African American travelers as they describe the emotional labor and atmospheric politics of race that structured their travel decisions, tourism practices, and automobile use patterns during state-sanctioned segregation, discrimination, and racialized violence on the road.

Jim Crow Journey Stories project

Study setting: the Beck Center

Empirically, this paper carries out a study of the counter-mobility work and the role of emotional labor of anti-racist car travel during the Jim Crow era. It does so by examining biographical tourism accounts of older African Americans based in Knoxville, Tennessee. These oral histories were collected through a series of semi-structured interviews about their experiences traveling by car out of town and overnight, whether they drove as adults, traveled as adult passengers, or traveled as children with parents who drove. Knoxville is located in the eastern portion of Tennessee, approximately 180 miles east of Nashville and is the third-most populated city in the state with over 187,000 people. The interviews, conducted in the summer of 2013, resulted from a partnership with a local African American museum and advocacy organization within Knoxville called the Beck Cultural Exchange Center. One of the co-authors of the paper (Kortney) conducted an internship with the Beck Center, which supported the collecting of oral histories about Black automobility, tourism and travel as part of the Center's larger mission of interpreting and preserving the histories of Knoxville's African Americans, who comprise almost 18% of the city's population.

Established in 1975, the Beck Center hosts public programs, archival collections, and heritage exhibits. Much of this activity is in the context of the 'memory-work' (Till, 2012) of recovering and retelling the story of those Knoxville Black neighborhoods and business districts razed from the 1950s to the 1970s as part of a urban renewal and slum clearance program meant to reinvigorate the downtown area and reverse capital flight from the center city. This 'urban renewal' program, termed by the Beck Center and local historians of color (e.g. Booker, 2017) as 'urban removal', was responsible for destroying three Black communities located in the eastern region of downtown and displacing hundreds of African American residents from homes and businesses unfairly blanketed with the label of 'blighted'. Knoxville's urban renewal/removal negatively altered African American spaces, quality of life, and belonging in the city, transforming 'Black neighborhoods and the nerve center of Black commerce into concrete highways, apartment buildings and public facilities, including the Civic Coliseum' ('Reclaiming Our Histories', 2018).

Partnering to collect, preserve, and analyze the Jim Crow car travel stories of Knoxville's African Americans supported the Beck Center's broader mission to carry out a broader critique of the impact of state-sanctioned racial segregation, discrimination, and dispossession on the spaces and geographic movements of African Americans. Black car travel is an important part of Beck's historical interpretation; its exhibits include many photographs of now demolished African American businesses that once served local residents and out of town tourists of color. One of our study's oral history participants, given the pseudonym Stokely (born 1941), recounted how his family's tourist home (a private home with rooms to rent) and restaurant were prominent parts of Knoxville's lost segregation-era travel geography. Understanding these Black geographies and mobilities through tourism-related oral histories supports the Beck's agenda of contextualizing Knoxville's urban renewal/removal as a wider project of racial control and inequality while also, more practically, gathering first hand testimony of this racialization before these witnesses die along with their memories of Jim Crow racial struggles.

The Beck Center has a special room highlighting the aforementioned *Green Book* travel guide, which includes a poster that summarizes some of the results of our Jim Crow Journey Stories oral history project. We elected to provide our results and produce this poster for the Beck Center to assist in their public history efforts before pursuing publication of this paper. This allowed us to gauge public reaction to our interpretations, which have been positive. We treated the Beck Center not merely as a study site or archive of information but as a partner in what we hoped would be socially relevant and helpful scholarship on behalf of an African American community institution.

The oral history interviews

Participants for oral history interviews were selected through purposive sampling based on race (they self-identified as African American), age (they were old enough to remember traveling by car during Jim Crow), and willingness to share personal stories of tourism with the researchers. The Beck Center's management staff played an important role in recruiting these participants by allowing the researchers access to a network of contacts and social relations with African Americans in the Knoxville community. Assisted by the Beck Center, we contacted 21 potential participants and were able to secure interviews with 12 participants, providing a yield rate of approximately 57%. Our analysis draws from 10 of those interviews; the remaining two oral histories were less helpful in excavating African American driving experiences and repeated many of the themes and details found in previously analyzed interviews, suggesting that data saturation had been reached.

The vast majority of oral history interviews were conducted on-site at the Beck Center, with just a few taking place in the homes of participants. The age range of the participants at the time of interviews varied from 66 years (born 1947) to 88 years (born 1925). Participants were split evenly by gender and they all described experiences of traveling by automobile out of town and over-night. They engaged in a wide range of tourism mobilities—including traveling across as well as outside of the American South, such as traveling back and forth to college or military assignments, on school-organized trips, family vacations, and often to visit family and friends in other cities. Because of the relatively advanced age of the study's participants, all had recollections of traveling by car during Jim Crow as adults and children, although there was variation in how often and far their parents drove because of expense and (un)willingness to leave familiar surroundings in the face of racism.

We did not ask specific questions about the income level of interviewees, but it was apparent that participants, before retirement, generally held middle class professions that afforded them the resources and time to engage in automobility. We make only passing reference to issues of income and class here, but they are important since navigating and circumventing Jim Crow through driving was not available to all social strata within Black communities. Moreover, the automobile, like other symbols of American consumerism, was deeply embedded in the now controversial ideology of racial uplift, in 'which black elites believed that racism could be conquered by convincing whites of the material and moral progress of African Americans' (Alderman & Inwood, 2014, p. 74).

Oral history interviews were recorded as audio files and then transcribed professionally to facilitate a critical reading and analysis of participants' responses. The identification of themes within the interviews was carried out by hand. All authors reviewed and interpreted transcripts, reaching an agreement on the prevailing interpretations of the data. We approached the interview analysis deductively, guided by broad a priori theoretical ideas about racialized atmospheres and emotional labor, but also inductively, allowing us to identify specific lived meanings, patterns, and struggles related to these broad ideas as they emerge from people's accounts. Our findings from these oral history interviews are not meant to be generalizable across all classes and cohorts of African American tourists, but are meant instead to identify, explore, and better understand the creative driving strategies and resilient decisions that our participants and their parents undertook to facilitate travel amid and in defiance of White supremacy. Throughout our critical reading of oral history transcripts we sought to understand how the travel patterns and behaviors of participants and their families were informed and influenced by the labor of regulating their feelings of fear, anxiety, and vulnerability, their exposure to the anticipated hostility of Whites, and the extent to which racism on the road may affect them physically and psychologically.

Interviews, both highly structured and more loosely organized, are widely used in tourism research (Hanna, Potter, Modlin, Carter, & Butler, 2015; Veal, 2017); however, oral histories remain underutilized within the field. Oral histories offer not only rich narratives for uncovering and preserving eyewitness accounts and memories of past tourism and leisure experiences but also insight into the meaning of those experiences to study participants as part of their wider biography (Trapp-Fallon, 2003). Unlike most standard interview scenarios, oral history interview methods offer more opportunities for researcher-participant interaction and reflexive sharing while giving a 'voice to individuals, often previously neglected by the social science research community' (Trapp-Fallon, 2003, p. 301). Indeed, in collecting these oral histories, we did not see or treat the interviews as merely data and information but as a vehicle for valuing the importance of telling and listening to the stories of people's often untold struggles, and using these narratives to expose, analyze, and challenge racist discourses that would otherwise forget and disregard the experiences of people of color (Solórzano & Yosso, 2002).

From a more practical standpoint, it is important to note differences in carrying out an oral history interview with participants about decades-old, emotion-laden travel behavior versus more standard interviews carried out with tourists concerning more recent travel experiences. Given that '[o]ral history interviews by definition rely on memory and the "use of personal testimony" in order to understand the social world' (Trapp-Fallon, 2003, p. 300), the interviewer may need to employ patient strategies to assist interviewees in remembering the past and engaging in the emotional ethics of helping the participant work through what can be painful memories in their own terms and at their own pace and order.

Our oral history interviewing required allowing participants to answer the same question multiple times during the interview so that they could add details and feelings to their recollection as they remembered them and felt comfortable sharing. When first asked about their feelings while traveling by car during Jim Crow, it was not uncommon to find participants initially downplay their feelings of anxiety and fear—which itself perhaps speaks to the emotional labor exercised by African Americans in defending against the intimidating and anxiety-creating power of racism and even the memories of racism. We would return to interview questions in different ways and at different times during the conversation, allowing participants to elaborate upon their response. We had a standard list of questions and prompts to guide the oral history interview, but interviews often moved beyond these questions and to take a different order than originally planned. The oral history process emphasized listening to and talking with participants rather than simply posing questions and record- ing responses.

Unpacking African American driving practices during Jim Crow

Our oral history interviews with each participant ranged from half an hour to almost two hours in duration. Participants are identified here using pseudonyms. Given space constraints, we offer a selective analysis of participant responses as they remembered and reflected upon their experiences as automobile drivers and passengers during the era of institutionalized segregation, discrimination, and racialized violence. In particu- lar, emphasis is placed on using their 'Jim Crow Journey Stories' to understand in his- torical geographic specificity a number of important themes: (1) the physical and emotional threats and consequences of driving that constituted an atmosphere of White supremacy on highways; (2) the emotional labor and affective politics underly- ing what appeared to be merely practical driving strategies, tourism decisions, and travel preparations; (3) how the everyday resilience and resistance of Black motorists was frequently tied to redefining the racialized atmospheric politics of the road as it was seen and experienced by their children.

Racialized atmospheres on the road

Smith et al. (2011, p. 65) note that racism and racial aggression 'operate as psycho- pollutants in the social environment and add to the overall race-related stress for Black men, Black women, and other racially marginalized groups'. Our interviews with participating African Americans reveal, sometimes in stark terms, the significant stress felt by motorists as they navigated and negotiated the racialized highways of the United States, even as they admitted that driving a private car gave them more free- dom and agency than racialized forms of public transportation. A number of partici- pants retold stories that, while several decades old, vividly captured their anxiety about driving long distances away from home and how being on the road increased their vulnerability to the physical, social, and psychological effects of racism. In describing the atmosphere of White supremacy that enveloped American highways, participants concretely connected their anxious feelings about traveling to real experi- ences of racial intimidation, harassment, and violence that they or others they knew had experienced. Importantly, the idea of the atmospheric politics of race is more than simply the mood or tone of Jim Crow America. Atmosphere captures the perva- sive and immersive way that racism engulfed and shaped every social, bodily, and emotive dimension of Black life. The construction and maintenance of this racialized atmosphere was part of rather than apart from the production of anti-Black violence, inequality, and controlled immobility. In describing experiences on the road, our inter- viewees recounted a history in which the automobile was a highly charged site for reminding African Americans of the precarious position they held within a white supremacist order, hence contributing to anxiety about their well-being while driving. Informing this anxiety were real instances of intimidation and violence precipitated by hostile White authorities and citizens.

Three Jim Crow Journey Stories relayed to us in oral history interviews shed light on the humiliations, intimidations, and injuries that undergirded the atmospheric politics of travel for people of color. In one of the most disturbing stories we collected, Adam (born 1931) described how a motor vehicle became a weapon for the racist control of an African American who had violated one of the central taboos of Jim Crow, engaging in sexual relations with a white woman. Adam recounted:

> [O]ne night our friend was liking this White girl, and … the White [man] pulled a chain around his neck, and tied him around the truck. And drug him down the highway … All the skin had come off. And he died. Cause he would touch a White girl.

This oral history testimony about the use of an automobile in lynching is instructive of the racism that could be associated so instrumentally with transportation, and how the atmosphere of Jim Crow roads could be a violent and highly affective assemblage of machines, social orders, built environments, sexual encounters, and the bodies of Whites and Blacks. While Adam's story is not typical of all oral histories we collected, it offers nonetheless an important glimpse into the raw brutality found on racist highways that we often do not hear about amid more common stories of African American travelers being refused places to eat, stay, or use the bathroom.

One of our participants, Bob (born 1942), offered his own highly evocative account of the bodily obstacles and threats one would encounter along Jim Crow's highways. While born and raised in east Tennessee and a resident of Knoxville for several decades, Bob's parents traveled out of town three to four times a year, often to visit extended family in Alabama. He described the denied service and racial slurs that his father endured at gas stations while trying unsuccessfully to have his car fixed after it broke down on a trip from Tennessee to Alabama. He also talked about the hostility and hate one might face, physically and emotionally, when driving through unfamiliar communities.

> I remember one time that I was traveling with my dad. I'm not sure where we were but, they [Whites] started throwing rocks and things up against the car. Broke the windshield and stuff like that. And it was just because you're Black, I mean, he didn't do anything. He just, he stopped at the wrong place.

Bob's biography, in particular, is illustrative of how African American automobility was seldom realized outside the history and experiences of anti-Black violence and threats to well-being. He noted that while he and his parents made regular trips to Alabama to visit his grandparents, most of the trips were done covertly in the dark of the night, in an attempt to go undetected by the town's sheriff. Bob's father had physically hurt the sheriff in retaliation for a lewd remark the officer had made about his wife (Bob's mother). His father was subsequently run out of his hometown in Alabama by the Ku Klux Klan. They fled by car, later relocating to Tennessee. For Bob and his family, how and when they traveled by automobile between Knoxville and Alabama was directly shaped by the threat of potential violence and the necessity of avoiding, subverting, and resisting that victimization.

While Jim Crow highways were certainly sites marked by violent discrimination, their oppressive atmospheric politics could be felt even when physical force was not actually exerted. Marjorie (born 1936) tells of such an experience, describing the police harassment that she and her friends faced on a trip returning from Chicago. She later moved and worked for many years in Chicago (and later Detroit) before retiring to her hometown of Knoxville.

> Some friends of ours who had a little motorcade, it was like three cars, and the cop got [behind us] ... .It was in Kentucky. And he started following us, and we kind of knew what was going on. So, he finally stopped us and said our friend was speeding. And we were all going about the same because we were like a little motorcade. He took us back in the woods somewhere and fined us [and gave us a ticket] .... And it was like two or three o'clock in the morning, so it was quite frightening. And I guess that's the worst experience I've ever had, as far as driving.

In hearing Marjorie's story, one is reminded of the tactics of intimidation employed by White authorities as they policed the social and spatial boundaries of racism. Going back into the woods to be ticketed was decidedly about engineering the affective atmosphere on the road to produce fear and anxiety among African American travelers and tourists. This anxiety was heightened not only by the uncertainty of what the 'cop' might do or not but, importantly, where he decided to take Marjorie's party. Wildlands, such as wooded areas, hold a powerful place in the African American social memory because of their negative association with racialized violence, from enslavement to lynching during Jim Crow (Johnson, 1998). In this respect, the racialized atmospheres of Jim Crow highways become intimately connected to the wider environments and emotional historical geographies of being Black, profiled, and threatened in America.

The emotional labor of driving during Jim Crow

For participants in our oral history study, the atmosphere or 'feel' of the Jim Crow era along highways was inseparable from an expectation that traveling by car would expose them to the harsh if not deadly realities and consequences of racism and the demeaning control of Black movements, bodies, and emotions. The affective potency of this racialized atmosphere, while realized through actual instances of discrimination and violence, was also due to the fearful uncertainty felt by drivers in not knowing whether, when, or where they might encounter white hostility. Hence, this uncertainty and anxiety about what may happen made traveling by automobile emotionally burdensome as drivers and their passengers stayed on guard when encountering others on the road, especially law enforcement officials. The emotional labor of uneasy anticipation and dread was especially evident in the words of many of our interviewees, especially an African American female (born 1925) named here as Florida,

> ...the whole time during and before civil rights [movement], you were always a little scared of being pulled over or stopped. Every time we saw a police car, they didn't seem to be friendly.

Florida's comments capture the extra emotional labor that African Americans had to perform versus their White counterparts. For Black motorists, tourism was not simply the physical and technological work of driving, but it is also required the emotional labor of managing the stress of driving within and against an atmosphere of

White supremacy that always carried with it the uncertainty of how, when, and where one might encounter racial hostility while traveling.

It is true that some African Americans resisted Jim Crow discrimination and managed the anxieties and stresses of racism on the road by simply refusing to travel (Jackson, 2018), but many chose to develop and carry out creative driving strategies that allowed them to exercise greater control over their journeys and the degree to which Jim Crow would affect them. These travel strategies, on the surface, would seem to be merely practical, commonsense decisions made by Black motorists to ensure that they reach their destinations. However, these decisions were never solely about making physical progress down the road; for African Americans, driving was always laden with emotions and affects that required managing. Our participant Florida, for example, described how she and her family chose to drive well after dark because 'we felt a little safer'. It was common for African American tourists to travel at night or early hours of morning to minimize their visibility and hence exposure to White law enforcement officers, who may or may not unfairly treat and even arrest Black motorists. Driving at night helped Florida and her family physically travel farther down the road, but this practice was also informed and guided by a deeper desire to defy, if not outright redefine, the affective atmosphere of Jim Crow. This creative driving strategy produced a time and a place on the highway where African Americans could feel safer and exercise self-determination over their lives. Driving, in this respect, was not just the work of regulating a machine and how one moved along roadways; it also constituted the labor of managing the travelers' emotional states and senses of fear and anxiety, as well as those of the White public, which could become hostile by seeing a Black family moving freely through their community.

The Jim Crow Journey Stories we collected reveal other driving strategies that are seemingly commonsense and ordinary, but which were informed and intertwined with the emotional labor of circumventing, subverting, and surviving the toll of White supremacy. For instance, most of our interviewees stressed how they or their parents made strategic choices about routes, duration of travel, and number of trips as way of managing their feelings of discomfort and uncertainty and not provoking the anger of Whites. A number of participants mentioned the necessity of minimizing one's time on the road in Mississippi, a state that held a strong place in their minds because of its reputation for rampant racial inequality and its brutalizing treatment of African Americans. Oral history participant Josenna (born 1936) recalled, for example, 'My dad would not go to Mississippi on any kind of trip. We'd go to Florida, we'd go to New York, we'd go to Detroit, but he would not go to Mississippi'.

For those Black motorists who, unlike Josenna's father, could not simply circumvent or avoid Mississippi and other places identified as being enveloped within a harsh atmosphere of White supremacy, it was common for them to drive through these locations non-stop without breaking to eat, sleep, or re-fuel. Marjorie (born 1936) captures the stress she felt when confronted with moving through Mississippi, her anticipation of encountering racial hostility, and how she and her family managed these feelings on the road by hurrying the pace of their travel.

> Once we drove to New Orleans and went through Mississippi, I really didn't feel comfortable … we didn't stop. We made sure we were gassed up to try to get straight

through there. Yes, I'm sure I would've probably been denied, and I had heard so much about those little places in Mississippi till I was just afraid. I really didn't give them an opportunity.

Marjorie's remarks suggest that the decision to drive quickly through Mississippi, while certainly motivated by feelings of fear, represented a more complex strategy of self-defense and everyday resistance. Believing that the likelihood of encountering racial hostility and discrimination was likely if they stopped, Marjorie saw non-stop driving as part of the labor of controlling her emotional and physical exposure to that racism, protecting her own sense of worth and subverting what she calls the 'opportunity' for a White supremacist society to deny her service and rights as a citizen. As much as it may seem that Marjorie and her family's mobility patterns were dictated and affected by the racialized atmosphere of Jim Crow, we argue that these uneven, power-laden practices on the road were much more nuanced when looking at them through the lens of emotional labor and affective politics.

Marjorie's account of driving through Mississippi also suggests that we revisit the strategic value of avoidance as a practice of resilience and resistance during the Jim Crow era. It might be easy to interpret the African American decision not to confront destinations that refused to serve Black tourists as a form of accommodation or acquiescence to White supremacy. Alderman and Inwood (2016) note that the line between accommodation and resistance is not so rigidly set in the lives of ordinary, working class African Americans whose political praxis is deeply couched within daily struggles for survival, self-expression, and opportunity. Because of what has come to count as Black resistance and activism within much of academic and popular thought, we often downplay the radical potential of everyday decisions and practices that are not overt forms of protest. In the case of Jim Crow automobility, we suggest that some African American travel decisions and practices are open to re-appraisal as moments of emotional and political agency and negotiation rather than merely impositions of racial domination.

To illustrate our point, we would like to turn to a subject frequently brought up by participants in the oral history project—travel preparations. As you might expect based on the popular memory that we have about tourism during Jim Crow, our interviewees stressed the need to be prepared for travel. Black motorists frequently carried food, water, and even some of the fuel that one would need for the journey across a White supremacist tourist landscape filled with unwelcoming and segregated restaurants and gas stations that would not even allow Black patrons to use their bathrooms. Experiencing racism is always intersectional and Stokely (born 1941) noted how women bore a disproportionate burden to the indignity of having no place to relieve oneself along highways. He said: 'It was easy for a man to go into the woods [along the road] to use the bathroom, but it was more difficult for a woman'. As Adam (born 1931) noted to us, it was customary for him and his family to carry jugs in the car for urinating in the automobile while in transit. A number of our oral history participants also remembered sleeping in their cars on the road, especially as they moved through unfamiliar cities and towns in which they did not have family or friends to provide lodging. It is worth noting that just one of interviewees indicated using *The Green Book* travel guide during Jim Crow to find accommodations and almost all did not know what the *Green Book* was. Interviewees suggest that most of their resilient navigation around racial inequalities on the road resulted from word-of-mouth directions and advice from fellow Black travelers, critically reading the landscape of segregation (i.e. identifying the Black side of town from the avoided White part), and their own resourcefulness in preparing physically and psychologically for the trip's obstacles.

While these extensive preparations were certainly necessary, as experienced African American travelers time and time again found no accommodations and limited service, Black motorists also saw these preparations as a means to avoid humiliating and abusive interactions with White merchants. Again, even the most mundane, practical tourism activity had an underlying emotional labor that informed the practice and made it affectively meaningful along with fulfilling the obvious need to get to one's destination. The wider emotionality behind preparations and planning was detectable in the comments of Marjorie (born 1936) describing social geographic intelligence that she and her family used on the road.

> We would map our trips out. And mostly, we were going to the same place. So, we had certain places that we stopped going and coming and we knew they were safe places, and certain places going back. ....We would stop at the same places and eat and gas up. And I guess that was a safe thing for us to do, and when we got to that certain destination that was a feeling of accomplishment, you know? Oh, we've gotten this far, we can get so much farther. So I guess we did a lot of planning.

Marjorie's recollections suggest that a well-planned, safe trip could assist not only in managing and mitigating feelings of fear and uncertainty about encountering racial discrimination but that this travel planning could also contribute to a 'feeling of accomplishment' and empowerment as they made material progress down the road. Marjorie's experience illustrates a transformative moment in the atmospheric politics of Jim Crow racism. She and her family used travel planning to produce an alternative geographic knowledge of the road to subvert the emotional control that White supremacy had over them—at least temporarily—and to redefine that atmosphere to include in some small way a place of self-determination and resilient everyday resistance.

Driving as parental management of children's emotions

The emotional labor of driving within and against an atmosphere of White supremacy was detectable in many of the stories and comments collected from our oral history participants from Knoxville, but none more so than when interviewees described how driving intersected with the politics of parenthood. Several participants recounted how they or their parents drove in certain ways and along certain routes to limit children's exposure to the physical and psychological effects of Jim Crow on the road. Historians note that some African American parents were especially mindful of protecting their children from seeing and experiencing the brutal, humiliating aspects of institutional segregation and discrimination, as well as how this racism demeaned and injured the image they had of their parents (Ritterhouse, 2006). Bob (born 1942) pointed to this fact in his oral history interview. His father viewed the freedom to drive and efforts to circumvent and subvert racism while traveling as important to parenting as well as his own psychological well-being.

> [Driving] gave him … flexibility, and I think it kept my dad at peace of mind with trying to be a Black man. Especially in the presence of his children. I mean he didn't like, and naturally no one would … to be denigrated and called boy and all that stuff, especially in our presence. He always taught us to try to be strong young men.

The emotional labor of navigating and negotiating the Jim Crow highway and its racialized atmospheres meant that African American parents were quite mindful of how, where, and when they drove might affect their children's vulnerability, not just in terms of witnessing racial discrimination but also to being a victim of those inequalities. This point was echoed repeatedly in the Jim Crow Journey Stories of Florida (born 1925), who often remembered the stress of driving at the height of segregation in terms of how it would have impacted her young, twin daughters and how she and her husband adapted their travel decisions regarding preparations and driving non-stop as a means of managing their children's exposure to the violence of White supremacy.

> We didn't ever feel really comfortable traveling, even though he [my husband] was used to traveling … from Knoxville back to Alabama, and Alabama to Knoxville. We just never felt that comfortable, and particularly, what would somebody try to do to us or to our children, who could not defend themselves [or understand what was going on]? … .We were even afraid at times to pull over and stop. We carried our water, and everything to eat, and everything.

In particular, Florida's remembrances were helpful in capturing the emotional labor that traveling African American parents faced in explaining the inequalities of White supremacy to their children and dealing with the stress of helping their children know the rules and unjust logics of how to negotiate safely the atmosphere of racial apartheid at destinations. She retold a powerful story of visiting a five and dime store and the mental anguish of helping her twin daughters, who are now almost 70 years old, understand why they could drink from the 'Colored' drinking fountain but not from the fountain reserved only for White patrons. According to Florida, 'Here are two children, and two water fountains. How do you tell a three-year-old, 'But see, you're Black, and that says White only?' One of her daughters never fully understood that day's lesson in navigating Jim Crow, and in Florida's words 'I just didn't want her to have to [understand]'. As Florida's journey story illustrates, navigating and negotiating tourist destinations carried with it, for African Americans, the identity labor of determining their place and limits within the prevailing racial order and atmosphere, while finding a means of coping with and making sense of racial aggressions and injustices. This identity labor can be highly stressful and emotionally and physically draining. The resilient embodied performances of driving for Black motorists was about being aware of not only the physical hazards of the road but also those places in the emotional geography of traveling and social learning that could pose difficulty for them and their children.

Concluding remarks

As demonstrated through the above words of African American travelers during the Jim Crow era, mobility was an intensely embodied and emotionally fraught struggle against White supremacy. Our analysis of their powerful Jim Crow Journey Stories yields three significant contributions to the literature on racialized mobility and tourism. First, the concept of emotional labor, largely applied to tourism workers in previous studies, can also be applied to understanding the actions and behaviors of tourists themselves, especially in politically charged destinations and as part of the identity work of marginalized groups. Second, African American travelers utilized everyday emotion-laden practices—such as carrying surplus supplies, planning the pace, timing, and route of driving, and stopping at strategically chosen locations—to navigate a hostile road and protect them and their families from potentially confrontational situations. Third, this paper demonstrates how oral histories can center the narratives and strategies of marginalized populations and the integral role these histories can have in the study of travel and tourism. The 10 oral histories analyzed by the authors reveal the highly contestable nature of travel during a time when the atmospheric politics of White supremacy created physically and psychologically violent conditions that travelers of color actively resisted against as they exercised their mobile agency. Layering this micro-level analysis of embodied travel practices and decisions with a macro, structural understanding of the atmospheric politics of racism offers a fuller unpacking of Jim Crow travel experiences than available through increasingly popular discussion of the *Green Book*.

Scholars increasingly interested in the role of emotions, feelings, and affects in tourism can benefit from revisiting the historical geographies of African American travel. The Black experience, particularly as it developed in and through automobility, sheds light on how tourism existed within and was heavily shaped by an affective politics of racial humiliation, intimidation, and sometimes violence that African American travelers have long labored under and, to some extent, still do today. The Jim Crow Journey Stories represented in this paper, while certainly set within the past and deployed here to analyze the historical racialization of tourism, point to the analytical and political value of examining the emotion-laden narratives of a broader array of travelers of color from other time periods, including the contemporary. Even now as #TravelingWhileBlack and #DrivingWhileBlack remain important social justice concerns (Dillette et al., 2018; Nicholson, 2016), there is a need to create spaces for racialized social actors and groups to engage in resistant storytelling about their embodied experiences on the road, the everyday resilience and contestation they carry out in traveling, and their own emotional labor strategies for managing their feelings and sense of place and mobility within the American travel landscape. Future work, based on the foundations laid out in this study, can make use of a storytelling approach to understand the emotional labor and counter-mobility work that present-day travelers of color embody and practice as they navigate a country that is still full of racialized attitudes, journeys, and violence. Any effort to achieve equity and reconciliation in tourism must ultimately be a political project attuned to the affective racial politics of mobility in America—past and present.

Disclosure statement

No potential conflict of interest was reported by the authors.

ORCID

Derek H. Alderman ⓘ http://orcid.org/0000-0002-5192-8103

References

Alderman, D. H. (2013). Introduction to the special issue: African Americans and tourism. *Tourism Geographies, 15*(3), 375–379. doi:10.1080/14616688.2012.762544

Alderman, D. H. (2018). The racialized and violent biopolitics of mobility in the USA: An agenda for tourism geographies. *Tourism Geographies, 20*(4), 717–720. doi:10.1080/14616688.2018. 1477168

Alderman, D. H., & Inwood, J. (2014). Toward a pedagogy of Jim Crow: A geographic reading of The Green Book. L. E. Estaville, E. J. Montalvo, and F. A. Akiwumi (Eds.), *Teaching Ethnic Geography in the 21st Century* (pp. 68–78). Washington DC: National Council for Geographic Education.

Alderman, D. H., & Inwood, J. (2016). Mobility as antiracism work: The "hard driving" of NASCAR's Wendell Scott. *Annals of the American Association of Geographers, 106*(3), 597–611. doi:10.1080/00045608.2015.1118339

Alderman, D. H., & Modlin, E. A. (2013). Southern hospitality and the politics of African American belonging: An analysis of North Carolina tourism brochure photographs. *Journal of Cultural Geography, 30*(1), 6–31. doi:10.1080/08873631.2012.745978

Algeo, K. (2013). Underground tourists/tourists underground: African American tourism to Mammoth Cave. *Tourism Geographies, 15*(3), 380–404. doi:10.1080/14616688.2012.675514

Barton, A. W., & Leonard, S. J. (2010). Incorporating social justice in tourism planning: Racial reconciliation and sustainable community development in the Deep South. *Community Development, 41*(3), 298–322. doi:10.1080/15575330903444051

Booker, R. (2017). *An Encyclopedia: Experiences of Black People in Knoxville, Tennessee, 1844-1974.* Knoxville, TN. Russell Printing Options.

Buda, D. M., d'Hauteserre, A. M., & Johnston, L. (2014). Feeling and tourism studies. *Annals of Tourism Research, 46*, 102–114. doi:10.1016/j.annals.2014.03.005

Butler, D. L. (2001). Whitewashing plantations: The commodification of a slave-free Antebellum South. *International Journal of Hospitality & Tourism Administration, 2*(3-4), 163–175. doi:10. 1300/J149v02n03_07

Butler, D. L., Carter, P. L., & Brunn, S. D. (2002). African-American travel agents: Travails and survival. *Annals of Tourism Research, 29*(4), 1022–1035. doi:10.1016/S0160-7383(02)00022-1

Carter, P. L. (2008). Coloured places and pigmented holidays: Racialized leisure travel. *Tourism Geographies, 10*(3), 265–284. doi:10.1080/14616680802236287

Cole, S. & Morgan, N. (Eds.) (2010). *Tourism and inequality: Problems and prospects.* Oxford: CABI

Dillette, A. K., Benjamin, S., & Carpenter, C. (2018). Tweeting the black travel experience: Social media counternarrative stories as innovative insight on# TravelingWhileBlack. *Journal of Travel Research*. doi:10.1177/0047287518802087

Edensor, T., & Sumartojo, S. (2015). Designing atmospheres: Introduction to special issue. *Visual Communication, 14*(3), 251–265. doi:10.1177/1470357215582305

Evans, L., & Moore, W. L. (2015). Impossible burdens: White institutions, emotional labor, and micro-resistance. *Social Problems, 62*(3), 439–454. doi:10.1093/socpro/spv009

Finney, C. (2014). *Black faces, White spaces: Reimagining the relationship of African Americans to the great outdoors.* Chapel Hill: UNC Press Books.

Finney, J. R., & Potter, A. E. (2018). "You're out of your place": Black mobility on Tybee Island, Georgia from civil rights to orange crush. *Southeastern Geographer, 58*(1), 104–124. doi:10.1353/sgo.2018.0007

Franz, K. (2008). The open road: Automobility and racial uplift in the interwar years. In B. Sinclair (Ed.), *Technology and the African American experience: Needs and opportunities for study* (pp. 131–153). Cambridge: MIT Press.

Gabriel, A. S., Daniels, M. A., Diefendorff, J. M., & Greguras, G. J. (2015). Emotional labor actors: A latent profile analysis of emotional labor strategies. *Journal of Applied Psychology, 100*(3), 863–879.

Gordon, T. S. (2015). 'Take Amtrak to Black History': Marketing heritage tourism to African Americans in the 1970s. *Journal of Tourism History, 7*(1-2), 54–74. doi:10.1080/1755182X.2015.1047804

Hague, E. (2010). 'The right to enter every other state' – The Supreme Court and African American mobility in the United States. *Mobilities, 5*(3), 331–347. doi:10.1080/17450101.2010.494839

Hanna, S. P. Potter, A. E. Modlin, E. A. Carter, P. & Butler, D. L. (Eds.) (2015). *Social memory and heritage tourism methodologies.* New York, NY: Routledge.

Henry, J. (2018). The unspeakable Whiteness of volunteer tourism. *Annals of Tourism Research, 76*, 326–327.

Hochschild, A. R. (1983). *The managed heart: The commercialization of feeling.* Berkeley, CA. University of California Press.

Inwood, J. F., & Alderman, D. H. (2018). When the archive sings to you: SNCC and the atmospheric politics of race. *Cultural Geographies, 25*(2), 361–368. doi:10.1177/1474474017739023

Jamal, T., & Camargo, B. A. (2014). Sustainable tourism, justice and an ethic of care: Toward the just destination. *Journal of Sustainable Tourism, 22*(1), 11–30. doi:10.1080/09669582.2013.786084

Jackson, A. T. (2018). Remembering Jim Crow, again–critical representations of African American experiences of travel and leisure at US National Park Sites. *International Journal of Heritage Studies, 25*(7), 671–688.

Johnson, C. Y. (1998). A consideration of collective memory in African American attachment to wildland recreation places. *Human Ecology Review, 5*(1), 5–15.

Johnson, C. Y., & Bowker, J. M. (2004). African-American wildland memories. *Environmental Ethics, 26*(1), 57–75. doi:10.5840/enviroethics200426141

Kahn, E. (2015). The 'Green Book' legacy, a beacon for black travelers. *New York Times*, August 6. Retrieved from https://www.nytimes.com/2015/08/07/arts/design/the-green-book-legacy-a-beacon-for-black-travelers.html

Kruml, S. M., & Geddes, D. (2000). Exploring the dimensions of emotional labor: The heart of Hochschild's work. *Management Communication Quarterly, 14*(1), 8–49. doi:10.1177/0893318900141002

Lee, K. J., & Scott, D. (2016). Bourdieu and African Americans' park visitation: The case of cedar hill state park in Texas. *Leisure Sciences, 38*(5), 424–440. doi:10.1080/01490400.2015.1127188

Lee, K. J., & Scott, D. (2017). Racial discrimination and African Americans' travel behavior: The utility of habitus and vignette technique. *Journal of Travel Research, 56*(3), 381–392. doi:10.1177/0047287516643184

Loewen, J. W. (2018). *Sundown towns: A hidden dimension of American racism*. New York, NY: The New Press.

Logan, R. W. (1965). *The betrayal of the negro: From Rutherford B. Hayes to Woodrow Wilson*. New York, NY: Collier Books.

Mandala Research. (2017). *The African American traveler, 2017 edition*. Alexandria, VA: Mandala Research.

Maruyama, N. U. (2017). Reunion or disconnection? Emotional labor among individual roots tourist who are second-generation Chinese-Americans. *International Journal of Culture, Tourism and Hospitality Research, 11*(3), 309–320.

Mitchell, J. T., & Collins, L. (2014). The Green Book: "Safe spaces" from place to place. *The Geography Teacher, 11*(1), 29–36. doi:10.1080/19338341.2013.854259

Nicholson, J. A. (2016). Don't shoot! Black mobilities in American gunscapes. *Mobilities, 11*(4), 553–563. doi:10.1080/17450101.2016.1211823

O'Brien, W. E. (2015). *Landscapes of exclusion: State Parks and Jim Crow in the American South*. Amherst: University of Massachusetts Press.

Ortlepp, A. (2017). *Jim Crow terminals: The desegregation of American airports*. Athens: University of Georgia Press.

Pesses, M. W. (2017). Road less traveled: Race and American automobility. *Mobilities, 12*(5), 677–691. doi:10.1080/17450101.2016.1240319

Philipp, S. F. (1994). Race and tourism choice: A legacy of discrimination? *Annals of Tourism Research, 21*(3), 479–488. doi:10.1016/0160-7383(94)90115-5

Pritchard, A., & Morgan, N. J. (2000). Privileging the male gaze: Gendered tourism landscapes. *Annals of Tourism Research, 27*(4), 884–905. doi:10.1016/S0160-7383(99)00113-9

Pryor, E. S. (2016). *Colored travelers: Mobility and the fight for citizenship before the Civil War*. Chapel Hill: UNC Press Books.

Reclaiming Our Histories: Urban Renewal Stories. (2018). Flyer advertising public storytelling program held April 28, 2018 at Carpetbag Theater in Knoxville, Tennessee. Retrieved from: http://www.carpetbagtheatre.org/events/urban-renewal-stories

Ritterhouse, J. L. (2006). *Growing up Jim Crow: How black and white Southern children learned race*. Chapel Hill: University of North Carolina Press.

Ruhanen, L., & Whitford, M. (2018). Racism as an inhibitor to the organizational legitimacy of Indigenous tourism businesses in Australia. *Current Issues in Tourism, 21*(15), 1728–1742. doi:10.1080/13683500.2016.1225698

Salman, D., & Uygur, D. (2010). Creative tourism and emotional labor: An investigatory model of possible interactions. *International Journal of Culture, Tourism and Hospitality Research, 4*(3), 186–197. doi:10.1108/17506181011067583

Seiler, C. (2006). "So that we as a race might have something authentic to travel by": African American automobility and Cold-War liberalism. *American Quarterly, 58*(4), 1091–1117. doi:10.1353/aq.2007.0015

Sheller, M. (2004). Automotive emotions: Feeling the car. *Theory, Culture & Society, 21*(4-5), 221–242. doi:10.1177/0263276404046068

Smith, W. A., Hung, M., & Franklin, J. D. (2011). Racial battle fatigue and the miseducation of Black men: Racial microaggressions, societal problems, and environmental stress. *The Journal of Negro Education, 80*(1), 63–82.

Solórzano, D. G., & Yosso, T. J. (2002). Critical race methodology: Counter-storytelling as an analytical framework for education research. *Qualitative Inquiry, 8*(1), 23–44. doi:10.1177/107780040200800103

Sumartojo, S. (2016). Commemorative atmospheres: Memorial sites, collective events and the experience of national identity. *Transactions of the Institute of British Geographers, 41*(4), 541–553. doi:10.1111/tran.12144

Sumartojo, S., & Pink, S. (2018). *Atmospheres and the experiential world*. London: Routledge.

Taylor, J., Levi, R., & Dinovitzer, R. (2012). Homeland tourism, emotion, and identity labor. *Du Bois Review: Social Science Research on Race, 9*(1), 67–85. doi:10.1017/S1742058X12000069

Till, K. E. (2012). Wounded cities: Memory-work and a place-based ethics of care. *Political Geography*, *31*(1), 3–14. doi:10.1016/j.polgeo.2011.10.008

Torabian, P., & Miller, M. C. (2017). Freedom of movement for all? Unpacking racialized travel experiences. *Current Issues in Tourism*, *20*(9), 931–945. doi:10.1080/13683500.2016.1273882

Townsend, J. (2016). How the Green Book helped African-American tourists navigate a segregated nation. Smithsonian. Retrieved from https://www.smithsonianmag.com/smithsonian-institution/history-green-book-african-american-travelers-180958506/

Trapp-Fallon, J. M. (2003). Searching for rich narratives of tourism and leisure experience: How oral history could provide an answer. *Tourism and Hospitality Research*, *4*(4), 297–305. doi:10.1177/146735840300400403

Tucker, C. N., & Deale, C. S. (2018). Embedded and exposed: Exploring the lived experiences of African American tourists. *Journal of Tourism and Cultural Change*, *16*(5), 482–500.

Veal, A. J. (2017). *Research methods for leisure and tourism*. Harlow: Pearson UK.

Veijola, S. (2009). Introduction: Tourism as work. *Tourist Studies*, *9*(2), 83–87. doi:10.1177/1468797609360748

Waterton, E., & Dittmer, J. (2014). The museum as assemblage: Bringing forth affect at the Australian War Memorial. *Museum Management and Curatorship*, *29*(2), 122–139. doi:10.1080/09647775.2014.888819

Weber, J., & Sultana, S. (2013a). The Civil Rights Movement and the future of the National Park System in a racially diverse America. *Tourism Geographies*, *15*(3), 444–469. doi:10.1080/14616688.2012.675515

Weber, J., & Sultana, S. (2013b). Why do so few minority people visit National Parks? Visitation and the accessibility of "America's Best Idea". *Annals of the Association of American Geographers*, *103*(3), 437–464. doi:10.1080/00045608.2012.689240

Williams, B. C. (2018). *The pursuit of happiness: Black women, diasporic dreams, and the politics of emotional transnationalism*. Durham, NC: Duke University Press.

Wong, J., & Wang, C. (2009). Emotional labor of the tour leaders: An exploratory study. *Tourism Management*, *30*(2), 249–259. doi:10.1016/j.tourman.2008.06.005

Zembylas, M. (2015). Rethinking race and racism as *technologies of affect*: Theorizing the implications for anti-racist politics and practice in education. *Race Ethnicity and Education*, *18*(2), 145–162. doi:10.1080/13613324.2014.946492

Decolonising the 'autonomy of affect' in volunteer tourism encounters

Phoebe Everingham and Sara C. Motta

ABSTRACT

Promotion of volunteer tourism is couched within notions of 'giving back', drawing on affective sentiments of 'care', 'compassion' and 'empathy', reinforced by neo-colonial and neo-liberal notions of developmental aid. It is not surprising then, that scholars are turning to theories of affect to make sense of the embodied, emotional aspects of the volunteering experience. We build on this emerging research trajectory by arguing that in drawing attention to the unequal geographies of international volunteering, the complexities and nuances of affect and emotion demand an engagement with theories that are more attuned to ambiguity, in order to open up dialogue for multiple possibilities. We critically engage with extant theorisations of affect as autonomous in volunteer tourism encounters to explore these possibilities. However we find a tendency within the conceptualisations of affect as autonomous (re)creates binaries, albeit in distinctive forms - with a focus on possibility - to the detriment of power. We therefore turn to decolonial feminist contributions to understand subjectivity, positionality and the pivotal role of the body in research in non-binary ways. We use this framing to reflexively re-engage with fieldwork six years on from a volunteer tourism site in Ecuador to demonstrate the nuances and complexities of theorising the affective aspects of volunteer tourism encounters. We focus this analysis around three key themes that arose in this re-engagement with the fieldwork: i) vulnerability and unlearning ii) critical intimacy and iii) affective closures. We conclude by arguing that the affective spaces in volunteer tourism are at once bound up in, and shaped by, the larger processes of neoliberalism and neo-colonial legacies, while at the same time, they contain borderland encounters of intersubjective relationalities and moments of vulnerability, care, critical intimacy and emergent decolonising connections.

摘要

志愿旅游的推广是在"回馈"的概念下进行的,利用"关怀"、"同情"和"同理心"等情怀,并通过新殖民主义和新自由主义的发展援助概念加以强化。因此,学者们开始求助于情感理论来理解志愿活动的具体情感方面也就不足为奇了。我们基于这一新兴的研究轨迹,认为在引起人们对国际志愿服务的不平等地理关注时,情感和情绪的复杂性和细微差别需要与那些更能适应模糊性的理论进行对话,以便开启多种可能性的对话。我们批判性地研究了现存的关于志愿旅游中自主情感的理论, 以探索上述诸多可能性。然而, 我们发现, 将情感概念化为自主性的趋势造成或者创造了情感的二元性, 这种二元性——尽管是以独特的形式, 侧重于可能性——损害了权力。因此, 我们转向去殖民女性主义的贡献, 以非二元性的方式了解主观性、立场性以及身体在研究中的关键作用。我们利用这一框架条件重新反思厄瓜多尔一个志愿旅游站点6年来的实地工作, 以展示将志愿旅游境遇的情感方面理论化的细微差别和复杂性。我们的分析围绕着三个主要的主题, 这三个主题是在重新参与田野调查时产生的:1)脆弱性和遗忘2)批判性亲密关系和3)情感封闭。我们得出结论认为志愿旅游的情感空间一度沉迷于,并且由新自由主义和新殖民主义遗产塑造的大过程,同时,它们包含主体间关系的模糊际遇和脆弱性、关怀、批判性亲密关系以及浮现出去殖民连接的诸多时刻。

Introduction

You use your time and energy to help others while exploring a different country and culture.

With us, you won't just help and explore as a volunteer, you'll discover what you're capable of
(Projects Abroad: https://www.projects-abroad.com.au/)

Volunteer tourism as 'responsible tourism' taps into a social consciousness concerned with rectifying the damage of mass tourism and is presented by the industry as a more ethical form of tourism. Volunteering is thus positioned as enabling tourists with more 'authentic' understandings of the challenges local communities in the Global South have in terms of poverty and inequality and gives tourists opportunities to 'give back' to the local communities they are visiting (Sin, 2009; Wearing, 2001). Volunteering also gives tourists a 'sensuous experience', through providing them with opportunities to embody 'other' places and people in 'being, doing, and touching' (Sin, 2009, p. 483). The marketing of volunteer tourism embeds these sensuous, affective and emotional aspects of the experience within altruistic desires by tourists to help 'others' represented as in 'need'. However, while these intentions may come from a conscious motivation of care and/or compassion, these projects tend to be couched within development aid models, reinforcing neo-colonial stereotypes of who is in need (the Global South and the subjects and communities to be voluntoured) and who can help (the Global North and the volunteer), in turn influencing the expectations of volunteers in terms of how they should be 'helping', and that they should even be helping at all (Everingham, 2015, 2016, 2018; Lough and Carter-Black, 2015; Palacios, 2010; Wearing, Mostafanezhad, Nguyen, Nguyen, & McDonald, 2018; Wearing, Young, & Everingham, 2017; Vodopivec & Jaffe, 2011) .

Within the context of this affective language of helping in the promotion of volunteer tourism, and the emotional and affective sentiments of 'altruism', 'care' and 'compassion', it is not surprising that scholars are turning to theories of affect to make sense of the embodied emotional aspects of the volunteering experience. As critical tourism scholars point out, emotions are central in mediating tourism encounters and are made sense of by tourists through their emotional and embodied entanglements in their experiences (see Buda, d'Hauteserre, & Johnston, 2014; Buda & McIntosh, 2012;

Tucker, 2016; Tucker & Shelton, 2018; Picard, 2012). Theorising affect in tourism spaces can provide 'new ways of understanding identity, place and power for tourism scholars' (Buda et al., 2014, p. 103), and gives researchers insights into how meaning is generated through subjectivities that are both individual and collective. Affect is connected to broader socio-cultural, economic and political framings of the world, in terms of how they shape our being-in-the-world and in doing so they alter how the world is experienced and our sense of who we are (Davidson & Milligan, 2004).

In the context of volunteer tourism, attention to affects and emotions can tell us much about how broader structures of power, poverty and injustice are (re)produced as well as turn our attention towards the 'more-than-rational' (Anderson, 2006), 'more-than-representational' (Lorimer, 2005) and 'more-than-volunteering' (Smith, Timbrell, Woolvin, Muirhead, & Fyfe, 2010) aspects of the experience. The 'more-than' refers to an expansion of how the social is typically theorised, and includes 'how life takes shape and gains expression in shared experiences, everyday routines, fleeting encounters, embodied movements, precognitive triggers, practical skills, affective intensities, enduring urges, unexceptional interactions and the sensuous dispositions' (Lorimer, 2005, p. 84). To make sense of the 'more-than-representational' and 'more-than volunteering' encounters that occur in volunteer tourism, we call for a reading of affect that complicates fixed universal understandings of the subjectivities of the volunteers and local communities and their encounters. We include non-universalist understandings of emotional registers (Tolia-Kelly, 2006) in our theorisation of affect and position the body, affect and emotion not as series of repeated (or separate/autonomous) moments but as 'an ongoing, incrementally altering chain' that influences 'the individual's capacity to act in the world' (Hemmings, 2005, p. 564).

In this article, we unpack the ways in which the affective aspects of volunteer tourism have been theorised thus far. On the one hand, affect in volunteer tourism is presented as a manipulation of neo-colonial and neoliberal forms of 'object-target power' (Griffiths, 2014, p. 2) that eases the anxieties volunteers may have about their privilege within uneven neo-colonial and neoliberal geographies (Crossley, 2012; Mostafanezhad, 2013, 2014; Vrasti, 2013). On the other hand, affect is presented as being autonomous from, or excessive/transcendent to these geopolitical orderings (Frazer & Waitt, 2016; Griffiths, 2014, 2015a, 2015b). We want to explore an analysis of affect in volunteer tourism encounters that does not frame them as either soley embedded within neo-colonial and neoliberal geographies or as autonomous/transcendent from these power dynamics. Instead we wish to explore the affirmative possibilities that these disentanglements from binaries in academic analysis provides, to explore moments of vulnerability where volunteers undergo an 'unlearning' of colonial ways of being-in-the world (even if only momentarily and emergent). At the same time however, we do not negate the influence that neo-colonial stereotypes and broader neoliberal logics have on these encounters. We focus on decolonial feminist frameworks because they seek to problematise binary framings of encounter and subjectivity without denying that binary hierarchies are existent.

We thus foreground decolonial feminist theorising to articulate affect as being embodied within the spaces of the in-between. We draw on the first author's fieldwork, of a volunteer tourism organisation in Ecuador, to reflexively re-engage with the encounters she experienced in the field through the in-between emergent languaging of Spanglish. Languaging refers to the creative and emergent aspects of language use (Chow, 2014) and is particularly pertinent in the context of creole languages such as Spanglish, where the contact zones between English and Spanish bring about 'interactive, improvisational dimensions' (Pratt, 1992, p. 7) of languaging. This embodied experience with languaging was a site of unlearning the colonial hegemony of English as an unthought linguistic medium, providing opportunities for both volunteers and the voluntoured to experience moments of what Motta (2014, 2017a) refers to as 'critical intimacy'. In these moments of critical intimacy there are emergent opportunities for unlearning the unthought colonial perpetuations of volunteer as expert/helper/White Saviour and local communities as deficit model. At the same time, the dominance of neo-colonial and neoliberal discourses of 'helping' is also present in these encounters, closing off some of the decolonial potentials for critical intimacy to mediate these tourism spaces. Affect circulates within the relationalities of the everyday encounters in volunteer tourism, and has the potential to reify these power relations as well as subvert them. While critical intimacy which encapsulates emotions such care and compassion can be become commodified in these spaces, as pointed out by Mostafanezhad (2013, 2014) and Sin (2009), we unpack how these emotions can also be a site of possibility for decolonising connections (Motta, 2016, 2017a,b,c, 2018). Affects in volunteer tourism are more ambivalent than any singular, monological (ethnocentric) logic can capture.

The spectrum of emotions and affects (and how we theorise them) in volunteer tourism

Volunteers embody a particular 'White' subjectivity in terms of how they inhabit these volunteering spaces, embedded within 'White' patriarchal capitalist-colonial legacies (see Ahmed, 2007; Motta, 2018). As Bandyopadhyay and Patil (2017, p. 654) argue, 'the racialised, gendered logics of volunteer tourism' emerges from a particular colonial environment of 'White Saviour' through the 'civilised masculinity of colonialist men'. The historic connection between volunteer tourism and the 'White Saviour' complex in popular media and academic critiques, is according to Wearing et al. (2018, p. 510), imbricated within contemporary forms of popular, neoliberal humanitarianism which highlights a 'desperate need for a more thorough and sustained analysis of race and class in the industry and its encounters'. Volunteer tourism is thus embedded within these broader structural power dynamics and this influences the emotions and affects that circulate between volunteers and local communities.

Affect has been utilised in the critiques of volunteer tourism, to emphasise the manipulation of the affective, emotional and embodied experiences of volunteers by neo-colonial and neoliberal forms of 'object-target power' (Griffiths, 2014, p. 2). In these critiques of volunteer tourism, affect is theorised as being 'engineered' to distract volunteers from broader issues of power or even ease the guilt volunteers may feel in the face of their privileged positions in these uneven neo-colonial and neoliberal geographies (Griffiths, 2014). Volunteering is understood as producing, sustaining and legitimising 'forms of subjectivity and social relations congruent with the ethos of neoliberal capital' (Vrasti & Montsion, 2014, p. 336), where volunteers learn to develop particular emotional responses to distant others as part of their 'flexible, cultural competencies', an inherent requirement of being a successful individual within neoliberal economies where individuals must be "'self-managing' and 'self-enterprising'" (Mostafanezhad, 2014, p. 106). In these accounts then, intimacy and emotional connection only work to buffer volunteers against an awareness or uncomfortableness of the perpetuation of inequalities within these neo-colonial (re)creations of power by drawing on orientalist ideas of the voluntoured as 'poor' yet 'happy' and 'exotic' (Crossley, 2012; Simpson, 2004). Volunteers are positioned as neoliberal foot soldiers governed by, and complicit in the (re)production an everyday affectivity of neoliberal order, that co-opts cosmopolitan care and empathy for 'the other' in order to perpetuate the expansion and ever deeper consolidation into individual subjectivities and desires, this global hegemony.

However, attention to affect and emotion in volunteer tourism has not only highlighted the (re)production of logics of containment and/of coloniality but also their transformative possibilities through attention to emotions such as empathy, compassion, pleasure, sorrow, anger, hope, and guilt (Everingham, 2016; Frazer & Waitt, 2016; Germann Molz, 2016; Guiney, 2018; Koleth, 2014; Mostafanezhad, 2013). Focus on such emotions illustrates not only the psychological mechanisms that perpetuate unequal geographies of volunteering but also opens up analysis towards the potential subversive affective elements of encounters between volunteers and hosts. Being attentive to these subversions however, requires an analysis that foregrounds a conceptualisation of power that is less codified and codifying than framing affect as being *either* complicit with *or* autonomous, excessive or transcendent of the neoliberal colonial order. Instead, we argue that these albeit momentary subversions of power through encounters in volunteer tourism inhabit in-between messy and non-containable moments and possibilities. In research on volunteering (more generally), Smith et al. (2010, p. 270) argue that exploring the intersections of embodied and emotional encounters in volunteering gives us expanded insights into how the spaces of volunteering function, through 'myriad prosaic, complex, tangible and intangible practices, emotions and embodiment, to spheres of politics or policy'. Focusing on the relational, intangible and affective components of 'doing' volunteer tourism can open up analysis towards affirmative possibilities in terms of intercultural connection and (un)learning (Everingham, 2015, 2016, 2018). However, as Judge (2016, p. 240) argues we must also remain cautious that an 'overemphasis on fluidity and the 'excess' of bodily experience can produce weak accounts of the actual politics of difference'.

Accordingly, in the next section we explore understandings of affect that problematize the reductive ways that affect and emotions have been theorised in the 'critical' work on volunteer tourism both to foreground more complex, *ambiguous* and affirmative ways that such encounters might be both theorised and are already-experienced, but also to highlight the ways in which these engagements are also in need of decolonisation in order to transgress the implicit (re)production of the very binaries they seek to contest.

The autonomy of affect in volunteer tourism

The trajectory of academic research into volunteering and affect has already begun to disrupt the homogenous and binary ways of understanding power in volunteer tourism spaces. For example, drawing on Massumi, Griffiths (2016) argues that there are dimensions of volunteering experiences that are 'outside of' or 'autonomous' from the representational, and not all encounters within these volunteering spaces can be understood as deferring to neoliberal 'object-target' forms of power (Griffiths, 2014). By privileging Massumi's notion of 'the autonomy of affect', Griffiths (2016, p. 8) urges researchers to move away from 'either/or conceptualisations of power-body relations in the volunteer-host encounter'. We now turn to a deeper reading of Massumi (1995, p. 89), to explore where the notion 'autonomy of affect' takes the analysis of volunteer tourism encounters, and to consider whether this theoretical framework is useful for taking the analysis beyond binary ways of codifying power in the affective realms of these encounters.

For Massumi (1995, p.89), affect is autonomous, and somewhat outside of social signification; affect is 'a suspension of action-reaction circuits and linear temporality'. In social life there is always a 'residue' or 'excess' that is left out in constructivist representations, that are 'not socially produced and constitutes the very fabric of our being' (Hemmings 2005, p. 549). In these conceptions, affect is both 'pre-conscious' and 'pre-individual'; there is an indeterminacy to affect which does not have a linear or deterministic relationship to structures of power (Clough, 2007). The body has an unpredictable autonomy in its encounters which critical (representational) enquiry fails to capture. In focusing on the 'autonomy of affect' between volunteers and local community, Griffiths (2014, 2015a, 2015b, 2015c, 2016) positions bodies in international volunteering spaces as having the capacity to be affected in ways that transcend discursive structures of volunteer tourism as neoliberal capitalism which relies on the oppression, exploitation, assimilation and misrecognition of 'other'. It is through the moments of intercultural connection that Griffiths describes in his fieldwork (see 2014, 2015a,b,c, 2016) where the 'excess' or 'autonomy' of affect in intersubjective moments of connection has 'the potential to subvert or resist neoliberalism' (Griffiths, 2016, p. 124).

While there certainly are aspects of these volunteer/host encounters that are 'not subject to the same market forces that shape more straightforwardly capitalist forms of labour and tourism' (Griffiths & Brown, 2016 p. 16), the boundaries between affect and broader formations of power are not clearly demarcated. These power relations then, can never really be 'transcended'. For Massumi, affects are not entirely 'asocial'; that is, affects are still attached to broader social structures (such as neo-colonialism and neoliberalism), and 'affective attachment frequently serves to satisfy drives or social norms' (Hemmings, 2005, p. 559).There is no clear line between moments when affect 'transcends' power relations and moments when affect reproduces and reinforces them. As Massumi (1995, p. 99) himself notes, it is difficult to conceptualise affect as being transcendent or immanent; instead, they flip over into each other: '[t]he trick is to get comfortable with productive paradox'.

This paradox then, would suggest Massumi's theorisation of affect could help academics move away from binary analyses of the role of affect in the intercultural embodied encounters in volunteer tourism. However, as Hemmings (2005) argues, while Massumi acknowledges the ways in which affect strengthens the hegemonic social order he does not pursue this in his analysis. Instead, he privileges the 'affective freedom' from social norms and structures. In Massumi's analysis, there is always an 'excess' to affect, which is separate from the cognitive. This suggests then, that Massumi falls back into dualistic thinking, by framing affect as separate/autonomous from the rational and cognitive aspects of epistemology (which Massumi implies is connected to the mind rather than the body). This mind/body dualism is further reified through Massumi's decision to separate emotion from affect: Massumi (1995, p. 88) defines affect, as 'intensity'. For Massumi, affect (as non-cognitive) follows different logics and pertains to different categorical orders than the realms of emotions (which are cognitive). According to Massumi (1995, p. 88), the socio-linguistic fixing of emotions to subjective personal experience renders them into the realms of the representational, as opposed to affect, which is non-representational. Affect, as 'non-representational', is 'unqualified' and '[a]s such, it is not ownable or recognisable, and is thus resistant to critique' (Massumi, 1995, p. 88).

We agree with the critique of Massumi's theorisation of 'affect' as put forward by Hemmings (2005). That is, we argue *against* Massumi's dualistic notion of epistemology and emotion (as cognitive and therefore rational) as separate from affect. Like Hemmings (2005, p. 557) we take on the definition of epistemology from the established body of feminist work as the 'inquiry into the relationship *between* the ontological, epistemological and transformative'. We argue there are ramifications for theorising emotion and affect, and affect and epistemology in ways that perpetuate dualistic thinking. In positioning affect as separate to emotion, affect as separate to epistemology and affect as autonomous from structural power relations, Cartesian dualisms that inherently underlie colonial thinking are perpetuated (Motta, 2017b, 2018). In utilising the productive possibilities of theorising affect in this paper then, we do not want to write out the placed body (or emotions and subjectivities as being connected to our raced, classed and gendered bodies). The affective spaces in volunteer tourism are at once bound up in and shaped by the forces and discourses of neoliberalism and neo-colonial legacies and presents (affective closures), while at the same time they contain intersubjective decolonial possibilities (affective openings).

It is thus important not to already pre-bound and codify volunteers and hosts as unified subjects that are necessarily in opposition to one another, nor internally unitary in desire, positionality or power. Part of the problem of such pre-codification is that the variety of volunteering organisations and volunteers are often glossed over (Benson, 2015; Everingham, 2017; Judge, 2017). However on a deeper more conceptual level, the homogenisation of these categories in volunteer tourism comes from the universalist sensibilities embedded within the history of critical Western ethnocentric social theory itself (Tolia-Kelly, 2006). The 'unified subject' is connected to this ethnocentric rational certainty and fixed hierarchical forms of subjectivity (Motta, 2011, 2013). What is needed is a denaturalisation of these dominant ways of seeing and being (in practise and in theorising), to make visible the relational processes of 'betweeness' to open up possibilities for radically disturbing the bounded and fixed categories of 'self' and 'other' (Motta, 2011, 2013).

In the next section we turn to decolonial feminist thinking to theorise affect in non-dualistic ways, from the edges and borders and the in-between. In doing so we also heed the call from Chambers and Buzinde (2015, p. 4) to delink tourism studies from Western epistemologies, a vital conceptual move needed for providing an 'other way of thinking, being and knowing [and doing] about tourism'.

Non-binary theorising of affect: emergent and in-between

Decolonial feminist thinkers such as Anzaldua (1987, 2002), Lugones (1992, 2010) and Motta (2014, 2017a, 2018) who can be thought of as contributing to the increasingly visible field of decolonial feminisms, all center the gendered, raced and classed nature of colonised (non)subjectivity in Western thought. Modernity as premised upon the attempted annihilation of the raced and feminised subaltern 'other', has resulted in a negation of agency, knowing and being. Critical theorising of affect has also tended to reinscribe these negations within either/or binaries which even in their most affirmative articulations speak over this raced and feminised 'other' through the positing of encounters as either being autonomous or transcendent (Spivak, 1998). In the context of volunteer tourism, affective theorising has centered on the circulation of affect at the macro level and within the volunteer tourists, yet little attention has been given to theorising the co-creation of affect through the relationalities *between* volunteers and local communities.

In turning our attention to the in-between, relational nature of affect we argue for a broadening of the parameters of *methodological* legibility (Vázquez, 2011) and the production of *credible, existent* possibilities (de Sousa Santos, 2014) to how we theorise affect in volunteer tourism spaces that are ambiguous, partial and messy. We call for a critique of the coloniality in the conceptualisation of volunteer tourism by academics that can prefiguaretely open up pathways for doing volunteering otherwise; by highlighting the 'possibilities of becoming 'other' in thought, practice and as embodied subjects' (Motta, 2017a, p. 38). We pay particular attention to the everyday moments of vulnerability, unlearning and recognition that open up embodied possibilities of critical intimacy, between volunteers and local host community members. At the same time, we uncover the affective closures that hinders this unlearning, recognition and critical intimacy between volunteers and hosts. As researchers we position ourselves within the in-between, of practice and theory, of our embodied positionality that influences how we affect in the field, and how we are affected. We argue for an affective attunement to betweeness, inter-relationality and inter-subjectivity in all stages of the research. We locate critical intimacy within the inter-subjective relationalities and dialogues that emerge in the affective spaces of the in-between: 'Dialogical construction breaks the domination of Monological thought, practice and being as it opens up a space for multiplicity, for doubts, questions, and discontent with the world as it is (both internal and external)' (Motta, 2017a, p. 41).

We look to moments in the field of the first author, where critical intimacy was embodied *between* volunteer/local through a fostering of dialogical spaces and co-constructing the conditions for voice, speaking and listening. Deep listening is also required, which involves being attuned to the 'insufficiency of representation' (Motta, 2017a, p. 41); that is, an attunement to the non-verbal, emotional and affective more-than-representational aspects of the social world. Reflexivity is key in order to develop practices that facilitate an inner voice and active listening between self and 'other'. From here it is possible to grow a collective that can enable 'their (our) transformation'. This also involves an attunement to pluriversality and a reflexive move away from universal knowing, a critique that opens up the parameters of legibility (de Sousa Santos, 2014) 'towards an embrace of multiple epistemologies, multiple subjects of knowing and multiple practices of creating knowledge' (Motta, 2017a, p. 42). The concept of unlearning is key for embracing multiple knowledges. It is through unlearning and decentering oppressors (colonial) logics where the taken-for-granted often unthought colonial ways of being in the world can be disrupted/disoriented in some way (Motta, 2017c). We argue that unlearning occurs in moments of vulnerability and critical intimacy, which enable emergent recognitions between volunteers and locals within these volunteer spaces.

In taking an affirmative approach to the affective moments of critical intimacy, unlearning and recognition in volunteer tourism spaces we are not negating the affective closures that can reproduce patriarchal colonial capitalism. These affective closures *also* circulate within the subjectivities of volunteers and host community members. Yet there are moments where volunteers may glimpse what it is like to be an 'other'; which is where we locate these decolonial moments and affirmative possibilities of connections between different 'others'. Emotions such as awkwardness for example, can signal a moment of vulnerability, a moment that opens the possibilities of emergent unlearnings of colonial certainty and confidence that comes from occupying a privileged subjectivity. For Motta (2017a) it is critical to make visible these vulnerabilities, as this is where the possibilities for decolonising transformation emerge: in the 'relationships of becoming, opening and integrity, which involves a reflexive crossing into the borderlands. These crossings are multiple and take us to the borders of self and certainty' (2017a, p. 42).

These liminal, affective, embodied zones of betweeness in the intercultural encounters in volunteer tourism opens up possibilities for theorising through the active practices of agency within the Self (and knowing-subjectivity) and the 'other (ed)' which by necessity do not and could not emerge from the cognitive as disembodied (as Massumi suggests when positing epistemology as separate from the body and separating emotions from affect) but rather from the disruptions and being touched by the 'other' through proximity and moments of critical intimacy. Proximity opens the possibilities for disruptive moments of being touched by 'other' so that that 'other' is recognised as human, and the loss embodied within colonising relationships for the self is felt (Motta, 2017b, 2018). This allows for mutual (if only momentary) processes of recognition through care, compassion and flesh.

Case study

The empirical section of this paper is based on the fieldwork of the first author who conducted fieldwork with a volunteer tourism organisation in Ecuador over two consecutive years, in 2012 (6 weeks) and 2013 (3 weeks). We now turn to outlining the case studies and methodology that underlie the empirical section of this paper.

The biblioteca (arte del mundo) baños Ecuador

Set amongst lush green mountains, volcanos and waterfalls, Baños Ecuador is a popular tourist destination and the setting for a small not-for-profit organisation called Fundacion Arte del Mundo. This is the real name of the organisation, who consented to be part of the research and for their real name to be used. The first author has a close relationship to the managers of this organisation, has since written blogs for them, and donates to the organisation each month. She believes this organisation represents best practice volunteer tourism because the focus is on community development as artistic expression and mutual learning, rather than development aid (see Everingham, 2015). The organisation runs a lively and creative space for children to come after school. A garage on the property was converted to a small theatre where travelling actors, artists and musicians are able to perform live shows for the local community, and where a projector can be set up to run film nights. The organisation also runs low cost English classes for adults and hosts a weekly intercambio (language exchange) where adults from the local community and volunteers come together to practice English and Spanish. The first author spent four weeks here as a participant observer in 2012 and three weeks as a participant observer in 2013, volunteering with the local children daily. In 2012 she also taught an English class to adults in the local community three nights a week. Several of these students had maintained a relationship with the organisation when she went back in 2013, whether it was through taking more English classes, attending the theatre shows and/or movie nights, and attending churascco (barbeque) parties that were held at the site, where volunteers and locals came together to eat, drink and dance; where Spanglish was the medium of communication.

Methodology and researcher as affected and affecting

Qualitative data was collected in the field using semi-structured in-depth interviews and autoethnography with anti-dualistic approaches that rejected either/or interpretations (Longhurst, 2016; Miller & Glassner, 2011). In-depth interviews provide access into different realities, particularly insights into the cultural frames that shape people's worldviews, to recognise and build on their interactive components rather than seek to control or reduce the interview (Miller & Glassner, 2011, p. 131). A total of 23 interviews were conducted and one focus group with ten local Spanish speaking students learning English. Questions for the volunteers were designed to understand their motivations, expectations and experiences of volunteering and the local adult English students were asked about their experiences participating in the volunteering spaces. All participants in the study were given information documents about the research and were aware of the research being conducted. Consent forms were signed before interviews were conducted. These documents were translated into Spanish for the Spanish speaking participants. All research participants were given pseudonyms for the purpose of anonymity.

Autoethnography was also conducted to map the first author's experiences doing participant observation. Autoethnography is conducive to affective theorising because it allows the researcher to explore emotions and subjectivities; all crucial for reflecting upon researcher positionality. In autoethnography, the analyses of the self undergoes the same process and scrutiny as the analyses of the 'other' (Ellingson & Ellis, 2008). Researching the self as an introspective process using journals, freewriting, fieldnotes and narratives of lived experiences, thoughts and feelings was a key site of knowledge production for the reflections on the first author's encounters discussed in this article (Ellingson & Ellis, 2008).

Attunement to affect in this research came from the embodied experiences of the first author, working through multiple positionalities while in the field. Her embodied positionality was fluid, moving between and within the borderlands of researcher/volunteer/tourist, woman/gringa/'other'. This methodological positionality of in-betweenness led to an analysis attentive to affect, emotions, the body and the importance of partial, or pluriversal analysis. The allusive nature of these aspects of the social world as emergings or becomings meant being attentive to the spaces in-between, where outcomes are not predetermined into either/or binaries and where the raced, classed and gendered body is key in the mediations of the encounters. Being attentive to the plurality of how different bodies affect and are affected leads us away from universalist and reductive theorising towards an analysis that is cognisant of the 'multitude of planes, immanent or other; upon which varied capacities to experience, to know and to shape are acted out, formed and lived through' (Tolia-Kelly, 2006, p. 216). To deeply engage with affect in this way politically orientates us away from universalism and ethnocentrism (Tolia-Kelly, 2006).

In bringing affect to the foreground of conceptualising encounters in volunteer tourism to disrupt fixed, bounded categories of subjectivities and power, we highlight not only the embodiments that occurred in the field, but also in the writing process itself and the embodied relationality between the two authors of this paper. We bring our own bodies into the research and reflexively unpack how different bodies have different affective capacities and different potentialities for affective (and decolonising) disruptions and agencies (Tolia-Kelly, 2006). In doing so we also want to messy the conceptual divisions between emotions and affects, and theorising itself, to demonstrate that the practise of theorisation and concept-making is itself embodied and becoming (Motta, 2017a, 2018). These embodied encounters between us as researchers six years later, and in a different location from where the fieldwork was conducted has led to a re-reading of the encounters and moments experienced in the field. In coming together to write this paper, we as colleagues and compañeras, disrupt the notion of 'disembodied contemplation' (Dewsbury, 2010, p. 324) and as we make sense of some of these encounters in the field together anew from afar (in both distance and time) we are both affected, and this in turn affects the writing up of the research.

The first author was acutely attuned to the embodied interactions with the local communities in Ecuador through the languaging of Spanglish, where emotions such as discomfort, awkwardness and vulnerability that came from not being able to express herself proficiently in Spanish mediated the experience and contributed to her experiences of unlearning her role as 'expert' volunteer and the centering of English as the medium of communication. In re-reading these feelings 6 years later within the encounter of conceptualising this paper with compañera/colleague, the notion of critical intimacy becomes another lens of understanding how she as researcher was affected in the field.

Encounters in the field

Volunteer tourism provides volunteers with a context of 'close proximity' to 'distant others', bringing what might be otherwise hidden to the fore. Volunteer tourism operates within the edges and borders of different cultures and worldviews coming together, where the individuals involved (volunteers and local community members) have opportunities to make sense of different 'others'. The linguistic barriers mean that emotions are central in navigating the boundaries of what feels comfortable and uncomfortable and our affective attunements towards critical intimacy within these intercultural encounters. The next section will outline how Spanglish, as languaging, mediated the intercultural contact zones in the fieldwork was a deeply embodied site of co-learning and co-communicating between volunteers and locals co-constructing moments (however fleeting) of critical intimacy between volunteers and local community members.

Critical intimacy through languaging

Outside the building at Arte del Mundo in Banos Ecuador there is a sense of excitement and anticipation amongst the children when they line up each day waiting for the big roller doors to open on the dot at 3 pm. Once the doors are open they bound in with big smiles and yelps of glee, go to the bookshelf, take a book out and find a bean bag. The smiles are inviting, anticipating their engagement with an attentive adult, and the volunteers go and sit with them to begin reading. The space generates feelings of inspiration and creativity, there is an abundance of colour throughout the building and children's artwork hangs on the walls. Even if the children cannot read they enjoy looking at the pictures in the books, helping the volunteers with their Spanish pronunciation as they read to them. The children are affectionate, they come over for cuddles, and play with my hair. I'm not quite sure how to navigate these touchy feely encounters but I go along with it. I'm taking their lead here, I'm attentive to being open with how these encounters play out. The children have agency in how these encounters unfold. As the days go on I become more comfortable and can anticipate, pre-empt these moments. I come to look forward to being touched, not only in a physical sense, but also through my sense of connection with these children. I *feel* that the children are happy in this space, and that makes me feel happy too. There is a contagious vibe of excitement and laughter. I catch a glint in a child's eye; we smile at each other.

The colourful library is inviting, there are so many beautiful books and the bean bags are comfortable. The books are written in Spanish where for the first half hour the children lie around on beanbags with the volunteers, reading books to the volunteers, or helping the volunteers with their Spanish pronunciation while the volunteers read to them. This act of reading is at once discomforting, humorous and educational for the volunteers who may feel embarrassed, awkward and vulnerable due to their limited linguistic competencies. However it gives the children a sense of purpose and pride in their roles as language teachers, subverting some of the neo-colonial stereotypes of who helps who in volunteer tourism (Everingham, 2015). As a global language English has elements of linguistic imperialism (Muhlhausler, 1994). In volunteer tourism, English (and particular native speaking norms) perpetuates linguistic imperialism through the English speaking volunteer as the knower, where English is often centred and unthought in these encounters. English teaching is also a popular form of volunteering, promoted as 'helping' or 'making a difference' despite the fact that no teaching experience is required. There is an unthought assumption that any intervention a volunteer can make in teaching local communities is better than none at all (Jakubiak, 2012).

In the case of reading Spanish with the children at Fundacion Arte del Mundo, these uncomfortable experiences of the volunteers not-knowing brings a certain vulnerability, uncertainty and unlearning to their ability to communicate via language, rather than taking English for granted as the medium of communication in these encounters. In the embodiment of the experience (rather than a codification of language learning in textbooks or curriculums) volunteers and local children are co-constructing and co-cultivating a language of betweeness leading to 'critical multilingual awareness, which disrupts designated language models and traditional ways of teaching' (Henderson & Ingram, 2018, p. 254) and they are unlearning and decentering English as the unthought medium of communication. Feminist decolonial thinkers remind us how discomfort and vulnerability plays a key role in learning to be affected by those who are potentially other(ed) in any encounter, and how such moments of discomfort can be moments of (un)learning prior assumptions and the affective attachments of those assumptions.

For Alex the Spanish practice he gets from reading with the kids has been the best part of volunteering and the children have agency in their role as 'teacher':

> I really enjoyed reading the books to the kids because I get to practice my pronunciation. That's really what I use that time for – and then trying to understand what I'm saying as I'm saying it, which is kind of hard, its good practice for speaking, doing those 2 things at once. So yeah, the whole Spanish acquisition thing…

These linguistic encounters as languaging in Spanglish demonstrate the 'deeply embodied interactive, improvisational and empathetic moments of 'in-betweeness' that mediates some of these encounters' in volunteer tourism (Everingham, 2018, p. 68). Languaging defies 'the boundaries of externally imposed, socially constructed (and containment) of languages' validating and normalising the wide range of often stigmatised bilingual/multilingual repertoire that underlies learning a second/other language (Henderson & Ingram, 2018, p. 254). The act of speaking Spanglish involves a range of non-verbal cues and ways of communicating, which are connected to emotions and depend upon an attunement to the affective registers of how these encounters are playing out in the moment. Speaking Spanglish might involve switching between English and Spanish, or muddling Spanish with English grammatical structures and pronunciation and vice versa. Spanglish is non-fixed, relational and thus always becoming. It is a language that inhabits and embodies linguistic and cultural borderlands.

The following exchange between the first author and a local adult English student demonstrates the in-between nature of Spanglish, and the ways in which critical intimacy underlies the dialogical, relational linguistic interaction. Lucia spoke about her experiences as a student in the English classes that were taught by the volunteers:

> P: and how was it when you had the other students in the class?

> L: I prefer to be lonely

I felt quite certain that Lucia doesn't mean she likes to feel lonely so I gently correct her:

P: you mean: the only one?

However in correcting Lucia she feels the need to apologise to me for her incorrect use of English:

L: yes, because the other students in class confuse me, he makes strange questions. For me better I am the only student. I hope for ever the only student. Sorry my English ...

In this encounter I am affected on numerous levels. Before I began my fieldwork I had spent 8 years as an ESOL (English second/other language) teacher. I was already uncomfortable with English being taught in a way that perpetuated the idea that learners should aim to speak like native English speakers. The number of people speaking English as a second/other language throughout the world far outweighs native English speakers (Warschauer, 2000) and what is 'normative' in English has transformed through the global/glocal use of the language. Yet the hegemonic ideal of speaking like a native speaker remains an unthought norm for those teaching and learning ESOL. One of the reasons I was drawn to South America as a tourist/English teacher and then later as a researcher/volunteer was because of my discomfort with teaching a language when I myself was a monolingual speaker. I wanted to learn Spanish. When choosing these volunteer organisations I believed I had an 'expertise' to share with my ESOL training, however this was something I had to also unravel and unlearn more deeply through because Spanglish more than English became the medium of teaching and communicating with the local adult English learners. Further, my awkwardness and vulnerability speaking Spanish with the students opened up my affective attunements to Lucia's journey with speaking a language she was not entirely comfortable with.

In this encounter I sensed her discomfort, awkwardness and vulnerability in making a mistake when speaking English because I have felt this way myself when speaking Spanish. I didn't want her to internalise any notion that speaking English equates to superiority, or that not speaking it correctly equates to inferiority. I wanted to reassure her and affirm her dignity through sharing my own inadequacy with Spanish – so that we could recognise ourselves in this moment of having an encounter that is human to human. As I write this now I am aware that this was not a disembodied cognitive process of affect as Massumi conceptualises it, but rather an affective moment of conscious recognition of emotions such as vulnerability, care, compassion and embodied within flesh. Reflecting on this moment six years later, in my encounter with compañera/colleague/second author we have rearticulated this moment through a lens of critical intimacy; a momentary intersubjective dialogue of deep listening and reflexivity that breaks the domination of English as the monological unthought linguistic medium. Yet in my encounter with Lucia none of this was spoken, demonstrating the importance of being attentive to the affective registers in embodied encounters that are beyond codification, and an attunement to the multiplicity of ways that humans connect and make sense of their relationalities.

I reach out to Lucia not physically through touch, but through a smile, I catch her eye and hope that she senses my kindness. I reassure her that she doesn't need to apologise, that I also make mistakes when speaking Spanish:

P:mi espanol no es muy bueno tambien.

(My Spanish isn't very good either).

While the other volunteers were also having their own languaging experiences, I cannot speak for their commitments in decolonising the colonial unthought medium of English and how much they are unlearning their own privileges. However from the interviews it is clear that for many of the volunteers Spanglish is the linguistic medium for all their encounters in the local communities, and with the locals participating in the volunteer programs.

For Kelly, a volunteer at Fundacion Arte del Mundo, the language barriers make her more patient. She gets more expressive with her hands, gesturing more to make herself understood. While many of the volunteers felt discomfort and unease when their intent could not be expressed so easily, for Kelly, speaking Spanglish took:

> the edge off sometimes – because you don't have to totally like express your personality – and commit to saying something in a certain way – you can be vague or more relaxed – and when you're around children it's kind of cool because you can kind of leave the floor open for them to come to you - or fill in those gaps for you, and that can be really interesting. I think it's really nice and really really rewarding when you feel like you've had a conversation that was correct in Spanish – or that your message got through.

The processes of Languaging are emergent and becoming, always manifesting differently regarding the code switching, the pronunciation, the grammatical errors, and how much is understood between the speakers. These linguistic encounters contain layers of emotions and are always emergent and relational. Kelly has articulated the importance of new forms of non-verbal reading of each other through the languaging of Spanglish which opens possibilities for different literacies and deep listening. This 'deep listening' involves being attuned to the 'insufficiency of representation' (Motta, 2017a, p. 41) and cannot be codified into monological binary understandings as being subsumed within or autonomous/transcendent of broader neo-colonial/neoliberal geographies. In the realms of the non-verbal, possibilities are opened up for connection through touch, play and experimentation. In beginning the processes of decolonising volunteer tourism spaces, these connections need to be fostered. As researchers we need to be attentive to the possibilities these affective attunements present and open up dialogue with the volunteer tourism industry to encourage opportunities for volunteers to critically reflect on these encounters.

Affective closures

Providing a space for reflection on these intercultural encounters is crucial to open up dialogue for how volunteer tourism can be otherwise to the unthought colonial perpetuations of volunteer as expert/helper and local communities as deficit model. Without critical reflections, these neo-colonial stereotypes are (re)produced and the encounters can become consolidated within neoliberal/neo-colonial circulations of affect. The framing of the volunteer experience by the industry as focused on the misguided altruism of the privileged volunteer means that the possibilities for transformational unlearning of colonial relationships are limited. While the above examples of languaging point towards the possibilities within these emergent co-constructed dialogic relationships for unravelling colonial binaries, there were also plenty of examples throughout the first author's fieldwork where neo-colonial stereotyping was present.

While Arte del Mundo did not frame their volunteering organisation in the 'helping model', the affective framing of 'altruism' within the industry as a whole is powerful in shaping the perceptions and thus experiences of some of the volunteers. Some of the volunteers mentioned that the children attending the afternoon activity space 'aren't so bad off', because their clothes are clean, they are wearing designer clothes and perhaps an expensive watch. One volunteer angrily questioned what she was even doing there, when she could be making more of a difference somewhere else with children who were 'more underprivileged'. The organisers had also mentioned having issues with previous volunteers being dissatisfied with their volunteering experience, because they didn't think the children were 'poor enough'. The implication being that in order to be 'voluntoured' the children need to conform to being a certain subject/object deserving of the volunteers' 'altruism'. A neo-colonial violence is perpetuated in these imaginings where interventions on certain populations becomes justified through the attempt to contain, 'develop' and 'civilise' (Motta, 2017b). In volunteer tourism these framings of 'self' and 'other' invisibles the cosmologies, knowledges and ways of life of the voluntoured and the neo-colonial development model remains the unthought in some of these encounters. The voluntoured are expected to perform certain impoverished identities for the volunteers, reproducing their invisibility as subjects. Misrecognitions of each other as human are perpetuated within these dualisms of self and 'other'. In these instances, often the volunteers experienced disappointment, that the programs did not live up to their imagined positionalities of 'White Saviour', leading to the loss of the potentiality of co- learning/(un)learning and critical intimacy that could create the conditions for possibilities (even if only momentarily) to decolonise these positionalities and encounters.

These encounters in the field demonstrate the inter-relational and intersubjective ways in which affects circulate through and between bodies, as well as through and between broader power relationships and bodies. Affect works in a multiplicity of ways, reproducing neo-colonial and neoliberal geographies as well as disrupting them. Fostering critical intimacy through active processes and pedagogies of critical reflexivity (Motta, 2017c) is key for dislodging presumptions and framings of the world, for volunteers and the voluntoured to be open to other framings and narratives about 'self' and 'other'. Volunteer tourism organisations need to actively facilitate encounters between volunteers and the voluntoured that foreground these unlearnings of the colonial ways of being-in-the world, and doing volunteering. Instead encounters that encourage deep listening, disruption, vulnerability, compassion, carefulness and critical intimacy should be deliberately fostered.

Conclusion

In this article we have traced the ways that attention to affect, embodiment and emotions have been theorised in volunteer tourism encounters. The affective turn in tourism studies has enabled scholars to further unpack the emotional and embodied aspects of tourism experiences and challenge assumptions that embodied feelings 'simply begin within-and belong only to-individuals' (Buda et al., 2014, p. 103). Rather, as Buda et al. (2014, p. 103) point out, '[w]hat is felt is both imagined and material, individual and collective'. The affective language of helping in the promotion of volunteer tourism highlights the ways in which affect is manipulated by the marketing of the industry which (re)produces neo-colonial and neoliberal geographies. Without critical reflections, these neo-colonial stereotypes are (re)produced and the encounters can become consolidated within neoliberal/neo-colonial circulations of affect. The framing of the volunteer experience by the industry as focused on the misguided altruism of the privileged volunteer means that the possibilities for transformational unlearning of colonial relationships are limited. While the examples of languaging point towards the possibilities within these emergent co-constructed dialogic relationships for unravelling colonial binaries, there were also plenty of examples of affective closures throughout the first author's fieldwork where neo-colonial stereotyping was present. It is thus pertinent for volunteer tourism scholars to utilise the insights from the affective turn in the social sciences to unpack the ways in which affect both (re)produces these object-target forms of power as well as how the affective experiences of encounters work to challenge and disrupt them.

In this article we have built on the research trajectory of volunteer tourism that highlights the ambiguity of these encounters. While acknowledging the importance of affect in (re)producing unequal geographies of volunteer tourism, we have argued that a more-than-representational analysis of these tourism spaces opens up analysis towards the potential subversive affective and decolonising elements of encounters between volunteers and hosts. We explored whether Massumi's notion of 'autonomy of affect' is a useful theoretical framework to explore the unpredictability and potentially subversive aspects of the embodied encounters in volunteer tourism, however we found limitations with this analysis. While Massumi does acknowledge the ways in which affect is attached to broader power structures, the emphasis on affect as being separate to cognitive rational epistemology and emotions reinforces the universalist and binary tendencies within Western ethnocentric social theory (Tolia-Kelly, 2006). We find these dualistic notions of affect in social theory particularly problematic in the ways they have underlined colonial thinking and in glossing over the ways in which racialized and gendered logics, bodies and subjectivities, underlie the unequal geographies of volunteer tourism.

In foregounding decolonial feminist voices of scholars such as Lugones, Motta and Anzaldua, we bring to conscious thought the always active practices of agency (broadly defined) which push back against the hierarchical binaries, bordering practices, and embodiments of codification that come from colonial divisions. Instead, we centre the possibilities that come from the inter-relationalities *between* volunteers and local community members; where embodied moments of vulnerability, unlearning and critical intimacy have the potential to disrupt the hierarchical binary logics, rationalities and relationalities that come from ordering the world around (neo)colonial axes and borders. These disentanglements from binaries that decolonial feminising brings to social analyses gives us another way of thinking about affective registers in the embodied encounters of volunteer tourism. We open up a politics of possibility for new ways of analysing volunteer tourism encounters through the lens of bodies, (b)orders, edges and in-betweeness.

In bringing our own embodiments into the research, both through the on the ground encounters, in the flesh moments of fieldwork for the first author, and through the encounters of the two authors as compañeras, and colleagues re-reading and re-articulating the fieldwork together six years later, we have argued that our capacity to affect and be affected as researchers, is also entangled within our embodied position-alities, relationalities and placed bodies. As such we are attuned to particular affective registers in our fieldwork and methodologies. In the field the first author experienced awkwardness and vulnerability speaking Spanglish which led to her exploring the affective aspects of languaging. Reflecting on these emergences and relationalities that underlie languaging six years later with compañera/colleague/second author, critical intimacy emerged as a key theme.

As researchers we have a significant role to play in prefiguring how the social world can be otherwise, however this means being attuned to how we 'situate' ourselves, how we are affected and our role in affecting the encounters in the flesh/field and in the writing process itself. In volunteer tourism researchers need to be attuned to *feeling* how affects and emotions circulate within and *between* broader structures of power, the volunteers and the voluntoured, and ourselves as researchers. An attentiveness to the in-between allows a 'process of dialogue as humanisation through recognition and embrace of radical difference' (Motta, 2015, p. 94). Finally, we attest to the importance of the volunteer tourism industry itself to decolonise their promotional language and practice, away from White Saviour volunteer as helper and voluntoured as the helped. Organisations must facilitate encounters and/as critical reflexivity that disrupt binary framings of self and other, and provide volunteers with opportunities for deep listening and critical intimacy. Providing a space for reflection on these intercultural encounters is crucial to open up dialogue for how volunteer tourism can be otherwise to the unthought colonial perpetuations of volunteer as expert/helper and local communities as deficit model.

Disclosure statement

No potential conflict of interest was reported by the authors.

References

Ahmed, S. (2007). A phenomenology of whiteness. *Feminist Theory, 8*(2), 149–168. doi:10.1177/1464700107078139

Anderson, B. (2006). "Transcending without transcendence": Utopianism and an ethos of hope. *Antipode, 38*(4), 691–710. doi:10.1111/j.1467-8330.2006.00472.x

Anzaldua, G. (1987). *Borderlands/La Frontera: The new mestiza consciousness.* Aude Lute Books.

Anzaldua, G. E. (2002). Now let us shift … the path of conocimiento … inner work, public acts. In G. E. Anzaldua & A. Keating (eds.) *This bridge we call home: Radical visions for transformation* (pp. 540–578). New York, NY: Routledge.

Bandyopadhyay, R., & Patil, V. (2017). 'The white woman's burden' – The racialized, gendered politics of volunteer tourism. *Tourism Geographies, 19*(4), 644–657. doi:10.1080/14616688.2017.1298150

Benson, A. (2015). Why and how should the international volunteer tourism experience be improved? *Worldwide Hospitality and Tourism Themes, 7* (2), 100–106. doi:10.1108/WHATT-01-2015-0001

Buda, D. B., d'Hauteserre, A.M., & Johnston, L. (2014). Feeling and tourism studies. *Annals of Tourism Research, 46*, 102–114. doi:10.1016/j.annals.2014.03.005

Buda, D. B., & McIntosh, A.J. (2012). Hospitality, peace and conflict: 'Doing fieldwork' in Palestine. *The Journal of Tourism and Peace Research, 2*(2), 50–61.

Chambers, D., & Buzinde, C. (2015). Tourism and decolonisation: Locating research and self. *Annals of Tourism Research, 51*(1), 1–16. doi:10.1016/j.annals.2014.12.002

Chow, R. (2014). *Not like a native speaker: On languaging as a postcolonial experience.* New York: Columbia University Press

Clough, P.T. (2007). Introduction. In P. T. Cough & J. Halley (Eds.), *The affective turn: Theorising the social* (pp.1–34). Durham: Duke University Press.

Crossley, É. (2012). Poor but happy: Volunteer tourists' encounters with poverty. *Tourism Geographies, 14*(2), 235–253. doi:10.1080/14616688.2011.611165

Davidson, J., & Milligan, C. (2004). Embodying emotion sensing space: Introducing emotional geographies. *Social & Cultural Geography, 5*(4), 523–532. doi:10.1080/1464936042000317677

de Sousa Santos, B. (2014). *Epistemologies of the South: Justice against epistemicide.* Boulder CO: Paradigm Publishers.

Dewsbury, J.D. (2010). Performative, non-representational, and affect-based research: Seven injunctions. In D. Delyser, S. Herbert S. Aitken, M. Crang and McDowell L. (Eds.) *The SAGE handbook of qualitative geography* (pp. 321–344). Thousand Oaks, California: Sage Publications Inc.

Ellingson, L., L., & Ellis, C. (2008). Autoethnography as constructionist project. In J. A. Holstein & J. F. Gubrium (Eds.), *Handbook of constructionist research* (pp. 446–467). New York, NY: The Guilford Press.

Everingham, P. (2015). Intercultural exchange and mutuality in volunteer tourism: The case of Intercambio in Ecuador. *Tourist Studies, 15* (2), 175–190. doi:10.1177/1468797614563435

Everingham, P. (2016). Hopeful possibilities in spaces of "the-not-yet-become": Relational encounters in volunteer tourism. *Tourism Geographies, 18*(5), 520–538. doi:10.1080/14616688.2016.1220974

Everingham, P. (2017). I'm not looking for a manufactured experience: Calling for decommodified volunteer tourism. In S. Filep, J. N. Albrechy, W. J. L. Coetzee (Eds.), *CAUTHE 2017: Time for big ideas – Rethinking the field for tomorrow* (pp 409–418). Dunedin: Otago University.

Everingham, P. (2018). Speaking Spanglish: Embodying linguistic (b)orderlands in volunteer tourism. *Emotion Space and Society, 27*, 68–75. doi:10.1016/j.emospa.2018.04.001

Frazer, R., & Waitt, G. (2016). Pain, politics and volunteering in tourism studies. *Annals of Tourism Research, 57*, 176–189. doi:10.1016/j.annals.2016.01.001

Germann Molz, J. (2016). Giving back, doing good, feeling global: The affective flows of family voluntourism. *Journal of Contemporary Ethnography, 46*(3), 334–360. doi:10.1177/0891241615610382

Griffiths, M. (2014). The affective spaces of global civil society and why they matter. *Emotion, Space and Society, 11*, 89–95. doi:10.1016/j.emospa.2013.08.003

Griffiths, M. (2015a). A compelling and flawed story of power-body relations. *Tourism Geographies, 17*(4), 627–629. doi:10.1080/14616688.2015.1053975

Griffiths, M. (2015b). I've got goose bumps just talking about it! Affective life on neoliberalized volunteering programmes. *Tourist Studies, 15*(2), 205–221. doi:10.1177/1468797614563437

Griffiths, M. (2015c). Transcending neoliberalism in international volunteering. In K. Dashper (Ed.), *Rural tourism: An international perspective*. Newcastle Upon Tyne: Cambridge Scholars Publishing.

Griffiths, M. (2016). Writing the body, writing others: A story of transcendence and potential in volunteering for development. *The Geographical Journal. 184*(2), 115–124. doi:10.1111/geoj.12200

Griffiths, M., & Brown, E.J. (2016). Embodied experiences in international volunteering: Power-body relations and performative ontologies. *Social & Cultural Geography 18*(5), 665–682. doi: 10.1080/146493

Guiney, T. (2018). 'Hug-an-orphan vacations': 'Love' and emotion in orphanage tourism. *The Geographical Journal, 184*(2), 125–137. doi:10.1111/geoj.12218

Hemmings, C. (2005). Invoking affect. *Cultural Studies, 19*(5), 548–567. doi:10.1080/09502380500365473

Henderson, K. I., & Ingram, M. (2018). "Mister, you're writing in Spanglish": Fostering spaces for meaning making and metalinguistic connections through teacher translanguaging shifts in the bilingual classroom. *Bilingual Research Journal, 41* (3), 253–271. doi:10.1080/15235882.2018.1481894

Jakubiak, C. (2012). "English for the global": Discourses in/of English language voluntourism. *International Journal of Qualitative Studies in Education, 25* (4), 435–451. doi:10.1080/09518398.2012.673029

Judge, R. C. (2016). Negotiating Blackness: Young British volunteers' embodied performances of race as they travel from Hackney to Zimbabwe. *Young, 24*(3), 238–254.

Judge, R. C. (2017). Class and global citizenship: Perspectives from non-elite young people's participation in volunteer tourism. *Tourism Recreation Research, 42*(2), 164–175.

Koleth, M. (2014). Hope in the dark: Geographies of volunteer and dark tourism in Cambodia. *Cultural Geographies, 21*(4), 681–694. doi:10.1177/1474474013519577

Longhurst, R. (2016). Semi-structured interviews and focus groups. In N. Clifford, M. Cope, T. Gillespie, & S. French (Eds), *Key methods in geography* (3rd ed., pp. 143–157). London: Sage.

Lough, B. J., & Carter-Black, J. (2015). Confronting the white elephant: International volunteering and racial (dis)advantage. *Progress in Development Studies, 15*(3), 207–220. doi:10.1177/1464993415578983

Lorimer, H. (2005). Cultural geography: The busyness of being 'more-than-representational'. *Progress in Human Geography, 29*(1), 83–94.

Lugones, M. (1992). On borderlands/La frontera: An interpretive essay. *Hypatia, 7*(4), 31–37. doi: 10.1111/j.1527-2001.1992.tb00715.x

Lugones, M. (2010). Toward a decolonial feminism. *Hypatia, 25*(4), 742–759. doi:10.1111/j.1527-2001.2010.01137.x

Massumi, B. (1995). The autonomy of affect. *Cultural Critique, 31*(2), 83–109. doi:10.2307/1354446

Miller, J., & Glassner, B. (2011). The "inside" and the "outside" finding realities in interviews. In D. Silverman (Ed.), *Qualitative research* (pp. 131–149). London: Sage.

Mostafanezhad, M. (2013). The geography of compassion in volunteer tourism. *Tourism Geographies, 15*(2), 318–337. doi:10.1080/14616688.2012.675579

Mostafanezhad, M. (2014). *Volunteer tourism: Popular humanitarianism in neoliberal times*. Farnham: Ashgate Publishing Limited.

Motta, S. C. (2011). Notes towards prefigurative epistemologies. In S. C. Motta & A. G. Nilsen (Eds.), *Social movements in the Global South: Development, dispossession and resistance* (pp. 178–199). Basingstoke: Palgrave MacMillan.

Motta, S. C. (2013). Spaces of transgressive possibility in the teaching of social and global justice. *Antipode, 45*(1), 80–10. doi:10.1111/j.1467-8330.2012.00995.x

Motta, S. C. (2014). Latin America reinventing revolutions, an other politics in practice and theory. In R. Stahler-Sholk, H. E. Vanden, & M. Becker (Eds.), *Rethinking Latin American social movements: Radical action from below* (pp. 21–44). Lanham: Rowman and Littlefield.

Motta, S.C. (2015). Becoming woman, on exile and belonging in the Borderlands. In Z. Rashiro & M. Barahonam (Eds.), *Women in Academia crossing North South borders: Gender, race & displacement* (pp. 89–116). London: Lexington Books.

Motta, S. C. (2016). Emancipation in Latin America: On the pedagogical turn: Emancipation in Latin America. *Bulletin of Latin American Research. 28*(1), 83–101.

Motta, S. C. (2017a). Decolonising critique: From prophetic negation to prefigurative affirmation. In A. Dinerstein (Ed.), *Social sciences for an other politics: Women without parachutes* (pp. 33–48). Basingstoke: Palgrave MacMillan.

Motta, S. C. (2017b). Latin America as political science's other. *Social Identities: Journal for the Study of Race, Nation and Culture, 23*, 6.

Motta, S. C. (2017c). Emancipation in Latin America: On the pedagogical turn. *Bulletin of Latin American Research, 36*(1), 5–20. doi:10.1111/blar.12526

Motta, S. C. (2018). *Liminal subjects: Weaving (our) liberation*. Lanham, MD: Rowman and Littlefield.

Muhlhausler, P. (1994). Language teaching = linguistic imperialism? *Australian Review of Applied Linguistics, 17*(2), 121–130.

Palacios, C. (2010). Volunteer tourism, development and education in a postcolonial world: Conceiving global connections beyond aid. *Journal of Sustainable Tourism, 18*(7), 861–878. doi: 10.1080/09669581003782739

Picard, D. (2012). Tourism, awe and inner journeys. In D. Picard & M. Robinson (Eds.), *Emotion in motion: Tourism, affect and transformation* (pp. 1–21). Oxford: Ashgate.

Pratt, M. (1992). *Imperial eyes: Travel writing and transculturation*. London: Routledge.

Projects Abroad. viewed 13th March 2019. Retrieved from https://www.projects-abroad.com.au/

Sin, H. L. (2009). Volunteer tourism: "Involve me and I will learn"? *Annals of Tourism Research, 36*(3), 480–501. doi:10.1016/j.annals.2009.03.001

Simpson, K. (2004). "Doing development": The gap year, volunteer-tourists and a popular practice of development. *Journal of International Development, 16*(5), 681–692. doi:10.1002/jid.1120

Smith, F., Timbrell, H., Woolvin, M., Muirhead, S., & Fyfe, N. (2010). Enlivened geographies of volunteering: Situated, embodied and emotional practices of voluntary action. *Scottish Geographical Journal, 126*(4), 258–274. doi:10.1080/14702541.2010.549342

Spivak, G. (1998). Can the subaltern speak? In C. Nelson & L. Grossberg (Eds.), *Marxism and the interpretation of culture* (pp. 271–316). Chicago: University of Illinois Press.

Tolia-Kelly, D.P. (2006). Affect an ethnocentric encounter? Exploring the 'universalist' imperative of emotional/affectual geographies. *Area, 38*(2), 213–217. doi:10.1111/j.1475-4762.2006.00682.x

Tucker, H. (2016). Empathy and tourism: Limits and possibilities. *Annals of Tourism Research, 57*, 31–43. doi:10.1016/j.annals.2015.12.001

Tucker, H., & Shelton, E. J. (2018). Tourism, mood and affect: Narratives of loss and hope. *Annals of Tourism Research, 70*, 66–75. doi:10.1016/j.annals.2018.03.001

Vázquez, R. (2011). Translation as erasure: Thoughts on modernity's epistemic violence. *Journal of Historical Sociology, 24*(1), 27–44. doi:10.1111/j.1467-6443.2011.01387.x

Vodopivec, B., & Jaffe, R. (2011). Save the world in a week: Volunteer tourism, development and difference. *The European Journal of Development Research, 23*(1), 111–128. doi:10.1057/ejdr.2010.55

Vrasti, W. (2013). *Volunteer Tourism in the Global South: Giving back in neoliberal times*. Routledge, London and New York.

Vrasti, W., & Montsion, J. M. (2014). No Good Deed Goes Unrewarded: The Values/Virtues of Transnational Volunteerism in Neoliberal Capital. *Global Society, 28*(3), 336–355.

Warschauer, M. (2000). The changing global economy and the future of English teaching. *TESOL Quarterly, 34*(3), 511–535. doi:10.2307/3587741

Wearing, S. (2001). *Volunteer tourism: Experiences that make a difference*. Wallingford: CABI.

Wearing, S., Mostafanezhad, M., Nguyen, N., Nguyen, T. H. T., & McDonald, M. (2018). Poor children on Tinder' and their Barbie Saviours: Towards a feminist political economy of volunteer tourism. *Leisure Studies, 37*(5), 500–514. doi:10.1080/02614367.2018.1504979

Wearing, S., Young, T., & Everingham, P. (2017). Evaluating volunteer tourism: Has it made a difference? *Tourism Recreation Research, 42*(4), 512–521. doi:10.1080/02508281.2017.1345470

Mexican women's emotions to resist gender stereotypes in rural tourism work

Isis Arlene Díaz-Carrión (iD) and Paola Vizcaino (iD)

ABSTRACT

Understandings of emotions and their role in ordering social life has been a fruitful feminist contribution to cultural and social studies. Under this theoretical perspective, affective or emotional responses illustrate women's strategies to cope with or resist productive and spatial limitations produced by traditional gender roles and stereotypes. Since the 2000s, tourism and gender researchers have turned their attention to emotions, although their intersection of gender stereotypes in rural tourism has been limited. We rely on Ahmed's framework on emotions and other theoretical contributions on socio-cultural spaces, embodied emotions, affective practices and gendered work to investigate gender roles, stereotypes and tourism productive and spatial relations in Mexican rural contexts. This context shed light on roles and gender stereotypes and their connections with the affective spatial practices experienced by women. A total of 49 Mexican women were interviewed from 2015 to 2018. Qualitative content analysis is employed to examine interview data, using inductive and deductive approaches. In addition, non-participant observation, document review, and field notes enrich and complement the interview data. Emotions are shown to mediate women's lived experiences of gendered rural tourism work and the potential of emotional responses to contest social norms in opening new paths to surpass women's relatively weaker positions in rural societies and to negotiate inequalities. Women continue to experience contradictory messages and tensions generated in both the family and the community, even with the growth in gender mainstreaming strategies; we propose a framework to contest traditional gender roles and to improve women's affective spatial practices in rural contexts.

摘要

研究情感及其在社会生活秩序中的作用是女权主义对文化和社会研究的一项卓有成效的贡献。根据这一理论观点,情感或情绪反应说明了妇女应对或抵抗传统性别角色和刻板观念所产生的生产和空间限制的战略。自2000年以来,旅游业和性别研究人员已经将他们的注意力转向情感,尽管他们对情感与性别刻板印象的交叉关系的研究一直很有限。本研究利用艾哈迈德情感研究的框架和诸如具身情绪,情感实践和性别化工作等其他社会文化空间方面的理论贡献,研究了墨西哥乡村的性别角色,刻板印象和旅游业的生产和空间关系。这一墨西哥乡村背景下的研究阐明了角色和性别定型观念以及它们与女性所经历的情感空间实践的联系。本研究从2015年到2018年,对总共49名墨西哥女性进行了采访。定性内容分析是使用归纳和演绎的方法来检查访谈数据。此外,非参与性观察、文献回顾和现场笔记也丰富和补充了访谈数据。研究结果强调了情感如何调解女性在性别化的乡村旅游工作中的生活经历,以及情感反应的潜力,以挑战社会规范,开辟新的道路,超越女性在农村社会中相对弱势的地位,并协商不平等。结束语侧重于妇女所经历的矛盾信息以及家庭和社区中产生的紧张关系,同时强调了性别主流化战略的重要性,并提出了一个框架,以挑战传统的性别角色和改善妇女在农村背景下的情感空间实践。

Introduction

The 'emotional turn' in human geography has highlighted the importance of emotions in the ways individuals experience and interpret the world in their quotidian lives (Bondi et al., 2007). Although some scholars have examined how tourism development contributes to shape the gendered and ethnic identities of Latin American women with some links to their emotions (Baab, 2012; Little, 2008; Wilson & Ypeij, 2012); an explicit analysis of the affective dimensions of tourism processes is lacking. Following recent calls to acknowledge the role of emotions in embodied tourism encounters and in tourism work (e.g. Buda et al., 2014; Hall, 2018; Picard, 2012; Tucker, 2007, 2009; Veijola, 2009), we seek to conduct an examination of women's emotions towards gendered work in rural tourism contexts and the implications of gender stereotypes in generating spatial divisions. The contribution of this study is to examine emotions as a form of cultural politics or world making (Ahmed, 2014), through which the affective practises of women may challenge traditional gender roles and stereotypes or inhabit social norms differently to overcome productive and spatial restrictions in a specific sociocultural context (rural tourism in Mexico).

Rural tourism is a growing and changing sub-sector of travel and tourism, closely related to natural, social and community values, as well as to rusticity and authenticity (Hernández et al., 2005; Little, 2008; Pérez-Ramírez et al., 2012; Sandoval-Quintero et al., 2017). Mexican scholars have highlighted rural women's incorporation as a result of public policy strategy to foster social change (Hernández et al., 2005; Pérez-Ramírez et al., 2012; Rodríguez & Acevedo, 2015), while promoting the conservation of natural resources (Martínez-Corona, 2003; Suárez-Gutiérrez et al., 2016).[1]

Similar to other regions of the world, rural tourism in Mexico is heavily grounded on the rural idyll, with traditional social norms playing an important role in attracting tourists (Baylina et al., 2016; Browne, 2011; Jiménez-Esquinas, 2017; Little & Austin, 1996; Serra & Ferré, 2006). A tension emerges between the work opportunities that rural tourism provides to local women and the gendered roles that women are expected to perform, as well as the spaces where they perform this work (i.e. often domestic spaces versus public tourism spaces). Scholars have examined the ways in which rural tourism can contribute to produce changes in gender norms mainly by generating work opportunities for women (Lenao & Basupi, 2016; Smritee & Brijesh, 2017). However, the literature has also shown that the economic changes produced by tourism development are not always accompanied by broader socio-cultural transformations (Kimbu & Ngoasong, 2016; Tran & Walter, 2014; Vizcaino-Suárez, 2018). Due to these tensions, even though rural women tend to appreciate the positive aspects of tourism work, the nature of such work and the prevalent gender expectations and stereotypes generate emotions with different outcomes at the individual and the social level (Ratten & Dana, 2017; Tran & Walter, 2014; Tucker, 2007). In line with tourism geographers and sociologists, who have called to acknowledge feelings and emotions in tourism research (see Cohen & Cohen, 2019; Picard, 2012), this paper conducts a qualitative examination of women's affective responses to traditional gender roles and stereotypes in rural tourism work, and to broader productive and spatial restrictions.

As Latin American scholars conducting research in Mexico, we are interested in analyzing women's participation in tourism production from a gender perspective. To problematize the affective practises embodied by women working in rural tourism, we pay close attention to the challenges and opportunities they face. Thus, two significant questions guide the present study: a) what are the implications of traditional gender roles and stereotypes for (Mexican) women who work in rural tourism? And given that emotions move us (Ahmed, 2014; Anderson, 2009; Bondi et al., 2007), b) what are women's emotional responses to gender stereotypes and broader productive and spatial restrictions? We seek to examine these questions through a qualitative study based on semi-structured interviews with 49 Mexican women who work in rural tourism. The aims of this paper are two-fold: first, it seeks to contribute to the literature on gender, emotions and tourism work, through an examination of traditional gender roles and stereotypes in rural tourism and the exploration of women's emotional responses to gendered work and spatial restrictions. Second, the paper advances a framework that seeks to improve women's participation, based on the lived experiences of Mexican women.

Conceptual background

Feminist understandings of emotions

Feminist theory has significantly contributed to social studies through the recognition of experience and subjectivity in the examination of gender issues, paying particular attention to the role of emotions in cultural values and beliefs, and in the construction of social relations and hierarchies (Dilley & Scraton, 2010; Waitt & Clifton, 2013; Wetherell, 2015; Wilson & Ypeij, 2012). In line with the transdisciplinary 'affective turn' in cultural and social studies, recent feminist scholarship on emotions has focused on exploring the critical links between affect, emotion and power relations based on gender, sexuality, race and class (e.g. Ahmed, 2014; Cvetkovich, 2003; Hemmings, 2005; Ngai, 2005; Waitt & Clifton, 2013; Wetherell, 2015). Similarly, feminist geographers have produced a body of work that looks at the impacts of emotions in the gendered socio-spatial spheres (Bondi et al., 2007; Browne, 2011). A common aspect of these studies is the examination of how emotions are negotiated in the public sphere (including the workplace), while being experienced through the body (Browne, 2011; Gorton, 2007). Feminist scholarship has also shed light on the social control of emotions (Lutz, 1996), while advancing the conceptualisation of emotions as a site of resistance to gendered norms that generate geographies of inequality and exclusion (Bondi et al., 2007; Browne, 2011; Hall, 2018; Waitt & Clifton, 2013; Wilson & Little, 2008).

Ahmed's (2014) work is particularly relevant for our analysis. The author adopts a multidisciplinary approach, drawing heavily from sociocultural theories rather than advancing a psychological explanation, to understand the way emotions interrelate with notions of culture and power. She focuses on how emotions shape people's affective practices in their quotidian life (Wetherell, 2015). In Ahmed's view, '[e]motions shape the very surfaces of bodies, which take shape through the repetition of actions over time, as well as through orientations towards and away from others' (2014, p. 4). In this sense, emotions create boundaries between the inside and the outside, and contribute to establish differences amidst the individual and the social. Emotions move subjects and can 'stick' them together, but they always involve particular readings of the world one inhabits (Ahmed, 2004, 2014). Thus, emotions, such as anger, fear, shame, joy or hope, can be construed as a form of cultural politics or world making, which interweaves the personal and the public. For example, anger can be a response to the pain produced by violence or to the injustice of racism, but it can also involve creativity and the capacity to imagine a different world (Ahmed, 2009). Fear can be structural and mediated as opposed to an immediate bodily response to danger (Ahmed, 2003; Wilson & Little, 2008). The feeling of shame, embarrassment or guilt may emerge from the experience of dispossession or degradation and involves the reshaping of bodily and social spaces; while hope can be a decisive element to bring about social change (Ahmed, 2014).

Gender and the affective practices in tourism

In concordance with some of Ahmed's theoretical proposals, feminist geographers have drawn attention to the impact of gender norms and stereotypes on women's affective practices and the complex and often unequal ways in which socio-cultural spaces are produced, interpreted and experienced (e.g. Bondi et al., 2007; Hopkins, 2009; Sharp, 2009). These 'emotional geographies' have contributed to opening new interpretations in the study of gender and emotions in tourism (see Cohen & Cohen, 2019; d'Hauteserre, 2015; Frazer & Waitt, 2016; Hall, 2018; Moyle et al., 2019; Picard, 2012; Tucker, 2009, 2016; Wilson & Little, 2008). For example, drawing from Ahmed's work on emotions, Buda et al. (2014) examined the notion of embodied emotionality or how emotions play a crucial role in the ways in which touring bodies interact with other subjects (i.e. hosts) and places in the context of dark tourism. By examining the embodied feelings and emotions of tourists and tourist guides, the authors shed light on how tourist experiences are socially constructed and shaped by prevailing social values. We use a similar premise in this paper when examining the rural idyll and women's affective practices.

Another recent work that draws from Ahmed's framework is Frazer and Waitt's (2016) on the sensual–emotional–affectual dimensions of volunteering. The authors conceptualise the pain experienced by volunteer tourists: 'as a distancing response that not only creates social and spatial borders between "selves" and "others," but also assigns meaning through the act' (p. 180). Through pain, volunteer tourists either repeat asymmetrical power relations or evoke an affective ethics of hope overcoming dominant power structures. The analysis highlights the ambivalence of emotions and their importance in the study of relational and spatial practices in tourism.

As illustrated in the previous examples, tourism scholarship has looked at the intertwined connections of affects (emotions and feelings) in tourism experiences and encounters, without necessarily distinguishing the gendered dimensions of affects. However, some gender and tourism scholars have sought to address this gap. Within the scholarship of women's experiences in tourism production, the work of Tucker (2007, 2009) has paid particular attention to the role of emotions. In her ethnographic studies in Göreme, Turkey, the author highlights the gender differences in the types of tourism entrepreneurial activities that local men and women have had access to, as well as the different levels of exposure to embodied encounters with tourists. According to local social norms, it is shameful for Göreme women to move around in public spaces due to the potential contact with strange men. In that sense, Tucker (2007) points to the need for Göreme women to 'undo' the feeling of shame in order for them to work comfortably in tourism spaces.

Johnston's work (2001, 2007) also identifies the role of pride/shame in the construction of lesbian tourism spaces. While exploring the performative practices of a woman's drumming group in Pride parades, Johnston is able to identify spaces of pride (i.e. welcoming spaces where fun and excitement are allowed) and shame (linked to Othering, the marginal body and heteronormalcy). In order to overcome shame participants employed humour, exaggerated femininities and masculinities, hid their personal identities and defied a tourist space that could be experienced as hurtful and shaming. Johnston's theorization of pride/shame has led to more comprehensive interpretations of affective performance by emphasizing the dynamics of emotions in the construction of space.

In looking at mountaineering, some authors have explored women's emotions in outdoor activities (Doran, 2016; Frohlick, 2006; Hall, 2018). Hall (2018) has relied on Ahmed's (2014) work to gain insights of emotions and to explore the affective dimensions of risk/fear. According to the author, women's weaker gender position and gender norms promote a sense of insecurity and fear of violence among them, which directly impacts their use of adventure tourism spaces. While analysing the emotional responses to risk/fear in a masculinized environment, Hall's findings endow risk with sensations of achievement and well-being. Her discussion of the 'sentient and emotional body' can be linked to some of the embodiment processes examined in Pritchard et al.'s book (2007). While focusing on the embodiment of two emotions (fear and achievement), Hall (2018) opens new interpretations of emotional geographies by legitimising alternative identities for women in gendered tourism spaces.

In another recent example, Jiménez-Esquinas (2017) interprets Abu-Lughod and Ahmed's work to examine pride and resistance among Galician women producing bobbin lace. Her narrative exhibits feelings and emotions faced by tourism scholars, a strand that has been addressed by Pocock (2015) and Bakas (2017) underpinning the affective turn in tourism studies. The main contribution of this work is the analysis of affective ambivalence as a series of fluxes generated by craftswomen who embrace but also react to gender stereotypes though their tourist performances.

The examination of gender stereotypes in rural tourism has been central to Mexican scholars (Hernández et al., 2005). Even though this line of research has not explicitly focused on the analysis of affects (emotions and feelings), some studies acknowledge an affective ambivalence in the strategies adopted by Mexican rural women as they try to reconcile their work in tourism with sociocultural restrictions in the use of tourism spaces (see Pérez-Ramírez et al., 2012; Rodríguez & Acevedo, 2015; Suárez-Gutiérrez et al., 2016).

Mexican rural women have been defined as highly grounded in the traditional social reproductive gender role of caretakers. The *mamá mexicana* (Mexican mother) is expected to devote herself to the family. This ideal of rural woman, emphasized through the rural idyll, is encapsulated in the archetype of *la doña*, which is a relevant conception in the Mexican imaginary. This concept has been used to depict the mythical figure of *Doña Marina*, also known as *La Malinche*, who represents an archetype of the national consciousness (González Hernández, 2002). *La doña* has also been used in a figurative sense to refer to a woman who promotes *machismo* (Rodriguez, 2015). Likewise, it has been appropriated by actress María Félix (*la Doña*, with capital letter to emphasize her importance) to craftily construct the notion of a strong woman (Ocasio, 2010). However, our use of the concept of *la doña* is closer to León-Portilla's (1993) archetype of a rural woman, depicted as a hard worker who supports her often extended family, both economically and emotionally. Her identity is grounded in a maternal role (*mamá mexicana)* that defines her emotions as always centred on others, while hiding or ignoring her own emotional needs.

This review aimed to show how the scholarship on gender and emotions in tourism has proposed novel perspectives to broaden our understanding of tourism processes. Some key insights from the literature point to the way affective practices emerge as a response to local gender dynamics, and how the acceptance of negotiation fluxes that women engage with through tourism processes have the scope to promote new identities. In such a process, women can translate these changes (e.g. new identities and ways of relating to others) to their socio-spatial context, where their marginal body can become more visible.

Methodological approach

The study employed a qualitative design in which Mexican women's work experiences were situated within the wider sociocultural context. Semi-structured interviews were conducted over four periods of fieldwork in several rural destinations in Mexico, spanning 16 months. The first period was from February to September 2015; the second one, from May to October 2016; the third, from September to November 2017; and the last one, from June to July 2018. Interviews allowed to explore the diversity of rural women's realities and focus on issues that were of particular concern to their lives (Hesse-Biber, 2016, 2006). Through this qualitative design, we attempted to co-produce situated knowledge grounded on the participants' experiences. In terms of positionality, we consider ourselves as insiders based on nationality (Mexican) and

Women are not interested in tourism	Provision of food and accommodation & production of foodstuffs
Women are not good at business Women are not interested in training Women do not like to make decisions Women do not know how to deal with tourists Women always criticize other women Women prefer to stay at home and take care of their families	Women feel safer while working closer to town Women like to work at the *comedor* (restaurant) or hostel Women do not have the skills to provide services for tourists Women do not like to interact with tourists A woman's place is in the kitchen
Production of folk arts	Provision of tour guiding services
Women can hurt themselves if they carve wooden handicrafts Women cannot do the physically demanding tasks of pottery production Painting and decorating pottery handicrafts is for women Knitting handicrafts is for women	Women do not know the *monte* (the hills, the outdoors) Women do not know how to handle animals Women do not like trekking Women are not strong Women do not like to take risks Women's reputation is endangered if they work with male tourists

Figure 1. Gender stereotypes in Mexican rural tourism. Source: Authors.

language (native Spanish speakers), but outsiders in terms of the cultural position within the areas of study (rural areas), and with sub-identities (Giwa, 2015) as mestiza, university-educated, middle-class, urban women.

The study reports the findings from 49 interviews with Mexican women who work in rural tourism. Research participants were identified during four different stages of fieldwork in the states of Baja California (8), Sonora (4), Querétaro (5), Mexico (18), Oaxaca (4) and Veracruz (10), and employing purposeful sampling, which consists on 'selecting information-rich cases strategically and purposefully' (Patton, 2002, p. 243). Snowball sampling was employed to contact additional participants who were referred to the authors by previous informants; interviews lasted 90 minutes on average. The majority of the interviews were conducted face-to-face (39). In addition, following the advantages and innovative uses of ICT in qualitative research (Janghorban et al., 2014; Krouwel et al., 2019; Lo Iacono et al., 2016; Longhurst, 2017; Tavakoli & Mura, 2015), we conducted some video-interviews (through diverse software that enables conversation), which were also transcribed (10). Participants were between 18–65 years old and worked in the following tourism and travel services: food and accommodation (12), handicrafts and foodstuff (29), and guiding services (8). Some of the participants were micro business owners (15), others worked in the family business (12), in a private company (10) or a community-based enterprise (12).

Qualitative content analysis was employed for the systematic examination of the interview data, using deductive and inductive approaches to coding. The deductive approach was deemed appropriate to re-examine the prevalence of gender stereotypes and emotions in rural tourism. Thus, initial codes, categories and themes were drawn from the review of Mexican gender and tourism scholarship (see Figure 1).

An inductive approach was employed to draw codes, categories and themes from the interview data to learn about participant's lived experiences (Camprubí & Coromina, 2016; Neuendorf, 2011) and emotional responses to the cultural stereotypes and gendered work. The data analysis process included both manifest and latent content analysis (Graneheim et al., 2017). During the manifest content analysis phase, we classified the visible and surface content of text; whereas in the latent content analysis, we coded the underlying meaning of the text, which requires a degree of researcher interpretation. Overall, the analysis process entailed categorizing and finding themes from key categories (i.e. gender stereotypes and women's affective/

emotional responses). In addition, non-participant observation, document review, and field notes enriched and complemented the interview data. Some strategies employed to avoid researchers' bias over the course of analysis and interpretation included: referring back to the conceptual framework, triangulating data (i.e. contrasting the interview data with the researcher observations and notes taken during the fieldwork), showing field notes to colleagues, and keeping research questions firmly in mind (Miles & Huberman, 1994). Ethical guidelines were followed to ensure that all participants understood the research objectives and the treatment that would be given to verbatim transcription of interview data. Pseudonyms were employed in lieu of participants' names and some demographic details were excluded in order to ensure anonymity and confidentiality.

Findings

Emotional responses to gendered rural tourism work

In general, tourism services and related productive activities (food, accommodation, handicraft production and guiding services) were positively valued by participants as a source of income despite their seasonal or irregular nature, because women thought this type of work was more attractive than other traditional economic activities available. This is consistent with the findings in other developing regions (e.g. Boonabaana, 2014; Tran & Walter, 2014) and in the Latin American context (e.g. Martínez-Corona, 2003; Rodríguez & Acevedo, 2015).

Even if the economic benefit generated by rural tourism is limited and their burden is increased, participants saw tourism as an opportunity to improve their lives (Hortensia, 45, married with 2 daughters, cooker, Las Margaritas, 2016; Susana, 32, married with 1 son, artisan, San Quintín, 2017; Teresa, 36, unmarried, ecotourist leader, Montepío, 2016). Sometimes they recognised the tensions produced by tourism work and experienced ambivalent fluxes which were negotiated or not (Jiménez-Esquinas, 2017; Johnston, 2007).

In some cases, women's participation in tourism work generated a sense of injustice and powerlessness. This is illustrated in the following account:

> At the beginning my husband told me that if I chose to work in tourism I must not neglect my family ... I felt stressed all time and also angry and sad too, this is also his family not only mine, but I didn't quit ... it was not easy ... and eventually he changed a little bit and I feel proud of what I have achieved (Marta, 42, married with 2 sons, rural gite owner, Montepío, 2016).

As tensions emerged, participants' struggles reflected an ambivalence when confronting the *status quo*. For example, the experience of shame, alongside with embarrassment and shyness, was commonly referred to in participants' accounts. Some interviewees recognised that rural communities tend to underestimate women's capacities to interact with strangers:

> we were very shy, we didn't like to talk with strangers ... we were not raised that way, here it is the man who talks ... it was difficult ... we were very hesitant but now ... now it is different when tourists come we don't stop talking (Olga, 40, divorced with 1 son and 2 daughters, ecotourism project leader, Roca Partida, 2017).

An important number of rural women who worked in tourism reported to struggle during the first years of their participation (e.g. Adriana, 25, unmarried, artisan, El Carrizal, 2016; Juana, doll maker, 50, married with 4 sons and 1 daughter, artisan, Santiago Mexquititlán, 2016; Sara, 43, re-married with 2 daughters, ecotourism partner, Bernal, 2017), but eventually used their work in tourism to gain self-confidence and overcome what was socially sanctioned as inappropriate activities/spaces for women.

In particular, participants who performed masculinised activities reported a constant comparison with male peers or the need to demonstrate that women could accomplish as much as men or could perform even better: 'you feel tired of always having to prove yourself... or show that you are better than men, sometimes it is exhausting...' (Laura, 34, single, adventure tourist guide, Jalcomulco, 2016). They also had to deal with the stereotype that 'women do not know the *monte* (the hills or outdoors)' and that 'their place is in the kitchen' (Patricia, 45, single with 1 daughter, B&B employee, Landa de Matamoros, 2016). So, women who wanted to access higher paying jobs in rural tourism such as tourist guides, faced this additional burden to prove that they were as capable as their male peers (Lucía, 20, single, ecotourist guide, Ruiz Cortinez, 2016; Manuela, 30, unmarried, adventure tourist guide, Jalcomulco, 2017). There is a reputational issue in rural Mexico regarding women who wander around the town interacting with men who are not from their communities, similar to what Tucker (2007) found in Turkey. This is exemplified in the following account: 'Some people think that a woman will lose her good reputation if they talk to male tourists that she ... may be looking for a man, it's frustrating I know, but I like what I do' (Patricia, op. cit.). In these cases, the feeling of shame can serve to maintain women's segregation in specific rural tourism activities.

The lack of recognition for women's work or the disregard for their contributions is also reported by those engaged in other activities rather than guiding: 'It is sad but sometimes I feel like my family is not recognising my work, the importance it has to me and to the rest of the community' (Margarita, 33, married with 2 sons, artisan, La Bocana, 2015). Participants also expressed disappointment when family members or members of the wider community disregarded their entrepreneurial efforts: 'Some people consider my effort as a secondary one, they minimise the hard work of being an entrepreneur.... "it is a hobby," they say, "it is not serious," "her business is tiny"...' (Lidia, 30, married, rural gite partner, Bernal, 2016).

Women felt unwarranted pressure to quit their activities when dealing with malicious gossip, which is used as a mechanism to limit women's mobilities in Mexican rural societies:

> I need to go to meetings, to talk to clients, to go out of the community, some people gossip and my husband was jealous, I told him to trust me... but some women quit or change because the husband forbid them to get out of their house or the community (Ana María, 37 years old, divorced, souvenir shop owner from Bernal, 2017).

The disregard for their contributions and work triggered mixed affective responses from women (e.g. anger, sadness or disappointment), while malicious gossip had repercussions on women's self-esteem and even caused some women to abandon their productive activities in tourism. In a clear recognition of their gender roles, participants frequently expressed feeling burnout or emotional and physical exhaustion, due to bearing the responsibility for care and domestic work in their households, in addition to the work they perform in the family business, private enterprise or community-based tourism venture (Adriana, op. cit.; Lucía, op. cit.; Margarita, op. cit.).

Other women's emotions towards their work emerged from a sense of accomplishment; from receiving recognition for their work (from family, other members of the community and visitors); and a sense of enjoyment or even passion (love) towards the activities they perform. Even though some degree of enjoyment derived from their work in rural tourism was experienced by most of the participants, the sense of passion was more evident among women who perform creative work in tourism (e.g. handicraft production or gastronomy), as demonstrated in the following account:

> Ah, on a personal level, I love it. It changed us all, it changed our lives because, come on, making handicraft pottery opens another world, right? Apart from the fact that we make a living out of this, we entered into a very special world. I think that knowing a lot of people of all types and social classes, I believe that one's work speaks for itself, but it did change our lives … I love my work. (Ana, 50, married with 2 daughters, potter, Metepec, 2016).

Other emotions as happiness and joy were also experienced by participants as a consequence of their work. Some women found in rural tourism the necessary spaces to expand their networks to gain support:

> So, you come here [to the workshop] and you interact with other *compañeras*, and you always have fun and you even finish the craft without noticing it. It is more pleasant than if I stay alone at home. The other day somebody turned on the radio and we ended up dancing (Julia, 37, married with 1 son, artisan, Ojoxapan, 2016).

In general, the social interactions with culturally aware or responsible tourists were also considered pleasant:

> When dinner is over, tourists stay at the *comedor* chatting with us or also when I am cooking, they ask me about the food, the town, my life…. we talk about many things; they tell me things too… all very interesting. I like to learn and have someone to talk to (Romira, 53, married with 1 son, cook, Benito Juárez, 2015).

Through transgressing traditional gender norms and roles, rural women have opened opportunities for change (Alba, 31, divorced with 1 son, tourist guide, Las Margaritas, 2015; Olga, op. cit.). Despite the fact that research participants did not see themselves as agents of change, it is important to recognise their quotidian acts of negotiation and the potential impact these acts can have not only in their own lives but in the lives of other women, as well as the diversity of emotions that they have experienced or embodied in different ways (Hall, 2018; Wilson & Little, 2008).

Feminist and gender scholars have called for the development of alternative gender roles in the context of rural tourism (Linehan & Walsh, 1999; Martínez-Corona, 2003; Rodríguez & Acevedo, 2015). Some of the research participants also reflected on the need to transform traditional gender roles, as illustrated in the following account: 'some people consider that women cannot be a rural tourist guide because they lack the strength or skills, but we are proving otherwise and our local guides feel very proud of it' (Marisa, 26, single, tourist guide, Jalcomulco, 2018). In this context, women experienced a range of affective or emotional responses due to the social pressure to conform to traditional gender roles and the prevalent gender stereotypes in tourism work (Jiménez-Esquinas, 2017). These findings are consistent with other studies that have explored the links between gender and tourism work in rural contexts (Hernández et al., 2005; Ratten & Dana, 2017; Suárez-Gutiérrez et al., 2016; Tran & Walter, 2014).

One of the most common stereotypes that emerged from the literature and was confirmed in the interviews was that 'women are not interested in tourism'. Participants' accounts illustrate how women were frequently left out of the community conversations around rural tourism initiatives:

> In this community the invitation to participate in tourism was given at the *ejido* [communal] meeting and since it is considered as a space for men, women were not invited - 'it is not for women' - they were saying (Rocío, 38, single with 1 son and 2 daughters, rural gite partner, Ruiz Cortínez, 2015).

Contrary to what the stereotype claims, women were not indifferent to the organization of tourism activities in their communities; in fact, they expressed anger or disappointment at not having been invited to these initial planning meetings (Lorena, 32 years old, single with 1 daughter, tourist guide from Las Margaritas, 2016; Olga, op. cit.).

Another common stereotype is that 'women are not good at business' and these extends to the notions that 'women are not interested in training' or 'they do not like to make decisions' (Rocío, op. cit.; Alba, op. cit., Ana, op. cit.), which are experienced as limitations and injustices (Ahmed, 2009). Most participants were well aware of these gender stereotypes and reflected on how they have overcome their emotions by gaining access to activities and spaces traditionally assigned to men: 'Through rural tourism we have been able to access places were only men used to participate, like the *Ejido* Assembly. I felt nervous and proud when I explained our recent project that involved the whole community in front of the Assembly members and others' (Alba, op. cit,).

A way in which women have been able to contest gender stereotypes is through the continuous interaction with people from outside the community (visitors and tourists) even if this is discouraged by local sociocultural norms (Tucker, 2007). The following account illustrates this: 'People from outside the community recognise our work and I like to see how they appreciate our work… you can do many things you weren't aware' (Juana, op. cit.).

Participants also reflected that their work in rural tourism was as valuable as the work performed by their male peers, but they also recognized some gendered constraints. Similar to what was reported by Johnston (2007) or Hall (2018), participants embodied more than one emotion in their performance of gendered tourism rural work. Some of them abandoned tourism activities, but others were able to negotiate the gender norms that underestimated them (Hall, 2018).

As stated before, feminist and tourist scholars have emphasized the role of emotions in power relations as a site of resistance to gender norms (Hall, 2018; Jiménez-Esquinas, 2017; Tucker, 2007; Wilson & Little, 2008). Our findings show that some women have taken advantage of tourism to negotiate gender norms and have experienced this improvement with a sense of pride as illustrated in the following account: 'I try to educate both my daughters and son not to maintain stereotypes' (Amalia, 50, married, embroiderer, Sontecomapan, 2015). Other women have used tourism to gain visibility and recognition in their communities: '...we have been able to get access to places were only men used to participate like the *Ejido* Assembly' (Olivia, 33, married with 1 daughter and 1 son, rural gite partner, Sontecomapan, 2015). We want to emphasize that the lack of family or wider community support makes the negotiation of gender roles even more challenging for participants: 'some women quit or change because the husbands forbid them to get out of their house or the community.... I feel sad for them' (Sonia, 29, married with 1 daughter, artisan jewellery, Jalpan de Serra, 2015). However, as stated by Martínez-Corona (2003) and Vizcaino-Suárez (2018), women's negotiations of gender roles to advance equality are a long-term project that leads to incremental changes over time, but these changes are not exempt from social backlash.

Likewise, women involved in tourism experience ambivalent fluxes (Jiménez-Esquinas, 2017; Johnston, 2007). In this study, women's affective and emotional responses were strongly intertwined with the productive and spatial restrictions established by gender roles (Wilson & Little, 2008). Tourism opened new possibilities and generated environments for women to embody emotions and transgress traditional gender norms in rural Mexico. However, the path is not straightforward, because women who negotiate established social norms are often disqualified and their emotions mistreated through public scolding and ridicule (see Ahmed, 2014).

Discussion: women's emotions and gendered work in Mexican rural tourism

In this study, emotions emerged in response to the social pressure to comply with social norms and these affective or emotional responses generated ambivalent fluxes (Jiménez-Esquinas, 2017). The emotional dimensions of gendered rural tourism work are influenced by complex processes and they have significant impacts on Mexican rural women's use of day-to-day spaces.

Our analysis identified some core affective or emotional responses by women in relation to their work in tourism. Shame was one of the most relevant emotions, and we consider it important because it is frequently employed by communities to restrict the use of public rural environments in Mexico. Shame is related to insecurity with a twofold meaning: a lack of self-confidence, but also a type of fear to outsiders. Similar to the experiences of Göreme women in Turkey (Tucker, 2007), Mexican participants had also begun to 'undo' the emotion of shame, slowly overcoming the sociocultural norms that attach shame to women's interaction with strangers (mainly male tourists or other male stakeholders, such as consultants, researchers, suppliers or trainers), to potentially work more comfortably in tourism environments. Furthermore, some of the women in our study used their emotions to negotiate gender stereotypes in a similar fashion to the participants in Johnston's (2007) study, who embodied affective performances to overcome their shame and transform it into pride. For example, Ana and Olga's initial shame or embarrassment of working in tourism led way to a feeling of entitlement to use public tourist spaces and other spaces in the community (like the Ejido Assembly), which generated happiness and joy.

Another finding we want to highlight is the role of emotions as a form of social control that defines the performance of tourism work. Some of the most relevant constraints rural women face take the form of gender stereotypes that interact with affective or emotional responses such as shame. The shame experienced by participants exposes a social mechanism to control not only the spaces where women move, but also the activities they can perform. Shame combined with local social norms are embodied by rural women and have an impact on their self-esteem, by: a) making them feel not capable of working with tourist/visitors; and b) having to avoid gossip that will damage their reputation. In this case, the affective performances promoted by the involvement in rural tourism can foster negotiations that allow women to gain self-confidence and a sense of accomplishment.

Responses linked to anger, disappointment or sadness also resulted from the prevalence of gender stereotypes, as women experienced the constraints of gendered jobs or gendered spaces in tourism work. This situation was more evident in the case of young women who became interested in activities traditionally ascribed to men. This was experienced by Marisa and Laura, tourist guides who have had to carve their place in the masculinised niche of adventure tourism; and also by Ana María, who faced a masculinised environment as entrepreneur. However, at the same time, emotions such as pride, accomplishment or joy are also reported by interviewees due to their participation in tourism, thus emphasizing the ambivalent fluxes that can confront women in tourism (Jiménez-Esquinas, 2017). Among our participants, these emotions were described as evidence of improvement in women's lives and employed to justify demands for further advancement. These ambivalent fluxes must not be oversimplified because according to our respondents, their involvement in rural tourism has not been free from contradictions or struggle.

A relevant example of these contradictions refers to the burden of care and emotional work, which continues to fall mainly on women. The traditional *mamá mexicana* and *la doña* are strong social constructions in rural Mexico and continue to be entrenched in rural tourism. Thus, strategies to improve women's participation in rural tourism and overcome gender stereotypes and embedded emotions, require a recognition of the value of care and emotional work, which turns out to be a core function of the maintenance of social life and a relevant factor of culture and power (Ahmed, 2004). In our view, this is the first step in reorganizing the division of labour in contexts where care and emotional work are both very important and very time consuming, such as the rural contexts we have examined. The sense of inequity is well founded in anger as an emotion generated by a lack of equitable arrangements in the division of labour, but a sense of achievement also emerges when women are able to overcome these inequities. In general, negotiation of care and emotional work generates affective ambivalences that can be experienced as an exhausting and controversial process: women can love their relatives but feel angry when their workload (in and outside of the house) increases.

The review of the literature and our findings also show that tourism has the potential to promote changes in gender stereotypes when correctly addressed. In our study, Mexican women recognised the role of rural tourism in opening spaces to negotiate gender stereotypes, but also as an activity that may reproduce or reinforce them. As

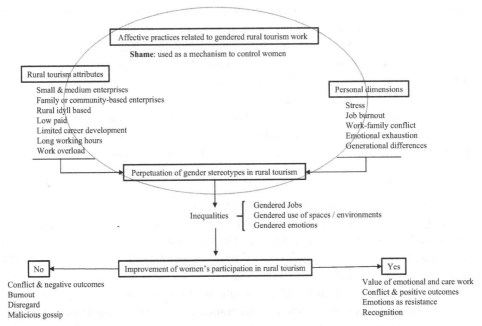

Figure 2. Framework for improving women's participation in rural tourism and overcoming gendered work. Source: Authors.

noted by Ahmed (2014), emotions reflect how social forms (such as traditional gender norms) are ingrained and difficult to transform because of repetition. In our opinion, even if rural tourism is a modern activity, the rural idyll and the quest for authenticity tends to reinforce gender stereotypes that devalue women's work. Therefore, we propose a framework to improve women's participation in rural tourism, accounting for their affective/emotional responses (see Figure 2).

The core of our proposal draws from Ahmed's notion of emotions as a source of movement and takes into account posterior work of emotions centred in tourism and gender studies. In that regard we have also considered the ambivalent fluxes (Jiménez-Esquinas, 2017), embodiment emotions (Hall, 2018), as well as Johnston's (2001, 2007) political dimension of emotions that interweave the personal and the public spheres of life.

As mestiza, middle-class, urban and university-educated Mexican women, we would like to highlight the relevance of avoiding gender stereotypes in rural tourism. However, not all the research participants construed the disparities that we examined as gender inequalities. This was especially evident when economic and monetary benefits were involved and trumped other sociocultural considerations. Following Ahmed (2014), emotions allow people to: 'feel their way' and 'the effects of 'not following' the scripts can be multiple' (p. 146) and may lead to social conflict. For women to negotiate gender roles effectively they must improve both their economic and socio-cultural standing, otherwise they will avoid any negotiation and maintain the *status quo*.

As stated by Ahmed (2004, p. 121) 'the circulation of signs of affect shapes the materialization of collective bodies', *las mujeres*, women who work in rural tourism in Mexico conform Ahmed's affective economy that materialised through an economic activity heavily centred in care work. *La doña*, a rural woman whose identity is primary restricted to the kitchen and the house, takes advantage of the skills that she has developed, which previously were demanded by the family in the domestic realm, and now are also offered to tourists in the public sphere.

Conclusions

The study of emotions has become a fertile area to promote critical tourism and gender studies. Some of the concepts highlighted by scholars, such as affective performance (Johnston, 2001, 2007), affective dimensions (Hall, 2018), ambivalent fluxes (Jiménez-Esquinas, 2017), and the embodiment of emotions (Ahmed, 2014; Tucker, 2007; Wilson & Little, 2008) have provided a useful framework to explore rural women's emotional responses to gendered tourism work. Since Mexican rural tourism can be anchored in local social norms and the rural idyll, participants in the study received contradictory messages and tensions emerged in the negotiation of new gender roles. From the point of view of participants, the possibility of gaining access to economic benefits was a strong motivation to participate in tourism; however, the availability of gendered occupations and reinforcement of gender stereotypes made some women question the transformational power of tourism work, leading to the emergence of ambivalent fluxes. Participation in rural tourism allowed participants to experience an affective performance, both in public and private spaces, where their emotions became a mechanism to negotiate gender roles.

Even though in general Mexican women appreciate the role of rural tourism in their lives, the implications of performing tourism work tended to go beyond the realm of the individual experience, and contradictions and tensions arose in the family and wider community spheres. As this experience shows, women cannot be left alone in the process of negotiating gender stereotypes and the need for wider social recognition and appreciation of the value of care and emotional work was identified. To contest the power of repetition and the 'stickiness' of social norms (Ahmed, 2014), it is crucial that all rural stakeholders are involved and incorporate gender mainstreaming strategies to improve women's participation in tourism. Enterprises also must work on introducing gender protocols to prevent occupational segregation in tourism work or the gendered use of tourism spaces. Scholars could also contribute to examining the gender dimensions of tourism work in rural contexts, monitor social change and share best practice. A relevant limitation of this research was focusing on binary gender identities and not considering other gender identities that tend to be rendered invisible in rural tourism studies. Furthermore, we suggest that the study of gender, work and emotions is expanded in the Latin American context and other emerging regions to explore affective practises and their implication in rural spaces.

Note

1. According to official data, 93.5% of rural women in Mexico lack access to education, health, other social services, adequate facilities and obtain 25% less income than rural men (CONEVAL, 2017). Rural women also bare the responsibility for family care and well-being.

Rural societies uphold deeply rooted values in Mexico and gender inequalities persist in both mestizo and indigenous societies (INMUJERES, 2017; Vásquez-García & Vargas-Vásquez, 2018).

Disclosure statement

No potential conflict of interest was reported by the author(s).

ORCID

Isis Arlene Díaz-Carrión (iD) http://orcid.org/0000-0002-0131-8163
Paola Vizcaino (iD) http://orcid.org/0000-0002-9691-9737

References

Ahmed, S. (2003). The politics of fear in the making of worlds. *International Journal of Qualitative Studies in Education*, *16*(3), 377–398. https://doi.org/10.1080/0951839032000086745

Ahmed, S. (2004). Affective economies. *Social Text*, *22*(2), 117–139. https://doi.org/10.1215/01642472-22-2_79-117

Ahmed, S. (2009). Embodying diversity: Problems and paradoxes for Black feminists. *Race Ethnicity and Education*, *12*(1), 41–52. https://doi.org/10.1080/13613320802650931

Ahmed, S. (2014). *The cultural politics of emotion* (2nd ed.). Edinburgh University Press.

Anderson, B. (2009). Affective atmospheres. *Emotion, Space and Society*, *2*(2), 77–81. https://doi.org/10.1016/j.emospa.2009.08.005

Babb, F. E. (2012). Theorizing Gender, Race, and Cultural Tourism in Latin America. A View from Peru and Mexico. *Latin American Perspectives*, *39*(6), 36–50.

Bakas, F. E. (2017). 'A beautiful mess': Reciprocity and positionality in gender and tourism research. *Journal of Hospitality and Tourism Management*, *33*, 126–133. https://doi.org/10.1016/j.jhtm.2017.09.009

Baylina, M., Garcia-Ramon, M. D., Porto, A. M., Salamaña, I., & Villarino, M. (2016). Women assess rurality — A tailored Rural Idyll. In K. Wiest (Ed.), *Women and migration in rural Europe. Labour markets, representations and policies* (pp. 25–43). Palgrave Macmillan.

Bondi, L., Davidson, J., & Smith, M. (2007). Introduction: Geography's 'emotional turn'. In M. Smith, L. Bondi, & J. Davidson (Ed.), *Emotional geographies* (pp. 2–16). Routledge.

Boonabaana, B. (2014). Negotiating gender and tourism work: Women's lived experiences in Uganda. *Tourism and Hospitality Research*, *14*(1-2), 27–36. https://doi.org/10.1177/1467358414529578

Browne, K. (2011). Beyond rural idylls: Imperfect lesbian utopias at Michigan Womyn's music festival. *Journal of Rural Studies*, *27*(1), 13–23. https://doi.org/10.1016/j.jrurstud.2010.08.001

Buda, D. M., d'Hauteserre, A. M., & Johnston, L. (2014). Feeling and tourism studies. *Annals of Tourism Research*, *46*, 102–114. https://doi.org/10.1016/j.annals.2014.03.005

Camprubí, R., & Coromina, L. (2016). Content analysis in tourism research. *Tourism Management Perspectives, 18*, 134–140. https://doi.org/10.1016/j.tmp.2016.03.002

Cohen, A. A., & Cohen, E. (2019). New directions in the sociology of tourism. *Current Issues in Tourism, 22*(2), 153–172. https://doi.org/10.1080/13683500.2017.1347151

Consejo Nacional de Evaluación de la Política de Desarrollo Social (CONEVAL). (2017). Informe de Evaluación de la Política de Desarrollo Social 2016. https://www.coneval.org.mx/Evaluacion/IEPSM/Documents/IEPDS_2016.pdf

Cvetkovich, A. (2003). *An archive of feelings: Trauma, sexuality, and Lesbian public cultures.* Duke University Press.

d'Hauteserre, A. M. (2015). Affect theory and the attractivity of destinations. *Annals of Tourism Research, 55*, 77–89. https://doi.org/10.1016/j.annals.2015.09.001

Doran, A. (2016). Empowerment and women in adventure tourism: A negotiated journey. *Journal of Sport & Tourism, 20*(1), 57–80.

Dilley, R. E., & Scraton, S. J. (2010). Women, climbing and serious leisure. *Leisure Studies, 29*(2), 125–141. https://doi.org/10.1080/02614360903401927

Frazer, R., & Waitt, G. (2016). Pain, politics and volunteering in tourism studies. *Annals of Tourism Research, 57*, 176–189.

Frohlick, S. (2006). 'Wanting the children and Wanting K2': The incommensurability of motherhood and mountaineering in Britain and North America in the late twentieth century. *Gender, Place & Culture, 13*(5), 477–490.

Giwa, A. (2015). Insider/Outsider issues for development researchers from the global south. *Geography Compass, 9*(6), 316–326. https://doi.org/10.1111/gec3.12219

González Hernández, C. (2002). *Doña Marina (La Malinche) y la formación de la identidad mexicana. [Doña Marina (La Malinche) and the formation of Mexican identity].* Ediciones Encuentro.

Gorton, K. (2007). Theorizing emotion and affect: Feminist engagements. *Feminist Theory, 8*(3), 333–348. https://doi.org/10.1177/1464700107082369

Graneheim, U. H., Lindgren, B.-M., & Lundman, B. (2017). Methodological challenges in qualitative content analysis: A discussion paper. *Nurse Education Today, 56*, 29–34. https://doi.org/10.1016/j.nedt.2017.06.002

Hall, V. (2018). Women Mountaineers and affect: Fear, Play and the Unknown. In Hayley & E. Waterton (Eds.), *Affective geographies of transformation, exploration and adventure: Rethinking frontiers* (pp. 147–164). Routledge.

Hemmings, C. (2005). Invoking affect. *Cultural Studies, 19*(5), 548–567. https://doi.org/10.1080/09502380500365473

Hernández, R., Bello, E., Montoya, G., & Estrada, E. (2005). Social adaptation. Ecotourism in the Lacandon forest. *Annals of Tourism Research, 32*(3), 610–627.

Hesse-Biber, S. N. (2016). *The Practice of Qualitative Research.* SAGE.

Hesse-Biber, S. N., & Leavy, P. (Eds.). (2006). *Emergent methods in social research.* Sage.

Hopkins, P. (2009). Women, men, positionalities and emotion: doing feminist geographies of religion. *ACME: An International E-Journal for Critical Geographies, 8*(1), 1–17.

Instituto Nacional de las Mujeres (INMUJERES). (2017). Día de las Mujeres Rurales. Objetivos Del Desarrollo Sostenible y Empoderamiento. https://www.gob.mx/inmujeres/articulos/dia-de-las-mujeres-rurales?idiom=es

Janghorban, R., Roudsari, R. L., & Taghipour, A. (2014). Skype interviewing: The new generation of online synchronous interview in qualitative research. *International Journal of Qualitative Studies on Health and Well-Being, 9*(1), 24152–24153. https://doi.org/10.3402/qhw.v9.24152

Jiménez-Esquinas, G. (2017). "This is not only about culture": On tourism, gender stereotypes and other affective fluxes. *Journal of Sustainable Tourism, 25*(3), 311–326. https://doi.org/10.1080/09669582.2016.1206109

Johnston, L. (2001). (Other) bodies and tourism studies. *Annals of Tourism Research, 28*(1), 180–201. https://doi.org/10.1016/S0160-7383(00)00012-8

Johnston, L. (2007). Mobilizing pride/shame: Lesbians, tourism and parades. *Social & Cultural Geography, 8*(1), 29–45.

Kimbu, A., & Ngoasong, M. (2016). Women as vectors of social entrepreneurship. *Annals of Tourism Research, 60,* 63–79. https://doi.org/10.1016/j.annals.2016.06.002

Krouwel, M., Jolly, K., & Greenfield, S. (2019). Comparing Skype (video calling) and inperson qualitative interview modes in a study of people with irritable bowel syndrome – An exploratory comparative analysis. *BMC Medical Research Methodology, 19*(1), 1–9. https://doi.org/10.1186/s12874-019-0867-9

Lenao, M., & Basupi, B. (2016). Ecotourism development and female empowerment in Botswana: A review. *Tourism Management Perspectives, 18,* 51–58. https://doi.org/10.1016/j.tmp.2015.12.021

León-Portilla, M. (1993). Lecturas de la palabra de doña Luz Jiménez [Interpretations of doña Luz Jiménez' words]. *Estudios de Cultura Náhuatl, 23,* 343–359.

Linehan, M., & Walsh, J. (1999). Senior female international managers: Breaking the glass border. *Women in Management Review, 14*(7), 264–272. https://doi.org/10.1108/09649429910291113

Little, J., & Austin, P. (1996). Women and the Rural Idyll. *Journal of Rural Studies, 12*(2), 101–111. https://doi.org/10.1016/0743-0167(96)00004-6

Little, W. E. (2008). Living within the Mundo Maya Project: Strategies of Maya Handicrafts Vendors. *Latin American Perspectives, 35*(3), 87–102. https://doi.org/10.1177/0094582X08315793

Lo Iacono, V., Symonds, P., & Brown, D. H. K. (2016). Skype as a tool for qualitative research interviews. *Sociological Research Online, 21*(2), 103–117. https://doi.org/10.5153/sro.3952

Longhurst, R. (2017). *Skype: Bodies, screens, space.* Routledge.

Lutz, C. (1996). Engendered emotion: Gender, power, and the rhetoric of emotional control. In R. Harré & W. Parrot (Eds.), *The emotions: Social, cultural and biological dimensions* (pp. 151–170). SAGE Publications.

Martínez-Corona, B. (2003). Género, sustentabilidad y empoderamiento en proyectos ecoturísticos de mujeres indígenas [Gender, sustainability and native women's empowerment through Ecotourism]. *La Ventana, 17*(Julio), 188–217.

Miles, M. B., & Huberman, A. M. (1994). *Qualitative data analysis: An expanded sourcebook.* Sage.

Moyle, B. D., Moyle, C., Bec, A., & Scott, N. (2019). The next frontier in tourism emotion research. *Current Issues in Tourism, 22*(12), 1393–1399. https://doi.org/10.1080/13683500.2017.1388770

Neuendorf, K. A. (2011). Content analysis—A methodological primer for gender research. *Sex Roles, 64*(3-4), 276–289. https://doi.org/10.1007/s11199-010-9893-0

Ngai, S. (2005). *Ugly feelings.* Harvard University Press.

Ocasio, R. (2010). La apropiación de María Félix del icónico personaje en Doña Bárbara de Rómulo Gallegos [María Félix's appropriation of Rómulo Gallegos' iconic character of Doña Bárbara]. *Romance Quarterly, 57*(4), 273–285. https://doi.org/10.1080/08831157.2010.496345

Patton, M. Q. (2002). *Qualitative research and evaluation methods* (3rd ed.). Sage.

Pérez-Ramírez, C., Zizumbo-Villareal, L., & Miranda-Contreras, S. (2012). Incorporación al Turismo Rural y Transformación del Habitus en la Mujer Campesina de San Pedro Atlapulco, México [Incorporation into rural tourism and transformation of San Pedro Atlapulcós, Mexico, peasant woman habitus]. *Rosa Dos Ventos, 4*(2), 158–177.

Picard, D. (2012). Tourism, awe and inner journeys. In D. Picard & M. Robinson (Eds.), *Emotion in motion: Tourism, affect and transformation* (pp. 1–19). Ashgate.

Pocock, N. (2015). Emotional entanglements in tourism research. *Annals of Tourism Research, 53,* 31–45. https://doi.org/10.1016/j.annals.2015.04.005

Pritchard, A., Morgan, N., Ateljevic, I., & Harris, C. (2007). Editor's introduction: Tourism, gender, embodiment and experience. In A. Pritchard, N. Morgan, I. Ateljevic, & C. Harris (Eds.), *Tourism & gender. Embodiment, sensuality and experience* (pp. 1–12). CABI International.

Ratten, V., & Dana, L.-P. (2017). Gendered perspective of indigenous entrepreneurship. *Small Enterprise Research, 24*(1), 62–72. https://doi.org/10.1080/13215906.2017.1289858

Rodríguez, G., & Acevedo, A. (2015). Cambios en la vida cotidiana de las mujeres a través de la incorporación al trabajo turístico en la Reserva de la Biosfera de la Mariposa Monarca [Changes in the daily lives of women through incorporating the tourism work in Michoacán, México]. *El Periplo Sustentable, 29,* 5–33.

Sandoval-Quintero, M. A., Pimentel-Aguilar, S., Pérez-Vázquez, A., Escalona-Maurice, M. J., & Sancho-Comíns, J. (2017). El turismo rural en México: Una aproximación conceptual al debate

suscitado sobre las políticas públicas desarrolladas, la irrupción de agentes externos y las nue-
vas metodologías de acción endógena y participativa [Rural tourism in Mexico: A conceptual
and critical approach to public policy, external agents and new endogenous and participatory
methodologies]. *Estudios Geográficos, 78,* 373–382.

Serra, I., & Ferré, M. (2006). El lugar del género en la geografía rural [Gender and its place in
Rural Geography]. *Boletín de la Asociación de Geógrafos Españoles, 41,* 99–112.

Sharp, J. (2009). Geography and gender: what belongs to feminist geography? Emotion, power
and change. *Progress in Human Geography, 33*(1), 74–80. https://doi.org/10.1177/
0309132508090440

Suárez-Gutiérrez, G. M., Bello-Baltazar, E., Hernández-Cruz, R. E., & Rhodes, A. (2016). Ecoturismo
y el trabajo invisibilizado de las mujeres en la Selva Lacandona, Chiapas, México. [Ecotourism
and the invisible work of women in the "Lacandona" jungle in Chiapas, Mexico]. *El Periplo
Sustentable, 31,* 1–24. http://www.redalyc.org/jatsRepo/1934/193449985008/193449985008.
pdf

Tavakoli, R., & Mura, P. (2015). Journeys in Second Life - Irani Muslim women's behaviour in virtual tourist destinations. *Tourism Management, 46,* 398–407. https://doi.org/10.1016/j.tourman.
2014.07.015

Tran, L., & Walter, P. (2014). Ecotourism, gender and development in northern Vietnam. *Annals
of Tourism Research, 44,* 116–130. https://doi.org/10.1016/j.annals.2013.09.005

Tucker, H. (2007). Undoing shame: Tourism and women's work in Turkey. *Journal of Tourism and
Cultural Change, 5*(2), 87–105. https://doi.org/10.2167/jtcc089.0

Tucker, H. (2009). Recognizing emotion and its postcolonial potentialities: Discomfort and shame
in a tourism encounter in Turkey. *Tourism Geographies, 11*(4), 444–461. https://doi.org/10.
1080/14616680903262612

Tucker, H. (2016). Empathy and tourism: Limits and possibilities. *Annals of Tourism Research, 57,*
31–43. https://doi.org/10.1016/j.annals.2015.12.001

Waitt, G., & Clifton, D. (2013). 'Stand out, not up': Bodyboarders, gendered hierarchies and negotiating the dynamics of pride/shame. *Leisure Studies, 32*(5), 487–506. https://doi.org/10.1080/
02614367.2012.684397

Wilson, E., & Little, D. E. (2008). The Solo female travel experience: Exploring the 'Geography of
women's fear'. *Current Issues in Tourism, 11*(2), 167–186. https://doi.org/10.2167/cit342.0

Wilson, T. D., & Ypeij, A. (2012). Introduction. Tourism, gender, and ethnicity. *Latin American
Perspectives, 187* (39/6), 5–16.

Vásquez-García, C. M., & Vargas-Vásquez, L. V. (2018). Foro Internacional de Mujeres Indígenas, &
Alianza de Mujeres Indígenas de Centroamérica y México. Situación general de las mujeres
rurales e indígenas en México [Serie Informes/País]. Coalición Internacional por el Acceso a la
Tierra (ILC) América Latina y el Caribe.

Veijola, S. (2009). Gender as work in the tourism industry. *Tourist Studies, 9*(2), 109–126. https://
doi.org/10.1177/1468797609360601

Vizcaino-Suárez, L. P. (2018). Tourism as empowerment: Women artisan's experiences in central
Mexico. In S. Cole (Ed.), *Gender equality and tourism: Beyond empowerment* (pp. 46–54). CABI.

Wetherell, M. (2015). Trends in the turn to affect: A social psychological critique. *Body & Society,
21*(2), 139–166.

Part II

Feeling places

Presence in affective heritagescapes: connecting theory to practice

Katherine Burlingame 🆔

ABSTRACT

A recent shift in tourism studies has focused on the emotional, affective, embodied, and performative dimensions of heritage landscape experience. However, such research often struggles to transform theoretical and conceptual discussions into practical and applicable terms that can be effectively implemented by site managers. The concept of presence is therefore proposed to identify emotional and affective dimensions of heritage landscapes through an embodied, observational, and collaborative approach. Inspired by landscape phenomenology, I share how my own embodied encounter in the Viking Age site of Birka in Sweden prompted further observations and reflections on the existing site experience to confirm that certain areas of the landscape have been largely unexplored for their affective and emotional potential. Practical strategies to utilize these new dimensions emerge from focus groups and interviews with site managers, re-enactors, and tour guides. I conclude that a more collaborative study of presence grounded in embodied and observational encounters provides a useful stepping stone to transform theoretical and conceptual discussions of emotion and affect into more practical heritage management strategies.

摘要

最近,旅游研究的一个转变集中在遗产景观体验的情感、情绪、亲身体验和展演方面。然而,这类研究往往致力于将理论和概念讨论转化为现场管理人员有效执行的实用而适用的术语。因此,本研究提出了在场的概念,并通过一个亲身观察和合作的方法来识别遗产景观的情感和情绪方面。受景观现象学的启发,我分享了我自己在瑞典比尔卡维京时代遗址的亲身经历,这促使我进一步观察和反思现有的当场体验,以证实该景观的某些区域在情感和情绪潜力上很大程度上未被挖掘。利用这些新维度的实用策略来自于我对焦点小组和现场管理人员、演员和导游的访谈。我的结论是,一个基于亲身实察经历的在场的更为协作性的研究,为将情感和情绪的理论和概念讨论转化为更实用的遗产管理策略提供了一个有用的跳板。

Introduction

> And there, quite suddenly and unexpectedly, I slipped a gear, or something like that. There was not me and the landscape, but a kind of oneness: a connection as though my skin had been blown off. More than that – as though the molecules and atoms I am made of had reunited themselves with the molecules and atoms that the rest of the world is made of. I felt absolutely connected to everything. It was very brief, but it was a total moment (Maitland, 2008, p. 63).

In *A Book of Silence*, Sara Maitland shares the story of her rather unexpected embodied encounter in the Isle of Skye's vast moorlands. Sitting on a rock gazing out at the landscape in front of her, she experiences a brief moment of oneness with the sky above and the ground below. Instead of thinking, sensing, or perceiving, she is merely *being*. Sam Harris describes a similar sensation challenging the 'illusion of the self' (2014, p. 82) in his book Waking Up while standing on the shore of the Sea of Galilee. He writes:

> As I gazed out at the surrounding hills, a feeling of peace came over me. It soon grew to a blissful stillness that silenced my thought. In an instant, the sense of being a separate self – an 'I' or 'me' – vanished. Everything was as it had been – the cloudless sky, sea, the pilgrims clutching their bottles of water – but I no longer felt separate from the scene, peering out at the world from behind my eyes. Only the world remained (2014, p. 81).

In these moments, the power of presence is often enough to banish our inner dialogue and to connect us to something greater than ourselves, which is why tourists often deliberately seek out such emotionally powerful places. As Laurajane Smith argues, they not only go to 'learn and/or to recreate' (2014, p. 125), but also to *feel* and experience something outside of the routine of daily life as demonstrated in the examples above.

An increasing body of research in tourism studies following geography's emotional turn (Birenboim, 2016; Buda, D'Hauteserre, & Johnston, 2014; Curtin & Kragh, 2014; Pearce, Strickland-Munro, & Moore, 2017; Pocock, 2015; Weaver & Jin, 2016) reveals the complexity of tourist encounters and thereby the importance of considering 'multivocal heritage processes' (Shea, 2018, p. 42). Such approaches challenge the traditional visitor experience structures dictated by what Laurajane Smith has called an 'authorized heritage discourse' (hereafter, AHD) (2006) through which 'experts' decide how visitors should engage and interact with certain sites based on different valued elements and the most common emotional responses they evoke. For example, while most visitors may encounter an overwhelming feeling of bliss in a certain landscape, others might experience fear, sadness, excitement, or any other range of emotions that stray far from the dominant narrative. This has been demonstrated by numerous authors including, for example, Tolia-Kelly's artistic work with post-migration communities in the English Lake District (2007, 2008), Buda's investigation of the 'death drive' in various tourist sites around Jordan (2015), or Shea's study of visitors' differing attachments and reactions to the past at an art installation in Derry/Londonderry (2018). As these works demonstrate, more attention must be given to heritage 'as a process understood, practiced *and experienced* on the ground by the people themselves' (Muzaini & Minca, 2018, p. 1, original emphasis) or what Robertson calls 'Heritage from Below' (2008) that highlights counter-hegemonic views and experiences in heritage landscapes. Similarly, others have called for a renewed focus not only on multivocal perspectives, but also multisensory dimensions through which senses are seen as 'affect-in-action' (Sather-Wagstaff, 2017, p. 13) and our bodies constantly navigate through physical, discursive, and affective spaces (Knudsen, 2011; Waterton & Watson, 2013).

Despite the increase in research that argues for more in-depth studies of emotional and affective dimensions of heritage landscapes, scholars often struggle to transform theoretical and conceptual discussions into practical and applicable terms that can be effectively implemented by site managers. I therefore propose the concept of presence as a useful stepping stone between academic and practical investigations of heritage landscape experience. As Eelco Runia argues, '... most makers of "experience museums" grope in the dark as to the nature of presence' (2006b, p. 309). This means that the visitor experience remains tethered to traditional components of the site (its historical significance and tangible remains), and there is little consideration for other affective and emotional dimensions. Therefore, I offer a new methodology for studying presence that combines embodied, observational, and collaborative research elements to explore these potentially overlooked affective and emotional landscape qualities.

Based on the creative writing and narrative styles increasingly employed within landscape phenomenology (Edensor, 2017; Wylie, 2005), I begin with my own embodied encounter with presence while exploring burial mounds in the Viking Age landscape of Birka. Observations of guided tours, paths, maps, and signs revealed that this area of the landscape is not included in the visitor experience despite its emotional and affective qualities. Reflective discussions on presence with site employees and volunteers (site managers, tour guides, and re-enactors) then resulted in new ideas and strategies to incorporate new affective and emotional dimensions of the landscape into the visitor experience. I conclude that more embodied, observational, and collaborative work on presence serves as an effective bridge between affective and emotional research and practical heritage management.

Defining presence

There are numerous theoretical and conceptual frameworks that might be used to study presence in heritage landscapes. Non-representational approaches (and those that are more-than-representational (Lorimer, 2005; see also Waterton, 2019)), for example, attempt to 'access, understand and communicate the ways in which people perform and embody the landscapes that surround them' (Waterton, 2013, p. 69) as well as how landscapes carry their own performativity in being able to *answer back* (Thrift, 2008; Thrift & Dewsbury, 2000). At the same time, there has also been a reemergence of 'Landscape Phenomenology' (Wylie, 2007), which focuses on the immediate, bodily experience of *being* in a lived world and 'the quality and intensity' of emotions that arise from embodied encounters (see Tuan, 1976, pp. 274–275). While all of these theoretical approaches may suffice in guiding us toward an understanding of presence, I first wish to discuss how different discussions of presence have emerged and how they have laid the groundwork for utilizing it as a conceptual tool for affective landscape analysis.

Inspired by early phenomenological ideas such as Heidegger's *Dasein*, Gumbrecht defines presence as something that is not temporal, but rather involves a 'spatial relationship to the world and its objects' (2004, p. xiii). The production of presence, he argues, involves the conditions under which objects affect human bodies. This understanding of presence resonates with Bennett's understanding of 'thing-power' and different objects having a 'live presence' or a certain vibrancy through which they have a capacity to affect us. For example, she describes encountering objects in a storm drain and says the 'stuff exhibited its thing-power: it issued a call, even if I did not quite understand what it was saying. At the very least, it provoked affects in me' (2010, p. 4). Eelco Runia has also extensively discussed presence in the philosophy of history where he defines presence as the 'living on of the past in the here and now' (2006b, p. 310). He argues presence is an active force that we pursue through the recognition of fleeting moments and the fascination of memory (2006a). More recently, Bjerregaard (2015) used presence in his work exploring the enduring fascination with objects in museums. He argues this neglects the role of space and the possibility of evoking a sense of presence that occurs before the meaning-making processes of traditional museum exhibitions.

Others have less explicitly discussed presence, but have used different words such as 'life awake' (Tuan, 1986), 'mindfulness' (Moscardo, 1996) or 'atmosphere' (Bille, Bjerregaard, & Sørensen, 2015; Bjerregaard, 2015; McCormack, 2013) to describe a certain level of awareness in the present moment and all the forces at play. Further work also discusses presence in terms of the absence of something – where there is a paradox between the absence of presence and the presence of absence (Degen & Hetherington, 2001; Goulding, Saren, & Pressey, 2018; Wylie, 2009). Research using the concept of haunting, for example, explores 'the dialogical experiences found between subject and object, presence and absence, past and future' (Degen & Hetherington, 2001, p. 2). Such research challenges spatial and temporal conceptions of landscapes by describing the atmosphere of a place as 'gestures in time and space reaching forwards and backwards and coming together in the fleeting moments in ways that unsettle a certainty in the linear flow of time' (Degen & Hetherington, 2001, p. 2).

As all of these different theoretical approaches and understandings reveal, the study of presence recognizes the unique way in which different people interact with and are affected by the spaces and objects around them. There is no one distinct way that emerges in how to use presence, but rather the recognition that it is inherently tethered to our active engagement with the seen and unseen world around us. It is therefore important to look into the literature that explores heritage landscape experience to identify the areas where a more critical application of presence might contribute.

Finding presence in research on affect and emotion

In tourism studies, presence has not been specifically researched as such, but rather first in the context of existential authenticity (also understood as something similar to Heidegger's *Dasein* – a connection discussed extensively in works by Pearce and Moscardo (1986) and Steiner and Reisinger (2006)). Existential authenticity first emerged out of a discussion regarding the many different layers of authenticity (and inauthenticity) in tourism identified primarily by MacCannell (1976). According to Wang (1999), similar to Runia's definition of presence, existential authenticity occurs in tourism because people want to get away from their everyday lives, and when the routine is broken they feel closer to their authentic selves. This aligns with Runia's stance that 'we *want* to be affected. We go to great lengths, and are willing to spend huge amounts of money, to *have* ourselves affected by the past' (2006b, p. 309, original emphasis). The 'presence of the past', he writes, 'makes me *feel* things, *think* things, and *do* things that are at odds with who I think I am – and so forces me to rewrite the story about myself' (2006b, p. 316, original emphasis). Therefore, a renewed focus on presence allows for the study of different modes of meaning-making outside of contested understandings of the authenticity of different tourist experiences.

Presence has also emerged in research that highlights the variability of visitors and their different interests and capacities to be affected or to be 'present'. Some have taken a more direct approach in categorizing visitors or offering strategies to engage them. For example, Moscardo developed a 'Mindfulness Model' to assess different factors that affected the visitor experience (1996), McKercher developed a typology of cultural tourists (2002) based on different visitor motives and the depths of their experiences, and Kantanen and Tikkanen (2006) looked at different persuasive strategies sites might use to engage different types of visitors from McKercher's typology. Their focus is on informative strategies, but they note that future work should also focus on possible affective strategies. McIntosh and Prentice also highlight the importance in studying 'experiential and emotive processes' (1999, p. 589) in tourists' interactions. Their study in British period theme parks revealed that tourists cared less about historical accuracy and more about a site's affective and personal dimensions.

Others have focused on the performative turn through which visitors gain more control over their experiences and the past is brought to life through hands-on encounters. For example, Moscardo notes it is important for visitors to have variety and control over their experiences, and she argues 'interpretation ... needs to *challenge* visitors, to question and encourage them to question' (1996, p. 392, my emphasis). Kirsti Mathiesen Hjemdahl (2004) came to a similar conclusion, demonstrating how school classes were more interested in Viking theme parks than traditional static museum exhibitions because they craved direct engagement rather than distanced observation.

Active engagement has also been discussed regarding the role of re-enactment events in fostering a sense of presence. For example, at an artillery re-enactment at the Dybbøl Battlefield Centre in Southern Denmark, four historical cannons were fired for ten minutes at maximum frequency. Mads Daugbjerg describes how one interview subject experienced a 'period rush' from physically feeling the 'thumps of the big guns ... and the confusion and lack of orientation brought about by the thick cover of the resulting smoke' (2017, p. 166). Other spectators, he notes, were completely captivated 'as they stared into something horrible, some of the horrible realities that are hard to communicate conventionally' (2017, p. 166). There was no other way to share the multisensory depth of such an experience without actually giving spectators a corporeal idea of what it felt like, sounded like, and smelled like. Through multisensory activities, the presence of the past 'can move you, [and] you can only tell from its wake that it has been there' (Runia, 2006a, p. 310). The power of evoking the past in the present through multisensory means has also emerged in similar literature on time travel, which involves a much deeper immersion of role-playing in a specific event or period in the past (Goodwin, 2017; Holtorf, 2017; Samida, 2017).

As these examples reveal, spaces are affective because we become *involved*. However, it is important to remember that every individual perceives and experiences meanings, symbols, and other elements in the landscape differently based on who they are, where they have been, and what they have experienced (Tuan, 1986). Given this variability and unpredictability in visitors' interests and backgrounds, it is often difficult to emotionally engage visitors who do not have an inherent cultural link or sense of belonging or identity with the place or its history (Poria, Butler, & Airey, 2003). Furthermore, the dominant and standardized way to experience a landscape might even exclude certain visitors from ever visiting in the first place, so it is vital to think of how to attract a wider spectrum of visitors who have the possibility to pursue their own interests while ensuring their unique, emotional encounters are also respected. As demonstrated in a study of Lake District tourism by Edmonds, one of the challenges in historic landscape management is giving the space for visitors 'to find their own connections and their own ways in' despite the fact that we continue to value landscapes with outdated perceptions of origin myths and a 'nostalgia for a past that never really existed' (2006, p. 185).

While all of these studies and others within the emotional turn effectively argue that visitors now use sites in many different ways for different purposes (Smith, 2014), perhaps what is broadly missed in the conclusion of these discussions is that it is good that visitors feel *something* regardless of the level of their engagement or capacity to be affected. Furthermore, given that emotional and affective encounters are based on active involvement within the landscape, there should be a renewed focus on the affective and emotional qualities of the landscapes themselves and the different strategies that might be employed to make different landscape elements more present within these performative engagements.

As I will discuss, studying presence first involves a landscape-based approach in which the landscape and its many ineffable qualities become the starting point of investigation. In this sense, the initial question posed is not how the landscape makes people feel, but rather, how *can* it make people feel (something). This also opens the door for a new methodology for studying presence in heritagescapes.

A methodology for presence

While Christopher Tilley once argued 'there is and can be no clear-cut methodology arising from [emotions and affect] to provide a concise guide to empirical research' (1994, p. 11), there are several worth mentioning. Barbara Bender, for example, analyzed landscapes in three different ways in order to capture different affective dimensions of how people relate to the world ('landscape as *palimpsest*; landscape as *structure of feeling*; and landscape as *embodied*' (1998, p. 32)). Mary-Catherine Garden also proposed a landscape-based approach called the 'heritagescape' method (2006). Moving away from the traditional approach of comparing sites using a template through which 'we impose a veneer of "sameness"' (Garden, 2009, p. 272), Garden's methodology analyzes three components that make up heritagescapes: boundaries, cohesion, and visibility. Though she criticizes the divide in research that separates material components and visitor experience, her focus remains on the site itself and identifying elements that distinguish different heritagescapes. Highlighting these qualities, she argues, identifies the site's unique 'personality' (2009, p. 272), and she emphasizes the need to study how individuals react to them. While Garden defines heritagescapes as social and interactive spaces, she still predominantly studies them as *visual* spaces. Therefore, more work must be done to understand the *experiential*, multisensory dimensions of heritagescapes beyond their boundaries and built features and in areas that Garden refers to as the landscape's 'empty spaces' (2009, p. 272). Though I will not employ the heritagescape as a method to explore presence, I will use it as a guiding concept following Garden's advice to 'describ[e] and think[] about those specific landscapes that make up a heritage site' (2006, p. 398).

Despite Garden's and others' efforts to develop these methodologies, however, there is still little effort in communicating these approaches to the site managers themselves. Traditional heritage management continues to focus on a site's geographical and historical dimensions and rarely engages with new strategies to explore emotional and affective possibilities. As demonstrated in Ankre, Fredman, and Lindhagen's study on visitor monitoring (2016), managers continue to resort to traditional methods because there is a lack of proper training and outreach with academic institutions or competent skilled workers who can help them learn more creative methods and techniques to study the visitor experience.

The concept of presence is therefore used to challenge both the traditional way of thinking about the visitor experience as well as the practice of heritage landscape management to make room for more affective and emotional possibilities. Studying presence, however, also poses a methodological challenge. Many have noted the difficulty in researching ephemeral qualities such as a site's atmosphere or powerful moments of presence (Bille et al., 2015). However, while existing methodologies tend to be vague, Bille et al. (2015) argue that this does not mean the research is weak. Rather, they argue that it has not yet been determined how to best study and write about fleeting moments. This was also discussed by Sarah Elwood who argued that 'affect, as a non-cognitive way of knowing, is … difficult to engage methodologically,' but this does not mean that it should not be studied. Instead, she argues we must 'extend qualitative methods beyond traditionally text-focused forms of evidence, modes of analysis, and ways of knowing' (2010, p. 110).

Existing research on presence involves a multisensory involvement and engagement with the world – whether in moments of intensity like those described at the beginning of this paper or in a simple awareness of the present moment. This was exemplified in Tilley's phenomenological work with ruins (1994) where he focuses as much on the whistling of the wind and the sound of a nearby waterfall as he does on the cultural elements. Since affective and emotional dimensions are often qualities of the site that cannot easily be grasped through representational modes of thinking, a study of presence fills the gap to consider the *more,* the *other*, and the vibrancy of the empty spaces – or the spaces in-between.

As noted previously, the field of tourism studies is increasingly rich with research revealing the complexity of visitor encounters and the different capacities for visitors to be affected in different ways, yet there is a lack of research that examines the affective capacity of the landscape itself. This is perhaps why such studies often lack a concrete engagement as to how the research outcomes might be implemented within the sites and landscapes studied. Similarly, despite the proven significance of such studies in bringing forth the emotional turn from geography to tourism studies and critical heritage studies (among others), there is still no concise methodology for emotional and affective research in heritage landscapes that can also be employed by site managers.

From existing literature on affect and emotion, there are two clear ways of approaching research on visitor and heritage landscape interactions: embodied or observational. Research on embodied encounters (Buda et al., 2014; Macpherson, 2016; Pocock, 2015; Tolia-Kelly, 2007; Vannini, 2015) explores the complexity of feelings in these interactions and the researcher's own reflexive role in untangling and deciphering them. This has been increasingly demonstrated using different narrative styles to explore the complexity in encounters between the self and landscape. John Wylie, for example, employs this approach during a coastal landscape walk (2005) while Tim Edensor explored the eerie presence of mundane urban spaces (2008) and the impact of light on the landscape experience (2017). Seeing his shadow, Edensor writes, 'affirms that my body impacts upon the landscape through which I move. I cannot be an abstracted, dispassionate entity who views and evaluates; rather, I am a body that even for a short time, is part of this landscape ... ' (2017, p. 631). However, such subjective approaches relying solely on the researcher's own feelings and encounters have been criticized for their limited scope especially with respect to neglecting others' voices (Edmonds, 2006; Harvey, 2015; Hill, 2013) and their 'excessive self-referentiality' (Butz, 2010, p. 142) that provides little meaningful insight to readers. Therefore, while they may provide the basis for affective investigations into the landscape, the question to be asked is: What can we do with this?

Other work is more observational in identifying tourist behaviors and perceptions, which are often explored through methods such as surveys (Wall-Reinius, 2012) and/or interviews (Poria et al., 2003; Smith, 2014). In these studies, while visitors might reflect on what they think is missing, it is difficult to derive from their answers what *else* could affect the visitor experience within the landscape. In this sense, it is difficult for a tourist to reflect on something they didn't know was there. As noted, this has created a lapse in identifying the emotional and affective potential of areas in the heritagescape not yet included in the visitor experience.

Therefore, guided by the different trajectories of research on emotion and affect with the goal of creating a more practical, landscape-based approach, I propose a new methodology to study presence through three stages: (1) embodied, (2) observational, and (3) collaborative. More specifically, the three stages involve an embodied evaluation of the landscape, an assessment of how it is currently being used by and presented to visitors, and collaborative work exploring new forms of engagement and how these might be implemented.

Embodied. Starting off with an embodied encounter in the landscape aligns with what Tilley refers to as a 'phenomenology of the landscape' (1994). This requires all the senses; it's 'a visionscape but also a soundscape, a touchscape, even a smellscape, a multi-sensory experience' (in Bender, 1998, p. 81). Consider, for example, the feeling of awe when you climb to the top of a mountain with a conquering view of the landscape below. You pause. You gaze. You no longer feel detached from the space around you, and you become one with the landscape. After the initial euphoria, you close your eyes and hear the howling wind moving across the rutted crevasses of the mountain. You feel the heat of the sun on your face. You hear distant echoes of a landscape alive.

Through our active participation we are able to 'better understand lived, sensed, experienced, and emotional worlds' (Watson & Till, 2010, p. 126). This stage involves an initial walk through the landscape to become familiar with the different sense impressions it might offer followed by writing detailed reflective field notes about emotional and/or affective dimensions encountered (see Ateljevic, Harris, Wilson, & Collins, 2005; Feighery, 2006). After the initial walk through the landscape, there should then be a more embodied engagement in which a deeper immersion is employed. Rather than simple observational notes of what the body encounters, it is necessary to consider other sense impressions that affect the present moment including a consideration of past landscapes and people. Consider, for example, Anders Lund Hansen's walking encounters in the urban environment. He writes, 'Through the rhythms of walking … one can observe and study myriad rhythms of modern society and the multiplicity of "footprints" that provide convergent and divergent spatiotemporal histories' (2008, p. 2).

For site managers, the difficult task is being open to new encounters and interactions with the landscape because they are already experts. This is also an opportunity to employ other methods to represent or reflect on affective places or moments such as taking pictures or drawing (see Mitchell, Theron, Stuart, Smith, & Campbell, 2011). Visits should take several hours over several days or longer in order to experience the landscape under different times of the day or even seasonal changes.

Observational. After exploring the researcher's own encounters, it is then important to study the visitor experience through observations of how and more importantly where visitors move within the landscape. While more creative participatory approaches such as map-making, drawing, and accompanied walks (Anderson, 2004; Macpherson, 2016) have allowed researchers to study how visitors react and respond to different areas of the site, these responses are often difficult to elicit due to the time constraints placed on visitors to certain sites. Furthermore, it is difficult to use this material to help guide practical changes due to the difficulty in generalizing visitors' unique, subjective encounters. As has been noted previously, short-term visitors also cannot be expected to point out elements they didn't know were there. Therefore, observing guided tours, different paths, maps, and visitor movements within the landscape helps to identify the areas of the site that are most valued, and more importantly, may confirm that certain affective areas of the landscape are not yet being utilized.

Collaborative. Finally, perhaps the most important stage in studying presence is the third, collaborative component through which the embodied and observational research is communicated and critically discussed with those responsible or involved with the visitor experience. Those responsible may also have completed the first two stages independently, and researchers and practitioners can then work together to develop new strategies. Collaboration is a vital piece of the presence puzzle because, as mentioned at the beginning of this paper, those responsible for the site experience grapple with how to actually approach presence and its multi-layered meanings. This is therefore the final stage of studying presence because it provides a platform to discuss how to deal with the affective and emotional dimensions uncovered in the first two stages. This can also be the point where different areas of the first two stages are re-visited for more in-depth studies or where practical strategies to employ within the landscape are developed. However, as I will discuss from my own fieldwork, collaborative work should start right from the beginning and continue throughout each stage so that different research techniques can be employed along the way and site managers can play an active role in the process.

Method

The fieldwork presented takes place in the UNESCO World Heritage site of Birka located on the island of Björkö outside of Stockholm, Sweden. Due to the narrow tourism season, the difficulty in getting to and from the island, and the limited options to stay on the island (there are a total of six residents living on the island and no formal lodging available), only two study visits were made – during the high tourism season in July 2018 and in the low season in early June 2019 for a total of one week.

There are less than 20 people working at the site during the high season and even fewer in the low season (re-enactors are only present during July). Tourist numbers are also limited due to the small island only being accessible by boat. There is one main tourist boat that runs daily from Stockholm, and several others depart from nearby ports – running intermittently for just over a month during the high season. Visitors may also come on their own boats and stay at the guest harbor. The ticket to travel roundtrip with the tourist boats includes the guided tour through the main archaeological field and access to the museum and reconstructed village. These visitors spend a total of three hours on the island. The guided tour takes approximately one hour, and the rest of the time is most often spent in the museum, the reconstructed village, and the restaurant. During both of my visits, the weather played an integral role in shaping how visitors engaged with the site, which should be considered a limitation for the reliability of my observations. However, I made sure to bring this up in subsequent discussions with site employees who confirmed that regardless of the weather the visitor experience remained largely unchanged with respect to the areas of the site most visited. During my first visit, the weather was unseasonably hot, and visitors mainly remained in the shade of the museum's pavilion after the guided tour to enjoy some ice-cream. During my second visit (already in the low season) there were less than 10 visitors on the island the first day due to torrential rain and cold temperatures, and the weather did not really improve for the remainder of my stay.

My first visit included walking through different areas of the site independently for several hours each day to explore different embodied encounters interspersed with participant and non-participant observations due to the high volume of tourists. Observations were made on the tourist boat, at the museum and reconstructed village, in the restaurant, throughout the historical landscape based on what was included on the site map, during guided tours, and in the wider landscape of the island beyond the main tourist paths. There were around 15 people working on the island (not including restaurant and other maintenance staff) during my first visit including site managers, tour guides, and re-enactors. They were all very occupied throughout the day, but once the tourist boats left, I moderated smaller group discussions in the reconstructed village and larger group discussions over dinner each afternoon and evening. During my second visit, there were only three tour guides (two were new that season) and the site manager and her family present on the island (besides restaurant/maintenance staff). Due to low tourist numbers, I often had the site completely to myself allowing for further multisensory interactions with different areas of the landscape in a more undisturbed state. While the first visit included group discussions about presence and shared experiences in different areas of the landscape, the second visit was the most collaborative. There was more time to sit together (in the Scandinavian way – usually over a very strong coffee) with the site manager and one of the more experienced tour guides to discuss how to implement ideas and strategies suggested during previous group discussions. A total of 234 photographs were also taken to supplement my observations and notes collected during group discussions and meetings.

Figure 1. Unmarked entrance to Hemlanden.
Source: Author.

Encountering presence in a viking cemetery

July 2018. It was a warm morning – no reprieve from the unseasonably hot weather that set the greater part of Scandinavia on fire in the summer of 2018. I had been on the island for several days observing tourists and following different visitor paths to understand the typical ways of experiencing the site. However, on that morning I set out to explore an area called Hemlanden (the largest Viking Age cemetery in Scandinavia (Magnus & Gustin, 2012)) adjacent to the open field where the city of Birka once stood. Tour groups only ever view Hemlanden from a distance because they remain on the opposite side of the field by the hillfort. Therefore, there are no signs, paths, or other informative elements typically present in a historical landscape (Figure 1).

After cautiously entering through one of the unmarked rickety metal gates aimed at keeping local grazers in their designated eateries for the day, I weaved my way up the hill around burial mounds of varying sizes worn down with age. The landscape levelled off and I had a panoramic view of the archaeological field, the hillfort, the sea, the harbor, and a few of the dwindling old houses and farms still in operation on the island. Behind me the forest grew more dense and the mounds more unkempt – covered with overgrown foliage beneath tall trees that swayed in the wind. Rays of sunshine danced on the ground, birds chirped overhead, and I could hear the distant sound of soft waves breaking on the island's rocky shores. I was content with the feeling of being surrounded by nature, and I understood why the people of Birka chose to bury their dead here. It was calm, and I embraced the silence (Figure 2).

Figure 2. From Hemlanden overlooking the main archaeological field with the hillfort in the distance.
Source: Author.

Moving further into the seemingly endless collection of mounds, however, I realized it *was* really quiet – too quiet, and I was alone. My imagination began to take over and it occurred to me that this is the kind of silence that results from being surrounded by the dead. 'Don't be silly,' the historian-archaeologist in me chided. I walked on trying to get back to the calm serenity I had experienced before, but my subconscious apparently found it difficult to ignore the eerie feeling that I was being watched as I determinedly continued deeper into the woods. Suddenly every footstep crunching on the parched ground below sounded like a cascading waterfall that enveloped the space around me. 'Stop it, you loon,' I pleaded in my own mind, and my rational side tried to remain focused at the task at hand. I intended to experience the site like a tourist and to offer some recommendations for how to get visitors to venture off and explore this area after the guided tour instead of immediately returning to the harbor with the museum, restaurant, and reconstructed village. I repeated the facts I knew: 1,600 burial mounds in such a small area, very little excavated, important Viking Age site, Vikings, … dead Vikings.

I couldn't shake the feeling of knowing I was alone, but somehow not *alone*. I thought if I listened closely enough I could faintly hear whispers of the past – of the people *inside* the mounds. Who were they? What was their life like in Birka? How did they die? How many were buried here? I looked around in vain for an informational sign or something to give me some answers, and I was reminded of a quote from Crang: 'The tourists seek to travel to be present at a place, but as we examine those places we find they are shot through by absences where distant others, removed in space and time, haunt the sites' (2006, p. 49). At a very visceral level, I now understood what he meant. A cracking sound from the forest sent a chill down my spine. Suddenly I was overcome with the feeling of being swallowed in this landscape of the dead, and with the open page of my field notebook still blank I quickly scurried back down the hill away from the clutches of the primordial tomb.

Close to the archaeological field I was compelled to sit on a rock under an old tree to reflect on what had just happened. I was rather dumbstruck because this encounter was *unexpected*. For several years I had talked to re-enactors who told me their favorite Viking sites were in Norway or other locations where the beautiful landscape plays a large role in their feeling a deeper connection with the past and a sense of belonging. Just as in monumental heritage sites, it is easy to feel something in those landscapes because there is less left to the imagination. Birka, however, is not a place where people seek out an awe-inspiring emotional connection with the landscape; yet in my encounter, somehow the landscape not only talked back, it woke up! The ethereal atmosphere enveloped me just by *being* there. True to Tilley's advice, still perched on my unexpectedly comfortable rock under the welcome shade of the tree, I started to record my experience in as much detail as I could. I returned to Hemlanden in June 2019 when the cows were in a nearby pasture and the sheep were lazily grazing throughout the cemetery. I was reassured. In case the dead awakened, I had company.

Awakening presence in Birka

Altogether I spent roughly three hours in Hemlanden, and during both visits I was completely alone. Hemlanden sits on the outer edge of the site with no signs, paths, or instructions as to how to experience the site, but it is capable of affecting visitors in a very powerful way. Yet most visitors never manage to go there because the tour boats only allot a certain amount of time for a guided tour, visit to the museum, and a Viking Age-inspired meal from the restaurant before departing. Perhaps the lack of tourists in Hemlanden is part of the reason why the site has such an enormous presence; the silence is at first deafening and then blaring with the voices of the past. While not every tourist needs to experience Hemlanden (since that would likely ruin the ethereal appeal) there should be at least some way to communicate this area more clearly to visitors who want to go beyond the allotted tourist route.

My discussions with site managers, re-enactors, and tour guides confirmed that Hemlanden is a significant area of Birka that must be considered for its emotional and affective dimensions, but those working at the site grapple with how to include it more seriously in the already time-constrained visitor experience. When I first (rather hesitantly) shared my early-morning encounter during a group discussion, several people were quick to tell their own stories of similarly eerie moments walking in Hemlanden. One re-enactor, a leather craftsman, told me that he believes the 'grave woods' are the most authentic part of the site because they have an 'ancient knowledge – a forgotten knowledge,' and being there is like having 'history sleeping underneath [your] feet' (personal communication, July 17, 2018). The woman working in the reconstructed village's garden told me her favorite time to go there is late in the evening when the light begins to slip away because that's when you really start to feel and hear things that you can't explain. Others shared similar stories of how Hemlanden was a unique place within the landscape where they would go to connect with the past, but also to feel *something*. One re-enactor who sometimes serves as a tour guide for private groups says he loves to take visitors there because it feels like going on a ghost walk. It was clear from our initial discussion that Hemlanden played an integral part in the experience of the landscape and its past, and I needed to investigate why it wasn't yet included in the main visitor experience and if it would be possible to do so.

During my observational research, I found that the museum does include some basic information about Hemlanden regarding previous excavations and some aerial photographs revealing the extent of the burial mounds across the island. This reveals its importance for the history of the island, but the area isn't labelled as a 'highlight' on the main site map. The only map that labels Hemlanden and includes a description is the smaller 'guide to Birka for the independent visitor'. Beyond a more prominent position on the main site map, it was discussed that a good start to encourage visitors to visit Hemlanden might simply be a few basic signs – both directional and informational – that point visitors in the right direction and give them a general idea of the significance and meaning of Hemlanden. While it does not need to be included in the guided tour (and likely should not be), the tour guides also mentioned that they frequently recommend a visit to Hemlanden to those who are more keen to explore a bit after the tour. Similarly, because there is a gravel road running alongside Hemlanden, this could also be communicated as a more accessible (and more interesting) route for visitors who are unable to follow the more rocky and uneven path of the guided tour.

The need for better orientation was brought up by several tourists I spoke to expressing feeling a bit lost within the landscape. The site itself occupies a large area with different points of interest, but several noted it is unclear if there is more to see once the guided tour ends. One visitor from South Africa, for example, felt like she missed out on different aspects of the site because there was a lack of signs, and she particularly wished that her senses had been engaged more since there aren't a lot of built elements throughout the site. For tourists with an untrained eye, it is difficult to independently engage with an empty landscape when it's not exactly clear what they should be looking for.

Since Birka is advertised online as a Viking City, visitors arrive with certain expectations of what they will encounter, and they can be disappointed if those are not met. In my discussions with tour guides, for example, they were quick to mention the underwhelmed reaction of visitors to Birka's archaeological field. I joined several of their tours each day to listen to how they describe the different areas of the site and to observe how the tourists respond to a landscape stripped bare of its original great Viking city splendor. Particularly with non-monumental sites, it is difficult to bring the landscape to life, which means visitors often struggle to imagine a thriving city in front of their eyes. When the guided tour finally arrives above the main field, tour guides scramble to keep the attention of the group by painting a picture of how it might have looked, how many occupants the city had at the height of the Viking Age, and what their daily lives might have been like. One guide tells visitors to close their eyes and imagine the clanging of metal from the smithy, to smell the smoke from the open fires, and to listen to the hum of daily life. Birka, he noted, is unique because 'you really *feel* something when you *try*' (personal communication, July 17, 2018). In those moments, the tour guides play an important role in bringing the landscape to life – especially in making the past more present.

Based on the affective possibilities Birka offers (such as Hemlanden's ghostly presence), further discussions with site managers, tour guides, and re-enactors were centered around developing ways of better communicating different dimensions of the site to appeal to a wider range of visitors. That is of course not to say that new strategies have not already been considered. For example, they hope to soon include audio guides so visitors can be more independent listening to the history of the site as they walk through the landscape themselves, which may give them more freedom if there is no longer a guided tour focused on one specific area. Yet this again poses the question of how visitors should experience the site and whether an audio guide somehow limits multisensory engagement and the possibility of experiencing a powerful moment of presence.

Crucially, one site manager noted that there are two different directions one can take in a non-monumental landscape: either high-tech or high-touch. While Birka and likely many other similar sites currently focus primarily on the archaeological and historical significance, she notes that in the future people will come to these sites because they want to 'put their cell phone away and listen to music or just silence' because the rest of the world will be too high-tech (interview, June 13, 2019). As similar research has shown, visitors want to feel *something* and have more control over their experiences that are more multisensory and hands-on. Therefore, identifying new affective and emotional dimensions of the site will be the only way to keep up with new generations of curious visitors seeking out these encounters.

When I asked what kind of ideas she has for the future, the site manager said she hopes to include more activities that bring people back to nature and provide the possibility to work and engage more with their hands. She imagines having burial mound meditations in Hemlanden, fishing groups, courses about the different flowers and other flora and fauna on the island, mushroom picking, bird watching, and historical craft workshops. Soon they will also begin creating a new exhibition in the museum showing replicas of some of the most important excavations from the main archaeological field and grave mounds that can help visitors more easily visualize what was once there and what continues to lie below the surface while they walk through the still predominantly unexcavated landscape.

Despite many different ideas, Hemlanden's fate remains questionable due to the limited time tourists can spend within an already very large archaeological landscape. Some guides are able to take private groups to Hemlanden, but they can only encourage other visitors who are able to walk over and explore a bit after the regular guided tour. There are ongoing discussions to include more areas of the landscape within the visitor experience including the possibility to visit the associated site of Hovgården on a nearby island called Adelsö; yet, time and funding continue to hinder progress. Nevertheless, this reveals that the site managers are constantly looking for more creative ways to utilize the resources they already have in the present while looking toward new possibilities in the future.

Similar to other findings from research on affect and emotion, visitors in Birka develop a sense of presence through active engagement and involvement within the fabric of the landscape. However, this research does not often have a direct impact in creating changes within the heritagescapes studied. This is often due to the more prominent focus on visitors' reflections, which may overlook certain areas of the landscape not included in the visitor experience. Similarly, the more abstract and theoretical conclusions that often emerge from this area of research are difficult to put into practice or communicate to site managers. As Mark Edmonds notes, research on affect and emotion needs to open itself up more to others' voices and must ultimately recognize that visitors need to find their own ways in to experiencing the landscape. Otherwise, he argues, 'the path simply takes us back to ourselves' (2006, p. 185).

By conducting an analysis of presence in three different yet intertwining stages in Birka, I have demonstrated how one powerful embodied encounter within the landscape guided observations and reflections on the existing site experience, and collaborative discussions fostered a diverse range of ideas and practical strategies to include a greater variety of activities and ways of interacting with the site. While previous research has stressed the importance of affective and emotional encounters in heritagescapes, I have suggested a more collaborative study of presence provides a stepping stone for these dimensions to be more effectively identified and implemented by site managers.

Presence in practice

The rise in adventure tourism, nature-based tourism, eco-tourism, and other new waves of tourism aimed at avoiding the standardized tourism experience all attest to an increasing desire in tourists to get off the beaten track, pursue places based on their own interests, experience different emotions, and encounter sites with more participatory and multisensory options. Particularly in non-monumental landscapes like Birka, visitors should be encouraged to explore the landscape beyond what has been designated as part of the tourist path and should be given different options to follow their own interests.

My encounter in Hemlanden evoked a similar sensation to that experienced by Sara Maitland and Sam Harris quoted at the beginning. It snapped me awake to an acute awareness of my senses, and I became entangled with the landscape around me. Yi-Fu Tuan once argued that the 'good life' is 'life awake' (1986, p. 24), and this comes in many forms – whether it's sitting on a rock eating a cheese sandwich in the Isle of Skye, pausing to take in the scene at the Sea of Galilee, walking through 'grave woods' with history sleeping below, or even standing in a group guided by someone trying to bring an archaeological landscape to life. At its core, tourism has always involved the pursuit of an experience that makes visitors *feel* something. It involves engaging with the world predominantly from an emotional curiosity through different levels of play, performativity, and meaning-making, and it challenges people to think about their own position in the world – what it means to play an active role in it, who they are, what shapes their identity, and where they belong.

While studying presence with a more concise methodology does not provide all the answers for developing and managing heritagescapes based on research on affect and emotion, I have argued that it serves as a useful concept for a more collaborative, landscape-based approach that can be implemented by site managers. Rather than developing sites strictly based on the traditional template and AHD, more affective and emotional elements can be identified that align with visitors' different motivations and interests to create more immersive, dynamic, varied, multivocal, and multisensory encounters where past and *presence* come together.

Acknowledgements

Thank you to Veronica Björkman from Strömma for the research support on Birka as well as to Lena Flodin from SFV for the accommodation. I also owe thanks to all of the Viking re-enactors and guides based on Birka for their kindness and willingness to be shadowed by me and my notebook – particularly Per, Johan, and Anton for the many rich stories and insights that inspired this article. Special thanks also to Tomas Germundsson for support on several drafts, and thanks to the anonymous referees for their challenging, yet insightful comments.

Disclosure statement

No potential conflict of interest was reported by the authors.

ORCID

Katherine Burlingame ⓘ http://orcid.org/0000-0002-1152-0189

References

Anderson, J. (2004). Talking whilst walking: A geographical archaeology of knowledge. *Area*, *36*(3), 254–261. doi:10.1111/j.0004-0894.2004.00222.x

Ankre, R., Fredman, P., & Lindhagen, A. (2016). Managers' experiences of visitor monitoring in Swedish outdoor recreational areas. *Journal of Outdoor Recreation and Tourism*, *14*, 35–40. doi: 10.1016/j.jort.2016.04.008

Ateljevic, I., Harris, C., Wilson, E., & Collins, F. L. (2005). Getting 'entangled': Reflexivity and the 'critical turn' in tourism studies. *Tourism Recreation Research*, *30*(2), 9–21. doi:10.1080/02508281.2005.11081469

Bender, B. (1998). *Stonehenge: Making space*. Oxford: Berg.

Bennett, J. (2010). *Vibrant matter: A political ecology of things*. Durham, NC: Duke University Press.

Bille, M., Bjerregaard, P., & Sørensen, T. F. (2015). Staging atmospheres: Materiality, culture, and the texture of the in-between. *Emotion, Space and Society*, *15*, 31–38. doi:10.1016/j.emospa.2014.11.002

Birenboim, A. (2016). New approaches to the study of tourist experiences in time and space. *Tourism Geographies*, *18*(1), 9–17. doi:10.1080/14616688.2015.1122078

Bjerregaard, P. (2015). Dissolving objects: Museums, atmosphere and the creation of presence. *Emotion, Space and Society*, *15*, 74–81. doi:10.1016/j.emospa.2014.05.002

Buda, D. M. (2015). The death drive in tourism studies. *Annals of Tourism Research*, *50*, 39–51. doi:10.1016/j.annals.2014.10.008

Buda, D. M., D'Hauteserre, A. M., & Johnston, L. (2014). Feeling and tourism studies. *Annals of Tourism Research*, *46*, 102–114. doi:10.1016/j.annals.2014.03.005

Butz, D. (2010). Autoethnography as Sensibility. In D. DeLyser, S. Herbert, S. Aitken, M. Crang, & L. McDowell (Eds.), *The SAGE handbook of qualitative geography* (pp. 138–155). London: Sage.

Crang, M. (2006). Circulation and emplacement: The hollowed-out performance of tourism. In C. Minca & T. Oakes (Eds.), *Travels in paradox* (pp. 47–64). Lanham, MD: Rowman and Littlefield.

Curtin, S., & Kragh, G. (2014). Wildlife tourism: Reconnecting people with nature. *Human Dimensions of Wildlife*, *19*(6), 545–554. doi:10.1080/10871209.2014.921957

Daugbjerg, M. (2017). Being there: Time travel, experience, and experiment in re-enactment and "living history" performances. In B. Petersson & C. Holtorf (Eds.), *Archaeology of time travel: Experiencing the past in the 21st century* (pp. 157–174). Oxford: Archaeopress.

Degen, M., & Hetherington, K. (2001). Guest editorial: Hauntings. *Space and Culture*, (11/12), 1–6. Retrieved from: https://sites.ualberta.ca/~rshields/sc/11-12%20Spatial%20cd/F1-6%20intro.pdf

Edensor, T. (2008). Mundane hauntings: Commuting through the phantasmagoric working-class spaces of Manchester, England. *Cultural Geographies*, *15*(3), 313–333. doi:10.1177/1474474008091330

Edensor, T. (2017). Seeing with light and landscape: A walk around Stanton Moor. *Landscape Research*, *42*(6), 616–633. doi:10.1080/01426397.2017.1316368

Edmonds, M. (2006). Who said romance was dead? *Journal of Material Culture*, *11*(1-2), 167–188. doi:10.1177/1359183506063019

Elwood, S. (2010). Mixed methods: Thinking, doing, and asking in multiple ways. In D. DeLyser, S. Herbert, S. Aitken, M. Crang, & L. McDowell (Eds.), *The SAGE handbook of qualitative geography* (pp. 94–114). London: Sage.

Feighery, W. (2006). Reflexivity and tourism research: Telling an(other) story. *Current Issues in Tourism, 9*(3), 269–282. doi:10.2167/cit/mp006.0

Garden, M.-C. E. (2006). The heritagescape: Looking at landscapes of the past. *International Journal of Heritage Studies, 12*(5), 394–411. doi:10.1080/13527250600821621

Garden, M.-C, E. (2009). The heritagescape: Looking at heritage sites. In M. L. S. Sørensen & J. Carman (Eds.), *Heritage studies: Methods and approaches* (pp. 270–291). New York, NY: Routledge.

Goodwin, H. (2017). The challenge of overtourism. Responsible tourism partnership working paper 4. Retrieved from https://haroldgoodwin.info/pubs/RTP'WP4Overtourism01'2017.pdf

Goulding, C., Saren, M., & Pressey, A. (2018). 'Presence' and 'absence' in themed heritage. *Annals of Tourism Research, 71*, 25–38. doi:10.1016/j.annals.2018.05.001

Gumbrecht, H. U. (2004). *Production of presence: What meaning cannot convey*. Stanford, CA: Stanford University Press.

Harris, S. (2014). *Waking up: A guide to spirituality without religion*. New York, NY: Simon and Schuster.

Harvey, D. (2015). Landscape and heritage: Trajectories and consequences. *Landscape Research, 40*(8), 911–928. doi:10.1080/01426397.2014.967668

Hill, L. (2013). Archaeologies and geographies of the post-industrial past: Landscape, memory and the spectral. *Cultural Geographies, 20*(3), 379–396. doi:10.1177/1474474013480121

Holtorf, C. (2017). Introduction: The meaning of time travel. In B. Petersson & C. Holtorf (Eds.), *Archaeology of time travel: Experiencing the past in the 21st century* (pp. 1–22). Oxford: Archaeopress.

Kantanen, T., & Tikkanen, I. (2006). Advertising in low and high involvement cultural tourism attractions: Four cases. *Tourism and Hospitality Research, 6*(2), 99–110. doi:10.1057/palgrave.thr.6040049

Knudsen, B. T. (2011). Thanatourism: Witnessing difficult pasts. *Tourist Studies, 11*(1), 55–72. doi:10.1177/1468797611412064

Lorimer, H. (2005). Cultural geography: The busyness of being "more-than-representational". *Progress in Human Geography, 29*(1), 83–94. doi:10.1191/0309132505ph531pr

Lund Hansen, A. (2008). Walking through a liquid forest of symbols. *Liminalities, 4*(1), 1–6. Retrieved from http://liminalities.net/4-1/index.html

MacCannell, D. (1976). *The tourist: A new theory of the leisure class*. Berkeley, CA: University of California Press.

Macpherson, H. (2016). Walking methods in landscape research: Moving bodies, spaces of disclosure and rapport. *Landscape Research, 41*(4), 425–432. doi:10.1080/01426397.2016.1156065

Magnus, B., & Gustin, I. (2012). *Birka and Hovgården*. (L. Johansson & A. Ragnarsson, Eds., A. Crozier & J. Tolk, Trans.). Karlstad: Swedish National Heritage Board and Votum.

Maitland, S. (2008). *A book of silence*. Berkeley, CA: Counterpoint.

Mathiesen Hjemdahl, K. (2004). History as a cultural playground. *Ethnologia Europaea, 32*(2), 105–124. doi: 10.16995/ee.934

McCormack, D. P. (2013). *Refrains for moving bodies*. Durham, NC: Duke University Press.

McIntosh, A. J., & Prentice, R. C. (1999). Affirming authenticity: Consuming cultural heritage. *Annals of Tourism Research, 26*(3), 589–612. doi:10.1016/S0160-7383(99)00010-9

McKercher, B. (2002). Towards a classification of cultural tourists. *International Journal of Tourism Research, 4*(1), 29–38. doi:10.1002/jtr.346

Mitchell, C., Theron, L., Stuart, J., Smith, A., & Campbell, Z. (2011). Drawings as research method. In L. Theron, C. Mitchell, A. Smith, & J. Stuart (Eds.), *Picturing research: Drawing as visual methodology* (pp. 19–36). Leiden: Sense Publishers.

Moscardo, G. (1996). Mindful visitors: Heritage and tourism. *Annals of Tourism Research, 23*(2), 376–397. doi:10.1016/0160-7383(95)00068-2

Muzaini, H., & Minca, C. (2018). Rethinking heritage, but "from below". In H. Muzaini & C. Minca (Eds.), *After heritage: Critical perspectives on heritage from below* (pp. 1–21). Cheltenham: Edward Elgar.

Pearce, J., Strickland-Munro, J., & Moore, S. A. (2017). What fosters awe-inspiring experiences in nature-based tourism destinations? *Journal of Sustainable Tourism, 25*(3), 362–378. doi:10.1080/09669582.2016.1213270

Pearce, P. L., & Moscardo, G. M. (1986). The concept of authenticity in tourist experiences. *The Australian and New Zealand Journal of Sociology, 22*(1), 121–132. doi:10.1177/144078338602200107

Pocock, N. (2015). Emotional entanglements in tourism research. *Annals of Tourism Research, 53*, 31–45. doi:10.1016/j.annals.2015.04.005

Poria, Y., Butler, R., & Airey, D. (2003). The core of heritage tourism. *Annals of Tourism Research, 30*(1), 238–254. doi:10.1016/S0160-7383(02)00064-6

Robertson, I. J. M. (2008). Heritage from below: Class, social protest and resistance. In B. Graham & P. Howard (Eds.), *The Ashgate research companion to heritage and identity* (pp. 143–158). Aldershot: Ashgate.

Runia, E. (2006a). Presence. *History and Theory, 45*(1), 1–29. doi:10.1111/j.1468-2303.2006.00346.x

Runia, E. (2006b). Spots of time. *History and Theory, 45*(3), 305–316. doi:10.1111/j.1468-2303.2006.00366.x

Samida, S. (2017). Performing the past: Time travels in archaeological open air museums. In B. Petersson & C. Holtorf (Eds.), *Archaeology of time travel: Experiencing the past in the 21st century* (pp. 135–156). Oxford: Archaeopress.

Sather-Wagstaff, J. (2017). Making polysense of the world: Affect, memory, heritage. In D. P. Tolia-Kelly, E. Waterton, & S. Watson (Eds.), *Heritage, affect and emotion: Politics, practices and infrastructures* (pp. 12–29). Abingdon: Routledge.

Shea, M. (2018). Troubling heritage: Intimate pasts and public memories at Derry/Londonderry's "Temple". In L. Smith, M. Wetherell, & G. Campbell (Eds.), *Emotion, affective practices and the past in the present* (pp. 39–55). Abingdon: Routledge.

Smith, L. (2006). *Uses of heritage.* New York, NY: Routledge.

Smith, L. (2014). Visitor emotion, affect and registers of engagement at museums and heritage sites. *Conservation Science in Cultural Heritage, 14*(2), 125–132. doi:10.6092/issn.1973-9494/5447

Steiner, C. J., & Reisinger, Y. (2006). Understanding existential authenticity. *Annals of Tourism Research, 33*(2), 299–318. doi:10.1016/j.annals.2005.08.002

Thrift, N. (2008). *Non-representational theory: Space, politics, affect.* New York, NY: Routledge.

Thrift, N., & Dewsbury, J.-D. (2000). Dead geographies—And how to make them live. *Environment and Planning D: Society and Space, 18*(4), 411–432. doi:10.1068/d1804ed

Tilley, C. (1994). *A phenomenology of landscape: Places, paths and monuments.* Oxford: Berg.

Tolia-Kelly, D. P. (2007). Fear in paradise: The affective registers of the English Lake District landscape re-visited. *The Senses and Society, 2*(3), 329–351. doi:10.2752/174589307X233576

Tolia-Kelly, D. P. (2008). Motion/emotion: Picturing translocal landscapes in the nurturing ecologies research project. *Mobilities, 3*(1), 117–140. doi: 10.1080/17450100701797372

Tuan, Y.-F. (1976). Humanistic geography. *Annals of the Association of American Geographers, 66*(2), 266–276. doi:10.1111/j.1467-8306.1976.tb01089.x

Tuan, Y.-F. (1986). *The good life.* Madison, WI: University of Wisconsin Press.

Vannini, P. (2015). Non-representational ethnography: New ways of animating lifeworlds. *Cultural Geographies, 22*(2), 317–327. doi:10.1177/1474474014555657

Wall-Reinius, S. (2012). Wilderness and culture: Tourist views and experiences in the Laponian World Heritage area. *Society & Natural Resources, 25*(7), 621–632. doi:10.1080/08941920.2011.627911

Wang, N. (1999). Rethinking authenticity in tourism experience. *Annals of Tourism Research, 26*(2), 349–370. doi:10.1016/S0160-7383(98)00103-0

Waterton, E. (2013). Landscape and non-representational theories. In P. Howard, I. Thompson, & E. Waterton (Eds.), *Routledge companion to landscape studies* (pp. 66–76). London: Routledge.

Waterton, E. (2019). More-than-representational landscapes. In P. Howard, I. Thompson, E. Waterton, & M. Atha (Eds.), *The Routledge companion to landscape studies* (2nd ed., pp. 91–101). London: Routledge.

Waterton, E., & Watson, S. (2013). Framing theory: Towards a critical imagination in heritage studies. *International Journal of Heritage Studies*, *19*(6), 546–561. doi:10.1080/13527258.2013.779295

Watson, A., & Till, K. E. (2010). Ethnography and participant observation. In D. DeLyser, S. Herbert, S. Aitken, M. Crang, & L. McDowell (Eds.), *The SAGE handbook of qualitative geography* (pp. 121–137). London: Sage.

Weaver, D. B., & Jin, X. (2016). Compassion as a neglected motivator for sustainable tourism. *Journal of Sustainable Tourism*, *24*(5), 657–672. doi:10.1080/09669582.2015.1101130

Wylie, J. (2005). A single day's walking: Narrating self and landscape on the South West Coast Path. *Transactions of the Institute of British Geographers*, *30*(2), 234–247. doi:10.1111/j.1475-5661.2005.00163.x

Wylie, J. (2007). *Landscape*. London: Routledge.

Wylie, J. (2009). Landscape, absence and the geographies of love. *Transactions of the Institute of British Geographers*, *34*(3), 275–289. doi:10.1111/j.1475-5661.2009.00351.x

Beyond 'a trip to the seaside': exploring emotions and family tourism experiences

Catherine Kelly (iD)

ABSTRACT

Family tourism is a key tourism segment, yet it is often taken for granted, and therefore passed over in contemporary research studies. Little research exists in the tourism literature that explores the experiential aspect of how families perform tourism in various spatial settings. Furthermore, the emotional aspects of such family tourism performances receive little attention. The concepts of existential authenticity and of 'interpersonal authenticity' are used to assess how families construct ideals of 'their real' (collective) selves, while on holiday at the beach, together. A case study of Brighton in the UK assesses family holiday experiences in a traditional British seaside resort. The primary research findings show that emotional connections are strengthened during family coastal holidays. These connections are not without complexity and contestation, particularly in terms of intra-family power relationships, gender and the social reproduction of domestic/holiday roles. The concept of quality time is revealed as a varied but important value in family tourism motivations. Wellbeing improvements (emotional, physical and psycho-social) are reported widely across the sample. The creation of memorable tourism experiences is shown to be a key driver for families as they attempt to come together away from the busyness of everyday stresses. Human-seascape interactions form a meaningful socio-spatial context for these explorations. The sea space itself facilitates the myriad of idealised expectations around family holiday connections. Deeper insights are therefore offered into a key tourism offering, 'the family holiday', through a lens that is often overlooked.

摘要

家庭旅游是一个重要的旅游市场, 但它往往被认为是理所当然的, 因此在当代的研究中被忽略。旅游文献中很少有研究探讨家庭如何在不同空间环境中进行旅游的体验。此外, 这种家庭旅游展示的情感方面也很少受到关注。本文运用存在真实性和人际真实性的概念评估家庭如何在海滩度假时构建"真实"(集体)自我的理想形态。本文以英国布莱顿为例, 评估在英国传统海滨度假胜地的家庭度假体验。主要研究结果表明, 家庭在海边度假时, 情感联系会得到加强。这些联系并非没有复杂性和争议, 特别是在家庭内部权力关系、性别和家庭/节日角色的社会再生产方面。在家庭旅游动机中, 黄金时间的概念被揭示为一种不同但重要的价值。情感、身体和心理社会的幸福感得到改善, 在本样本中广泛报道。创造难忘的旅游体验是家庭的主要驱动力, 因为他们试图聚在一起, 远离日常的繁忙压力。人与海的相互作用为这些探索形成了有意义的社会空间背景。海洋空间本身促进了无数对家庭假期联系的理想化的期望。因此, 通过一个经常被忽视的镜头, 我们对一个关键的旅游项目——"家庭度假"有了更深入的了解。

Introduction

This article seeks to contribute to touristic spatialities of emotion, specifically through the locus of the coastal environment, and via the lens of 'the family'. The role of emotions has until recently (e.g. Buda et al., 2014; d'Hauteserre, 2015; Kearns & Collins, 2012; Pritchard et al., 2011; Servidio & Ruffolo, 2016), been relatively overlooked in the field of tourism studies. This paper seeks to redress the role of emotions and touch on corporeality (or embodied feelings) in often taken-for-granted family tourism encounters and tourism spaces. The sea, the coast and the beach are key loci for tourism performances and tourism experiences. Affective forces of encounter at the sea involve sensory engagement with sight, smell, touch, and emotion. The affective atunement between human and the non-human physical elements of the beach, the coastal space and indeed the water itself have yet to be sufficiently explored by researchers within tourism studies. All arguably contribute to memorable tourism experiences, where families connect emotionally in specific ways, temporarily, in coastal spaces. This work explores some of these connections, how they are often constructed as more authentic than everyday experiences, and questions the role of the coastal setting itself.

This research has two central objectives – (i) to analyse the differential nature of emotional connections and experiences in family coastal tourism using a UK case study approach; and (ii) to discuss existential and interpersonal authenticity as forms of psycho-social family tourism outcomes. Adjunct explorations consider how the above contribute to 'memorable tourism experiences', as perceived and constructed by families on holiday at the coast. The paper also discusses the role the coast itself plays in family tourism experiences and emotions.

This research argues that the coast itself can be more closely examined to deconstruct specific spatialities that are valued and that elicit certain responses. The paper explores the family-emotion-identity nexus as it plays out through and is shaped by the sea. The family is chosen as a unit of tourism study to assess the importance of memorable tourism experiences and their associated emotional expectations, connections and realities. Notions of existential, or 'real family authenticity' are unpacked as we discover what being on holiday can do to temporarily transform, or emotionally ameliorate everyday busy-life realities.

The sensory material reality of the biophysical world of the coast actively contributes to the symbolic value of the coast in constructing family stories, as well as offering emotional connectivity in itself. Watching the sea come into view at the end of a long car or plane journey, feeling the sand beneath bare feet, smelling the salty air, allowing the shoulders to relax, water touching skin and hearing the sound of the waves all elicit an emotional sensory response that is, arguably, the *essence* of many coastal tourism experiences.

In the next section, this paper will review literature related to the themes outlined in the paper's objectives – i.e. emotions and family tourism, existential and interpersonal authenticity, as well as ideas around memorable tourism experiences, and the role of the coast/sea as a space for performing (family) tourism. Thereafter, a conceptual framework is presented using some of the concepts above. A methodology section then presents a case study of one British seaside resort, Brighton, on England's south coast, using sixty interviews from sample families on or near the beach. A qualitative analysis of the research findings follows, where a thematic analysis of interviews and observations is presented. A final discussion and conclusion draw together key outcomes and suggestions for future research directions in family coastal tourism geographies.

Literature review

Emotions and family tourism

Tourism research has presented family tourism mainly in terms of taken-for-granted market analysis, package tourism preferences and decision making (Minnaert & Jens, 2017). Little, however, has been said about the emotional aspects of the need for holidays as forms of family respite, nor the emotional investment that is involved symbolically, and psychologically. Scope exists therefore to delve into the *feelings* that create the perceived need for a holiday. These can be explored in terms of the anticipatory emotions leading up to the trip, those felt while on the holiday itself, and those reflective feelings post-trip, that in turn become memorable tourism experiences. These are complex, multifaceted and difficult issues to deconstruct – particularly across cultures, time, gender and space. It is acknowledged that humans are also not passive recipients of emotions. Given the challenges of this subject matter, the emotional affect of many elements of family holidays is often not explicitly extracted from tourism studies.

The relationship between families and emotions are usually private, internal interplays in the realm of the home- yet the arena of tourism allows for some of these to be considered and overtly displayed in public spaces, such as the beach. Indeed, Obrador (2012) notes that one reason for the invisibility of the family in tourism studies is the very notion that the family's place is mainly the home, which is contrary to the dominant focus of tourism investigation. This research will examine some of the experiences, emotions, performances and affect of family holidays, with the sea/coast/water as a repository co-agent for such expressions.

Tourism studies have often taken the notion of family for granted. It is seen as a key 'market segment', but there is much more scope for exploring how families organise themselves, behave, perform emotions, and construct memorable tourism experiences according to their own self-identities and values. The family can be viewed as a form of social group, one held together by a common purpose, and one that is different to other types of groups in society. Day et al. (1995) argue that family members may be more intensely bonded through emotional ties, and that there is often a shared family paradigm or world view. There is further scope in tourism studies to correlate self-constructs of family paradigms to tourism behaviours – families who self-identify as 'the adventurous family, 'the cultural family, 'the fun family' and so on.

Constructs of 'the family' are dynamic and changing as societal structures become more fluid. Modern families range from heteronormative 2.4 children formats, to same sex parents with children, single parent families, blended families with children from multiple marriages and a spectrum of high-to-low levels of extended familial support. From an economic perspective, it is one of the fastest growing and most consistent tourism markets, with 80% of respondents in a 2017 industry survey citing 'quality family/children time' as a key motivation to travel (Schanzel & Yeoman, 2014; Shaw, 2010). Quality time in itself, is a contested term. Snyder's (2007) research on how parents themselves defined or constructed quality time showed differential results. She classified quality time into 3 categories, based on her research; 'structured planning', 'child-centred', and 'time available'. For this paper, structured-planning parents are key. They define quality time as 'time specifically set aside from normal daily routines for special family activities, such as a vacation' (p.327). This idea of quality time, particularly in terms of holiday making, has become part of our cultural discourse, and is for some, synonymous with what it means to be 'a good parent', or indeed, 'a happy family'. This becomes evident in the findings section of this paper.

Such quality time however, may be fraught with complex expectations, gendered holiday/domestic labour performances and unrealistic projected ideals of delineated time and space. Cheong and Sin (2019) discuss the concept of 'happy families' on holiday. They question how exactly the 'happy family' materialises through tourism practices? What is it about the tourism time-space that differentiates it from home, transforming the ordinary family holiday into an extraordinary obligation that desires to be performed? Obrador (2012) explores how homely feelings and idealizations of the family are formed and performed on holiday, noting that family holiday processes can highlight the importance of tourism in the reproduction of social networks and relations of domesticity. Gender and power relationships around social reproductive roles are something that also require more attention overall in family tourism studies. Mothers may often be the ones who influence the choice of holiday type, and may do the majority of menial tasks of laundry, packing, cleaning and cooking both at home and on (particularly self-catering) holiday. Therefore, family holidays are experienced differentially within a family unit in terms of relaxation and chores undertaken.

Everyday realities for modern families are often fraught with multi-tasking working parents, commuting, childcare logistics, and juggling school-age children's activities, homework and caring challenges. Because of this, the role of the family holiday becomes loaded with expectation and projected constructs of what it means 'to be a family', to relax together, to bond and to enjoy time away from 'normal life' stressors. Family tourism interestingly allows for the intertwined relationships of affect with everydayness to be considered. We may feel threatened in not having something that constructs our existence, because we feel undefined with its absence (Gregg & Seigworth, 2010), which may partially help to explain the notion of not feeling like 'a real family', without going on a 'proper family holiday'. Families where parents are no longer together may also feel this need for idealised quality time, if they share holiday-making opportunities during the year. Affective tourism approaches give further opportunities to explore such internal drives (Buda, 2015).

Family tourists are also, as Obrador-Pons (2003) notes, situated and embodied subjects whose lives unfold in reciprocal interactions with their environment. Notions of affect, emotions and feelings between humans in the family unit, and the coastal space itself plays an important role in deeper understandings of this tourism segment. Families can create affective resonance, among themselves and with the sea, where we accept the affective premise of a lack of distinction between person and environment (Gregg & Seigworth, 2010; Massumi, 2015). Questions can be posed therefore about how the coast acts as a repository for/facilitates manifestations of emotion and familial authenticity.

Existential and inter-personal authenticity

Authenticity is an important notion, and it is closely related to the ability to express our true emotions (Belhassen & Caton, 2006). The concept of authenticity however, is socially constructed. It is not an objective quality of a thing, place or experience, but rather, a discourse through which certain practices (or objects) are made meaningful through a socially constructed system. One of the most common sources of anxiety, malcontent and stress in contemporary society is the feeling of not being able to live our life with purpose, the life we really want (or have constructed in our minds as reflective of who we are/our values), engaging in daily activities, work or connections that allow us to be our 'real selves'. Sociologists would argue that there is no such thing as a real or authentic self – that the self is a social construct and the effect of social performances (Goffman, 1990). However, there *is* merit in thinking about this as a personal construct, in so far as many tourists have indeed emphasised this idea of 'just being free to *be myself* on holiday' (see findings later in this paper).

The concept of expressing authentic self-identity (existential authenticity) through holiday destination or activity choices has been presented by some tourism researchers (Kirillova & Lehto, 2015; Wang, 1999). However, challenges still remain conceptually, to understand why the 'holiday self' might be seen or experienced by some tourists as more 'real' than an everyday/work/parent self. Perhaps the answers lie in the removal of stress (deadlines, commuting, parenting) and/or the mundanity of repetitive work or domestic tasks. The idea of not having to perform our professional roles, work to schedules, or perform emotional labour - when on holiday may lead to an improvement in personal wellbeing for some. Others may struggle to let go of their professional personas, or to unwind sufficiently without structure. For some tourists, escape from everyday pressures may result in the hedonistic behaviours of release or excess, often associated with mass tourism. Therefore, there is potential for 'differential versions of the self' to be performed in different contexts and almost certainly in different holiday contexts, settings and groupings. Existential authenticity, or feelings of really being oneself, are therefore complex and problematic in essence.

Individual senses of existential authenticity are socially constructed across gender, culture, age, life experiences, education, personal awareness and reflexivity. When this is examined at the level of the family unit however, the concept of 'inter-personal authenticity' is important. Kim and Jamal (2007) propose the idea Inter-Personal Authenticity (IPA) which examines emotional bonds, intimacy in family relationships and the pleasure derived from such human connections. Let us consider the varied opportunities for this in everyday life versus holiday time. Collectively, families often suffer from a dearth of everyday quality time (Snyder, 2007) where parents and children are physically present and even temporarily, emotionally connected through a common sense of purpose or engagement. Therefore, in addition to seeking idealised locations for family holidays, there is the added emotional need for collective bonding, and the desire 'to feel like a proper family', or to perform roles such as the 'good wife', or the 'attentive husband', 'the present father', or 'the loving child'. In other words, an opportunity to perform better versions of ourselves. These notions of idealized holiday spaces and family roles or performances are socially determined, through external forces such as the media, marketing imagery and even peer behaviours. The problematics of idealized constructs of (our)selves, and ourselves as families, as we perform certain holiday roles are complex but interesting considerations.

Methods

A conceptual framework

Whilst 'families on holiday' are an often taken for granted tourism segment, as we have seen, they are far from simple when attempting to understand how their emotional interrelationships, social reproductive roles and constructs of authentic identity are performed.

This primary research presented in the following sections explores

- emotional connections between family members as they partake in coastal tourism – emotional connections with the coast itself
- constructs of authenticity (existential and interpersonal) through performances of family tourism
- how the above help to create memorable tourism experiences that therefore reinforce potentially positive emotional connections and family bonding
- engagement with coastal spaces themselves as a form of connection

Figure 1, below offers a framework for exploration.

This framework links concepts from the literature, with interview themes in the qualitative methodologies employed for this coastal case study.

This research used the locus of the coast for its data collection, and the family as a unit of investigation, through which to meet its objectives. The coast in question was that bounded by the city of Brighton and Hove, on the Sussex south coast of England. Families were approached on the beach itself, whilst walking along the seafront promenade, and via a 'stop and chat about the sea' point set up at a traditional wooden beach hut.

Bachelard's phenomenological methodologies are key in this research, whereby we remain with the vital details of particular experiences or images in order to allow readers to imagine the experiences, that is, to live, embody them (Bachelard, 1969, cited in

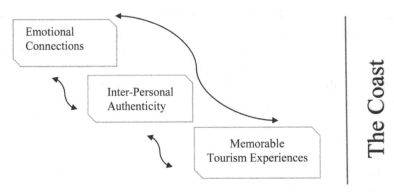

Figure 1. Family tourism at the sea: an exploratory framework.
(Source: author).

Game & Metcalf, 2011). Where possible, therefore, the words and feelings of the respondents are described and contextualised without excessive re-interpretation. The grouping of the family, the spaces of the coastline-beach-sea, and temporality of the present (that day) and past (other coastal holidays) constitute the 'who, where, when' aspects of investigation. Semi-structured interviews covered the key issues reflected in the research objectives and literature review.

Semi structured interviews were used to ask family groups about a variety of issues including-

- *their visit* (duration, family composition, origin, motivations, activities engaged with)
- the *emotional values* such experiences held for family members
- emotions and *emotional connections* felt on the holiday
- how their coastal holiday made them feel in relation to their own *identity as a family.*
- *differential experiences* of their trip within the family
- the *spaces engaged with*
- their coastal *experiences (expectations, motivations, feelings, bodies, activities and wellbeing)*
- *past* important family holidays by the sea
- what makes a family visit to the sea *a memorable experience*

Interviews took between 15 and 25 minutes each to conduct. The work is conceptually framed by theories and ideas discussed earlier, in relation to emotions, familial authenticity, memorable tourism experiences, and emotional-coastal connections.

Sixty interviews in total were achieved, divulging a wealth of qualitative responses. A variety of day trippers, weekend and longer-duration holiday visitors from the UK and abroad took part. Interviews were carried out over a 5-month period from June to September 2018, and across weekdays and weekends. Within a family grouping, the mother primarily responded in 70% of interviews (female voice), the father in 10% (male voice) and a mixture of both parents with interjections from other relatives (grandparents, aunts, and children- 'extended family or child voices') in the remaining 20%. It is acknowledged that the maternal voice is dominant in the sample responses as a result. Children were not sought out specifically to answer interview questions, but sometimes involuntarily 'chipped in' with soundbites. Permissions and ethical considerations were adhered to throughout the process.

Attempts were made to ensure a varied demographic of responses (male/female, origin and so on) during interviews, but often, given the fluid nature of the outdoor environment, especially for interviews held on the beach – one adult needed to watch over the children during an interview. Poria and Timothy (2014) pose the question 'where are all the children in tourism research?', and this research includes their voice where it arose (-although future work would be very valuable if focusing on children's perspectives only!). Of the 60 families, 32 were from south east England, 15 were from outside the UK (Germany, France and Holland), and the remining 13 were from the immediate local area. Therefore 45 families, or 75% of respondents were British. This is important in that cultural differences exist in how the coast is experienced. The beach is performed differently in many parts of the world, in terms of weather responses, clothing, and phenomenological practices (playing games, making sandcastles, fishing, surfing, swimming, paddling). Therefore, no universal claims are made in this work about definitive family behaviours at the coast.

In addition, the spatial uniqueness and complexity of the chosen case study site, Brighton and Hove – is recognised here (Shields, 1990). Brighton has a long history of coastal tourism. The health tourists of the 17/1800s arrived following Richard Russell's work on the value of saltwater. The city has a colourful, raffish reputation (Shields, 1990) and was famous in the 1960s for mods and rocker encounters and clashes. In the current climate its coastline is a heterogenous space associated with gay tourism, London day-trippers, young urban weekenders, cultural tourists seeking out Regency architecture, and family tourism. Over time, social constructions of the beach as a place to be, to avoid or to have fun, have changed considerably. Baerenholdt et al. (2004) evaluate this changing landscape and review the historical contextualization of the beach as 'a place in process'. And although not the focus of this work, the seaside can in many places in the UK, host an array of socio-economic problems, far from the Instagram scenes of holiday company social media platforms. There is no reduction therefore of Brighton beach to classify it as being a particular 'type of beach', - rather, the focus here is on one category of user, the family tourist.

Results and discussion

Findings are presented thematically in the next sections. Respondent voices lead the narrative in keeping with the qualitative nature of this work. The two objectives of the paper – to explore emotional connections, and constructs of authenticity in family coastal tourism – form the structure of the analysis that follows. The nature of memorable tourism experiences and the role of the coast itself are contributory, additional narratives that emerged strongly in the interviews. The boundaries between these themes are somewhat arbitrary in that the interviewees themselves leapt between themes of feelings, family experiences, the sea, the beach and memories in an often-ad hoc manner. Their voices show interesting insights to how family tourism is experienced, felt and performed.

Figure 2. Word cloud: emotions and the sea.
(Source: author).

Emotional connections by the sea

Respondents were asked about emotions in a number of ways – what emotional value they placed on family holidays, what emotions they felt on the holiday, and how emotionally connected they felt to each other. Interestingly, the idea of emotions that emerged in the interviews displayed a temporal element and can be classified as (i) anticipatory emotions, (ii) embodied/present emotions, and (iii) reflective emotions.

Holidays are key moments in family life, where expectations and emotions are high. This theme emerged in all the research interviews undertaken in Brighton and Hove. Work by Ashe (2012) shows that perception of emotional need-fulfilment is an important aspect of holiday decision making, and this is borne out by many responses in this study, feeding into the anticipatory emotions category noted above.

> "when we book our holiday, just the thought of it keeps me going, for months sometimes. It's something to look forward to, where we can just switch off and be together" (respondent mother xxxi)

Other, London daytrip visitors relished the thought of a Sunday visit to sea, as a way to get through the busy working week in the city.

> "I've been thinking of this moment all week when I've been squashed on the underground. It's kept me going. Coming out of the train station in Brighton and just catching your first glimpse of that sea. You can almost feel the cold water on your feet before you even get to the beach".

Hedonic wellbeing, or 'an increased emotional state of happiness', was a strong self-reported outcome in this work — 100% of the sample expressed positive emotions or feelings when asked how it felt to be by the sea. These were almost all expressed in terms of present moment/embodied emotions – during the interview itself. Figure 2 below shows the most commonly expressed terms and emotions in relation to a question on 'how being at the sea makes you feel'. The emotions expressed are primarily positive and include multiple mentions of 'happy', 'joy', 'together', 'fun', 'relaxed', and 'family'.

Interestingly, these expressed emotions link back to Snyder's (2007) work on parental constructs of quality time. Her key focus is on what constitutes quality family time, but an interesting perspective here is *where* quality time takes places. For many respondents, enjoyable quality family time takes places outside the home, and for some, has temporal connotations, which is reinforced in the findings with references to 'Sunday afternoons' or 'on holiday'. These are times when visits to the sea usually take place. Snyder usefully refers to quality time classifications such as recreation (quality time as break from everyday life), bonding (quality time as an emotional connection), active leisure quality time (where family members are interacting and physically active) or place-based quality time (e.g. away from home).

These ideas reinforce the interviewee responses to the question on emotional values and family holidays by the sea. There was a sense of importance for many respondents – not just a frivolity, but a need – to carve out this time together. Bonding, connection, and doing things together are mentioned many times by respondents.

One dad noted that 'it's often too hectic to be that nice to each other during the week. There is a lot of shouting, hurrying and organising in our life. Getting everyone to where they need to be, on time. Its nice to come down here and have time to feel good, and enjoy ourselves and not to worry about all that for a bit'. Therefore, emotional connections may improve, as the holiday and the coastal space allow more relaxed interactions to take place.

Family identities: existential and interpersonal authenticity

An important aspect of this research centred on the relationship between family holidays and authenticity. Theories of psychological wellbeing, call upon people to live in accordance with their true self (Ong, 2009), although as discussed earlier, this is an often-contested concept (Goffman, 1990). The idea of existential authenticity as a psychological phenomenon (Kirillova & Lehto, 2015) is central to family tourism in so far as respondents themselves voice the desire 'to feel like a real family'. Perhaps one of the factors that allows families on holiday to construct or differentiate the idea of 'authentic selves or existential authenticity' are the notions of presence, connection and (even accidental) mindfulness.

When tourists feel fully connected to the world, these moments can have a profound effect on them (Hom Cary, 2004). Such 'mindful authenticity' is a real outcome of much sea-based family tourism – in the moment, connected to the water, nature, and each other. It is both a simple and yet profound experience, as this research has shown.

"being here by the sea, makes you feel alive, and when you are in there, in the waves, with the kids, you can't think about anything else – your commute, the work project, you are just catching the next wave, seeing if you can stand on it, laughing when you fall in" (respondent father, xxxx)

And,

"When we are all here, I really *see* my kids – notice them, you know? I appreciate them all over again. Just playing, covered in ice-cream or whatever, being themselves. And I look at my husband and remember how lucky we are to have them, and each other I suppose. This is what it's all about, isn't it?" (mother, vii)

The two interview themes centring around 'how respondents' coastal holidays made them feel in relation to their own identity as a family', and 'differential experiences of their trip within the family' yielded interesting results. Kim and Jamal (2007) discussion of Inter-Personal Authenticity (IPA), noted earlier, involves emotional bonds, intimacy in family relationships and the pleasure derived from connections. IPA emerged as an important framework in this research where three key themes recurred amongst respondents- 'who we are as a family', 'who I am as a parent', and 'what my kids' childhood means to me', all emerged as recurring respondent themes. These aspects of inter-personal authenticity are reflective, perhaps of Day et al. (1995) notions of shared family paradigms. These self-constructs of idealised authentic roles and interplays are interesting at a family level.

Trips to the sea (regardless of length, interestingly) symbolized togetherness and a chance to do things 'that matter' – again reinforcing Snyder's theories of quality time. Perhaps an additional construct could be offered here – the notion of 'real family time'. Many respondents alluded to the idea of being a real family, and also to quality time. Combining these elements into a notion of real family time allows temporality and authenticity to be co-aligned more strongly. Despite some sociological theories to the contrary, many parents did express this 'splitting' of self – their home/everyday self, and their holiday/better-parent self. Perhaps this is facilitated by time, open space, fresh air, water, scope for fun and relaxation? This is not an unproblematic construct if it is examined more closely. It is also fair to say that not all family members experience this scope for relaxation and bonding equally.

Again, the work of Obrador (2012) and Cheong and Sin (2019) on the idealization of 'the family' on holiday is useful here. Everyday conflicts over labour sharing at home were for some, softened on holiday ('he can help me more on holiday because he isn't at work'), but for others they were reinforced and led to discontent for mothers ('it's the same old story, I just do everything', as one revealed). Many fathers said they enjoyed having time to spend with their children, playing and just 'hanging out'. Some mothers noted that their partners chose the more fun options on holiday, such as playing with the children in the water, or making sandcastles, while they were left to repeatedly organise snacks, bags, and sort out wet swimsuits and towels. As noted earlier, assessing how social reproductive roles change (or do not) while on holiday is of interest here, albeit in a limited sense of interplay at the coast itself. Gendered power relationships are complex and where they came up in conversation (not all respondents talked about them), they varied greatly.

Questions were asked about inter-family (mother and father) roles, expectations and feelings around coastal holidays. It emerged that 80% of mothers in this survey had organised, booked or planned the trip/holiday to the beach. Mundane tasks such as applying sunscreen, and handing out water bottles were largely maternal actions (observed and noted during interviews). Indeed, Obrador Pons (2003) observes that the most relevant embodied practices through which we become tourists are everyday, and ordinary. This is particularly true of family tourism where children's home routines, and preferences are often replicated on holiday, especially for very young children. Mothers overwhelmingly prioritised the needs and preferences of their children, beyond their own needs.

Feelings of contentment were high when children were happy, although some expressed feelings of frustration at the replication of domestic gendered roles on holiday There was also conflict over who 'deserved' a break most, in some instances, and the subtleties of paid versus hidden domestic labour emerged for some respondents

"I work all week, so it's nice to get down here and relax and do nothing" (dad, xi) – followed by his wife's reply (mother, xxvii): "So you think I *don't* work all week? I wonder who looks after the children and keeps the house going then? Or who organised this trip, packed this picnic, this sunscreen, these buckets and spades?!"

Another mother noted on a very similar theme, "I do everything on holiday, same as at home – I packed everything, got us sorted at the hotel, organise all the beach stuff, dry and change the kids after being in the sea, sort out their wet things when we get back. It's not much of a rest really, just a different background". Yet, there seemed to be a resigned acceptance of these inequalities, offered up in the name of positive quality time for the whole family, particularly the children.

"Yes, it's not much of a rest for me really, but you do it for them – and spending family time together here is more important than us arguing over who's doing what".

These gendered power relations are also *emotional*. Pocock (2015), suggests that while tourism involves physical travel, it does not always concurrently involve emotional change – our domestic emotional states around caring from children, parenting and inter-parent conflict may well be carried with us as we holiday. Buda and MacIntosh (2012) similarly note that emotions travel with us, and through us. Mothers who did the majority of childcare at home, seemed to replicate this on holiday, and also displayed more emotions of worry – so while the sea was seen as a largely positive presence, for some it meant a safety hazard in terms of water, and strangers. 'My kids are still small, so you have to go with them to the shore, and you have to keep looking, or they might wander off with someone, you can't be too careful', one mother noted. Therefore, family coastal holidays can be complicated emotional encounters, where predicted idealisms of loving, bonded experiences are sought out, but sometimes are diluted by the continuation of everyday family labour roles and interactions.

The interviews explored the kinds of activities and experiences the families had on their seaside trip and how they felt about them. Bondi and Davision (2003) advocate that encounters are not given, rather, they are produced by the experience of the agents involved. These intricacies of children and parental interplay, and performative experiences in coastal spaces were explored.

"there's more freedom at the beach, isn't there? I mean, yes, you have to keep an eye on them in the water for sure, but they're just happy in there. I don't have to keep shouting at them not to get wet or dirty, because that's the point really, isn't it? Let them be kids … they don't get much of a chance to do that anymore with all that's on. When they come down to the sea, they can just be kids again, even the big ones." (respondent mother, xi)

Positive psycho-social wellbeing seemed to emerge through family-coastal encounters. Emotions run high for family tourism experiences, they matter – and they have huge symbolic meaning that forms intricate narratives of family identities, values and family histories.' We look forward to our holidays every year, it keeps us going', said

Table 1. Classification of responses/descriptor benefits.

Psychological	Social
mental health	togetherness
brain/head	family (& 'being' a family)
stress	bonding
downtime/time out	quality time
rest/a break	the children being children
relaxation	connecting
Clarity	sharing, enjoying

(Source: Author).

one mother, 'especially in the winter, when you are all cooped up together indoors, you can imagine yourself there on the beach, or you can look back on last year's photographs – Facebook is great for that, the reminders'.

Interview transcripts dealing with positive emotional responses were content analysed and then classified into psychological and social categories.

Table 1 loosely categorizes responses to questions about how family holidays/trips to the sea affected them (emotions/connections/wellbeing). Phrases such as 'It's great to rest and relax', 'it's so good for my headspace', 'coming down here is like a family mental health boost!' and 'its' just lovely to be together, we can connect with each other again' – were simplified and classified below.

Across the sample the most often quoted responses to how coastal holidays made families feel, were, interestingly, the social wellbeing aspects of togetherness, connection and family (supporting Snyder, 2007); and the psychological aspects of rest, a break from the everyday and relaxation by the sea. Authenticity descriptors such as 'children being children', and 'time to be a family' were also commonly cited. These ideas of 'real family time' and 'authentic childhoods' are reinforced once more.

What is more complex to ascertain in the research, is the differential importance placed on the holiday itself (any holiday?), the togetherness of the family trip, and the coastal setting itself, across different family groups. More work is needed on this. In summary, an important outcome of this research shows that authenticity is a key factor in coastal family holidays – in terms of the collective self-identifying unit of 'the family', parental roles within the family, and the construction of 'real childhood experiences'. Existential authenticity or 'real familiness' is afforded a temporary and temporal opportunity in seaside holiday performances.

Coastal spaces

Although presented as a separate category here, in reality the sea, the beach and the water were mentioned in most discussions, regardless of the question asked. Positive emotions associated with bluespace emerged as a strong theme in the interviews for this research, supporting Gesler (1992) ideas of 'therapeutic landscapes', or places that essentially improve our wellbeing. This research shows again that humans value the coast, and especially the water itself, as a fluid form of subjective wellbeing. It may even enable them to feel better, and connect better with each other, due to reduced stress levels, and the performance of 'quality time'. Bell et al. (2015) suggest that emotional attachments to the coast can develop through the accumulation of diverse individual and/or shared coastal experiences. The shared coastal experience is pertinent to family tourism in particular and is seen in these findings.

"We all just feel better when we come down to the sea; there is no question about not getting in, never mind the weather. Just the feel of the cold water hitting your skin, hearing the kids shriek, splashing, swimming, - there is nothing to beat it really. It makes us all feel happy, and we get along better with each other." (respondent mother xii)

Kah et al. (2020) reinforce this role of the *sensory* in memorable tourism experiences. These 'sensoryscape factors' they speak of are central to experiential engagement at the sea. Some parents did not get into the water themselves, but just enjoyed the chance to sit on the beach and watch their children, or to gaze at the sea itself. Contemplative and aesthetic experiences also therefore contributed to bluespace wellbeing. This restorative immersion in seascapes and spaces (both reported by respondents and observed by the researcher) supports Kaplan's (1995) ideas on restoration, where stress is reduced by the presence of/engagement with nature, or in this case, coastal bluespace.

"I just sit here on the beach, looking out. Honestly, that is all I need. With all the hustle and bustle of our week at home, afterschool clubs, work, and the house, I never get to just sit and do nothing. The sea lets you do that, it's just there." (respondent mother xiv)

We can compare looking out to sea with encountering infinity, or at least, a world beyond oneself. The quietness of a pause, to look without purpose, is restorative and healing.

The results showed the type of spaces engaged with by respondents, and revealed a classification of usage by the respondents that elicited different experiences and emotions. There appeared to be somewhat of a continuum of emotional response – related to the sea, the beach, or the coast more generally – and also the geographical 'prepositions of place' became important in our analysis as 'near', 'next to', and 'in', the sea, also generated different emotions. This requires further attention in future work as it was an unexpected but interesting finding. For some respondents it was all about being in the sea, for others (notably the European families) – being next to ('the very cold British sea) water was enough. Grandparents were often parked on benches nearby on the promenade, overlooking things, particularly where steep beach shingle slopes made for unsteady ground.

In addition, the space of the body itself, was the starting point for feelings generated in tourism encounters. Our first, most immediate and intimately felt geography is the body, the site of emotional experience and expression (Davidson & Milligan, 2004, cited in Buda et al., 2014). The body, immersed in cold British seawater, certainly elicited enthusiastic responses.

'I can't wait to get myself in the sea! As soon as we get to the beach, I just take everything off, and run in! Even if it's freezing cold at first, I don't care. It's so exciting!' (respondent child, ii)

'It's sooooo cold, I can't feel my fingers or toes, but I don't care – it's brilliant!'

(respondent child, i)

This intertwining of body and beach and sea is fluid and typical in tourism encounters. The body itself is spatial, it creates places by means of uniting us directly with

Scale

COAST (near/next to)	WATER (in)	BODY/EMOTION
Crowded, quiet, busy, empty, open, long, secluded, services	Wavy, calm, bouncy, crashing, strong, flat, cold, fresh, warm, salty	Body: exposed, covered, flabby, fit, free, pale, tanned, unfit, goosebumps, cold, warm
Stony, sandy, pebbly, slopey, flat, warm, windy, cold, breezy	Clear, murky, blue, green, translucent	Emotions: Invigorated, free, joyful, carefree, childlike, alive, happy, myself, content, calm

Figure 3. Content analysis of external/internal descriptors of coastaland emotions. (Source: Author).

people, spaces, and things-and it is not distinct from the environment in which it dwells (Obrador-Pons, 2003). This is particularly true when bodies inhabit the sea or ocean – body and marine aquatic space as mutually defining.

Figure 3, below collates content mentioned by respondents at different spatial scales to reflect their own descriptions of the coast, the water and their bodies at the seaside. ('how would you describe this beach, the sea, and yourself, here today?')

The emotive spatialities of proximity to or immersion in the sea showed the clear interrelationship between space and body, the material and emotional. Many described the human conditions of the beach, according to how many others were there (busy, or quiet), whilst also describing the physical conditions of the coast or beach (pebbly, sandy, the weather that day). Descriptions of the water blurred with emotive responses, facial expressions and voices rose and fell when asked to describe the water and how it felt to be in the sea. Children sometimes butted in to parental interviews here, excitedly describing how they used their bodies to jump or catch waves, to swim underwater, getting knocked down, swallowing water and so on. Colours, and how the water itself was acting or behaving that day were important in held conversations. Bodies were often described self- judgementally (by mothers), or in relation to temperature – but in complete contrast, the *emotions* expressed were overwhelmingly positive (invigorated, free), see Figure 3. This interplay between space and human response emerged strongly throughout, supporting d'Hauteserre's (2015) call for reintroducing corporeality and the role of emotion into accounts of tourism realities. She notes, rightly, that the notion of embodied (or corporeal and emotional) performative engagement produces more nuanced understandings of tourists' experiences and allows one to look at the role of all participants in the co-creation of behaviours and practices in the tourist zone.

"we love it when we can all go in the sea, we can jump and shout, and get wet or sandy, and nobody minds. It's so fun, the best thing ever" (respondent child, iv).

Obrador-Pons (2007) also refers to this sensuality of bodily engagement with the beach and the sea – and the importance of touch. 'Letting the sun get in, feeling the coolness of the water on the skin and playing with sticky textures of the sand are some of the main delights that people find on the beach – touch holds the key to bringing back life, sensation and enjoyment to the beach' (p.138). Children in particular found joy in this sensory release of touch, liberated from clothes and everyday spatial enclosures.

Emotional expressions of joy and contentment, - hedonic wellbeing, peppered all of the interviews held. These overlap with terms expressed in Figure 2 earlier.

"I just love it here, it makes me happy, pure and simple"

(respondent grandmother i)

"you can just switch off when you come down to the sea, it just comes in and goes out, up and down the beach, no matter what we do. There's peace in that"

(respondent mother viii)

The theme of existential authenticity also arises in these narratives of sea and identity. 'I come home to myself a bit when we are here by the water', one mother noted. These themes were expressed throughout many of the interviews, and speak to the strong socio-psychological potential of place, bonding and sea connections. The sea, it can be argued, is very much a co-agent in constituting and structuring these family emotional experiences on holiday.

Memorable tourism experiences

A final coming together perhaps of all the aforementioned themes, can be found in the expression of memorable tourism experiences. To feel joy, freedom and connection and to later reflect on those feelings through recall, shared stories, photographs and videos create important points of reference for family milestones. MTEs-Memorable Tourism Experiences (Kim et al., 2012), are central in the story of any family (Tung & Ritchie, 2011), and here, emotional connections, quality time, constructs of authenticity, the coast and the water are central actors in these stories.

Nichols (2012) notes that some of our best memories were formed near the water, in the water – with our friends and our loved ones, 'my brain', he says, 'is full of water memories, and they form who I am'. These ideas of self-identity link to place-identity and lived space, an affective attunement that is fluid and yet firm.

"I can't imagine us going on any holiday that isn't by the sea. It's what we do, and what we have always done," (respondent mother, iii)

The expression of 'it's what we do', emphasises once again the idea of familial existential authenticity – and the shared family paradigm. Self-identifying as a 'coastal holiday family' reinforces the collective memorable tourism experience. Place is important here and interviewees often referred to other seaside holidays whilst speaking. The tendency to romanticize past holidays is also part of this creation of memories. 'Do you remember when' was a phrase often interjected throughout the interview processes. Anecdotes and shared memories of past holidays help to reinforce feelings of existential familial authenticity. An important nuance, might be to note that such per-sonal memories do not necessarily symbolise 'what all/real families do', rather what 'our family' did. Meaning and authenticity are therefore constructed within, to some extent, when examined through the temporal lens of the remembered past.

Strong emotional connections to landscape have been built up across multiple gen-erations, and are reinforced by personal experiences (Collins & Kearns, 2010). In over 50% of the British interviewees, respondents had been taken to Brighton on family holidays as children themselves, so the idea of legacy and continued family traditions was strongly evident. Continuity and legacy therefore also serve to reinforce the notion of familial authenticity. Strong family identities can be expressed and shared when grandparents, for example, participate in holiday-making.

Obrador (2012) also observes the importance of the family holiday in 'home-making practice'. The home and domestic realm, are connected to the holiday and the beach, through the vessel of the family. Tourism, it is noted, does not always have to be about escaping home, it can also be about *making* home, through different forms of displacement. The family, at the beach, still need to eat, to play and interact, look after their children, help them dress, supervise their safety and many other normative domestic actions. The proximity of the sea and sunshine can potentially elevate the mundane to the joyful, excited and possible. The ritual of return visits reinforces the legacy of the family holiday practice.

> "my nan used to bring us down here from London when I was a lad, I took my son, and now we come here with the grandchildren, its changed lots since my day, but its lovely" (respondent grandfather, ii)

It can be argued that certain spaces are more prone to produce certain kinds of emotions than others – and this was shown to be true of the coast. The love of the sea (or indeed fear of the sea) is a social construction, often conveyed through the medium of the family, performed in leisure time and space. Many parents conversa-tionally referred to the idea of showing their children the beaches, coves and seaside towns they had been to as children themselves. Others valued the passing on of coastal skills of their own, teaching their children to surf, to fish, to collect mussels, or go crabbing. So, memory-making was performed through both place-meaning and recreational performances.

Regardless of specific family roles, it was clear that a love of coastal space expressed here is a key element of childhood experiences, Game and Metcalf (2011), suggest our chronological past, and particularly our maternal connections, influence our current enjoyment of meaningful spaces. The beach is for many -symbolically, a place of childhood freedom, fun and excitement. 'It's got to be the seaside, every time – surely?' declared one grandmother, 'it's got everything for the nippers, and all free, nothing like it is there?' As discussed earlier, a key parental motivation for choosing family holiday experiences is the aim of creating these positive childhood experiences, and these in turn become identifying family memories. Togetherness and memory-making are key drivers according to Gram (2005), while Servidio and Ruffolo (2016) assert that emotional involvement is a critical aspect of memorable and lasting tour-ism experiences. Sthapit and Coudounaris' (2018) work has shown, similar to this research – that measurements of memorable tourism experiences are strongly corre-lated with meaningfulness and happiness (eudomonic and hedonic wellbeing).

Conclusion – beyond 'a day at the seaside' in tourism and leisure narratives

So, what can be said of all these experiences, these emotions and the coastal spaces that allow them to flow? This exploratory research has reviewed aspects of connection, family, emotions, bodies, authenticity and coastal spaces. All overlap to create a fluid-ity of experience, of dynamic, socio-spatial emotions. The importance of narrative must not be overlooked in tourism studies– who we are, what we enjoy, what this place, this trip, this beach, this water -makes us feel like, what it means to us individu-ally or as a family, and how we remember it, are core issues for deepening our under-standing of the *human* condition of tourism. Humans are in essence, emotions and thoughts contained in corporeal spaces, albeit affected by a myriad of external social constructs – but our quest for connection with other significant humans in our lives, and with nature itself are core existential conditions. They are not *secondary* to other aspects of tourism behaviour, rather, they inform, filter and differentially affect our experiences in time and space.

This work aimed to explore the emotions and experiences related to coastal tour-ism encounters in one UK site, and it has shown the largely positive, joyful expressions of its respondents. A diverse set of experiences were reported within specific spatial contexts of the coast, the beach and the water itself. Thick dialogue, rich descriptions and animated performances brought the importance of this coastscape to the fore-front of real and imagined family stories, memories and legacies. The paper also dis-cussed family narratives and emotional experiences in the context of coastal tourism. It has shown that these spaces can ameliorate or indeed sometimes replicate family dynamics in many cases – where mundane domestic issues either become suspended and improved, or for others, simply transposed. For some respondents, there was a continuation of the private rhythms of the family, into the outdoor, temporal, public, beach setting. Idealized projections of family inter-personal authenticity were unpacked and discussed. For many families, the notion of 'being a real or proper fam-ily' was expressed, often through the construction of 'quality time' encounters. Performing parenting roles that fed into socially constructed notions of 'good mothers and fathers', connecting to their children in fun and/or meaningful ways was highly valued. Gender and power relationships around social reproduction issues were expressed by many. For some parents, a seaside holiday represented a break from the mundane chores of 'home'; for others it meant 'more of the same'. For many families however, the beach holiday epitomised idealized space and time, a place for quality time, bonding, relaxation and togetherness, without the distractions characterised by everyday places. As a result, psychosocial wellbeing increased across all interviewees – and the effect of these interconnected emotions, spaces and the water itself, made almost everyone *feel* better.

Memorable tourism experiences are important in the story of most families. These experiences are emotional and emotive. They are often strengthened by the connections that are enabled in the spatial setting of the coast, the beach, the water. Quality time is critical in family tourism practices, but constructed differentially within various parenting styles and values. The connection between the concepts of 'time' (quality, temporary, or suspended) and tourism, warrants more attention.

Meaning, emotions and existentialism all need to be considered in more depth within the tourism academy, given that tourism is an important dimension in how we conduct and perform our family lives. These issues are indeed beyond 'a trip to the seaside', they are the components that help to shape family identities. Families 'doing family' as a particular configuration of human connection is an important aspect of all tourism performances. How tourists imagine and perform 'familiness' in the context of coastal tourism is complex, as this paper has shown, but warrants deeper research. Future research needs to delve deep inside the feelings evoked by tourism spaces and their associated social connections. More tourism studies need to be conducted on families and emotions and on the voice of children and *their* experiences of family holidays (especially new forms of families – single parent, blended step-families, homosexual parent families, bereaved families and more). More work is also needed on the interaction and gendered power relationships between parents as they perform family holidays. In the realms of the coastal, more succinct questioning is needed on the geography of coastal prepositions – the differential experiences felt beside or in the sea itself. Perhaps there is scope for a more central acknowledgement of the sea space itself within themes of emotion, authenticity and connectivity. To conclude on this note, citing Nichols (2012): 'when we are staring at the sea, watching it, it takes away our stress, it reduces our anxiety, it connects us to ourselves. When we go to the sea, we connect to *ourselves*, at the edge of the water. When we go to the ocean with friends, with *our families*, we form these deep, blue, *memories* that become *who we are*- that *connect* us with the people we love, in the *places* we love.' A fitting synopsis perhaps, of the emotional value of family holidays by the sea.

Disclosure statement

No potential conflict of interest was reported by the author(s).

ORCID

Catherine Kelly (iD) http://orcid.org/0000-0002-7776-1874

References

Ahmed, S. (2004). Collective feelings: Or, the impressions left by others. *Theory, Culture and Society, 21*(2), 25–42. https://doi.org/10.1177/0263276404042133

Ashe, J. (2012). Understanding feelings can help hotels improve guest experiences. *Loughborough Echo*, 3.

Bachelard, G. (1969). *The poetics of space*. Beacon Press. https://doi.org/10.1086/ahr/74.4.1389

Baerenholdt, J'., Haldrup, M., Larsen, J., & Urry, J. (2004). *Performing tourist places*. Taylor and Francis.

Belhassen, Y., & Caton, K. (2006). Authenticity matters. *Annals of Tourism Research*, *33*(3), 853–856. https://doi.org/10.1016/j.annals.2006.03.009

Bell, S. L., Phoenix, C., Lovell, R., & Wheeler, B. W. (2015). Seeking everyday wellbeing: The coast as a therapeutic landscape. *Social Science & Medicine (1982))*, *142*, 56–67. https://doi.org/10.1016/j.socscimed.2015.08.011

Bondi, L and Davidson, J, (2003). Troubling the Place of gender, In Anderson, K. (ed.) *The Handbook of Cultural Geography*. Sage: London

Brown, S. D., & Tucker, I., (2010). Eff the ineffable: Affect, somatic management and mental health service users. In M. Gregg & G. J. Seigworth (Eds.), *The affect theory reader* (pp. 229–403). Duke University Press.

Buda, D. M. (2015). *Affective tourism; dark routes in conflict*. Abingdon.

Buda, D. M., d'Hauteserre, A.-M., & Johnston, L. (2014). Feelings and tourism studies. *Annals of Tourism Research*, *46*, 102–114. https://doi.org/10.1016/j.annals.2014.03.005

Buda, D., & MacIntosh, A. (2012). Hospitality, peace and conflict: Doing 'fieldwork' in Palestine. *The Journal of Tourism and Peace Research*, *2*(2), 50–61.

Cheong, Y. S., & Sin, H. L. (2019). Going on holiday only to come home: Making happy families in Singapore. *Tourism Geographies*, 1–22. https://doi.org/10.1080/14616688.2019.1669069

Collins, D., & Kearns, R. (2010). It's a Gestalt Experience' – Landscape values and development pressure in Hawkes Bay, New Zealand. *Geoforum*, *41*(3), 435–446. https://doi.org/10.1016/j.geoforum.2009.11.010

d'Hauteserre, A. M. (2009). L'altérité et le tourisme: Construction du soi et d'une identité sociale. *Espace Populations Sociétés*, *2*, 279–291. https://doi.org/10.4000/eps.3693

d'Hauteserre, A. M. (2015). Affect theory and the attractivity of destinations. *Annals of Tourism Research*, *55*, 77–89. https://doi.org/10.1016/j.annals.2015.09.001

Davidson, J., & Milligan, C. (2004). Embodying emotion: sensing space: Introducing emotional geographies. *Social & Cultural Geography*, *5*(4), 523–532. https://doi.org/10.1080/1464936042000317677

Day, R., Gilbert, K., Settles, B., & Burr, W. (Eds). (1995). *Research and theory in family science*. Brooks-Cole.

Game, A., & Metcalf, A. (2011). My corner of the world. *Bachelard and Bondi Beach. Emotion Space and Society*, *4*(1), 42–50. https://doi.org/10.1016/j.emospa.2010.10.002

Gesler, W. (1992). Therapeutic landscapes: Medical issues in light of the new cultural geography. *Social Science & Medicine (1982))*, *34*(7), 735–746. https://doi.org/10.1016/0277-9536(92)90360-3

Goffman, E. (1990). *The presentation of the self in everyday life*. London and New York: Penguin Books.

Gram, M. (2005). Family holidays. A qualitative analysis of family holiday experiences. *Scandinavian Journal of Hospitality and Tourism*, *5*(1), 2–22. https://doi.org/10.1080/15022250510014255

Gregg, M., & Seigworth, G. J. (2010). *The affect theory reader*. Duke University Press.

Hom Cary, S. (2004). The tourist moments. *Annals of Tourism Research*, *31*(1), 61–77. https://doi.org/10.1016/j.annals.2003.03.001

Kah, J. A., Shin, H. J., & Lee, S.-H. (2020). Traveler sensoryscape experiences and the formation of destination identity. *Tourism Geographies*. https://doi.org/10.1080/14616688.2020.1765015

Kaplan, S. (1995). The restorative benefits of nature: Toward an integrative framework. *Journal of Environmental Psychology*, *15*(3), 169–182. https://doi.org/10.1016/0272-4944(95)90001-2

Kearns, R., & Collins, D. (2012). Feeling for the coast: The place of emotion in the resistance to residential development. *Social & Cultural Geography*, *13*(8), 937–955. https://doi.org/10.1080/14649365.2012.730150

Kelly, C. (2018). 'I need the sea and the sea needs me' – Symbiotic policy narratives for sustainability and wellbeing. *Marine Policy*, *97*, 223–231. https://doi.org/10.1016/j.marpol.2018.03.023

Kim, J. H., Brent Ritchie, J. R., & McCormick, B. (2012). Development of a scale to measure memorable tourism experiences. *Journal of Travel Research*, *51*(1), 12–25. https://doi.org/10.1177/0047287510385467

Kim, H., & Jamal, T. (2007). Touristic quest for existential authenticity. *Annals of Tourism Research*, *34*(1), 181–201. https://doi.org/10.1016/j.annals.2006.07.009

Kirillova, K., & Lehto, X. (2015). An existential conceptualization of the vacation cycle. *Annals of Tourism Research*, *55*, 110–123. https://doi.org/10.1016/j.annals.2015.09.003

Massumi, B. (2015). *Politics of Affect*. Cambridge: Polity Press

Minnaert, L., & Jens (2017). *Family Travel Survey*. Family Travel Association. NYU School of Professional Studies. Online report. file:///C:/Users/User/AppData/Local/Packages/Microsoft.MicrosoftEdge_8wekyb3d8bbwe/TempState/Downloads/P1718-0036-2017_Family_Travel_Survey%20(3).pdf

Nichols, W. J. (2018). *Blue mind: How water makes you happier, More connected and better at what you do*. Abacus.

Nichols, W. J. (2012). *Exploring our blue mind*. TedX Talk, San Diego. https://www.youtube.com/watch?v=7n95ylBq6jo

Obrador, P. (2012). The place of the family in tourism research: Domesticity and thick sociality by the pool. *Annals of Tourism Research*, *39*(1), 401–420. https://doi.org/10.1016/j.annals.2011.07.006

Obrador-Pons, P. (2003). Being-on-Holiday: Tourist Dwelling, Bodies and Space. *Tourist Studies*, *3*(1). 47–66.

Obrador-Pons, P. (2007). A haptic geography of the beach: Naked bodies, vision and touch. *Social & Cultural Geography*, *8*(1), 123–141. https://doi.org/10.1080/14649360701251866

Obrador-Pons, P. (2009). Building castles in the sand: Repositioning touch on the beach. *The Senses and Society*, *4*(2), 195–210. https://doi.org/10.2752/174589309X425139

Ong, A. (2009) On the measurement and mismeasurement of happiness: Contemporary theories and methodological directions. In: A. Dutt, & B. Rudcliff (Eds.), *Happiness, economics, and politics: Towards a multi-disciplinary approach* (pp. 33-44). Northampton: Edward Elgar.

Pocock, N. (2015). Emotional entanglements in tourism research. *Annals of Tourism Research*, *53*, 31–45. https://doi.org/10.1016/j.annals.2015.04.005

Pons, P. O. (2003). Being-on-holiday: Tourist dwelling, bodies and space. *Tourist Studies*, *3*(1), 47–66. https://doi.org/10.1177/1468797603040530

Poria, Y., & Timothy, D. J. (2014). Where are the children in tourism research? *Annals of Tourism Research*, *47*, 93–95. https://doi.org/10.1016/j.annals.2014.03.002

Pritchard, A., Morgan, N., & Ateljevic, I. (2011). Hopeful tourism: A new transformative perspective. *Annals of Tourism Research*, *38*(3), 941–963. https://doi.org/10.1016/j.annals.2011.01.004

Schanzel, H. A., & Yeoman, I. (2014). The future of family tourism. *Tourism Recreation Research* , *39*(3), 343–360. https://doi.org/10.1080/02508281.2014.11087005

Servidio, R., & Ruffolo, I. (2016). Exploring the relationship between emotions and memorable tourism experiences through narratives. *Tourism Management Perspectives*, *20*(2016), 151–160. https://doi.org/10.1016/j.tmp.2016.07.010

Shaw, S. M. (2010). Diversity and ideology: Changes in Canadian family life and implications for leisure. *World Leisure Journal*, *52*(1), 4–13. https://doi.org/10.1080/04419057.2010.9674617

Shields, R. (1990). The 'system of pleasure': Liminality and the Carnivalesque at Brighton. *Theory, Culture and Society*, *7*(1), 39–72. https://doi.org/10.1177/026327690007001002

Snyder, K. A. (2007). A vocabulary of motives: Understanding how parents define quality time. *Journal of Marriage and Family*, *69*(2), 320–340. https://doi.org/10.1111/j.1741-3737.2007.00368.x

Sthapit, E. & Coudounaris, D.N. (2018) Memorable tourism experiences: antecedents and outcomes, Scandinavian Journal of Hospitality and Tourism, *18*(1), 72–94. http://doi.org/10.1080/15022250.2017.1287003

Tung, V., & Ritchie, J. (2011). Exploring the essences of memorable tourism experiences. *Annals of Tourism Research*, *38*(4), 1367–1386. https://doi.org/10.1016/j.annals.2011.03.009

Wang, N. (1999). Rethinking authenticity in tourism experience. *Annals of Tourism Research,* *26*(2), 349–370. https://doi.org/10.1016/S0160-7383(98)00103-0

White, M., Smith, A., Humphryes, K., Pahl, S., Snelling, D., & Depledge, M. (2010). Bluespace: the importance of water for preference, affect, and restorativeness ratings of natural and built scenes. *J. Environmental Psychology, 30*(4), 482–493. https://doi.org/10.1016/j.jenvp.2010.04.004

Dystopian dark tourism: affective experiences in Dismaland

Maria Sofia Pimentel Biscaia ⓘ and Lénia Marques ⓘ

ABSTRACT

In dark tourism affects are generated in a relational manner by the tourists and the locations visited by them. Exploring affective meanings of Banksy's *Dismaland* via socio-spatial theories of emotion and affect is a way to contribute to the understanding of dystopian tourism. The dystopian touristic experience of Dismaland evolves from the interaction of a dystopian atmosphere, a displacement strategy and productive negative intensities. Whilst the affects produced vary according to the artist's intentions, through innovative and politicised forms of dystopian dark tourism, Banksy creates atmospheres where productive negative intensities are able to be developed. In spite of the shades of dystopia and darkness in the artist's work, a hopeful form of tourism could be generated. The implications are that affect in the dark tourism context has different layers of meaning where the materialising dystopian experiences, as simulacra, range from pure attraction to social change. Dismaland's dark tourism experience reveals the role that political and ethical matters play in socio-affective encounters as exemplified by the commodification of the tourism industry, the Mediterranean refugee crisis and the glorified/sorrowful death of Diana, princess of Wales.

摘要

在黑暗旅游中, 游客和他们访问的地点是以一种关系的方式产生了感情。本文通过情绪和情感的社会空间理论探索班克斯的恐怖迪士尼的情感意义, 有助于理解反乌托邦式旅游。恐怖迪士尼的反乌托邦式旅游体验是从反乌托邦氛围、错位策略和产生的负面对比强度的相互作用演变而来的。尽管根据艺术家的不同意图, 班克西通过反乌托邦式的黑暗旅游的创新和政治化形式所产生的情感也有所不同, 但是班克西创造了一种氛围, 在这种氛围中, 生产性的负面对比强度能够被开发出来。尽管在艺术家的作品中有反乌托邦和黑暗的阴影, 但一种充满希望的旅游形式可能会产生。这意味着, 在黑暗旅游背景下的情感具有不同层次的意义, 其中物化的反乌托邦体验, 作为拟像, 从纯粹的吸引物到社会变革广泛存在。恐怖迪士尼的黑暗旅游体验揭示了政治和伦理问题在社会情感遭遇中的作用, 本文通过旅游业的商品化、地中海难民危机和威尔士王妃戴安娜的荣耀而悲伤的死亡等实例进行了说明。

"In affect, we are never alone."

- Brian Massumi (2002, p. 6)

"Disneyland: a space of the regeneration of the imaginary as waste-treatment plants are elsewhere, and even here. Everywhere today one must recycle waste, and the dreams, the phantasms, the historical, fairylike, legendary imaginary of children and adults is a waste product, the first great toxic excrement of a hyperreal civilization."

- Jean Baudrillard (1981 [1994], p. 13)

Introduction

What does a traveller visiting Jim Morrison's tomb in Paris have in common with a pilgrim gazing upon 5000 human skulls on display in the Bone Chapel of Saint Francis's Church in Évora, Portugal? What does someone who takes a tour to the Dharavi slum in Mumbai share with those who crawl their way through the war tunnels of Cu Chi and Ben Duoc in the jungles of Vietnam? What impulses are triggered when one witnesses the killing of a bull at a Mexican bullfight or attends the Ground Zero site in New York? What kind of tourists visit Fukushima Daiichi area so profoundly devastated by earthquake, tsunami and nuclear disaster in 2011? At first glance, it seems like these types of tourism are markedly different, encompassing cemetery, religious, slum, war and disaster tourism as well as even blood sports tourism and memorialisation. And yet, it is instinctively clear that a common "darkness" pervades them all.

In this conceptual paper we aim to study what affective negotiations can be involved in dystopian dark tourism. As a case study, we will use Banksy's 2015 dystopian pop-up theme park (De Visser-Amundson et al., 2016) *Dismaland: Bemusement Park*, which constituted a political, artistic and touristic endeavour. Dismaland was built on an abandoned lido site in Weston-Super-Mare, North Somerset, England. The doors of this pop-up art installation were opened for 5 weeks in 2015, having 58 artists on show and attracting 150,000 visitors (Banksy, n.d.), with an estimated revenue of 20 million pounds for the town (BBC, 2015). Informed by different media, such as newspaper articles, videos, as well as websites, this conceptual paper critically debates affective meanings of Dismaland via socio-spatial theories of emotion and affect, thus hoping to contribute to the understanding of dystopian tourism.

We will argue that this work arose from conflating two traditional types of tourism: English seaside tourism and Disneyland. However, unlike more conventional views might suggest, Banksy used the project to both emphasise the repressed affects of these types of tourism and reignite specific affects relating to contemporary themes such as migration and spectacle. We argue that the affects generated both by the tourists and the location, a dismayed theme park, evolve from the interaction of a dystopian atmosphere, a displacement strategy and productive negative intensities. Our focus in this paper will be specifically on the refugee boat installation, *Mediterranean Boat Ride,* and Cinderella's coach crash.

Shades of "darkness"

Dark tourism practices are by no means new. It has been claimed that the Romans began "the age of tourism" (Perrottet, 2003, p. 5) and that all roads led *from* Rome. The most infamous form of entertainment used to satisfy the tourist gaze was the games: human and exotic animal slaughter, chariot races and, of course, gladiator fighting. Blood was a necessary ingredient for many a tourist. This type of motivation can also be seen in nineteenth century Britain which, using the structures put in place by the all-consuming empire, fed the orientalist (Said, 1978 [2003]) imagination of explorers, adventurers and tourists who flocked to the "darkest" corners of the empire with the view of filling their halls with stories of bravery and their curiosity cabinets with souvenirs. Undoubtedly even pre-modern tourism was vested with dehumanising traits, since souvenirs could have been as gruesome (and exciting) as a shrunken human head or a mummy repurposed as a meal (Larson, 2014; Noble, 2011; Sugg, 2015).

Malcolm Foley's and John Lennon's (1996) introduction of the dark tourism concept brought new perspectives to tourism studies.

Their major contribution refers to the actual conceptualisation of the term 'dark tourism' and to its contextualisation as a service and an activity referring to places of death, disaster, and atrocities. Since then, the typology and conceptualisations of dark tourism have greatly changed with dark tourism literature blossoming and now thriving (e.g. Biran & Buda, 2018; Hooper & Lennon, 2016; Magee & Gilmore, 2015).

As a byproduct of postmodern desires and fears, dark tourism departs from a specific relationship with death. Due to overwhelming mediatisation death, along with its counterparts of violence, grief and trauma, has been naturalised and neutralised. Our time is one of technological progress with mass consumption marking current information societies. Tourism occurs within this context and can be viewed as a sign-value, a prestigious product, a sign of distinction, status, power and social rank (Baudrillard, 1976). In the very aptly titled *Symbolic Exchange and Death* (1976), Baudrillard argues that the linearity of capitalist thinking transforms death into the opposite of life and therefore a type of waste and consumable good. Controversially, he proposes a break with capitalist values of production and economic relations; this he calls a "symbolic exchange", a form of resisting capitalist values of utility and hardcore profit in favour of cultural values (Baudrillard, 1976). This capitalist framework is designed, organised and operated along anthropocentric philosophies of reason. His formulation on simulacra and spectacle offer an alternative avenue which when discussed along theories of Affect which recognise the role of the unconscious in social relations and production of collective meaning gain further force.

Foley and Lennon emphasise the role of reproduction and spectacle for dark tourism, in line with Baudrillard's idea of the postmodern world (third order of simulacra), as a place where the "real" is preceded by its representation, making them indistinguishable; the simulation of the "real" prevails instead because of the success of spectacularism (Baudrillard, 1981 [1994]).

Both dark tourism (Foley & Lennon, 1996; Lennon & Foley, 2000) and thanatourism (Seaton, 1996) evolve from the accepted premise of the phenomenon as a dependant of the economic and cultural milieu of market capitalism and consumerism. Seaton's

(1996) point of departure being heritage tourism can lead to an interpretation that is narrower than dark tourism, as also highlighted by Light (2017).

The literature in Tourism Studies has provided different overviews of approaches to dark tourism (e.g. Light, 2007; Sharpley, 2009; Golańska, 2015; Light, 2017; Martini & Buda, 2020). Light (2017) provides a critical overview of the studies that have been developed on dark tourism and thanatourism, with their different emphases on motivations, types of place, practices, forms of experience or heritage-based. According to Light (2017), there are overlaps between the different concepts as many of the so-called dark forms of tourism fall under the umbrella of heritage tourism. Although there is most often a direct link between tangible or intangible heritage, a certain geographical location and the dark happening, it would be restrictive to amalgamate all forms of dark tourism within heritage tourism. Dark tourism has, however, developed beyond heritage tourism in a myriad of ways, for example, in events and festivals (e.g. Podoshen et al., 2018). In light of these developments, there is a need for a more profound reflection upon the central role played by the tourists' motivations and the affects surrounding dystopian dark touristic experiences at particular geographical locations.

Tourists' motivations are graded in topoi related to death which can range from atrocity, tragedy, brutality, violence and dismay. In this framework, the recent trend of affective dark tourism (Buda, 2015; Golańska, 2015; Holst, 2018; Martini & Buda, 2020) is particularly productive. The debate would benefit from expanding the discussion with other concepts of practical philosophy such as dystopia, hyper-realism, spectacle and simulation.

Affective dark tourism

The increasing scholarly attention given to dark tourism is matched, if not superseded, by the boom in Affect Studies which has taken the Humanities and the Social Sciences worlds by storm. This concept was theorised in the 1960s by a psychologist, Silvan Tomkins (1962), but it has outgrown this field, particularly with Brian Massumi who provided a reflective distinction between affect and emotion, thus highlighting the importance of intensity:

> An emotion is a subjective content, the socio-linguistic fixing of the quality of an experience which is from that point onward defined as personal. Emotion is qualified intensity, the conventional, consensual point of insertion of intensity into semantically and semiotically formed progressions, into narrativizable action-reaction circuits, into function and meaning. It is intensity owned and recognized. It is crucial to theorize the difference between affect and emotion. If some have the impression that it has waned, it is because affect is unqualified. As such, it is not ownable or recognizable, and is thus resistant to critique. (Massumi, 1995, p. 88)

Massumi argues that there is a gap – as well as a connection – between the content (quality) and the effect (intensity) of an image, experience or situation. Such experiences might be short-lived, but nevertheless have a long lasting intense affective impact. Building on this concept, Seigworth and Gregg (2010) point out the difficulty of studying affect precisely because it does not exist in an absolute, pure or original form. Affect "arises in the midst of *in-between-ness*", "in the capacities to act and be acted upon", a transient (or not so transient) state of relations or its intensities (Seigworth & Gregg, 2010, p. 1. Italics in the text). Affect resides in the realm beyond the conscious; it is something that cannot be named nor qualified, but which nevertheless has a bodily expression as the body reacts to the intensities it experiences. Such stimuli occur before the process of cognition is initiated and, therefore, a conscious registration cannot be made at that stage. It is always already escaping us (Massumi, 2002, p. 35). Affect should not be reduced to emotions nor be controlled by conscious thought, although both are always present in the social connections one forms, thus transcending the individual and rooting itself in the networks of belonging to others. This being said, there are various approaches to affect, including critical discourses of emotions (Seigworth & Gregg, 2010). Sara Ahmed (2004, p. 9) points out a "model of sociality of emotion" where emotions are theorised as social and cultural practices and not mere psychological forms. As emotions circulate over time, they acquire affective value:

> the cultural politics of emotions is not only developed as a critique of the psychologising and privatisation of emotions, but also as a critique of the model of the social structure which neglects the emotional intensities, which allow such structures to be reified as forms of being" (Ahmed, 2004, p. 12).

Ahmed's affective model of emotion includes an important component of shame. Theorists of affect, and certainly Ahmed and Massumi, refocus on questions of corporeality and embodiment in combination with the political. Matter once again comes to the forefront of philosophical thought and experience, in tune with the New Materialist turn theorised by feminists of the embodied subject, such as Rosi Braidotti (1994; 2002) and even Sara Ahmed herself (2004).

In this context, Affect Studies seem particularly apt as a critical tool to approach dark tourism with. Given our gradual desensitisation in the face of brutal deaths shown on our numerous TV and computer screens, as well as its excessive representation and reproduction, affect as an unqualified intensity is waned. While the commodification of death has resulted in its affective mitigation, it has also produced new ways to consume it and thus to refresh and transform associated affects.

In some ways, dark tourism can be seen as death's phoenix-like transformation where it arises reinvigorated. The simultaneously consuming and creative aspect of affect (Massumi, 2002; 2015), as connecting with others and the world, is made possible through dark tourism. Buda (2015) has further developed the studies on dark tourism by relating experiences in conflict territories to affect. The idea of an encounter comes back in a recent study by Martini and Buda (2020, p. 4) where it is stated that dark tourism "experiences arise through explicitly sought after encounters, whereby tourists are receptive to the networks of affects arose by the connections with death and its representations", which are referred to as "affective socio-spatial encounters" (2018, p. 1).

Accordingly, Hazel Tucker speaks of empathy (2016) and points to the need to debate tourisms according to paradigms of moral encounters, social justice and peace (2016, p. 15). Like Ahmed, she elaborates on shame which, according to Tucker, is not only productive but also reflective, as empathy can itself be commodified, for instance, in situations promoting the voyeuristic neo-colonialist gaze. Tourism can thus be material in developing a politically charged form of "ethical empathy" contributing to imagining a more hopeful future (Tucker, 2016, p. 40). Rekindling affects as well as emotions is politically and culturally required for societies to engage with their pasts, transgenerational traumas and to reinterpret spaces. Tourism is one way of doing this.

Tourism and utopian places

Since the 2000s particular attention has been given to relations of living, leisure and tourism practices as well as to a certain social responsibility towards humanity and the planet. McLaren and Jaramillo (2007) bring attention to the need for reshifting focus in terms of a critical praxis in the face of danger to humanity's own survival, the destructive effects of global neoliberal capitalism and the continued exploitation of "Third" World workers. Following Zygmunt Bauman (2005), McLaren and Jaramillo (2012) argue that we have turned from political citizens to market consumers. As such, we see our desires unquestioned and legitimised as we are deformed by a system which, conveniently, we feel we cannot change. An examination of the extent to which our thinking is complicit with the "discourses and communities that grant them value" is, therefore, needed, while bearing in mind that these do not shape the world independently from the "forces of capitalist production and class struggle" (McLaren & Jaramillo, 2012, p. xxvii). Change requires disrupting this system, informed agency or, in McLaren and Jaramillo (2012, p. xxvii) words, "critical pedagogy". When one refers to tourism then, critical "transformative pedagogy" (2012, p. xxxiii) is at stake which is founded on class consciousness, self-affirmation, as well as on solidarity with the sub-altern and the proletariat (2012, p. xxxv).

In this context, creativity is deemed a necessity to overcome capitalism and a logic of self-centredness must be replaced by one of relationalisation (being in the relation with others). Ateljevic et al. (2012) present this shift as the critical turn in tourism studies where tourism would be hopeful, focused on social justice, equality and anti-oppression. Active hopeful tourism is about rejecting patriarchal models (dynamic feminine), "a global consciousness which recognises our interdependencies, vulnerabilities and responsibilities to each other" (transmodernity) and the multiple co-creative trans-generational relations (worldism) (Pritchard & Morgan, 2013, p. 5).

This perspective is not concomitant with utopianism although it seems understandable that many forms of tourism develop according to utopian logic. Numerous examples spring to mind in relation to theme parks or resorts: Hobbit Land, The Wizarding World of Harry Potter, Las Vegas and, of course, all the Disney parks from Orlando to Hong Kong. The key feature of these utopias is unaccountability in an escapist world where the tourist gives in to her/his desires without consequences. This has been referred to as "unconscious guilt" (Podoshen et al, 2015, p. 317).

However, many of these utopian places thrive *because* they magnify problems which plague contemporary Western societies: the infantilisation of adult populations, extreme forms of financial risk, patriarchal exploitation of female bodies as well as the all-consuming oppression of global brands. As d'Hauteserre (2015, p. 81) remarks, the "affective capacities of any given atmosphere are signified unequally as bodies belong to socialized subjects (e.g. gendered, racialized, sexualized, etc.)". Utopia is, therefore, never far from dystopia where a critical turn is taken. Regarding Las Vegas, for instance, R. Belk writes: "resorts jointly participate in a theatrical farce meant to infantilize their adult patrons by creating a fantastic liminal time and place. Infantilized adults make better gamblers and consumers" (2000, p. 101). And Belk later completes: "Disneyland and Las Vegas celebrate stylized versions of long-standing myths of the Western world (the exotic savage, knightly chivalry, winning the West, fabulous riches, utopian futures, and far away times and places)" (2000, p. 104).

Dark tourism might be a means to integrate the suppressed aspects of tourism, particularly in the form of dystopian dark tourism, as, on the one hand, it incorporates the notion of tourism in terms of consumption and consumerism – for instance Podoshen et al. (2014) whose dedication to the prolific field of Black Metal led them to develop a model of analysis – and on the other hand, it highlights the need to bring back the question of morality. In this respect, though dark tourism has been accused of merchandising and trivialising death, particularly when intertwined with recreational activities, it nevertheless has a "potential role [...] within an emotion–morality framework" (Stone, 2009, pp. 59–60). In secular societies which have been alleviated of religious pressures, the individual feels "morally confused" and "isolated" (Stone, 2009, p. 60). Dark tourism thus plays a mediating role in this framework of secularism, individualism and moral confusion, where dualistic conceptualizations are no longer sufficient to account for the experiences of these affective spaces (Golańska, 2015).

Taking Dismaland as a case study, we will argue that dark tourism addresses head-on these issues and that it can, therefore, "project moral meaning" and be "a new moral force" to our existence (Stone, 2009, pp. 62–63). Since this is a conceptual paper, Dismaland has been the source which inspired reflection on the complex experiential, sociological, emotional and affective dystopian experiences in tourism. The information used in this paper was obtained through several forms of publicly available media, such as newspapers, websites and videos. More than a deductive analysis of the data, these sources were used in an inductive manner mainly to illustrate and feed the theoretical reflection.

Dystopian and disconsolate Banksy: Dismaland

Banksy, whose identity is unknown, has been described as a "graffiti master, painter, activist, filmmaker and all-purpose *provocateur*" (Ellsworth-Jones, 2013). The artist's provocative art has led to a world-wide recognition. Since starting in Bristol in the 1990s, Banksy's actions have been subversive (when not disruptive), inquiring and confronting the public with pieces of (street) art questioning the establishment and the norm. With very clear links to geographical locations, this *provocateur*'s art should be interpreted as a confrontation with society paradoxes, including those of tourism.

Dismaland: Bemusement Park opened on the 21st of August 2015 and closed on the 27th of September the same year. It had popped-up on an abandoned lido site built originally in 1937 to serve the seaside population of Weston-Super-Mare in North

Somerset, England. After many repurposings of the site the Tropicana Pleasure Beach entertainment complex (1983) was eventually closed down, and on its remains Dismaland later emerged as part of an ongoing reconfiguration and rebranding of the site. Being a part of the touristic tradition originating prior to the Second World War this project had both coalesced with its local identity and rebranded it. However, it did not focus on typical British seaside tourism. Dismaland gave continuity to the already embedded sense of a disheartened tourism experience hidden in the rubble of the previously unsuccessful entertainment complex. Darkness was already there to be amplified.

Since Dismaland had closed its doors, the site riding on its coattails has undergone a "renaissance" and a rebranding as a pop-up amusement park, Funland: a venue for various cultural shows, street art, food and music festivals. For all of Dismaland's sub-versiveness it appears that in a carnivalesque manner (Bakhtin, 2009), institutionalised order was restored and, in the process, the site absorbed the political power of carnival itself. In 2019, the now renamed Tropicana Weston boasts being a "hub of arts and culture" and a "unique creative community project" (Tropicana, n.d.), which has been successful in attracting to the premises celebrities such as Laurel and Hardy but, as part of the Dismaland project, as well as artists like Damien Hirst, Damon Albarn, Pussy Riot and, of course, Banksy (photos can be now seen in http://www.dismaland. co.uk/).

The *Walled Off Hotel* – Banksy's other piece of dystopian dark tourism in war-struck Bethlehem – and Dismaland could be viewed as immediate subversive examples of Banksy's work which relate to tourism, forms of leisure and urban regeneration. The pertinent question, however, remains: was *Dismaland* really that subversive?

One can view it as a form of transformative pedagogy, political agency, and ultimately Banksy's attempt at engaging in hopeful tourism and leisure. The field is, therefore, broad for the negotiation of emotions and affects. Dystopia can be considered here to some extent in parallel to Tucker's (2016) "productive shame". A case could also be made for Dismaland as a productive dystopia.

Consideration of Dismaland must inevitably start with Disney as it is not a coincidence that both experiences start with Dis-: Dis-ney on the utopian side; Dis-maland on the dystopian side. This was not the first time that Banksy used Disneyland as an inspiration since in 2006 he had installed a piece titled *Banksy at Disneyland* in Disneyland, California, as a form of what some have considered to be "culture jamming" (Harzman, 2015). Dismaland was a step further in the subversion of the utopian world of Disney.

Standing at the entrance of Dismaland, Rhys Williams describes a "dilapidated gothic parody of a Disneyland sign", a "miserable" sight but, in contrast, the queuing public seemed to be enthusiastic about a show which they anticipated would give them food for thought (Williams, 2016). Dismaland's gloomy space extends well beyond the Tropicana site to form a caricatural theme park. Staff members have been coached to have a matching attitude and whether they are selling tickets or are on site to provide assistance, their demeanour is ... dismaying.

Barry Cawston's touring exhibition *Dismaland and Others* (2019) aptly reproduces that affect through photos such as "The Perfect Fish & Chips", "Make My Day", as well

Figure 1. *Mediterranean Boat Ride.* Photo by Florent Darrault, 23 August 2015, under the Creative Commons Attribution-Share Alike 2.0 Generic license. No changes were made.

as with various photos of demoralised Mickey Mouse-eared employees. The latter provide the perspective of underpaid female and/or ethnic workers who are usually behind the façade of Disney's show of happiness. Perhaps the queuing public did not feel that there was that much food for thought after all, as the readings were too easily graspable. The theme of security (or lack of it in a world where the alarming signs of terrorism are prevalent) is already present at the entrance with fake metal detectors and check points; the full-blown Disney castle on a lake displays a warped Ariel (a technique also used by Cawston for the poster of his exhibition though applied to a staff member on her/his break wearing the infamous Mickey Mouse ears); human excrement floats in the water; a boat with plastic refugees is adrift; police hoses stands for a fountain; a Ferris wheel is also there; a killer-whale jumping through a hoop into a toilet starkly reminds us that Willy was never freed.

The impression of dismaying dystopia is overwhelming. Death itself rides a dodgem car with disco music in the background; a miniature city, eerily reminiscent of Peter Carey's short story "American Dreams", shows a community in turmoil with police cars blocking the roads but where, nonetheless, a busy Burger King can be spotted; a foetus is code branded; a nuclear bomb has mistakenly materialised as a cloud and a stairway to heaven is at one's reach too; a swarm of oncomice is in view (what is it about ears in Dismaland?); the Cookie Monster leads an African armed group; a woman is violently attacked by birds like in the famous Hitchcock film. In the short promo film, we witness the white parents who were previously awaken from their Suburbian coma to go to Dismaland, now leaving the place in tears. In contrast, the children, a boy and a girl (what else?), are ecstatic. The library on site is empty (another mouse-eared woman is

Figure 2. Cinderella's coach crash. Photo by Byrion Smith, 20 August 2015, under the Creative Commons Attribution-Share Alike 2.0 Generic license. No changes were made.

presented looking utterly bored); banking facilities are provided so that children could put their pocket money at risk from an early age. There are "clashings of consumerism and nature" as well as "[t]ensions between soft and hard, natural and human, cartoon whimsy and grim realism are prominent" (Williams, 2016).

All good disheartened fun aside, there are two elements which make this politically invested dystopia a critically relevant piece of dark tourism. The first is *Mediterranean Boat Ride* (see Figure 1) and the second is Cinderella's coach crash (see Figure 2), alluding respectively to the post-2013 refugee crisis in Europe and to Princess Diana's fatal car accident in Paris, 1997.

Boats of shame in the pond

Though the identity of the artist remains elusive, Banksy's concern for themes of migration, social integration and justice have long been manifested in the artist'swork. According to Attimonelli (2016), Banksy is an actor of artivism. Highly engaged works include Cosette from *Les Misérables* (a novel by the French 19th century writer Victor Hugo) being gassed as immigrants in Calais were (London, opposite the French embassy); a black girl in Paris painting pink flowery patterns over a swastika which was later vandalised and painted over (2018); also in the City of Lights, Napoleon rides his white horse but his head is covered with a red veil which is arguably an allusion to the French Government's legislation regarding Islamic veils (2018); Steve Jobs in the Jungle, Calais, highlights the creative potential of migrant forces as his father was a Syrian immigrant; also in Calais one finds Banksy's take on Théodore Géricault's *The Raft of the Medusa*, but here the boat carries refugees trying to get attention of a cruise ship and, therefore, drawing attention to the Mediterranean as an affective socio-spatial encounter, on the one hand, of abundance (cruise tourism) and, on the other, of impending death (for the asylum seekers).

The most significant piece in Dismaland regarding the refugee humanitarian crisis is the installation of asylum boats, eerily adrift on a pond. The plastic look affords this piece the dehumanising reaction which the asylum seekers frequently receive from the Europeans. These boat people are rooted to the spot standing upright as they are aimlessly taken by the tides to and fro. In the water we see bodies floating without attracting anyone's attention. The background music causes greater dissociation between this scene of multiple deaths and what it suggests: exotic and exoticising (Said, 1978 [2003]) holidays in the sun, somewhere in the Pacific Islands.

In Dismaland's specific cultural productions of the migrant boat Banksy is creating a socio-affective encounter of productive shame. Ahmed (2004) has theorised that shame both acts as a mode of recognising emotional injury caused to others and as a form of nation-building. Shame is produced as a "double play of concealment and exposure" but paradoxically one feels shame as s/he tries to cover something that is already out: "[s]hame in exposing that which has been covered demands us to re-cover, such a re-covering would be a recovery from shame. [...] Shame involves the intensification not only of the bodily surface, but also of the subject's relation to itself, or its sense of itself as self" (2004, p. 104). Shame thus evolves from the relation of the self to itself and to others. Whereas the correlating affect of guilt is about violating some rule, shame is about the quality of the self, a quality that becomes under inspection (2004, p. 105).

Ahmed's model of sociality of emotion is further developed as she recognises that shame intrinsically depends on who one feels exposed to. Only some others can be witnesses to the action that makes one ashamed (2004, p. 105) and that is precisely the productive aspect of displacement in Dismaland: as a British person surrounded by other Britons, you recognise in the other a valid witness to your shame for the death of asylum seekers (as much as for the beloved Princess Diana). Shame is present when an ideal fails to bind subjects together; and that is what happens as British Dismaland visitors, collectively, witness the fatal results of their idealisation of Britishness. But Ahmed (2004) tells us that by expressing its shame, a nation can transform that shame into an identity, i.e. "a narrative of reproduction":

> The nation is reproduced through expressions of shame in at least two ways. First shame may be 'brought onto' the nation by illegitimate others (who fail to reproduce its form, or even its offspring), such as queer others [...], or asylum seekers [...]. Such others are shaming by proxy: they do not approximate the form of the good citizen. As citizens they cannot reproduce the national ideal. Second, the nation may bring shame 'on itself' by its treatment of others; for example, it may be exposed as 'failing' a multicultural ideal in perpetuating forms of racism [...]. These actions get transferred to the national subject; it becomes shamed by itself. In this instance, the nation may even express shame about its treatment of others who in the past were read as the origin of shame. (Ahmed, 2004, p. 108)

As a politically invested cultural product, the tourist experience in Dismaland is appealing to the affect of shame as a means for Britain to reconcile with itself. National shame provides the possibility of reconciliation by collectively bearing witness and, therefore, mutually identifiyng what is wrong as well as wanting to do better (Ahmed, 2004, pp. 107–110). One of the failed ideals which Dismaland tourists bear witness to and feel ashamed by is that of multiculturalism. The then Prime Minister David Cameron, a one-nation Tory, had, in fact, proclaimed war on multiculturalism in 2011 on the grounds that it had helped to promote home-grown Islamic extremism.

Though Dismaland does not attempt a reconciliation so successful that it turns into national pride (as Ahmed suggests), it nevertheless creates intensities of productive shame which urge the British to engage in a process of tackling head-on the failure of national ideals (and national politicians) and to come together to work towards building a nation which is actively proud of such ideals. It is in this sense that one can speak of productive dystopian dark tourism and where Ahmed and Baudrillard meet: the narrative of reproduction, the approximation to an ideal identity, is more effectively achieved through simulacra, the plastic figures. Copies are more exact than the referent, more "real" (Baudrillard, 1981 [1994] , p. 107); the "sovereign difference" between the original and the copy fades away (Baudrillard, 1981 [1994], p. 2) and only then can shame be productively generated.

Banksy also acts on this shame. Upon the closing of *Dismaland* he decided to send the material from the project to Calais where it was intended to be reused as shelters. In addition, one of Dismaland's migrant plastic boats was raffled to support refugee organisations. Quite significantly, the final concert in the dismal theme park was given by the well-known band and social activists, Pussy Riot, who launched a new song "Refugees In", emphasising the need not only for the British but for the Europeans in general to be involved in productive shame. Some verses include "Met in Europe by razor wires/Governments here fucking liars/Desperate people who need to flee/Seeking refuge by land and sea/Push for borders, get no peace" as well as "Push, push borders away!/Push borders, do it today!/Human beings, not a swarm/Injustice – government norm" (https://www.youtube.com/watch?v=FDoVdLjCjoM).

The tragic story of cinderella's coach crash

The second piece with relevance to dystopian dark tourism studies is that of Cinderella's tragic death. It was staged in a darkened room to amplify the flashes of the paparazzi cameras.

Princess Diana had previously been the subject of Banksy's attention, namely with the creation of £10 notes issued by Banksy of England instead of by a bank, where her face replaced that of Queen Elizabeth II. The commodification of Princess Diana's image suggests an uncomfo? reading: her face, her body, are profitable. For some at least, a less uncomfortable reading is made: she could have replaced the Queen giving force to anti-monarchist feelings but, more likely, to the disappointment of many British citizens with the Royal family's behaviour in the aftermath of Princess Diana's car accident. Until 2017 there was speculation as to whether *Diana in the Tower* in Croydon (showing her mournfully locked away inside) was Banksy's work, however, in August that year this rumour was dispelled by the announcement that it was the work of Rich Simmons. In Dismaland, however, the theme of Princess Diana's fatal accident is fully developed. Cinderella/Princess Diana has had an accident and her pumpkin-coach has been brutally smashed open. One of her white horses is frozen in a moment of pain, whilst the other seems dead.

The princess's body is limp, hanging out – rather too gracefully – of the coach's window. Imitating real life, paparazzi click their cameras without approaching to help: the spectacle of death requires only one participant, one celebrity. In "Dark Detours: Celebrity Car Crash Deaths and Trajectories of Place", Gary Best argues that "the moral paradigm of engagement" in situations of celebrity car crashes (2013, pp. 205–206) is directly connected to a relativised individual moral compass which is charted by the collective framework created by the dark tourist experience.

If the value of the individual experience becomes a "means of energizing moribund frameworks" (Best, 2013), then the death of Princess Diana surely fits the bill. The fascination of the tourist rests upon the death of the notion of Princess Diana as a fairy tale princess: from the innocent blushing bride to a scandalous divorce and her ultimate demise while driving away at great speed with her very publicly non-white partner, Dodi Fayed. In the aftermath, the paparazzi were often blamed for the fatality. However, many of the distraught fans have failed to realise that their insatiable appetite for the princess's image was as much of a contributing factor. As such, Best (2013, p. 212) says, that a Princess Diana dark tourist itinerary must include "those darker sites where she was most pestered, most harassed, most annoyed" and even a Mercedes Benz ride to the tunnel under the Place de l'Alma in Paris.

The dark tourist experience can help with dealing with grief (Best, 2013, p. 213), but the shades of darkness and lightness of experiences truly depend on questions of cannibalisation of post-mortem image. Matters of aesthetics aside, they are materialised from her memorialisation in Harrods to the Diana, Princess of Wales Memorial Fountain in Hyde Park, and to Althorp House, the residence of the Spencers, where Diana is remembered in a silhouetted bust. Thus, the perspective will define what role each site has in building place identity.

Did then, the recapturing of Diana as a princess at the very moment she meets her death contribute to the "resurgence of moral vitality" as Stone (2009, p. 60) suggested? Again, one goes back to the issue of tourists' motivations and affective experiences (Miles, 2014; Golańska, 2015; Zhang et al., 2016). The first Dismaland visitors were most likely surprised, perhaps even shocked, by the staging of Princess Diana's death in the guise of Cinderella.

As word spread, the surprise element was removed and Dismaland visitors became voyeurs, each one replicating with her/his intentional presence the princess's death and the consuming gaze immediately following the accident. Here the fascination is acknowledged, and the mimicry of death becomes an example of purposeful dark tourism supply. But what could be said of the fact that Weston-Upon-Mare is, without a doubt, not Paris and, therefore, not the actual site of the tragedy? In instances such as various dungeons from San Francisco to Shanghai via London or the Old Melbourne Gaol which once held the criminal-come-national hero Ned Kelly, the affective attunements depend on being in the place. However, these examples of dark tourism supply have neutralised the atrocities which had occurred on site, including executions. The intensities have been played down so that death can become commodified and adequate for family fun. It could be argued that *because* Banksy had displaced the princess's death and brought it home, the affective connections with the British were reanimated and a second opportunity invested with a moral vitality was created. This is done, of course, ambivalently: though there can be a release from guilt because the viewer is not actually witnessing the death, nevertheless Banksy dares her/him to engage with the affects of shame for still seeking the thrill of witnessing the death of a celebrity princess. The comment by Baudrillard about the film *Crash*

(Cronenberg, 1996) is here also applicable: "The automobile crash had made possible the final and longed-for union of the actress and the members of her audience" (1981 [1994], p. 188).

In addition, in the way that tourism motivated by pilgrimage may lead grievers to the same site and the affect is generated by the collective but non-simultaneous experience, seeing Cinderella/Princess Diana dying once again reinforces the sense of communal experience, of emotional contagion which, theoretically, can be an idea of "working through" trauma, as Sigmund Freud has put it, through remembering and repeating. In this case, Banksy's installation could help to mediate death and work through the national trauma as a form of edutainment but which, as Body Worlds, is open to accusations of disrespectful exploitation of death. In any case, making the absent death present is the very foundation of dark tourism and the symbolic materialisation of death does not necessarily need to take place at the site of the event in question, as it can be notably stronger where a network of affective intensities can be activated, as in this case, by the British. As Martini and Buda (2020, p. 6) have stated, the tourist is primarily affected by mediatised events due to mobilisation, digitalisation and social media which "make consumption of death and disaster events immediately accessible, and *unfiltered*" (italics added). This might not have been so acute in 1997, but the fatal accident was constantly on magazine covers and TV channels. Dark tourism might provide the means for creating an affective response shared by an imagined community (Anderson, 1983), a concept which describes an idea of a nation formed not so much by a sense of kinship or geography, but by cultural conventions resulting in a sense of shared identity and belonging which has been made possible because of advancements in communication technologies.

Sharpley and Stone (2009) also address the question of dark tourism as part of nation-building whilst Martini and Buda (2020, p. 7) argue as well that dark tourism "produces a *displacement* that transforms places and intentionalities" (italics in the text) in the sense that specific narratives of atrocities, disasters or death are favoured over other narratives with a view to meet the touristic demand for specific affects.

Staging McDisneyified dystopian experiences

Both with the refugee boat and the Diana/Cinderella installation, Banksy displaces the subjects/victims of the dark moment so to more intensely satisfy and resist that demand and activate affective empathy, shame, catharsis, shock or exhilaration. As Podoshen (2013, pp. 265–267) states "dark tourism favours the visual and the experiential over the historic" and its affects are, consequently, augmented through the phenomenon of emotional contagion ("an involuntary spread of feelings without conscious awareness") and empathy which in this case could only be invoked with intensity in the United Kingdom. Simulation of Diana's death would always fall short of creating affect and therefore a performance of the tragedy can arguably be more stimulating.

Tourists hope to "revisit the emotions aroused by images from the destination" but because of the emotional contagion phenomenon, the displacement of the princess's demise to her homeland engages in stronger affective attunements through dystopian dark tourism or through memorialisation (d'Hauteserre, 2015, p. 83). This is in line with Podoshen and Zheng in "Dystopian Dark Tourism: An Exploratory Examination" (2015) who not only recognise a reformulation of our connection with death in the present time in view of the specific forms of its consumption (technological, massive, desensitised) but also a shift of focus from site to motivation.

This connects as well to debates over authenticity in tourism as a negotiated, co-creating process between visitor and site (Cohen & Cohen, 2012; Bryce et al., 2017). Authenticity is produced by tourists; they go so far as to say that "subjects are 'interpellated' in relation to objects in a plenitude of 'authencities', manifested in dispersed consumer culture" and that tourists are offered "quality assurance of *versions* of original objects, experiences and places" (Bryce et al., 2017, p. 50. Italics in the text). And to recover Baudrillard in this discussion, in the context of late capitalism consumer culture, replicas can therefore be more "authentic" than the original, particularly if affects are activated. The same goes for the location; the commodification of such places and the narratives created with a view to capitalising the event, embody a removal from historical facts.

Dark events are sometimes inaccurate or trivialised, distancing them from values of authenticity. However, dark events such as Diana's death and the humanitarian crisis in the Mediterranean presented as a dystopian dark experience provide a sense of authentication. Fully aware of the inauthenticity of postmodern living, the tourist engages in a quest to find that s/he desires: authenticity.

As the tourist is paramount in creating authenticity, a process which has been referred to as authentication (Xie & Wall, 2008), it can be generated in a variety of places and not necessarily where the original event occurred: "authenticity is not a given, measurable quality that can be applied to a particular place, event or experience" and it recognises "the need for an emotive, affective" element (Sharpley & Stone, 2009, p. 116). This perspective is in line with Rickly-Boyd (2013) when highlighting that place matters in existential authenticity (more than an objective state, it is about Being).

Dismaland introduces first and foremost an affective element meant to strip Disney theme parks of their immature construction of bliss. Dismaland, and in particular the Disney related features such as Mickey-Mouse eared employees and Cinderella, are more authentic than the originals insofar as they reveal the latter as simulacra and a "frozen, childlike world" (Baudrillard, 1981 [1994], p. 12).

Baudrillard's well-known discussion on Disneyland and its counterparts is based upon the premise that The United States are themselves not real and Disney theme parks are the "imaginary" so as to hide the unreality of the country. It belongs instead to "the hyperreal order and to the order of simulation". The argument is that it is not a matter of falsely representing reality but of concealing that the real has become unreal:

> The imaginary of Disneyland is neither true nor false, it is a deterrence machine set up in order to rejuvenate the fiction of the real in the opposite camp. Whence the debility of this imaginary, its infantile degeneration. This world wants to be childish in order to make us believe that the adults are elsewhere, in the "real" world, and to conceal the fact that true childishness is everywhere - that it is that of the adults themselves who come here to act the child in order to foster illusions as to their real childishness (Baudrillard, 1981 [1994], p. 13).

In addition to the concept of simulacrum, in the framework of our discussion on tourism another conceptualisation becomes key: George Ritzer's (1983, 1993)

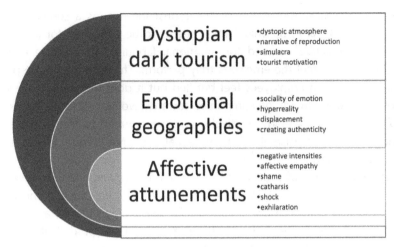

Figure 3. Productive dystopian dark tourism: the McDisneyified experience.

formulation on the McDonaldization of society. It derives from a profound rationalisation of the postmodern Western society and its model is McDonald's and the fast food restaurant. A rationalised society, and therefore a McDonaldised society, emphasises the following features: efficiency, predictability, calculability, substitution of non-human by human technology and control over certainty.

According to Ritzer and Liska (1997, p. 97), "following Weber, [McDonaldisation] has a more dystopian emphasis upon the increasing irrationality of rationality". As every other aspect of our age, tourism has also been McDonaldised. Because it has been Disney who has most successfully applied the principles of McDonaldisation to the industry, Ritzer and Liska speak of the McDisneyisation of tourism. This process is not only dehumanising, mostly unsustainable, but also a quest for sameness. Though many will actively seek difference and therefore represent a need in the tourist industry to de-McDonaldise, the comfort of the rationalised system in the other aspects of their lives offers comfort to many a tourist. McDonaldised tourism infers homogenisation instead of diversity. And in Baudrillard's suit, they argue that the tourist is now totally immersed in simulacra and therefore unable to identify authentic experiences also because inauthentic experiences are disguised as authentic.

These debates and paradoxes can be therefore understood as McDisneyified dystopian experiences, where different levels of the experience are constructed from outside-inwards, starting by the most visible, a form of dystopian dark tourism, the most expressive form related also to the place, emotional geographies; and finally, affective attunements (Figure 3).

Developing Ritzer's theories, Bryman (2004) expands on the four dimensions of the phenomenon which are reflected in other aspects of our lives: theming of places of consumption such as restaurants; hybrid consumption as forms of consumption appear in other than their traditional places; merchandising; and performative labour (Bryman, 2004, p. 2). However, Bryman (2004) argues that where McDonalds strives for homogeneity, through spectacle and drama, Disney strives for diversity as a means to increase profits. We would say however, that Disney promotes forms of cramped diversity as the range of variation is carefully surveilled and controlled. Rightly Bryman argues that emotional labour is key to the tourist industry as a source of differentiation (2004, pp. 103–105) but what Banksy seems to be criticising, for instance, is the callous and manipulative demand for emotional labourers to produce deep acting, whereby they train to feel the emotions they perform. This results in more profitability for companies to which employees feel bonded but it does not necessarily result in a more profound commitment of companies towards workers. If in Disneyfied theme parks around the world, employees display and are required to feel happiness, enjoyment, and pleasure, in Dismaland they reveal the "real" emotions of precarious employees: dismay and disillusionment.

Dwelling in a universe of simulations, when one is a tourist one will crave for simulations as well. After all, surviving in the wild on food, s/he can find the experience "authentic" but it is often too uncomfortable for the average tourist; a meal at a fast-food restaurant is well more desirable (Ritzer & Liska, 1997, p. 107). It is also in this sense that, despite being limited to the reflection of one single dystopian experience, Dismaland is a milestone and brings together a series of acting concepts that contribute to see tourism experiences through new lenses.

In this conceptual paper, a critical exploration of affective attunements of Banksy's Dismaland via socio-spatial theories of emotion and affect was proposed, leading to an understanding of the complexity of a McDisneyfied experience, within a productive dystopian dark tourism. In Dismaland, Banksy exposes the layers of in/authenticity which we as citizens and tourists have naturalised. The refugee plastic boat and Cinderella's crash are powerful instances of simulations which have the potential to develop intensities and an emotion-morality framework.

The death of thousands of refugees or the tragedy of a princess driven to her demise have been played down by the incessant repetition of the "real" events. As those copies/replicas' impact wanes as well, through an innovative and politicised form of dystopian dark tourism Banksy creates atmospheres where productive negative intensities can develop. The success of suchefforts is not guaranteed as affects can only emerge with the tourist's commitment. Therefore, depending on the motivations different affects are produced but because of the shades of dystopia and darkness of Banksy's work, a hopeful form of tourism might have been generated.

Acknowledgements

The authors would like to thank Dr Rhys Williams from the University of Glasgow for kindly having provided access to his article "Radical Politics, Recent Exhibitions, and Utopianism Now".

Disclosure statement

No potential conflict of interest was reported by the author(s).

Funding

This work was partly supported by the Project *Bodies in Transit 2: Difference and Indifference*, Ref.: FFI2017-84555-C2-2-P, MINECO-FEDER.

ORCID

Maria Sofia Pimentel Biscaia (iD) http://orcid.org/0000-0001-5455-9983
Lénia Marques (iD) http://orcid.org/0000-0002-6360-9919

References

Ahmed, S. (2004). *The cultural politics of emotion*. Routledge.

Anderson, B. (1983). *Imagined communities: Reflections on the origin and spread of Nationalism*. Verso. https://doi.org/10.1086/ahr/90.4.903

Ateljevic, I., Morgan, N., & Pritchard, A. (Eds.). (2012). *The critical turn in tourism studies: Creating an academy of hope*. Routledge.

Attimonelli, C. (2016). Artivism and migration: JR and Banksy a mediological analysis of the transfrontier practices of refugees in Europe and the Mediterranean. *Localities*, *6*, 9–31. https://doi.org/10.15299/local.2016.11.6.9

Bakhtin, M. (2009). Rabelais and his World (Hélène Iswolsky, Trans.). Indiana UP.

Banksy. (n.d.). *Dismaland*. http://www.artbanksy.com/dismaland.html

Baudrillard, J. (1981 [1994]). *Simulacra and simulation* (S. F. Glaser, Trans.). University of Michigan Press.

Baudrillard, J. (1976). *Symbolic exchange and death* (S. F. Glaser, Trans.). University of Michigan Press.

Bauman, Z. (2005). *Liquid life*. Polity.

BBC. (2015, September 27). *Banksy's Dismaland 'leaves £20m tourism boost' [online]*. http://www.bbc.com/news/av/uk-34372662/banksy-s-dismaland-leaves-20m-tourism-boost

Belk, R. (2000). May the Farce be with you: On Las Vegas and consumer infantalization. *Consumption Markets & Culture*, *4*(2), 101–124. https://doi.org/10.1080/10253866.2000.9670352

Best, G. (2013). Dark detours Celebrity car crash deaths and trajectories of place. In L. White & E. Frew (Eds.), *Dark tourism and place identity: Managing and interpreting dark places* (pp. 202–216). Routledge.

Biran, A., & Buda, D. M. (2018). Unravelling fear of death motives in dark tourism. In R. Stone, P., Hartmann, R., Seaton, T., Sharpley, R. & White, L. (Eds.), *The Palgrave handbook of dark tourism studies* (pp. 515–532). Palgrave Macmillan.

Braidotti, R. (1994). *Nomadic subjects: Embodiment and sexual difference in contemporary feminist theory*. Columbia University Press.

Braidotti, R. (2002). *Metamorphoses: Towards a materialist theory of becoming*. Blackwell Publishers.

Bryce, D., Murdy, S., & Alexander, M. (2017). Diaspora, authenticity and the imagined past. *Annals of Tourism Research*, *66*, 49–60. https://doi.org/10.1016/j.annals.2017.05.010

Bryman, A. (2004). *The disneyization of society*. Sage.

Buda, D. M. (2015). *Affective tourism: Dark routes in conflict*. Routledge.

Cohen, E., & Cohen, S. (2012). Authenticity and commoditization in tourism. In E. Cohen (Ed.), *Contemporary tourism* (pp. 101–114). Elsevier.

Cronenberg, D. (Director) (1996). *Crash* [Motion picture]. Canada/UK.

De Visser-Amundson, A., De Korte, A., & Williams, S. (2016). "Chill or thrill": the impact of the "polarity paradox" on hospitality and tourism. *Journal of Tourism Futures, 2*(1), 71–78. https://doi.org/10.1108/JTF-12-2015-0053

d'Hauteserre, A. M. (2015). Affect theory and the attractivity of destinations. *Annals of Tourism Research, 55*, 77–89.

Ellsworth-Jones, W. (2013, February). The story behind Banksy. *Smithsonian Magazine*. https://www.smithsonianmag.com/arts-culture/the-story-behind-banksy-4310304/

Foley, M., & Lennon, J. (1996). JFK and dark tourism: A fascination with assassination. *International Journal of Heritage Studies, 2*(4), 198–211. https://doi.org/10.1080/13527259608722175

Golańska, D. (2015). Affective spaces, sensuous engagements: in quest of a synaesthetic approach to 'dark memorials. *International Journal of Heritage Studies, 21*(8), 773–790. https://doi.org/10.1080/13527258.2015.1020960

Harzman, J. C. (2015). Banksy at Disneyland: Generic participation in culture jamming. *Kaleidoscope: A Graduate Journal of Qualitative Communication Research, 14*(3), 17–26.

Holst, T. (2018). *The affective negotiation of slum tourism: City walks in Delhi*. Routledge.

Hooper, G., & Lennon, J. J. (Eds.). (2016). *Dark tourism: Practice and interpretation*. Routledge.

Larson, F. (2014). *Severed: A history of heads lost and heads found*. Liveright.

Lennon, J., & Foley, M. (2000). *Dark tourism: The attraction of death and disaster*. Continuum.

Light, D. (2007). Dracula tourism in Romania cultural identity and the state. *Annals of Tourism Research, 34*(3), 746–765. https://doi.org/10.1016/j.annals.2007.03.004

Light, D. (2017). Progress in dark tourism and thanatourism research: An uneasy relationship with heritage tourism. *Tourism Management, 61*, 275–301. https://doi.org/10.1016/j.tourman.2017.01.011

Magee, R., & Gilmore, A. (2015). Heritage site management: from dark tourism to transformative service experience? *The Service Industries Journal, 35*(15–16), 898–917. https://doi.org/10.1080/02642069.2015.1090980

Martini, A., & Buda, D. M. (2020). Dark tourism and affect: framing places of death and disaster. *Current Issues in Tourism, 23*(6), 679–614. https://doi.org/10.1080/13683500.2018.1518972

Massumi, B. (1995). The autonomy of affect. *Cultural Critique, 31*(31), 83–109. https://doi.org/10.2307/1354446

Massumi, B. (2002). *Parables of the virtual: Movement, affect and sensation*. Duke University Press.

Massumi, B. (2015). *The politics of affect*. Polity Press.

McLaren, P., & Jaramillo, N. (2007). *Pedagogy and praxis in the age of empire: Towards a new humanism*. Sense Publishers.

McLaren, P., & Jaramillo, N. (2012). Foreword: Dialectical thinking and critical pedagogy–towards a critical tourism studies. In I. Ateljevic, N. Morgan & A. Pritchard (Eds.), *The critical turn in tourism studies: creating an academy of hope* (pp. xvii–xxxix). Routledge.

Miles, S. (2014). Battlefield sites as dark tourism attractions: An analysis of experience. *Journal of Heritage Tourism, 9*(2), 134–147. https://doi.org/10.1080/1743873X.2013.871017

Noble, L. (2011). *Medicinal cannibalism in early modern English literature and culture*. Palgrave Macmillan.

Perrottet, T. (2003). *Pagan holiday: On the trail of ancient roman tourists*. Random House.

Podoshen, J. S. (2013). Dark tourism motivations: Simulation, emotional contagion and topographic comparison. *Tourism Management, 35*, 263–271. https://doi.org/10.1016/j.tourman.2012.08.002

Podoshen, J. S., Venkatesh, V., & Zheng, J. (2014). Theoretical reflections on dystopian consumer culture: Black Metal. *Marketing Theory, 14*(2), 207–221. https://doi.org/10.1177/1470593114523446

Podoshen, J. S., Venkatesh, V., Wallin, J., Andrzejewski, S. A., & Jin, Z. (2015). Dystopian dark tourism: An exploratory examination. *Tourism Management, 51*, 316–328. https://doi.org/10.1016/j.tourman.2015.05.002

Podoshen, J. S., Yan, G., Andrzejewski, S. A., Wallin, J., & Venkatesh, V. (2018). Dark tourism, abjection and blood: A festival context. *Tourism Management, 64* (2), 346–356. https://doi.org/ 10.1016/j.tourman.2018.07.009

Pritchard, A., & Morgan, N. (2013). Introduction: Creating an academy of hope: An enquiry–learning–action nexus. In I. Ateljevic, N. Morgan, & A. Pritchard (Eds.), *The critical turn in tourism studies* (pp. 43–52). Routledge.

Rickly-Boyd, J. M. (2013). Existential authenticity: Place matters. *Tourism Geographies, 15*(4), 680–686. https://doi.org/10.1080/14616688.2012.762691

Ritzer, G. (1983). The McDonaldization of society. *The Journal of American Culture, 6*(1), 100–107. https://doi.org/10.1111/j.1542-734X.1983.0601_100.x

Ritzer, G. (1993). *The McDonaldization of society*. Pine Forge.

Ritzer, G., & Liska, A. (1997). McDisneyization' and 'post-tourism': Complementary perspectives on contemporary tourism. In C. Rojek & J. Urry (Eds.), *Touring cultures: Transformations of travel and theory* (pp. 96–109). Routledge.

Seaton, A. V. (1996). Guided by the dark: From thanatopsis to thanatourism. *International Journal of Heritage Studies, 2*(4), 234–244.

Said, E. (1978 [2003]). *Orientalism*. Penguin.

Seigworth, G., & Gregg, M. (2010). An inventory of shimmers. In M. Gregg & G. Seigworth (Eds.), *The affect theory reader* (pp. 1–28). Duke University Press.

Sharpley, R. (2009). Shedding light on dark tourism: An introduction. In R. Sharpley & P. R. Stone (Eds.), *The darker side of travel: The theory and practice of dark tourism* (pp. 3–22). Channel View Publications.

Sharpley, R., & Stone, P. R. (Eds.). (2009). *The darker side of travel: The theory and practice of dark tourism*. Channel View Publications.

Stone, P. R. (2009). Dark tourism: Morality and new moral spaces. In R. Sharpley & P.R. Stone (Eds.), *The Darker Side of Travel: The Theory and Practice of Dark Tourism* (pp. 56–72). Channel View Publications.

Sugg, R. (2015). *Mummies, cannibals and vampires: The history of corpse medicine from the renaissance to the victorians*. Routledge.

Tomkins, S. (1962), Affect Imagery Consciousness: Volume I, The Positive Affects. Tavistock.

Tropicana. (n.d.). Welcome to the Tropicana Weston. http://tropicanaweston.co.uk/

Tucker, H. (2016). Empathy and tourism: Limits and possibilities. *Annals of Tourism Research, 57*, 31–46. https://doi.org/10.1016/j.annals.2015.12.001

Williams, R. (2016). Radical politics, recent exhibitions, and utopianism now. *Science Fiction Studies, 43*(1), 183–187.

Xie, P. F., & Wall, G. (2008). Authenticating ethnic tourism attractions. In A. Fyall, B. Garrod, A. Leask & S. Wanhill (Eds.), *Managing visitor attractions: New directions* (pp. 132–147). Butterworth-Heinemann.

Zhang, H., Yang, Y., Zheng, C., & Zhang, J. (2016). Too dark to revisit? The role of past experiences and intrapersonal constraints. *Tourism Management, 54*, 452–464. https://doi.org/10.1016/j. tourman.2016.01.002

Summers of war. Affective volunteer tourism to former war sites in Europe

Siri Driessen 🆔

ABSTRACT

An important aspect of contemporary volunteer tourism is generated by the possibility of having personal, emotional and affective encounters and experiences. Volunteer summer camps on former war sites, organized by the German Action Reconciliation Service for Peace (ARSP), can be regarded as an expression of a contemporary form of tourism, which consists of the development of a personal, affective, and immersive approach to learning and volunteering on former war sites. A performative approach to studying emotion is applied, and helps to locate and understand the social, cultural, and political components that instigate the desire for affective volunteer tourism. For this study, 26 semi-structured in-depth interviews have been conducted with participants of ARSP volunteer summer camps that focused on conserving and maintaining former war sites in Italy, Lithuania, and France. The results indicate that volunteers expect war themed summer camps to be impactful (in terms of work) and emotional (in terms of personal experiences). Yet, the sought-after impact and emotion are not always found, which gives rise to contradictory feelings and tensions. Feelings of guilt about unmet expectations have caused volunteers to re-evaluate their motives and look for different ways to make the summer camps meaningful to them. Participants were encouraged to critically reflect, on this form of volunteer tourism in particular, and on societal debates about war and volunteer tourism in general.

摘要

当代志愿旅游的一个重要方面是有可能产生个人的、情绪的和情感的遭遇和经历。由德国和平行动调解服务处(ARSP)组织的在以往战场的志愿者夏令营, 可以被视为一种当代旅游形式的表现, 其中包括发展一种个人化的, 情感的, 沉浸式的方法, 在以往战场进行学习与志愿活动。本研究采用展演性方法来研究情感, 并帮助定位和理解激发情感性志愿旅游愿望的社会、文化和政治因素。为了这项研究, 对ARSP志愿者夏令营的参与者进行了26次半结构化的深入访谈, 重点访谈在意大利、立陶宛和法国以往战场的保护和维护活动。结果显示, 志愿者们期望以战争为主题的夏令营活动, 就工作来说具有冲击性, 就个人经历来说具有情感性。然而, 他们所追求的冲击和情感并不总能找到, 这就产生了矛盾的感觉和紧张感。没有达到预期的内疚感促使志愿者们重新评估自己的动机, 并寻找不同的方式使夏令营对他们有意义。本研究鼓励参与者不仅批判性地反思这种特定形式的志愿旅游, 而且还要更广泛地反思关于战争和志愿旅游的社会辩论。

Introduction

Every August, a group of volunteers travels to the wooded hills of Tuscany, Italy. Secluded between trees and bushes, they settle in a historical farmhouse where they work and live together for two weeks. The house is not only a monument to traditional Tuscan farm life, but also knows a more unsettling history. In March 1944, as an act of retribution, fascist forces from Siena captured and executed nineteen partisan fighters, who had taken shelter in the farmhouse. The volunteers who come here dedicate their time to preserving the memory of these events, by working on the maintenance of the memorial site, and by learning about its history. At the end of the two weeks, they will do the same in Sant'Anna di Stazzema, the village where Nazi German Waffen SS killed more than 500 villagers and refugees in 1944 (Di Pasquale, 2012). These killings served as revenge for the assumed support of the villagers to the Partisan resistance (Pezzino, 2012, p. 128). Here, the volunteers meet with survivors, historians and contemporary refugees, to connect the past to the present. As such, an important part of the summer camps consists of personal and direct contact with war history. By spending time on a former war site while doing physical work, meeting eyewitnesses, and scrutinizing violent histories, the volunteers develop a specific affective relationship with the site and its past.

Every year, volunteer summer camps like this one take place on various sites all over the world, like military cemeteries or war memorials. Volunteers of different ages and nationalities dedicate their free summer to work at places associated with war and death. Their work consists of maintaining monuments and war sites, cleaning, preserving and documenting cemeteries, or assisting war survivors with their daily chores. Most of the European summer camps are initiated by the Action Reconciliation Service for Peace (ARSP), a German organization with roots in the protestant peace movement and antifascist activism (Huener, 2001). Since the early 1960s, ARSP has been organizing volunteer projects, starting with one in Oświęcim (Auschwitz), Poland. Nowadays, around 25 summer camps take place each year, at locations such as St. Petersburg, Sarajevo, and Berlin. The costs of participation in these camps range from €40 to €130 for a two-week stay, depending on the participant's country of origin, and include food and excursions. The remaining costs are paid for by the ARSP, which is funded by different institutions and organizations: the church, the German government, the EU, international volunteering organizations, and by individual donations and contributions as well (Aktion Sühnezeichen Friedensdienste 2020). Compared to the traditional design of the ARSP summer camps, which focused on symbolic retribution and reconciliation, the current camps take a more international humanist perspective. Next to the manual work and leisure activities, the summer camps are dedicated to studying the past and discussing contemporary issues like migration, memory politics and right-wing extremism. Thus, their goal is to educate the participants about the effects and consequences of war and conflict in the past and present. This is done with work-shops, discussions, encounters with eyewitnesses and descendants of war victims, and by visits to memory sites. Although the camps are open to people of all ages and backgrounds, most of the participants and team leaders (who are involved in the creation of the daily program) are female European young adults. The camps can be regarded as an expression of a contemporary form of war tourism, which consists of the development of a personal, affective and immersive approach to visiting, learning and volunteering on former war sites (e.g. Buda, 2015).

Research on war-themed volunteer summer camps is limited. Besides Huener (2001), who discusses the ideology and politics of the ARSP from a top-down perspective, no recent studies have been conducted on this form of tourism. This raises questions about the present characteristics of the summer camps and their place within contemporary volunteer tourism to former war sites. Specifically, a bottom-up perspective could inform us about the way in which, nowadays, (young) European volunteer tourists engage with war history nowadays. Knowledge about volunteer tourism to former war sites helps to assess the potential value of war themed summer camps as a means for historical and civic education through personal, tangible, and emotional encounters with the past.

Whereas the emotional responses of day tourists to former war sites have recently been examined (Biran et al., 2011; Isaac et al., 2017; Nawijn & Fricke, 2015), less is known about tourists who spend a longer period at such places. In this article I will provide insight into the emotions and affects that are evoked through this immersive tourist experience. By focusing on the time spent at a site, the contact with tangible remnants of war, and the affective responses of the volunteers, I will discuss the often complex and contradictory emotions and affects related to this specific type of tourism. Debates about war and 'dark' tourism often have a moral and normative undertone that obscures deviant voices and experiences. By examining the personal experiences and emotions of volunteer tourists on war sites in-depth, I aim to give room to these experiences. Moreover, discussions about volunteer tourism often focus on the problematic dynamic of tourists from the global North who volunteer in the global South. Because these dynamics are less present in the ARSP summer camps, it is interesting to see which possible experiences of privilege, helping, or inequality arise in this specific case, and how these experiences affect the volunteers' self-image.

This paper contributes to empirical research on emotion and affect in both volunteer and war tourism. As such, this study adds to the emerging field of research that focuses on affective tourism to sites associated with war and conflict (cf. Buda, 2015). The theoretical contribution of this study lies with nuancing existing ideas about the nature of volunteer, 'dark', and war tourism. Also, it broadens the understanding of the appeal of auratic traces of the past. The study is based on 26 in-depth interviews with participants of three summer camps that took place in 2016 and 2017, in Italy, Lithuania, and France, and focused on conserving and maintaining former war sites. The camps were dedicated to different episodes of European war history: fascism and resistance in Italy, Jewish culture and the Holocaust in Lithuania, and migration in the Spanish civil war and the Second World War in the French-Spanish border area. What motivates participants to do volunteer work on former war sites? What kind of connection do they establish with the place and its history? Which emotions and affective experiences do they have, and how do these experiences relate to the development of a self-image?

Volunteer tourism: motivations and morality

Volunteer tourism is usually regarded as a popular form of 'alternative tourism' – a form of tourism that diverges from activities commonly associated with mass tourism (McIntosh & Zahra, 2007). Traditionally, the intention of 'alternative tourists' is explained as the urge to contribute to host countries and communities (Stoddart & Rogerson, 2004). As a sub-category of alternative tourism, volunteer tourism has been researched from various perspectives. Many studies focus on the motivations of the volunteers and the impact of the experience: why do they wish to volunteer abroad and what do they expect to obtain from their stay? The main motivations distinguished in these studies include the desire to contribute something somewhere (e.g. Conran, 2011; Koleth, 2014), the search for personal development and transformation (e.g. Wearing, 2001), the urge to learn, travel and have authentic experiences of a place (Sin, 2009) and even the convenience of an organized holiday (Sin, 2009).

The impact of the volunteer experience has been discussed from two angles: the impact of the experience on the volunteer, and the impact on locals and communities in the host countries (McGehee & Santos, 2005; Sin, 2010). The impact on the volunteers is mostly seen as positive: through volunteering, volunteers develop social awareness, work on their international network and adapt a more activist attitude in their home country (McGehee & Santos, 2005). Yet, some volunteer experiences are characterized by feelings of powerlessness, forcing the volunteers to invent new strategies to deal with witnessed misery (Gius, 2017). The impact of the presence of volunteers in host countries is more ambivalent: while some communities are positive about the attention they receive from volunteers, it is questionable whether their work contributes something in a sustainable manner (Sin, 2010). Wishes of the volunteers might clash with the needs of local communities, and in the selection of the places, albeit well intended, volunteers are inclined to move to the places that they think are the most in need, thereby leaving out other sites (Sin, 2010).

Some scholars regard volunteer tourism as a neoliberal phenomenon in which power hierarchies are reinforced and where the volunteer work becomes a commodified, neoliberal experience (Burrai et al., 2017; Conran, 2011; Germann Molz, 2017; Mostafanezhad, 2013). Other scholars argue for a related research perspective in which volunteer tourism, and especially its relationship with gender, 'race', and religion, is seen as an exponent of broader political, historical and cultural developments and discourses (Bandyopadhyay & Patil, 2017). Yet, these perspectives have been criticized by some for being too normative or deterministic (Everingham, 2016). Everingham adopts a 'hopeful' approach to studying volunteer tourism, an approach in which the complexities, ambiguities and deviant experiences of volunteer tourism are recognized (p. 521, 523, 525). This call for more focus on individual, deviant and ambiguous touristic experiences is significant, as the exploration of possibilities, hopes, and imagination might open up new perspectives in tourism studies (Pritchard et al., 2011). Still, the critical and hopeful approaches are not direct opposites, they may, in my opinion, strengthen each other when investigating the diverse experiences of volunteer tourists.

Affective volunteer tourism to former war sites

Contemporary volunteer tourism is generated by the possibility of having personal, emotional and affective encounters and experiences. Volunteer tourists are eager to undergo emotional experiences in order to provoke personal growth (Germann Molz, 2017). By putting themselves in situations that are designed for intimate encounters (Conran, 2011) and even cathartic responses (McIntosh & Zahra, 2007), volunteer tourists hope to build on their personality and gain 'emotional capital' (Germann Molz, 2017, p. 340). Yet, these experiences predominantly apply to encounters with people, pain, or poverty in the global South. When thinking about confrontations with remnants of war and violence, different affects, emotions and experiences are at play. Nevertheless, visits to places associated with war and violence are often emotional (Martini & Buda, 2020; Nawijn et al., 2016). As such, the combination of volunteer and war tourism presents a relevant case for researching affect and emotion in tourism.

Koleth (2014) discusses the affective responses of volunteer tourists who visited Cambodia's war heritage. These trips served as excursions for the volunteers who were working on activities like teaching and medicine. The confrontation with physical traces of horrific events caused the volunteers to develop a different attitude toward their work in Cambodia. Their initial idealism, roughly defined as 'I want to contribute to a better world', changed into a more immersed and realistic attitude, in which the limitations of volunteers' capacities to contribute to that better world were also included (Koleth, 2014, p. 688). In this way, confrontations with tangible war history affected the volunteers' perspective on their work and self-image.

In the last decade, various researchers have studied the emotional responses of day tourists to former war sites. In their work on visitors to Auschwitz, Biran, Poria and Oren state that aspirations for emotional experiences formed a key part of the motivations of the tourists to visit the site, next to the desire to be educated (2011, p. 836). Nawijn and Fricke (2015) investigated the 'positive' and 'negative' emotional responses of visitors to the Neuengamme concentration camp memorial, and found that the 'negative' emotions (shock, sadness, anger) overshadowed the positive ones (fascination and positive surprise). 'Negative' emotions were also felt more intensely (p. 226). Although such a binary division of positive and negative emotions is questionable – feeling sad is not necessarily something negative – their study did find that day tourists were content with their visit, despite the 'negative' emotional experiences (p. 226). These results expose the complexity and ambiguity of emotional experiences undergone at former war sites, as well as the subjectivity of interpreting emotional experiences.

Studies like these illustrate that the desire to be affected is an important part of the volunteer and war tourists' motivation to visit a site. Yet, much remains unclear about the way these affective experiences are formed. Do tangible war sites indeed 'impress' feelings on their visitors (Buda et al., 2014, p. 108), or is affect rather created in the open-ended encounter between tourist and site (Everingham, 2016, p. 525)? In what ways do previous experiences and socio-cultural contexts shape tourists' affective responses? Where earlier studies tend to concentrate on the experiences of day tourists, in this paper my focus is on tourists who spend a significant period of time on former war sites. In this way, I intend to get a better understanding of the processes underlying these tourist experiences.

A discussion of affective volunteer tourism to former war sites brings up questions about terminology. These visits are often framed as a form of 'dark tourism' (Foley & Lennon, 1996). Tourism to sites related to twentieth-century conflicts, in particular, is studied from the perspective of 'dark tourism' (Light, 2017, p. 280). This has resulted in a large number of quite similar case studies about tourism to 'dark' locations (Light, 2017). Despite the popularity of the concept, its applicability has been questioned (e.g. Biran et al., 2011; Dunkley et al., 2011). Critiques of the concept include its lack of theoretical substantiation, its assumptions about the sensationalist and voyeuristic attraction of death and disaster, its minor differences from 'heritage tourism', and its normativity (Light, 2017). For these reasons, I will refer to 'war tourism'; although this is a rather descriptive concept, it allows me to explore a wider range of (emotional) experiences than the typical 'dark' tourist ones, which are framed by the morbid attraction of everything that is assumed to be 'dark'.

Conceptualizing affect and emotion

The recent 'affective turn' in tourism studies has brought forward a cluster of research that focuses on the emotional and affective responses of visitors to former war sites, some of which has been discussed above. Emotion and affect have only recently been included in tourism research, and applicable theories of emotion and affect are in development (Buda, 2015, pp. 25–29; Martini & Buda, 2020). When discussing affect and emotion in tourism, scholars rely on studies done within a broad range of scientific fields, such as critical theory, feminist studies, geography, psychology or neuroscience. A main point for discussion is the difference between affect and emotion. While some scholars see little need to differentiate between affect and emotion (see Gorton, 2007, p. 334), others underline the necessity of separating the two notions (Massumi, 1995, p. 88). Massumi regards affect as an 'intensity', while emotion serves as a 'qualified intensity'. In his view, 'affect' is abstract and autonomous, while 'emotion' refers to affect in its cultivated, subjective state (p. 88). Massumi's approach to affect and emotion can be associated with a Deleuzian perspective on affect, in which affect involves a certain transition from one phase to another. Here, affect is also seen as an intensity, yet an intensity that takes form in movement (Thrift, 2009, p. 83). Affect thereby pertains to impersonal and unexpressed experiences – that are nevertheless corporeal – while emotions can be regarded as the personal, social and cultural expressions of these experiences (see Probyn, as quoted in Gorton, 2007).

Instead of concentrating on the exact differences between the notions of affect and emotions, other scholars study emotions and affect from a performative point of view. Ahmed famously argued for asking 'what emotions do, instead of what they are' (Ahmed, 2004, p. 4). In her work, Ahmed not only emphasizes the quality of emotions as cultural practices, which are shaped in contact with others (p. 10), but also dis-cusses how hierarchy, power and privilege are inherent to the possibility of being emotional (pp. 2–4). As such, they have the power to in- and exclude (groups of) peo-ple. In a similar way, Berlant takes on a performative approach to studying collective, social and political manifestations of affect. In her work on compassion, she defines the term compassion as 'an emotion in operation' (Berlant, 2004, p. 4). This approach to defining compassion does allow us to ask what compassion does, how it operates within power structures, and how it manifests itself within different contexts. Thus, the attention Ahmed and Berlant pay to the performative quality of emotions assists in conceptualizing emotions as situated and cultivated practices that are constituted by power relations and social discourses.

I look at the aforementioned popularity of experience oriented, emotional and affective volunteer tourism in the light of these arguments. When considering volun-teer tourism to former war sites as an expression of a contemporary desire to be touched, a performative approach to studying emotion and affect helps to locate and understand the social, cultural and political components that instigate this desire. By focusing on what emotions 'do', it becomes possible to address their performative qualities on different levels. We can explore the ways in which emotions are shaped and reshaped during touristic encounters, and to deepen the understanding of emo-tion and affect as experienced in the specific socio-cultural setting of the volunteer summer camps.

Methods

This study is based on data obtained in interviews and during participant observation conducted during three volunteer summer camps: one in Lithuania (2016), one in France (2017) and one in Italy (2017). I joined the 2017 camps, while a research assist-ant participated in the 2016 camp. Both of us signed up as participants and joined all activities. During our weeklong stay, we conducted semi-structured, in-depth inter-views with 26 participants, including the team leaders. We wrote down field notes, and had many more informal conversations. The three summer camps were selected because of their content and their variety in terms of location. This has resulted in a diverse sample in which the chosen camps address different facets of war: Jewish cul-ture and the Holocaust in Lithuania; migration and refugees in France; ideology and violence in Italy.

The Lithuanian summer camp took place in Švenčionys, a small town on the north-east border with Belarus. During the Second World War, Nazi German troops built a ghetto in the town, where they captured and killed the Jewish residents living in the area, or transported them to extermination camps. This resulted in the deaths of thou-sands of Jewish persons in the area (Arad, 2009). One of the remnants of the former presence of the Jewish community is an 18th-century cemetery that can be found at the edge of Švenčionys. Yet, the cemetery is neglected and now and then vandalized. ARSP volunteers spent two weeks at the cemetery, cleaning the vegetation off the tombstones and documenting the names of the deceased. According to Jewish burial tradition, the overgrown tombstones cannot be moved and are left to nature, which evokes a romantic atmosphere.

In France, volunteers stayed at a 12th century monumental priory in the eastern Pyrenees. Under the guidance of a specialist, they worked on the dry-stone walls that protect the monument, by first dissecting the old and collapsed walls, and then rebuilding them. Whereas the volunteer work in Lithuania was directly connected to the place we stayed at, this was different in France, as the priory did not have a clear connection with refugees of either the Spanish civil war or of the Second World War. Still, the connection with history was sought by hiking along routes in the mountainous area that had been used by refugees.

The Italian summer camp took place at two different sites in Tuscany. The first site was the aforementioned old farmhouse, not far from Siena, which was used as a partisan shelter during the Second World War. Nowadays, the house serves as a monument to the partisans who were captured and executed by the fascist militia. During the summer camp the volunteers worked on the preservation of the house by doing light manual work. The second site was the village of Sant'Anna di Stazzema, where volunteers studied the history of the village and met with Italian relatives of the victims of the Waffen SS.

All interviews took place during the summer camps, had an average duration of 45 minutes, and were conducted in English. The participants could choose the location of the interview. In this way, we were able to interview in a setting that was comfortable for the interviewee. Meanwhile, this also allowed us to speak about the motivation for selecting a specific place, which generated knowledge about the reasons for feeling at ease on specific spots on site. The interviews were based on an interview guide that contained questions about the motivation to join a summer camp, expectations, the meaning of the (local) historical events to the participants, working with tangible history, emotional responses, as well as the personal developments that took place during the camp. Semi-structured interviewing allows for flexibility while at the same time preserving the coverage of all designated topics (Kvale & Brinkmann, 2007). Such flexibility was necessary in order to adapt to the different phases the volunteers were in: from a more forward-looking perspective during the first days of the camps to a more reflective stance during the later days.

All 26 interviews have been recorded and transcribed verbatim. All participants have consented to collaborate in this study, and the project was approved by the ethics committee. The persons who wished to preserve their anonymity were assigned a pseudonym. I have analyzed transcripts and field notes with an inductive thematic approach (Braun & Clarke, 2006). Through different rounds of open and selective coding, four different themes have been found, that I will elaborate on below. During the analysis, specific attention has been paid to deviating voices, by contrasting individual stories to existing narratives of war and volunteer tourism.

Unavoidably, this study knows limitations. English was not the native language of any of the interviewees, nor of the interviewers, who are Dutch and Moldovan. Though the interviewees' level of English differed, most of them were able to express themselves well. Still, two of the interviewees mentioned at the end of the interview that they would have liked to tell more, but had been unable to, because of the language barrier. While our presence during the summer camps provided us with a frame of reference that allowed us to partially overcome these language issues, the interview answers should be regarded as being produced in a setting that is neither a reflection of daily life nor a completely artificial setting (Michael, 2017, p. 35). The interviewees were primarily highly educated German women in their twenties. Although this demographic is similar to the population of the ARSP summer camps, the results have to be read with this in mind. Additionally, our presence during the camps and our openness about our purposes might have influenced the group dynamics. However, there are many benefits to such an immersive approach: it is not only easier to interview in the setting of the camps and get back to specific topics at a later moment, but it also facilitates observation of whether the interviewees' attitude and behavior during the camp matched their answers. Most importantly, by participating in the camp, we gained an atmosphere of trust and mutual understanding that was beneficial when speaking about difficult topics.

Motivations, attitudes, and (moral) responses

When looking at the motivations of summer camp volunteers, two types of volunteers can be discerned. The majority of the participants signs up for the camp because of an interest in history, but without any specific concern for the country or the wartime event. For them, the camp's value lies in increasing their historical knowledge, in meeting new people, and in doing something good in general. Then, there is a smaller group of people with a specific interest in the history of the site. Most of these volunteers have had earlier experiences with working on former war sites and memorials, either by participating in a previous summer camp or by engaging in a long-term volunteer project.

An important part of the motivation to join a volunteer summer camp is formed by the desire to have an impact, to contribute something of value to a society or community. During the interviews, this desire to have an impact through volunteer work surfaced often. Working hard and doing important work was a main incentive for all participants. This echoes the results of earlier studies on volunteer tourism (e.g. Conran, 2011; Koleth, 2014). Some interviewees also regard the reactions of the communities they are supporting as a valuable aspect of their work. Yet, not everyone spoke about such need for recognition. Maike talked about the way in which she dealt with her initial urge to focus on personal achievements during the work:

> And for example at first I, kind of stupid but I ... The first three or four stones I cleaned, I actually counted them, and then I was like 'Wait, that's absolutely not what it's about', like saying that I cleaned like 150 gravestones or anything, and I was just like 'No, that would make it, like kind of a proud or self-righteous thing, a bit'. So, at some point I was like 'No, I don't ... that's not how I want to do it, I want to be here and do this work and be here in the moment'. (Maike, 25, Germany)

Maike's remark contains a question that many of the volunteers struggled with: what attitude should you adopt as a volunteer? Should you focus on doing hard and impactful work, on the effect the work has on others, or is it better to focus on your personal state of mind? These questions about attitude are coming from conflicting expectations about the impact of the work and disappointment about the actual amount and quality (Gius, 2017). Many participants had higher expectations, both in terms of impact and in terms of the time spent on the volunteer work. For Miri, the limited possibility to work during the summer camp even resulted in feelings of guilt:

> I don't feel like, that's one thing I'm not feeling good about, that I don't work that much, (.) and also I get food, and I can stay here for free, and I don't feel that I'm giving enough back. (Miri, 22, Germany)

Miri clearly worried about the idea of reciprocity. She wanted to do something in return for her stay in Italy, but has no insight into the way the ARSP pays for the stay of the volunteers. Other participants, too, mentioned that they would have liked to work more, so as to feel better about their cheap stay. Interestingly, where doing volunteer work is sometimes seen as a way to deal with feelings of guilt about experienced privilege (Germann Molz, 2017), involvement in an ARSP summer camp did not resolve such guilt. Instead, participation made the volunteers conscious of the commodified character of the summer camps and volunteer work in general. Such consciousness caused discomfort with the experience as a whole. This discomfort was strengthened by feelings of uneasiness about the nature of war tourism (see Gius, 2017, p. 1626). When participants experienced that the logic of giving and paying back did not work out for them, they were confronted with their position as war tourists, and the societal discourse of sensationalism and voyeurism that surrounds this form of tourism (Buda & McIntosh, 2013). Additionally, feelings of disappointment and guilt were reinforced by the original aim of the ARSP to have German volunteers doing work on war sites affected by Nazi-German aggression as a symbolic means of reconciliation and reparation: when confronted with the futile character of such reparations, participants feel powerless. Moreover, for some of the volunteers, a general sense of shame and guilt about Germany's war history played a role as well.

Still, feelings of disappointment and guilt did not cause the volunteers to turn away from the summer camps. Instead, such feelings made participants re-evaluate their initial expectations, adjust attitudes, and search for different ways to make the camp relevant to them. Gius (2017) names three strategies for the re-evaluation and legitimization of a volunteers' presence abroad: 'the sympathetic response', 'the overturn' and 'taking charge'. The 'sympathetic response' implies a focus on the establishment of emotional relationships with communities and the gratitude of these communities toward the volunteers. This sympathetic response is visible in the volunteers who emphasize the gratitude of local communities. The 'overturn' and the 'taking charge' strategies entail a shift in focus to the volunteers' personal development and agency, either through emotional growth (e.g. Germann Molz, 2017; McIntosh & Zahra, 2007), or by employing a more activist attitude in the home country (e.g. McGehee & Santos, 2005). In both cases, the volunteers have accepted their position as spectators of suffering (Gius, 2017, p. 1627). In the case of the summer camp volunteers, these strategies are discernible too, but with a stronger focus on increasing one's historical knowledge and the search for personal connections with the past.

Personal connections and identification

Besides the manual work, an important part of the summer camps is dedicated to studying the (war) history of the sites the volunteers visit and stay at. As mentioned, many participants join the camps because of a general interest in history. Yet, some volunteers said that their personal background had also influenced their motivation to join. Franziska, for example, a 29-year old German volunteer, explained her interest in war history as rooted in frustrations about the nonpolitical household that she grew up in. Because of the absence of a political attitude within her family, Franziska has assigned herself with the task of paying attention to the life stories of others. It is not only important for Franziska to do volunteer work on war heritage sites, but also to pass her story on to people who come from a similar situation and show them that it is possible to disengage from one's background. In doing so, she articulates a moral understanding of the volunteer experience (Burrai et al., 2017).

For many participants, such a connection between one's personal background and the history of a country or region shaped their experience of the summer camp. Obviously, because of the different backgrounds of the participants, the way this connection is sought for and established differs, and ranges from highly political or activist to more imaginary. In some cases, however, identification with historical events also caused tensions. Some volunteers explicitly mention that they experienced difficulties with their identification as German citizens and the history of the Second World War. They indicated that their choice to join a summer camp about Italian fascism was rooted in the desire to not be confronted with their German background in any explicit way. As Lisa told the interviewer:

> Yeah, I think that's the reason, it's overwhelming and here [in Italy] you can deal with it, and you're not personally affected. In a way, you are personally affected when you are German and going to Auschwitz, in a way. You are, you know? (.) I think I could never stand to go to Auschwitz, actually, because I don't know, I just, I'd just cry all the time actually. I don't know that it would deepen my knowledge of this history. (Lisa, 27, Germany)

Where a visit to Auschwitz would only result in an overwhelming yet unproductive emotional experience, studying fascism from an Italian point of view allowed her to distance herself. Hence, where for some of the participants a connection with their (national) past served as a means to make studying the past relevant to them and 'take charge', others expect to experience such a connection as being too confronting. For them, visiting war crime sites as a citizen of the perpetrating country is seen as too burdensome. This exposes an interesting dynamic in relation to what Boltanski (1999) has called 'distant suffering' – the assumed (mediatized) attraction of the simple, far-away suffering of others. A similar logic is often found in 'dark tourism' research (e.g. Stone, 2009). Yet, such logic does not seem to apply here. On the one hand, Lisa indeed seems to be looking for an impersonal confrontation with war history. On the other hand, this confrontation is her only way to deal with her national background and (learned) feelings of guilt. Rather than being 'attracted' by the suffering of others, learning about this suffering allows her to access and reflect on her personal situation. Here, less personal emotional responses to confrontations with war history seem to be more productive than the very personal and overwhelming ones. As such, here we could see the difference between the desire for an emotional response and an affective response to visiting a former war site.

Experiencing sites of conflict

Identification with past events functions as a means to make the volunteering and the study of the past more relevant to the participants. Yet, staying on a tangible war site also gives rise to specific experiences. Places associated with war and conflicts are thought to impress specific experiences on their visitors (Buda et al., 2014). The confrontation with material and 'authentic' traces of the past is thereby seen as auratic (Jones, 2010, p. 189). Seeing and touching material remnants of the past, with all their references to earlier times and users, causes people to establish personal relationships with those remnants and the networks they belong to (p. 181). As such, material objects serve as points of connection within larger networks that help persons to reflect on themselves. Furthermore, auratic experiences of 'authenticity' are closely connected to affect (Carter, 2019). Visitors are inclined to be affected by auratic experiences of places, objects, or people: through these experiences, long-lasting memories of places and encounters are created (p. 312). Hence, on-site experiences and emotions are created in a negotiation between the site, its network, and the visitor, and have the potential to create long-lasting memories of specific places and encounters.

According to all interviewees, staying on a tangible site provided something extra to their experience and increased their knowledge about the past, precisely because of the physical closeness of the past. Again, the proximity of historical traces allows for making war history more personal, emotional, and memorable. Jacob explained how this worked for him:

> Yeah, you know, and you feel somehow... people are buried here and they're... all of them have a history and personality and it's not just a number... Like, usually when you read about the Holocaust it's just numbers... So you have one grave – that's one person, that's one life... So, for example, this cemetery has around, like, 2000 tomb stones, and in comparison to the numbers you normally hear, it's quite a small number. But if you're at the cemetery and see that it's a big area, territory, you... you... it's more individual. (Jacob, 22, Germany)

Many interviewees had experiences similar to those of Jacob. Contact with physical traces of the past caused them to think about individuals who lived in the past and 'feel' their presence. Traces of their lives, such as a name on a gravestone, thereby function as triggers of their imagination. Even volunteers who were located on sites with fewer historical traces were present still felt encouraged to use their imagination. For instance, the summer camp in France took place in a 12th century priory, yet this specific site had nothing to do with refugees in the Spanish civil war and the Second World War, the topics of the camp. Here, it was only an indistinct mountainous landscape that referred to refugee routes in those wars. Lisa, a 20-year-old German student, talked about how she was still able to imagine the past on this site:

> Even though you don't see anything at all, it's just the imagination that makes you understand a little more what this, the people's situation was... (Lisa, 20, Germany)

Like Lisa, many interviewees were convinced that a visit to a former war site makes the past more real and more understandable. This image of the past is mainly about obtaining information that is not present in a history book, details that seem too unimportant or too common to write about. By seeing the consequences of past violence, it is easier to believe that such violence took place. Importantly, it is not only seeing these consequences that matters, but also feeling them. Desislava explained:

> We visited Sant'Anna, the city that's been burnt down, where everyone was killed and so on. And you go and you see it with your own eyes, because even now people aren't living there. There are not, not some, it's like a dead city. And then you see what it really means that everyone was killed, because if so many people have been killed it doesn't matter how many years ago, still – like, it's empty. You get the feeling. (Desislava, 22, Bulgaria)

In Desislava's account, a corporeal understanding of the events at Sant'Anna is present. This understanding is not directed at the committed crimes, but rather at the consequences of these crimes. By visiting a village that still breathes a feeling of violence because of its emptiness, Desislava affectively understood what happened to the place. The time spent on site plays a role in this: by gradually learning about a place, and by discovering more and more details on site, the past becomes more real, and, as a consequence, more emotional. As such, an affective relationship with the past is developed in phases, and new layers of emotions, feelings, reflections, and memories are continuously added to the experience.

Encounters with physical remnants of the past 'do' something to their visitors. They work on their imagination, even if those remnants are mainly geographical, and help them to understand and remember specific histories better. The shared belief in the fact that physical remnants contain traces to a more realistic past is fascinating. Lisa's description of how an indistinct landscape triggered her historical imagination illustrates that, at least in her case, not many historical remnants are needed to invoke an image of the past. Here, it is rather a series of personal and cultivated associations that make up this image of the past (Jones, 2010). Auratic experiences seem less important, at least for Lisa. Still, this does not undermine the (affective) power of seeing and feeling the consequences of war and violence on site – for many other volunteers, the encounters with auratic traces of the past were, indeed, powerful and affective. An important factor that impacts the experience of the volunteers is the period of time spent on a war site. By being confronted with the same site for a long(er) period than a few hours, the emotional and affective responses of the volunteers become more layered. Importantly, such a longer period of time spent on site sometimes also results in the development of more contradictory experiences. As we will see in the next section, this also has consequences for the volunteers' behavior during the summer camp and their reflection on their experiences.

Feeling (un)touched

One of the reasons participants join war themed summer camps is to search for emotional experiences. They want to be touched by stories about events that occurred in the past. This desire for affective experiences was noticeable, for example, in the way in which some of the participants reflected on the historical explanations we obtained. They emphasized that these explanations were nice but it did not make them 'feel' anything, even though they were expressed on the site where the historical events took place. The way participants spoke about encounters that were more personal, such as meeting different eyewitnesses and survivors of the Second World War, revealed that they valued these experiences the most, precisely because they said to have 'felt' something. The same goes for visits to places of extreme violence, like the Rivesaltes transit camp in France or the village of Sant'Anna di Stazzema in Italy. Sites with strong symbolic meaning were also said to be highly affective. Hence, for the participants, 'feeling' something is a key element in the evaluation of their experience, and such feelings are more easily obtained through personal encounters and confrontations with traces of and references to extreme violence.

When speaking about their affective responses to the places visited during the summer camps, interviewees often referred to earlier visits to other former war sites, with which they could compare their experience. Especially the German participants had been on quite a number of school visits. Miri spoke about how a trip to the former Stasi prison Hohenschönhausen in Berlin had affected her in a physical way:

> We went there and it was horrible, it was like the worst place I've ever been to. I felt it [emphasis on felt], I felt it like everything in me like froze and wanted kind of like I wanted to make myself short and small, and I was in a really horrible setting, there was nothing horrible anymore there, sure there were the buildings, but they didn't, there was nobody like actually doing me any harm, but it felt like somebody would do that at the moment. I was scared it would happen like any second, and it was so bad that I actually had to leave and take a break. (Miri, 22, Germany)

Miri's description of the disturbing experience she had in Hohenschönhausen is a clear example of the bodily quality of affect, in this case in a quite literal sense, as Miri even felt she wanted to make herself small. Franziska, who took part in multiple summer camps, talked in a related way about how tremendously the Jewish cemetery she had to work on scared her. Yet, by returning to a similar cemetery years later, she had also experienced that her anxiety to work on such a site had disappeared:

> I've, I've had different phases, let's say … Like four years back, I'd be anxious about going to the cemetery, because it would confront me with death … And I hated that. (.) After one day or two, we ended up not working on the cemetery, but in their garden … I was so, so incredibly relieved about that, you can't imagine … (.) And last year, it kind of changed, last year I… It was such a beautiful work, we were such a nice team, so I was like sitting quietly on that cemetery, I would be like listening to music all the time, painting all day long… (.) It gave me like a really peaceful feeling being on the cemetery, so I kind of lost all the anxiety I had before … (Franziska, 29, Germany)

Hence, for Franziska, her repeated presence on a cemetery made her to get used to being close to references to death and dying, and made her develop an attitude that allowed her to feel relaxed and peaceful. Again, the development of an affective relation with the work and the place here occurred here in phases, and emotions changed because of earlier emotions. Importantly, Franziska mentioned the nice team that she was part of during the second time she volunteered at a cemetery. Here, the attitude and emotional state of other members of the group volunteers had an impact on how she felt on the cemetery and gave her a positive experience. Hence, group dynamics make up a significant part of the volunteer experience. Thus, while auratic experiences of the past are important to the volunteers, group dynamics have an equally important impact on the volunteer experience. Daniele, a 29-year-old volunteer from Italy, explicitly alluded to the fact that group processes play a role in the way emotions are transmitted on site:

> Yeah, if you, if you go there, if you see where it happened … And it's important to do this experience in a group, I think that it can contribute to the transmission of emotion … (Daniele, 29, Italy)

Daniele was convinced that being in a group helps in getting feelings across, and as such, making those feelings more intense. Moreover, Daniele regarded being emotional as something valuable, something that you want to happen. Yet, while Daniele had no difficulty feeling it affected, others had much more problems with this, in which on might distinguish a mechanism of in- and exclusion (Buda et al., 2014). From my own observation, mentioning not to feel involved or affected incited negative judgment by some of the group members. Noteworthy, Miri, who was so impressed by her visit to the former Stasi prison, told me she had not felt much during the summer camp. Realizing that she was not affected as much as she had expected even troubled her at night:

> On the second night [of the summer camp] I couldn't sleep well, because I thought about that, well, because it didn't bother me at all, and I kind of feel that because I expected to be feeling bad about it, and that was what was keeping me awake, because I kind of wanted it to bother me, but it didn't. (Miri, 22, Germany)

Worries about not feeling affected were present in the accounts of other interviewees too. While they expected to feel a great deal during the summer camp, reality was different. Some of the German volunteers mentioned that they felt extremely numb earlier on, due to their extensive German education about the Second World War, which had saturated them with historical information. Nele even related this saturation to her desire to learn about that war in a different, more personal way during the summer camp in Italy:

> I don't know whether it's maybe because it doesn't seem to be so cruel in, in comparison to other things that happened in the World War. Or just, I mean, I heard a lot about some massacres and stuff in school, and also afterwards … It's maybe not that sensitive to me anymore. And then I thought maybe when I come here and see the places, that will change. But it, it doesn't seem like it's really here. I don't know, it, it doesn't seem to be very close. (Nele, 21, Germany)

Miri's and Nele's remarks about feeling untouched concerned the first week of the Italian summer camp, when the places associated with mass atrocity, such as the village of Sant'Anna, had not yet been visited. Still, their accounts reveal their struggle to deal with their unmet expectations. This struggle was confronting to them, as it gave rise once more to questions about their motivation and guilt about their incapacity to relate to 'smaller' histories of violence and death, histories less saturated with recognizable symbolic references to war and violence. Here, the unbalance in the dynamics of giving and taking as formed by the experience of volunteering on a former war site seems to be resurfacing, yet this time concentrating on absent emotional responses. As a consequence, a self-judgment is distinguishable, related to the preferred (or imposed) reaction to being part of a war themed summer camp. However, as was the case with the question of the desired impact of the work, the inner debates also caused some volunteers to reevaluate their motivation, adjust their attitude, and shift their focus (e.g. Gius, 2017; Koleth, 2014). Such shifts in focus took the form of obtaining historical knowledge and focusing on the beauty of a site, separated from its history. This resulted, for example, in lyrical descriptions of the Lithuanian cemetery as beautiful, magical, or romantic, or in developing a caring relationship with the partisan refuge in Italy. In this way, the volunteers were able to create a more layered narrative about the sites and their experience of the summer camp. Here, we see the impact of a longer stay on a former war site. By having the time to explore, reflect, and re-evaluate one's expectations and experiences, different stories are created – stories that surpass the traditional narrative of the 'dark' or war tourist.

Conclusion

In this article, I have discussed the motivations, expectations and emotional experiences of volunteer tourists who participated in war-themed summer camps at different European locations. I focused on the different forms and outcomes of emotion and affect, as generated within a specific socio-cultural context. As argued, volunteers join war-themed summer camps in search of emotional experiences. They hope to find these experiences by employing a personal, embodied and located approach to studying the past. The ARSP summer camps provide a framework for combining this urge for emotional experiences with the possibility to do something in return: volunteer work. In this way, participants can symbolically pay for their stay, education, and experiences. The unmet expectations about the impact of the volunteer work reveal that for a part of the participants, this logic of a symbolic payback did not work out. Still, witnessing the limited impact of the work did something to the participants: it made them re-evaluate their motives and expectations, and made them think critically about this form of volunteer tourism. Volunteers found new ways to relate to volunteering after having witnessed places of (former) suffering, either by becoming more realistic in their expectations about having a significant impact, or by shifting their attention to their personal development and identity building. This is in line with the findings of Gius (2017) and Koleth (2014).

With regards to the sought emotional experiences, a similar process took place. Once volunteers realized that they remained untouched by a local history, they began to deliberate on their urge to be affected and started to look for different ways to make the summer camp meaningful to them. In both cases, confrontations with unfulfilled expectations and desires could be regarded as moments of personal growth, and in that sense, as a positive consequence of the volunteer tourist experience. Still, not everyone wants to be overwhelmed by war history: sometimes, distancing oneself from one's personal and socio-cultural background is more productive. Here, we see a difference between the desire to be emotionally touched and the desire to be affected.

Auratic experiences of place are closely linked to affect (Carter, 2019). And indeed, the volunteers regarded the tangible encounters with traces of war as an opportunity to be affected or emotionally touched. This research indicates that personal expectations, cultural codes, the design of the site, as well as group dynamics play an important role in the volunteers' emotional experiences. Hence, research about affect and emotion needs to take these dynamics into account. Moreover, studies on visitors to former war sites predominantly discuss day tourists who only spend a few hours on site (e.g. Biran et al., 2011). This study shows that the time spent on site has a considerable impact on the tourist experience; thus, it is an important factor in research on tourists' emotional and affective responses.

This study includes a limited number of summer camps organized by a single German organization. To gain a better understanding about this particular type of tourism, further research should focus specifically on its relation to emotion and affect. Longitudinal research would be necessary to gain more insight into the impact of the summer camps on the lives of the volunteers, their self-image, and their experiences of privilege. In addition, studies about the influence of the presence of volunteers on local (mnemonic) communities could add to the understanding of the impact of the summer camps on a local level. As experienced emotions are dependent on the cultural background of the participants, it would be interesting to conduct this research in different cultural settings.

A focus on 'what emotions do' makes it possible to expose various and deviant experiences of volunteer and war tourism. By paying attention to the processes that underlie individual tourist experiences, the opportunity arises to explore the changes, complexities, and ambiguities of emotional and affective experiences on former war sites.

Acknowledgements

The research reported here has received funding from the Erasmus University Rotterdam under the Research Excellence Initiative program, 'War! Popular culture and European heritage of major armed conflicts'. The author would like to thank all interviewees for their cooperation. Special thanks to Victoria Balan for assisting with the fieldwork. Thanks to Stijn Reijnders and Maria Grever for their supervision of this project. Thanks to the reviewers for their useful comments to this paper.

Disclosure statement

No potential conflict of interest was reported by the author.

ORCID

Siri Driessen http://orcid.org/0000-0002-6778-8977

References

Ahmed, S. (2004). *The cultural politics of emotion*. Edinburgh University Press.

Aktion Sühnezeichen Friedensdienste. (2020). Finanzierung. Retrieved September 14, 2020, from https://www.asf-ev.de/ueber-uns/organisation/finanzierung/

Arad, Y. (2009). *The Holocaust in the Soviet Union*. University of Nebraska Press; Yad Vashem.

Bandyopadhyay, R., & Patil, V. (2017). 'The white woman's burden' – The racialized, gendered politics of volunteer tourism. *Tourism Geographies*, *19*(4), 644–657. https://doi.org/10.1080/14616688.2017.1298150

Berlant, L. (2004). Compassion (and withholding). In L. Berlant (Ed.), *Compassion: The culture and politics of an emotion*. Routledge.

Biran, A., Poria, Y., & Oren, G. (2011). Sought experiences at (dark) heritage sites. *Annals of Tourism Research*, *38*(3), 820–841. https://doi.org/10.1016/j.annals.2010.12.001

Boltanski, L. (1999). *Distant suffering: Morality, media, and politics*. Cambridge University Press.

Braun, V., & Clarke, V. (2006). Using thematic analysis in psychology. *Qualitative Research in Psychology*, *3*(2), 77–101. https://doi.org/10.1191/1478088706qp063oa

Buda, D. M. (2015). *Affective tourism: Dark routes in conflict*. Routledge.

Buda, D. M., d'Hauteserre, A.-M., & Johnston, L. (2014). Feeling and tourism studies. *Annals of Tourism Research*, *46*, 102–114. https://doi.org/10.1016/j.annals.2014.03.005

Buda, D. M., & McIntosh, A. J. (2013). Dark tourism and voyeurism: Tourist arrested for 'spying' in Iran. *International Journal of Culture, Tourism and Hospitality Research*, *7*(3), 214–226. https://doi.org/10.1108/IJCTHR-07-2012-0059

Burrai, E., Mostafanezhad, M., & Hannam, K. (2017). Moral assemblages of volunteer tourism development in Cusco, Peru. *Tourism Geographies*, *19*(3), 362–377. https://doi.org/10.1080/14616688.2016.1236145

Conran, M. (2011). 'They really love me!' Intimacy in volunteer tourism. *Annals of Tourism Research*, *38*(4), 1454–1473. https://doi.org/10.1016/j.annals.2011.03.014

Carter, P. L. (2019). Looking for something real: Affective encounters. *Annals of Tourism Research*, *76*, 200–213. https://doi.org/10.1016/j.annals.2019.04.004

Di Pasquale, C. (2012). Massacre, trial and 'choral memory' in Sant'Anna di Stazzema, Italy (1944–2005). International Journal of Transitional Justice, *6*(3), 486–501. https://doi.org/10.1093/ijtj/ijs025

Dunkley, R., Morgan, N., & Westwood, S. (2011). Visiting the trenches: Exploring meanings and motivations in battlefield tourism. *Tourism Management*, *32*(4), 860–868. https://doi.org/10.1016/j.tourman.2010.07.011

Everingham, P. (2016). Hopeful possibilities in spaces of 'the-not-yet- become': Relational encounters in volunteer tourism. *Tourism Geographies*, *18*(5), 520–538. https://doi.org/10.1080/14616688.2016.1220974

Foley, M., & Lennon, J. (1996). JFK and dark tourism: A fascination with assassination. *International Journal of Heritage Studies*, *2*(4), 198–211. https://doi.org/10.1080/13527259608722175

Gius, C. (2017). Facing the pain of others: Perspectives on international volunteer tourism between agency and spectatorship. *Current Issues in Tourism*, *20*(15), 1620–1632. https://doi.org/10.1080/13683500.2015.1047330

Germann Molz, J. (2017). Giving back, doing good, feeling global: The affective flows of family voluntourism. *Journal of Contemporary Ethnography*, *46*(3), 334–360. https://doi.org/10.1177/0891241615610382

Gorton, K. (2007). Theorizing emotion and affect: Feminist engagements. *Feminist Theory*, *8*(3), 333–348. https://doi.org/10.1177/1464700107082369

Huener, J. (2001). Antifascist pilgrimage and rehabilitation at Auschwitz: The political tourism of Aktion Sühnezeichen and Sozialistische Jugend. *German Studies Review*, *24* (3), 513–532. https://doi.org/10.2307/1433413

Isaac, R. K., Nawijn, J., van Liempt, A. & Gridnevskiy, K. (2017). Understanding Dutch visitors' motivations to visit concentration camp memorials. *Current Issues in Tourism*. https://doi.org/10.1080/13683500.2017.1310190

Jones, S. (2010). Negotiating authentic objects and authentic selves. *Journal of Material Culture*, *15* (2), 181–203. https://doi.org/10.1177/1359183510364074

Koleth, M. (2014). Hope in the dark: Geographies of volunteer and dark tourism in Cambodia. *Cultural Geographies, 21*(4), 681–694. https://doi.org/10.1177/1474474013519577

Kvale, S., & Brinkmann, S. (2007). *InterViews. Learning the craft of qualitative interviewing.* SAGE.

Light, D. (2017). Progress in dark tourism and thanatourism research: An uneasy relationship with heritage tourism. *Tourism Management, 61,* 275–301. https://doi.org/10.1016/j.tourman. 2017.01.011

Martini, A., & Buda, D. (2020). Dark tourism and affect: Framing places of death and disaster. *Current Issues in Tourism, 23*(6), 679–692. https://doi.org/10.1080/13683500.2018.1518972

Massumi, B. (1995). The autonomy of affect. *Cultural Critique, 31,* 83–109.

McGehee, N. G., & Santos, C. A. (2005). Social change, discourse and volunteer tourism. *Annals of Tourism Research, 32*(3), 760–779. https://doi.org/10.1016/j.annals.2004.12.002

McIntosh, A., & Zahra, A. (2007). A cultural encounter through volunteer tourism: Towards the ideals of sustainable tourism? *Journal of Sustainable Tourism, 15* (5), 541–556. https://doi.org/ 10.2167/jost701.0

Michael, J. (2017). *Negotiating normalcy and difference: Discourses on cultural taste and symbolic boundaries.* Erasmus University.

Mostafanezhad, M. (2013). The geography of compassion in volunteer tourism. *Tourism Geographies, 15*(2), 318–337. https://doi.org/10.1080/14616688.2012.675579

Nawijn, J., & Fricke, M. C. (2015). Visitor emotions and behavioral intentions: The case of concentration camp memorial Neuengamme. *International Journal of Tourism Research, 17*(3), 221–228. https://doi.org/10.1002/jtr.1977

Nawijn, J., Isaac, R., van Liempt, A., & Gridnevskiy, K. (2016). Emotion clusters for concentration camp memorials. *Annals of Tourism Research, 61,* 244–267. https://doi.org/10.1016/j.annals. 2016.09.005

Pezzino, P. (2012). *Memory and massacre: Revisiting Sant'Anna di Stazzema.* Palgrave MacMillan.

Pritchard, A., Morgan, N., & Ateljevic, I. (2011). Hopeful tourism. A new transformative perspective. *Annals of Tourism Research, 38*(3), 941–963. https://doi.org/10.1016/j.annals.2011.01.004

Sin, H. L. (2009). Volunteer tourism – 'Involve me and I will learn?' *Annals of Tourism Research, 36*(3), 480–501. https://doi.org/10.1016/j.annals.2009.03.001

Sin, H. L. (2010). Who are we responsible to? Locals' tales of volunteer tourism. *Geoforum, 41*(6), 983–992. https://doi.org/10.1016/j.geoforum.2010.08.007

Stoddart, H., & Rogerson, C. M. (2004). Volunteer tourism: The case of Habitat for Humanity South Africa. *GeoJournal, 60*(3), 311–318. https://doi.org/10.1023/B:GEJO.0000034737.81266.a1

Stone, P. (2009). Making absent death present: Consuming dark tourism in contemporary society. In R. Sharpley & P. Stone (Eds.), *The darker side of travel. The theory and practice of dark tourism* (pp. 23–28). Channel View Publications.

Thrift, N. (2009). Understanding the affective spaces of political performance. In M. Smith, J. Davidson, L. Cameron, & L. Bondi (Eds.), *Emotion, place and culture* (pp. 79–95). Ashgate.

Wearing, S. (2001). *Volunteer tourism: Experiences that make a difference.* CABI.

Appendix. Overview of 26 interviewees

Švenčionys, Lithuania, 2016.

Name	Age	Nationality	Gender
Andrea	27	German	f
Franziska	29	German	f
Hanna	24	Belorussian	f
Jacob	22	German	m
Jan	26	German	m
Julian	20	German	m
Maike	25	German	f
Miriam	26	German	f
Nele	19	German	f
Sammy	24	German	f

Marcevol, France, 2017.

Name	Age	Nationality	Gender
Chrisoula	49	Greek	f
Lisa	20	German	f
Manon	23	French	f
Mina	24	German	f
Seyit	24	Turkish	m
Smaragda	20	Greek	f

Montemaggio/Sant'Anna di Stazzema, Italy, 2017.

Name	Age	Nationality	Gender
Alicja	63	Polish	f
Daniele	29	Italian	m
Desislava	22	Bulgarian	f
Jana	22	German	f
Justine	24	German	f
Laura	23	German	f
Lisa	27	German	f
Mevisa	26	Albanian	f
Miri	22	German	f
Nele	21	German	f

Traveler sensoryscape experiences and the formation of destination identity

Junghye Angela Kah, Hye Jin Shin and Seong-Hoon Lee

ABSTRACT

Every destination needs to create a unique identity to sustain competition. However, it is difficult to create a destination identity between alternatives which share the same market and have similar environments. As creating the destination identity for travelers requires a memorable tourism experiences for travelers. From the perspective of experiential approaches, the sensory is one of the most vital entity of the destination based on his/her perception elements of an experience and therefore it is a powerful key to identify the destination characteristic. To become destination with distinct characteristics, they should provide positive tourism experiences by stimulating effectively five senses such as sight, sound, smell, taste and touch. This study was aimed to find out the effects of sensoryscape factors on creating destination identity. With this aim, a total of 322 questionnaires were distributed to those who visited Nami Island and 300 copies of questionnaires were used for the empirical analysis. The results can be summarized as follows. First, this study found two single senses including vision and touch are most positively associated with all types of travel destination identity. Second, the result showed the effects of interaction of two senses on travel destination identity and obtained that when combining the senses, the vision and smell are the most effective to create a travel destination identity rather combinations of vision and touch, which are effective senses when acting individually. This study is meaningful in that the study of sensory perception, which was mostly done in retailing setting, was carried out targeting travelers in a destination.

摘要

每个目的地都需要创造一个独特的身份来维持竞争。但是，在面对相同市场和具有相似环境的备选方案之间很难创建目的地独特的身份，因为为游客创造目的地身份需要为游客提供难忘的旅游体验。从经验方法的角度来看，感官是目的地基于体验的感知要素中最重要的实体之一，因此它是识别目的地特性的有力钥匙。要成为特色鲜明的旅游目的地，必须通过有效地刺激视觉、听觉、嗅觉、味觉、触觉等五种感官，提供积极的旅游体验。本研究旨在探讨感官景观要素对目的地身份创造的影响。为了达到这一目的，本研究一共发放了322份问卷给南怡岛的游客，并使用了300份问卷进行实证分析。结果总结如下：首先，这项研究发现包括视觉和触觉在内的两种单一感觉与所有类型的旅游目的地身份最相关。第二，结果显示了两种感官的交互作用对旅游目的地身份的影响，得出了视觉和嗅觉结合是最有效的创造旅游目的地身份的方式，但不是视觉和触觉的结合，这是单独行动时的有效感官。本研究的意义在于，对感官感知的研究主要是在零售环境中进行的，针对目的地旅行者的研究较少。

1. Introduction

Every destination needs to create a unique identity to sustain competition. However, it is difficult to create a destination identity between alternatives that share the same market and have similar environments. Diţoiu et al. (2014) explained that due to the technological evolution, it is becoming harder to differentiate destinations based on their nature resource, and therefore, providing memorable experiences is considered important to help make a unique association with the destination. From the perspective of an experiential approach, the sensory experience is one of the most vital entities of the destination. It is also a powerful key to identify the destination's unique and distinct characteristic (Guzel & Dortyol, 2016). A tourist experiences a destination through five sensory channels and the sensory experience further generates the emotional connection to help differentiate and distinguish a destination from other similar destinations (Diţoiu et al., 2014; Son & Pearce, 2005). Therefore, it can be stated that for tourism marketers, the challenge lies in identifying specific senses that have the power of consciously and unconsciously embedding themselves in the process of the tourism experience (Agapito et al., 2013).

According to Lindstrom (2005), vision is the most important persuasive cue, with a share of 58% by branding, smell is the second most important one with a proportion of 45%, hearing for 41%, taste for 31%, and touch for 25%. However, several studies have stated that all five senses are, at least, equally important (Dann & Jacobsen, 2003; Gretzel & Fesenmaier, 2003; 2010; Markwell, 2001; Son & Pearce, 2005). It comes as no surprise that marketers have become increasingly interested in the role of sensory marketing that uses the five sensory stimuli in the environment of the store (Shabgou & Daryani, 2014). Hulten et al. (2009) asserted that sensory marketing approaches should be based on the assumption that a firm can create a brand identity and establish a brand value through different sensorial strategies for sight, sound, smell, taste, and touch. In Krishna (2010, p. 2), sensory marketing is defined as "marketing that engages the consumers' senses and affects their behaviors". That is, sensory marketing implies "marketing that engages the consumers' senses and affects their perception, judgment and behavior". Sensory marketing is a relatively new concept in the tourism industry, despite the fact that travelers have always experienced a destination with their five senses (Dann & Jacobsen, 2003; Markwell, 2001; Pan & Ryan, 2009; Urry, 2002). To be precise, the question "Which of the five senses is the most heightened?" has been a significant one among general marketing researchers and practitioners, and yet it receives limited attention in tourism literature. As stated previously, the reasons behind different identities of destinations could theoretically be related to what tourists sense at the destinations. From this perspective, the destination identity that is perceived in its entirety by the tourist is the outcome of receiving, selecting, organizing, and interpreting the sensory input (Andreu et al., 2000). The experiential paradigm used to conceptualize travel destinations has turned the attention of destination marketers to the five sensory dimensions and its application. This focus will help strengthen the core themes of a destination, and creating a unique destination identity that eventually translates into specific emotional responses (Agapito et al., 2013). Consequently, sensory marketing in a tourism context is understood as a "bridge" between the destination's stimuli and tourist's emotions, and aims to reduce the gap between the destination's projected image and the traveler's perceived destination identity (Diţoiu et al., 2014).

Most previous studies focusing on the sensory systems have investigated an individual component of sensory stimuli, and the visual sense is the most frequently mentioned sensation (Guzel & Dortyol, 2016). However, the senses work not only as a single entity, but also in interaction and combination with each other (Miller & Stoica, 2004). Lindstrom (2005) emphasized the positive synergy across and between each of the five senses. Lindstrom (2005) states that it is important for the brand to trigger a higher number of sensory appeals, in order to make a strong bond between the brand and consumer. However, later Lindstrom (2009, p133) argued that the more stimulus that is conveyed, the harder it is to capture customers' attention to specific messages, because the human focus is limited. In this regard, it is important for tourism researchers and marketers to recognize how the sensory experiences play a role in identifying a destination, as well as how a destination highlights the ability to use the senses synergistically to create more positive travel responses. Therefore, this study investigates the effect of sensory experiences on the identification of a travel destination. In this study, travelers' sensory experiences of smell, sound, sight, taste, and touch are examined in isolation, as well as in combination.

2. Literature review

2.1. Destination identity

Tourism is a phenomenon in the place context, which creates its own brand that has social and emotional appeal (Hall, 1998; Morgan et al., 2006; Urry, 1990; 1995). A tourism destination can be branded with considerable care by transferring branding principles to a tourism destination concept. Researchers who have investigated the destination branding model have stressed the importance of understanding the concept of destination identity to explain destination branding (e.g., Cai, 2002; Hankinson 2004; Kaplanidou & Vogt, 2003; Risitano 2006; Konecnik and Go 2008; Konecnik & de Chernatony, 2013). For example, Kaplanidou and Vogt (2003) developed a destination brand model to create and manage the destination's value, which in turn has an impact on the tourist's perspective. Their study incorporated many components that work together to form the destination brand concept, and found that the core of the model is the defining and building of destination identity. The destination identity indicates a unique set of destination brand associations that can be used by tourists to differentiate a destination from its competitors (Tsaur et al., 2016). Researchers have explained that brand identity is a combination of visual, auditory, and other sensorial experiences that create recognition and provide differentiation (Aaker et al., 2004; Hudson & Ritchie, 2009). Worlu et al. (2015) added that a destination with a distinct identity is created by appealing to the different senses and emotions of tourists. It is important for destination marketers to understand tourist-brand relationships, as it has emerged as being crucial in building and achieving long-lasting relationships with customers.

Many studies have made an effort to disclose the construct of destination identity (e.g., Bagozzi & Dholakia, 2006; Balmer & Liao, 2007; Bergami and Bazzoci, 2000; Berrozpe et al., 2017; Choi & Um, 2011; Han, 1995; Kim, 2014; Kim & Park, 1999; Lam et al., 2010; 2012; 2013; Yuksel et al., 2010). In general, the cognitive and affective dimensions are most essential. Tourist destinations with their tangible and intangible attributes and numerous functional and symbolic advantages are increasingly regarded and managed as brands (Ekinci & Hosany, 2006; Morgan et al., 2002). The strategic use of destination identity can make a destination more attractive to visitors, and offer an edge over competing destinations. Lee and Lee (2012) proposed that this concept can be applied to tourism. The researchers specifically constructed a destination identity scale for Insa-dong, and explored two dimensions, viz. artistic identity and traditional identity. Their study focused on the cognitive attributes of Insa-dong along with traditional and cultural characteristics, to define the destination identity. In this study, Insa-dong was considered a destination for tourists to purchase and view art items, and to experience unique paths and historical sites that have existed since time immemorial. Jeong (2012) conceptualized the destination identity, reflecting three dimensions of psychological stability, nature beauty, and culture learning. The study constructed a scale to measure the destination identity of Jeju Olle using its cognitive and affective attributes that include tranquility, nature landscape, and culture and history learning (Han, 1995; Choi & Um, 2011). According to the research, tourists identified Jeju Olle as a walking trail with natural beauty, calm, and unique culture. Skinner (2018) emphasized that destination brand is not owned in the same way a commercial brand is owned, and added nature and activity elements to build destination identity.

2.2. The sensory experiences and destination identity

A traveler spends a period of time at a destination, and creates the destination identity through reception, selection, organization, and interpretation of the information about the destination (Mayo & Jarvis, 1981). Since the destination identity perceived by a traveler is a reflection of the sensory information they receive (Stringer, 1984), it is necessary to concentrate on creating destination identity through all the five sensory dimensions, that is sight, sound, smell, taste, and touch, as well as a combination of multiple senses.

2.2.1. Sight

In tourism marketing, visualization is used as an effective communication strategy to persuade the traveler, even before they make the decision to visit the destination (Pawaskar & Goel, 2014). With the emergence of photo-sharing websites, it is easy to motivate people to visit a destination (Gibson, 2012). It is also possible to visualize goods and services, and create a destination image through a virtual tour of the service landscape. Regarding a visual experience of the tourism setting, Urry (2002) emphasized the significance of sightseeing through tourism activities. In addition, cultural, historical, and architectural museums and places serve as the visual symbols of destination identity (Cvitkovic & Kline, 2017; Zukin, 2004). The Statue of Liberty in Manhattan, a symbol of freedom and an American icon, and the Eiffel Tower, a symbol of Paris and, by extension, of France, are good examples of monuments that shape destination identity. According to a study by Guzel and Dortyol (2016), people create positive memories about a destination, mostly through the visual sensory stimuli. Scenic beauty, such as that provided by oceans, lakes, waterfalls, mountains, and flora and fauna, attract tourists who seek an emotional connection with a destination. New Zealand's majestic beauty and beautiful natural environment encourage visitors to understand the distinctive appeals of the destination. However, visual pollution through improper development or uncontrolled visitation, especially at prime locations like beachfronts, special views, and mountains, serve to damage the destination's image and identity (Kreag, 2001).

2.2.2. Sound

It is apparent that sound can provide a holistic experience and favorable atmosphere. In Guzel and Dortyol's research (2016), auditory, the third most commonly mentioned stimulus by tourists after sight and taste, is linked to emotions and feelings of fun and peace. Theme music through the entire Disney World universe stimulates the interest of children and awakens the heart of adults (Lindstrom, 2005, p. 74). Theme music and familiar melodies are an essential part of the total experience of Disney World. A destination has its own sound. In European towns during carnivals, musical instruments are everywhere; from Irish pipes to Gypsy music, and on market days, the noise of the market brings out the vital identity of the city (Garrioch, 2003). Music has a powerful influence on memory and place identity. For example, Vienna is world-renowned for classical and popular music (Bohlman, 2011, p. 74). Cohen (2013) explored the relationship between rock music, collective memory, and local identity by focusing on events of Liverpool city, which is internationally known for its music, and for being the birthplace of the Beatles. The study provided that memories of rock music are actively produced and attached to heritage through various events and media, and such musical memories are used to form local identity (Cohen, 2013). Silence, the opposite of noise, is defined as "lack of sound," or "an absence of an expected sound" (Stockfelt, 1991), and can be used to identify a destination such as the silence of a forest in a hectic city.

2.2.3. Smell

From a destination marketing point of view, this highlights the potential for scent in helping to build the destination identity and conceptualize service products. The sense of smell is intensely associated with the dining experience at a destination (Dann & Jacobsen, 2003). Additionally, smell is strongly related to the character of a place (Porteous, 1985). For example, in Son and Pearce's study (2005), respondents remembered the smell of the sea, Asian food, and fresh air, when they thought of

Australia. Visitors to Manchester China Town can have a unique identity to the place by detecting the strong smells of cooking, which is considered a characteristic of Chinese society and food culture (Henshaw, 2013: 98). The smell of a certain place, which may not be usually be noticed by local people, could be a strong sensory experience for visitors (Dann & Jacobsen, 2002). Henshaw et al. (2016) argued that while the same odor may carry a positive connotation for one person, it might be considered a pollutant by another. In this regard, they suggested that if smell is introduced into a place for marketing purposes, it is necessary for it to be targeted towards individuals who previously agreed to receive the olfactory stimulus using various marketing communication tools and channels, such as social medial chat room, and smell map. These tools are used by the travelers wherein they can post their smell experiences obtained during a trip around the world (British Broadcasting Corporation, 2009). However, lack of boundaries in a space, uncontrollable conditions, and the features of the place itself, present a challenge in targeting specific individuals in relation to the smell sense. This reflects that smell marketing needs to be in a well-planned space, in order to be effective and attract new visitors (Isacsson et al., 2009).

2.2.4. Taste

Pawaskar and Goel (2014) pointed out that the sensorial strategy of taste is hard to introduce in the tourism industry, because of its tangible characteristics. Obviously, research on taste marketing at a destination is at an early stage, and the integration of taste sensory and destination identity is hardly seen. However, several studies have noted that consuming local food and dining at destinations is essential for international travelers (e.g., Hjalager & Richards, 2002; Mintz & Bois, 2002; Telfer & Wall, 2000). Hong Kong which has over 15,000 restaurants promotes itself as "the culinary capital of Asia" by providing detailed information on a variety of foods and dining places on its tourism website for tourists (Tsai, 2013). In a similar vein, Italy is known as the culinary tourism destination where tourists can taste local gastronomy, ranging from fruits, vegetables, sauces, meats etc. Consumption of local food and dining at destinations is a pleasurable sensory experience. Such pleasure is an appealing cue, and hence a strategic destination marketing tool that must not be undervalued (Kivela & Crotts, 2006). Food reflects a destination, and its cultural and social identity (Sengel et al., 2015). As explained by Getz (2000), culinary experience for travelers is understood as a social and cultural interaction, since it gives them an insight into the local. Therefore, tasting local food has played an important role in motivating tourists who desire to experience and understand the culture of a destination they visit (Fields, 2003; Ryu & Jang, 2006; Sparks et al., 2003). Given the fact that local cuisine is the major driving factor for travelers to visit a destination, studies claimed that tasting local food is also critical in shaping the destination image, and differentiating it from its competitors (e.g., Tsai, 2013; Quan & Wang, 2004; Ab. Karim et al., 2009; Leong & Karim, 2015). It is therefore comprehensible that travelers can recall the taste experience at home, which serves to strengthen the gastronomic image of the destination (Jandala & Hercz, 2016).

2.2.5. Touch

In the travel business, it is obvious that touch experience is significant. Such reasoning is demonstrated in how many firms try to offer customers the best feel. For example, hotels offer exceptional professional services, such as therapeutic massage and spa experience features. Hotels also provide customers with a cozy duvet and pillow, which can enhance the touch experience. Natural resources, such as beaches, plant and wildlife, provide attractive nature activities, such as sunbathing, hiking, and fishing that are ideal features of touch experience. Hot springs provide an experience of touching natural hot thermal water through the entire skin. According to Son and Pearce's study (2005) one of the most memorable experiences for travelers in Australia is the touch of animals, such as kangaroos, koalas, snakes, and sheep. There is lack of evidence to demonstrate the isolated effect of touch sensation on creating a destination identity. However, previous studies emphasize that the brand is supported by the product (Diţoiu et al., 2014), and that the touch sense is essential to understanding how customers identify a product and its quality (Hulten et al., 2009). It can therefore be assumed that a traveler's destination identity depends on the quality of tourism goods and services, perceived through the touch sense.

2.2.6. Multiple senses. Of the five senses of sight, smell, taste, sound, and touch, sight and sound have so far dominated sensory marketing. Researchers have called for more studies to investigate the interaction of senses, because senses rarely function in isolation (e.g., Krishna, 2012; Puccinelli et al., 2009; Wright, 2006). Indeed, there have been studies on multi-sensory events, including vision and sound (Houston et al., 1987; Russell, 2002), vision and taste (Hoegg & Alba, 2007), vision and touch (Balaji et al., 2011), sound and smell (Henshaw & Bruce, 2012; Mattila & Wirtz, 2001; Spangenberg et al., 2005), sound and taste (Yorkston & Menon, 2004), smell and touch (Krishna et al., 2010), taste and smell (Stevenson et al., 1999), and touch and taste (Kishna & Morrin, 2008). Overall, these studies found that one sense seems to enhance the ability to detect the other. For example, Hulten et al. (2009) explained that touch reinforces sight, as the touch sense allows people to re-experience what they have seen. A study of taste and smell by Stevenson et al. (1999) demonstrated the effect of odors on taste perception.

3. Method

3.1. Instrument and data

A survey questionnaire was applied to tourists who had spent at least one hour in the area under study. This study used data collected from travelers in Nami Island, Korea, from August 20 to August 25, 2016. The survey was conducted between 1:00 pm and 6:00 pm, with tourists over 20 years old, after the tour of Nami Island. The investigator conducted a self-administered questionnaire, after giving the survey respondents sufficient explanation of the purpose and content of the survey. A total of 322 questionnaires were distributed, and all were collected. A total of 300 valid samples were used for the empirical analysis.

Nami Island was chosen as a tourist destination, because many tourists visit it every year due to its geographical proximity to Seoul, and the characteristic of harmony between the natural human environment. To visit Nami Island, visitors must board a ship at the marina. Nami Island is 5 km in circumference, and of about 460,000 square meters.

3.2. Measures

The group of questions used in this study included five sections and one open-ended question section based on direct elicitation, (Gretzel & Fesenmaier, 2010), in order to capture the five senses' impressions regarding the tourists' overall experience in the rural area under study. This study used a twelve constructs survey questionnaire, including five factors of senses (vision, sound, taste, smell, touch), four factors of travel destination identity (nature type, activity type, functional type, emotional type), travel attitude, travel satisfaction and travel behavior intention. Vision was assessed by using four items: green, bright, sunny, and spacious. Sound was assessed by using two items: silent and delicate. Taste was assessed by using three items: sour, spicy, and salty. Smell was assessed by using three items: stink, fish smell, and fusty. Touch was assessed by using four items: hot, warm, smooth, and soft.

Of the four types of travel destination identity (nature type, activity type, functional type, emotional type), to assess a nature type of travel destination identity, four items were adapted from previous research: 1) feel nature (mountain, sea, walking trails etc.), 2) natural scenery is beautiful, 3) natural scenery is in harmony with its surroundings and 4) there are many pedestrian-friendly walking trails. To assess an activity type of travel destination identity, seven items were adapted from previous research: 1) performances and exhibitions, 2) festivals and events, 3) cultural experience programs, 4) gallery, auditorium, experience facilities, 5) recreational facilities and ride things, 6) a variety of sights to see and enjoy, and 7) a variety of food. To assess functional type of travel destination identity, four items were adapted from previous research: 1) convenient facilities (tourism information center, rest areas etc.), 2) good accessibility, 3) reasonable costs, and 4) safe place. To assess an emotional type of travel destination identity, seven items were adapted from previous research: 1) peaceful place, 2) interesting place, 3) attractive place, 4) unique place, 5) comfortable place, 6) a good place to travel with travel companions, and 7) a good place to make precious memories with travel companions. All constructs were measured using a Likert-type five-point scale, where 1 = never, and 5 = very much so. Three items representing traveler characteristics were used: visit frequency, hours of stay, and the number of persons who accompanied them. Four items were used to control demographic characteristics: gender, age, education level, and monthly income level.

4. Results

Table 1 shows the results of the frequency analysis to determine the demographic characteristics (gender, age, monthly average income, and accompanied relationship) of the 300 tourists visiting Nami Island. Females represented 56.7% (n = 170) and

Table 1. Traveler characteristics.

PROFILES	Total ($n = 300$)
Gender	
Female	56.7%
Male	43.3%
Age	
20 ~ 29	39.0%
30 ~ 39	21.7%
40 ~ 49	15.6%
50 ~ 59	18.7%
Over 60	5.0%
Monthly income	
Less than 2 mil	51.3%
2 mil ~ 4 mil	39.1%
Over 4 mil	9.6%
Accompanied relationship	
Families	42.3%
Friends	40.0%
Club members	13.7%
Others	4.0%

males 43.3% (n = 130). The largest number of respondents i.e. 117 (39.0%) respondents ranged (20–29) years old, followed by 65 (21.7%) respondents who ranged (30–39) years old, 56 (18.7%) respondents ranged (50–59) years, 47 (15.6%) respondents ranged (40–49) years old, and lastly there were 15 (5.0%) respondents who ranged age $\geq$ 60 years old. About a half (n = 154, 51.3%) of the participants reported a monthly average income of less than 2 million KRW (equivalent to 2,000 USD); another more than one third (n = 117, 39.1%) indicated a monthly income between 2 million and 4 million KRW ((2,000 and 4,000) USD); and the last one tenth (n = 29, 9.6%) reported a monthly income greater than 4,000,000 KRW (equivalent to 4,000 U.S. dollars) Most accompanied relationships were families (n = 127, 42.3%), followed by friends (n = 120, 40%), club members (n = 41, 13.7%) and others (n = 12, 4%).

This study examined the effects of sensory experience on travel destination identity (nature, activity, functional and emotional types), which was conducted with SAS 9.2. Along with single sensory experiences, multi-sensory experiences were also considered.

Table 2 shows the regression estimation results for the effects of single sensory experiences on each of the four types of travel destination identity (nature type, activity type, functional type, emotional type). Demographic characteristic variables, such as gender, age, education, and monthly income, were controlled for in the estimation. The gender variable was coded 1 for male, and 2 for female respondents. The age variable was coded as real age. The education variable was coded as 1 for high school degree, 2 for college degree, 3 for undergraduate degree, and 4 for graduate degree. Monthly income was coded as 1 for respondents with a monthly income of less than 1 million KRW (1,000 won is roughly equivalent to 1 USD), 2 for between (1 and 2) million KRW, 3 for between (2 and 4) million KRW, 4 for between (4 and 5) million KRW, and 5 for more than 5 million KRW.

The senses perceived by tourists are composed of visual, sound, smell, taste, and touch senses. The results of the effects of single sensory experiences on each of the four types of travel destination identity are as follows. The explanatory power for the effect of single sensory experiences on the nature type of travel destination identity

Table 2. The effect of single sensory experiences on travel destination identity.

VARIABLES	Nature	Activity	Functional	Emotional
		Travel destination identity		
Vision	0.4114***	0.2816***	0.2035***	0.4141***
	(7.4368)	(3.6561)	(3.1486)	(7.4282)
Sound	0.0731*	0.0186	0.1491***	0.1266***
	(1.8069)	(0.3297)	(3.1537)	(3.1051)
Taste	0.1138**	−0.1060	0.0406	0.1161**
	(2.3868)	(−1.5960)	(0.7276)	(2.4153)
Smell	0.0496	−0.1098*	0.0749	0.0303
	(1.0405)	(−1.6544)	(1.3449)	(0.6310)
Touch	0.2088***	0.1277**	0.1476***	0.1385***
	(4.7370)	(2.0815)	(2.8664)	(3.1188)
Gender	−0.0203	−0.0109	−0.0783	−0.0936
	(−0.3361)	(−0.1299)	(−1.1098)	(−1.5374)
Age	0.0079***	−0.0001	0.0002	0.0048*
	(2.9962)	(−0.0408)	(0.0741)	(1.8162)
Education	0.0379	0.0214	−0.0021	0.0366
	(1.0220)	(0.4152)	(−0.0487)	(0.9775)
Income	0.0090	−0.0215	0.0053	0.0109
	(0.3953)	(−0.6795)	(0.2013)	(0.4768)
Visit frequency	0.0048	−0.0569	−0.0212	−0.0535*
	(0.1599)	(−1.3533)	(−0.6000)	(−1.7574)
Stay hours	−0.0455**	0.0551*	−0.0567**	−0.0275
	(−2.0184)	(1.7536)	(−2.1524)	(−1.2083)
Constant	1.0151***	2.2846***	1.7423***	1.0697***
	(3.1956)	(5.1662)	(4.6937)	(3.3417)
Observations	300	300	300	300
R-squared	0.361	0.154	0.180	0.349
Adjusted R^2	0.337	0.121	0.148	0.324
F	14.82	4.754	5.728	14.02
Prob > F	0.00	0.00	0.00	0.002

t-statistics in parentheses.
***$p < 0.01$, **$p < 0.05$, *$p < 0.1$.

was 36.1%, and its F value was 14.82, indicating that the regression equation was statistically significant (p <.001). The explanatory power of the dependent variable on activity type was 15.4% and the F value was 4.754, indicating the regression equation was statistically significant (p <.001). The explanatory power of the dependent variable on functional type was 18.0% and the F value was 5.728, indicating the regression equation was statistically significant (p <.001). The explanatory power of the emotional type, which is a dependent variable, was 34.9%, and the F value was 14.02, and the regression equation proved statistically significant (p <.001). Vision and touch were positively associated with all four types of travel destination identity with high significance. Sound was positively associated with the nature type of travel destination identity with weak significance, and functional type and emotional type of travel destination identity with strong significance. Taste was statistically significant and positively associated with only the nature type and emotional type of travel destination identity. Smell was negatively associated with the activity type of travel destination identity. In general, we confirm that five single senses have positive effects on each of the four travel destination identities. Of the control variables, the age variable was statistically significant and positively associated with the nature and emotional type of

Table 3. The effect of multi-sensory experiences on travel destination identity.

VARIABLES	Travel destination identity			
	Nature	Activity	Functional	Emotional
Vision*Sound	−0.0135	0.0087	−0.0169	0.0104
	(−0.3721)	(0.1720)	(−0.3946)	(0.2812)
Vision*Taste	−0.0054	−0.1822**	−0.1105	−0.0221
	(−0.0933)	(−2.2830)	(−1.6314)	(−0.3776)
Vision*Smell	0.1696***	0.2888***	0.1364*	0.1162*
	(2.8272)	(3.4625)	(1.9263)	(1.9025)
Vision*Touch	−0.0164	−0.0320	0.0604	0.0340
	(−0.3948)	(−0.5553)	(1.2345)	(0.8052)
Sound*Taste	−0.0400	0.1876**	0.1782**	0.1316**
	(−0.6695)	(2.2587)	(2.5266)	(2.1645)
Sound*Smell	−0.0153	−0.2656***	−0.1291*	−0.1226**
	(−0.2505)	(−3.1250)	(−1.7891)	(−1.9708)
Sound*Touch	0.0986***	0.0811*	0.0239	0.0226
	(2.9901)	(1.7705)	(0.6137)	(0.6741)
Taste*Smell	−0.0456*	−0.0640*	0.0039	−0.0309
	(−1.7140)	(−1.7302)	(0.1253)	(−1.1420)
Taste*Touch	0.1153**	0.0507	−0.0399	−0.0435
	(1.9855)	(0.6281)	(−0.5827)	(−0.7360)
Smell*Touch	−0.1369**	−0.0570	−0.0171	0.0146
	(−2.2545)	(−0.6752)	(−0.2390)	(0.2370)
Gender	−0.0258	−0.0088	−0.0827	−0.0934
	(−0.4309)	(−0.1053)	(−1.1685)	(−1.5297)
Age	0.0065**	−0.0015	0.0008	0.0049*
	(2.4842)	(−0.4082)	(0.2445)	(1.8413)
Education	0.0269	0.0080	−0.0105	0.0295
	(0.7325)	(0.1566)	(−0.2428)	(0.7872)
Income	0.0127	−0.0072	0.0064	0.0149
	(0.5552)	(−0.2271)	(0.2356)	(0.6387)
Visit frequency	0.0114	−0.0484	−0.0225	−0.0557*
	(0.3766)	(−1.1545)	(−0.6310)	(−1.8138)
Stay hours	−0.0466**	0.0477	−0.0564**	−0.0265
	(−2.0856)	(1.5341)	(−2.1398)	(−1.1653)
Constant	2.6474***	2.8339***	2.7603***	2.5409***
	(11.3782)	(8.7625)	(10.0529)	(10.7321)
Observations	300	300	300	300
R-squared	0.388	0.191	0.198	0.363
Adjusted R^2	0.353	0.145	0.152	0.327
F	11.20	4.176	4.360	10.09
Prob > F	0.00	0.00	0.00	0.00

t-statistics in parentheses.
***$p < 0.01$, **$p < 0.05$, *$p < 0.1$.

travel destination identity. The hours of stay variable had a statistically significant negative effect on the nature and functional type of travel destination identity, while it showed a weak positive effect on activity type.

Table 3 shows the regression estimation results for the effects of multiple sensory experiences on each of the four types of travel destination identity. Demographic characteristic variables, such as gender, age, education, and monthly income, were controlled for in the estimation, as in the previous regression. The multiple senses perceived by tourists are composed of combinations of two out of the five sensory experiences, including vision and sound, vision and taste, vision and smell, vision and touch, sound and taste, sound and smell, sound and touch, taste and smell, taste and touch, and smell and touch.

The results of the effects of multiple sensory experiences, on each of the four types of travel destination identity were as follows. The explanatory power for the effect of multiple sensory experiences on the nature type of travel destination identity was 38.8%, and its F value was 11.20, indicating that the regression equation was statistically significant (p <.001). The explanatory power of the dependent variable on the activity type was 19.1% and the F value was 4.176, indicating the regression equation was statistically significant (p <.001). The explanatory power of the dependent variable on the functional type was 19.8%, the F value was 4.360, and the regression equation was proved to be statistically significant (p <.001). The explanatory power of the emotional type, which is a dependent variable, was 36.3%, the F value was 16.09, and the regression equation was proved to be statistically significant (p <.001). A combination of vision and taste was negatively associated with the activity type of travel destination identity with 5% significance level. A combination of vision and smell was positively associated with nature type and activity type of travel destination identity with strong significance, and the functional emotional type of travel destination identity with weak significance. A combination of sound and taste was statistically significant and positively associated with all types of travel destination identity, except the nature type. A combination of sound and smell was statistically significant and negatively associated with all types of travel destination identity, except the nature type. A combination of sound and touch is positively associated with natural and activity type of travel destination identity. A combination of taste and smell was negatively associated with nature type and activity type of travel destination identity with weak significance. A combination of taste and touch was positively associated with nature type of travel destination identity with 5% significance level. A combination of smell and touch was negatively associated with nature type of travel destination identity with 5% significance level. As a control variable, age had positive effects on the nature and emotional type of travel destination identity, while the variable of hours of stay showed negative effects on the nature and functional types. In sum, we confirmed that combinations of the five senses influence travel destination identity.

5. Discussion

Although previous research in retailing discussed how senses associated with products or places affect brand identity, emotions, perceptions, preferences, and consumption behavior, there is still the need to explore sensory experiences and their application in the tourism industry. As suggested by Krishna (2010), there may be differences in people's sensory arousal. It can be postulated that the variances in travelers' sensorial experience at destination create different destination identities. In addition, a study by Lindstrom (2005) suggests that the more positive the synergy between the senses, the more effective and memorable the experience. It is therefore important for destination marketers to discover a balanced combination of sensory inputs to design a destination identity that will in turn result in competitive advantage. That is, a destination marketer should design destination experiences that include specific sensations, feelings, cognitions, and behaviors (Govers et al., 2007).

The results of this study are summarized as follows. First, this study found the effects of vision and touch sensory on all four types of travel destination identity of nature type, activity type, functional type, and emotional type. In addition, this study showed the partial effects of the other sensory experiences on travel destination identity. Specifically, sound was positively associated with three types of travel destination identity, viz. nature type, functional type, and emotional type. Also, taste showed significant relationships with nature and emotional type of destination identity, while smell was negatively related to activity type of travel destination identity. We confirmed that four single senses of vision, touch, sound, and taste have effects on each of the four travel destination identities, but among the five senses, vision and touch, respectively, are the most effective senses to create a destination identity. Second, the study showed the effects of the interaction of senses on travel destination identity. To be more specific, a combination of vision and smell was positively associated with all types of travel destination identity. A combination of sound and taste was positively associated with three types of travel destination identity, except the nature type. A combination of sound and smell was negatively associated with three types of travel destination identity, including activity, and functional and emotional type. In addition, a combination of sound and touch was positively associated with two types of travel destination identity, viz. natural and activity types, while a combination of taste and smell was negatively associated with those types of travel destination identity. A combination of taste and smell was negatively associated with the nature and activity types of travel destination identity. A combination of taste and touch was positively associated with only the nature type of travel destination identity, while a combination of smell and touch was negatively associated with the nature type of travel destination identity. Lastly, a combination of vision and taste was negatively associated with the activity type of travel destination identity. In sum, we confirmed that combination of the senses of vision and smell are most effective in creating a travel destination identity, but a combination of vision and touch that were most effective as single senses, are no longer effective. In addition, we found that many combinations of senses come with negative effects, and that only a few combinations have positive effects on travel destination identity.

The many results mentioned above can be summarized as follows. First, this study found that two single senses, viz. vision and touch, were most positively associated with all types of travel destination identity. Only smell does not have any positive effect on travel destination identity. Second, we showed the effects of interaction of two senses on travel destination identity, and obtained an interesting finding. That is, when combining senses, vision and smell were found to be most effective in creating a travel destination identity rather than combinations of vision and touch, which are effective senses when acting in isolation.

The results of this study provide several implications for a travel destination marketer using different sensorial strategies to create destination identity. First, as Krishna and Schwarz (2014) emphasized, not all stimulations can exert an influence through an identical pathway; in this study, sight and touch have been the most dominant sensory vehicles for creating destination identity. For a long time, marketers have emphasized the positive effect of the vision sense of the consumer, and such a phenomenon is expected to continue. As mentioned earlier, an individual's vision is made up of a number of visual sense expressions, such as color, light, and theme. Therefore, the formation of the space to differentiate itself from the competitors is one of the most significant challenges of sensory marketing in visualizing a destination identity. In this regard, Hulten et al. (2009) have emphasized that in order to be visually prominent among many similar tourist spots, a destination has to be seen much more easily and clearly than ever before. Simplicity can be a suitable strategy, in an environment where countless possible combinations of sight expression, such as color, light, and theme, can be made. In addition, whilst senses other than vision have been largely ignored in previous discussions of sensory marketing, (Henshaw et al., 2016) this study opens up opportunities for a destination marketer to adopt tactile marketing to establish destination identity, since the results of this study presented that touch solely affects all types of travel destination identity. Tactile marketing relies on individual participation, and can contribute to special touch impressions and form the foundation of brand identity (Hulten et al., 2009). Balaji et al. (2011) indicated that consumers are motivated to touch, and such physical examination can generate the product identity. Indeed, a supermarket chain could remove the wrappers from several brands of toilet paper, so that shoppers could feel and compare textures (Lindstrom, 2005). However, unlike physical stores, where consumers rely on sense of touch to make more accurate product judgement (Peck & Childers, 2003), in travel business the absence of touch cues in the pre-trip decision process cannot provide an opportunity for product/service evaluation through touch. Peck and Shu (2009) showed that for both buyers and non-buyers, only imagining the touch experience can increase perceived ownership of the product, which suggests tactile information can contribute to the choice process. Therefore, it is necessary for a destination marketer to utilize a sensorial touch strategy in communicating with the potential traveler during the decision-making process. In retailing, it turned out that consciously using texture in sensory marketing can increase the perceived value of brand for customers (Hulten et al., 2009). A study by Berger et al. (2006) specified the sense expressions, such as material, temperature, and steadiness, are important for the tactile experience. Consequently, it is of great importance for a destination marketer to understand what kind of tactile experience is engendered by a destination. Above all, as discussed earlier, tactile marketing is based on physical access; therefore, it becomes more important for travel destinations to be accessible to enable a physical activity, interaction with nature, and cultural learning, which are the core components of the travel experience (Viren et al., 2017).

In this study, the empirical analysis included all five senses, which was novel to this study, and not covered in previous studies. Interestingly, unlike the well-known fact that smell affects emotion and behavior in general, this study revealed that smell alone does not affect any type of tourist identity. One reason for the inefficient result can be the difficulty in controlling obvious olfactory input, as compared to visual and tactile input. Krishna and Schwarz (2014) have explained that since having the same intensity of smell input across participants is complex, the exploration of the olfactory sense requires a different degree of smell intensity, or require that participants be asked to imagine a smell and desire for a destination. It should also be mentioned that people who stay in a destination for a long time may become less sensitive to a particular scent (Hulten et al., 2009). Therefore, this fact should be taken into consideration when a destination marketer plans to utilize scent. However, despite the fact that the influence of smell alone is not found in creating destination identity, one of the most important observations from our research is the effective sensory interaction of the smell and vision to the traveler's experience of a destination. In other words, the smell sense enhances the visual sense or vice versa, in a destination. As explained by Krishna et al. (2010) that a distinctly scented object enhances recall for other attributes of the objects, there is no doubt that scents can play a part in creating a destination identity. This study also demonstrated that a combination of smell and vision was effective, and therefore, goods and service providers have opportunities to use smell as an important element in sensory marketing.

6. Recommendation and limitation

There are limitations to this study. First, this study examined the effects of single sensory and multiple sensory experiences on travel destination. It would be more informative to examine the effects of sensory experiences on travel attitude and travel satisfaction via the channel of travel identity. Second, the survey was conducted during the hot summer in a specific tourist spot. It would be useful if the results are supported by further studies in other seasons at other travel destinations. Additionally, Nami Island is a travel destination not only for Koreans, but also for foreigners. However, there have been no attempts yet to study sense expressions across nationalities or cultures. In future research, a study should be conducted on how senses and destination identity are perceived differently, due to differences in nationality or culture. Lastly, this study not only highlighted the positive aspects of sensation, but also its negative aspects. Future research could examine how negative aspects engender the unique destination's identity, and distinguish it from other places. This will enable us to establish an effective sensory marketing strategy.

Disclosure statement

No potential conflict of interest was reported by the author(s).

Funding

This paper is financially supported by College of Public Policy at Korea University Grant in 2020.

References

Aaker, D. A., Kumar, V., & Day, G. S. (2004). *Marketing research*. John Wiley and Sons.

Ab. Karim, M. S., Chua, B. L., & Salleh, H. (2009). Malaysia as a culinary tourism destination: International tourists' perspective. *Journal of Tourism, Hospitality and Culinary Arts, 1*(3), 1–16.

Agapito, D., Mendes, J., & Valle, P. (2013). Conceptualizing the sensory dimension of tourist experiences. *Journal of Destination Marketing & Management, 2*(2), 62–73. https://doi.org/10.1016/j.jdmm.2013.03.001

Andreu, L., Bigne, J., & Cooper, C. (2000). Projected and perceived image of Spain as a tourist destination for British travelers. *Journal of Travel & Tourism Marketing, 9*(4), 47–67. https://doi.org/10.1300/J073v09n04_03

Bagozzi, R. P., & Dholakia, U. M. (2006). Antecedents and purchase consequences of customer participation in small group brand communities. *International Journal of Research in Marketing, 23*(1), 45–61. https://doi.org/10.1016/j.ijresmar.2006.01.005

Balaji, M. S., Raghavan, S., & Jha, S. (2011). Role of tactile and visual inputs in product evaluation: A multisensory perspective. *Asia Pacific Journal of Marketing and Logistics, 23*(4), 513–530. https://doi.org/10.1108/13555851111165066

Balmer, J. M., & Liao, M. N. (2007). Student corporate brand identification: An exploratory case study. *Corporate Communications: An International Journal, 12*(4), 356–375. https://doi.org/10.1108/13563280710832515

Bergami, M., & Bagozzi, R. P. (2000). Self-categorization, affective commitment and group self-esteem as distinct aspects of social identity in the organization. *British Journal of Social Psychology, 39*(4), 555–577. https://doi.org/10.1348/014466600164633

Berger, G., Katz, H., & Petutschnigg, A. J. (2006). What consumers feel and prefer: Haptic perception of various wood flooring surfaces. *Forest Products Journal, 56*(10), 42–48.

Berrozpe, A., Campo, S., & Yagüe, M. J. (2017). Understanding the identity of Ibiza. *Journal of Travel & Tourism Marketing, 34*(8), 1–46. https://doi.org/10.1080/10548408.2016.1272525

Bohlman, P. (2011). *Music, nationalism, and the making of the new Europe* (2nd ed.). Routledge.

British Broadcasting Corporation. (2009). *Follow your nose on web scent map*. Retrieved January 20, 2019, from http://news.bbc.co.uk/2/hi/asia-pacific/7823820.stm

Cai, L. A. (2002). Cooperative branding for rural destinations. *Annals of Tourism Research, 29*(3), 720–742. https://doi.org/10.1016/S0160-7383(01)00080-9

Choi, M. J., & Um, S. H. (2011). Measuring the place identity of a tourist destination. *Journal of Tourism Sciences, 35*(6), 15–34.

Cohen, S. (2013). Musical memory, heritage and local identity: Remembering the popular music past in a European Capital of Culture. *International Journal of Cultural Policy, 19*(5), 576–594. https://doi.org/10.1080/10286632.2012.676641

Cvitkovic, S., & Kline, M. (2017). Skopje: Rebranding the capital city through architecture and monuments to remake the nation brand. *Sociologija i Prostor, 55*(1), 33–53. https://doi.org/10.5673/sip.55.1.2

Dann, G., & Jacobsen, J. K. S. (2002). *Leading the tourist by the nose. The tourist as a metaphor of the social world* (pp. 209–235). CAB International.

Dann, G., & Jacobsen, J. K. S. (2003). Tourism smellscapes. *Tourism Geographies, 5*(1), 3–25. https://doi.org/10.1080/1461668032000034033

Diţoiu, M. C., Stăncioiu, A. F., Brătucu, G., Onişor, L. F., & Botoş, A. (2014). The sensory brand of the destination. Case study: Transylvania. *Theoretical and Applied Economics, 21*(5), 37–50.

Ekinci, Y., & Hosany, S. (2006). Destination personality: An application of brand personality to tourism destinations. *Journal of Travel Research, 45*(2), 127–139. https://doi.org/10.1177/0047287506291603

Fields, K. (2003). Demand for the gastronomy tourism product: Motivational factors. In *Tourism and Gastronomy* (pp. 50–64).

Garrioch, D. (2003). Sounds of the city: The soundscape of early modern European towns. *Urban History, 30*(1), 5–25. https://doi.org/10.1017/S0963926803001019

Getz, D. (2000). *Explore wine tourism: Management, development and destinations.* Cognizant Development Corporation.

Gibson, C. (2012). Geographies of tourism: Space, ethics and encounter. In Julie Wilson (Ed.), *The Routledge handbook of tourism geographies* (pp. 72–77). Routledge.

Govers, R., Go, F. M., & Kumar, K. (2007). Virtual destination image: A new measurement approach. *Annals of Tourism Research, 34*(4), 977–997. https://doi.org/10.1016/j.annals.2007.06.001

Gretzel, U., & Fesenmaier, D. (2003). Experience-based internet marketing: An exploratory study of sensory experiences associated with pleasure travel to the Midwest United States. In Andrew J. Frew, Martin Hitz, Peter O'Connor (Eds.), *Information and communication technologies in tourism* (pp. 49–57). Springer-Verlag.

Gretzel, U., & Fesenmaier, D. (2010). Capturing sensory experiences through semi-structured elicitation questions. In Michael Morgan, Peter Lugoci, Brent Ritchie (Eds.), *The Tourism and Leisure Experience: Consumer and Managerial Perspectives* (pp. 137–160).

Guzel, O., & Dortyol, T. (2016). Exploring the Multi-sensory based memorable tourism experiences: A study of Adam and Eve Hotel in Turkey. *Journal of Marketing and Consumer Behaviour in Emerging Markets, 2*(4), 28–39. https://doi.org/10.7172/2449-6634.jmcbem.2016.2.2

Hall, C. M. (1998). *Introduction to tourism: Development, dimensions and issues.* Longman.

Han, S. I. (1995). *A study on the tourist's cognition of destination identity: A case of Gyeongju National Park* [Doctoral thesis]. Graduate School Hanyang University.

Hankinson, G. (2004). Relational network brands: Towards a conceptual model of place brands. *Journal of Vacation Marketing, 10*(2), 109–121. https://doi.org/10.1177/135676670401000202

Henshaw, V. (2013). *Urban smellscapes: Understanding and designing city smell environments.* Routledge.

Henshaw, V., Medway, D., Warnaby, G., & Perkins, C. (2016). Marketing the 'city of smells. *Marketing Theory, 16*(2), 153–170. https://doi.org/10.1177/1470593115619970

Henshaw, V., & Bruce, N. (2012). Smell and sound expectation and the ambiances of English cities. In *2nd International Congress on Ambiences* (pp. 449–454).

Hjalager, A. M., & Richards, G. (2002). *Tourism and gastronomy.* Routledge.

Hoegg, J., & Alba, J. W. (2007). Taste perception: More than meets the tongue. *Journal of Consumer Research, 33*(4), 490–498. https://doi.org/10.1086/510222

Houston, M. J., Childers, T. L., & Heckler, S. E. (1987). Picture–word consistency and elaborative processing of advertisements. *Journal of Marketing Research, 24*(4), 359–369. https://doi.org/10.1177/002224378702400403

Hudson, S., & Ritchie, J. B. (2009). Branding a memorable destination experience. The case of 'Brand Canada. *International Journal of Tourism Research, 11*(2), 217–228. https://doi.org/10.1002/jtr.720

Hulten, B., Broweus, N., & van Dijk, M. (2009). *Sensory marketing.* Palgrave Macmillan.

Isacsson, A., Alakoski, L., & Bäck, A. (2009). Using multiple senses in tourism marketing: The Helsinki expert, Eckero line and Linnanmaki Amusement Park cases. *Tourismos, 4*(3), 167–184.

Jandala, C., & Hercz, A. (2016). The role of the gastronomy in the tourism image of a destination. *Journal of Business Insights and Transformation, 9*(1), 18–22.

Jeong, G. R. (2012). *A study on tourists' motivation, place identity and satisfaction: Focused on four Jeju Olle courses.* [Master thesis]. Graduate School Jeju National University.

Kaplanidou, K., & Vogt, C. (2003). *Destination branding: Concept and measurement.* Travel Michigan and Michigan State University, Department of Park, Recreation and Tourism Resources, 1–7.

Kim, J. H. (2014). The antecedents of memorable tourism experiences: The development of a scale to measure the destination attributes associated with memorable experiences. *Tourism Management, 44*, 34–45. https://doi.org/10.1016/j.tourman.2014.02.007

Kim, K. D., & Park, M. R. (1999). A study on the tourist's destination identity and tourism development in Kyoungju. *Kyongju University Community Development Research Institute, 2*, 49–62.

Kivela, J., & Crotts, J. C. (2006). Tourism and gastronomy: Gastronomy's influence on how tourist experience a destination. *Journal of Hospitality & Tourism Research, 30*(3), 354–377. https://doi.org/10.1177/1096348006286797

Konecnik, M., D., & Chernatony, L. (2013). Developing and applying a place brand identity model: The case of Slovenia. *Journal of Business Research, 66*(1), 45–52.

Konecnik, M., & Go, F. (2008). Tourism destination brand identity: The case of Slovenia. *Journal of Brand Management, 15*(3), 177–189. https://doi.org/10.1057/palgrave.bm.2550114

Kreag, G. (2001). *The impacts of tourism.* Minnesota Sea Grant.

Krishna, A. (2010). *Sensory marketing: Research on the sensuality of products.* Routledge.

Krishna, A. (2012). An integrative review of sensory marketing: Engaging the senses to affect perception, judgment and behavior. *Journal of Consumer Psychology, 22*(3), 332–351. https://doi.org/10.1016/j.jcps.2011.08.003

Krishna, A., Elder, R. S., & Caldara, C. (2010). Feminine to smell but masculine to touch? Multisensory congruence and its effect on the aesthetic experience. *Journal of Consumer Psychology, 20*(4), 410–418. https://doi.org/10.1016/j.jcps.2010.06.010

Krishna, A., Lwin, M. O., & Morrin, M. (2010). Product scent and memory. *Journal of Consumer Research, 37*(1), 57–67. https://doi.org/10.1086/649909

Krishna, A., & Morrin, M. (2008). Does touch affect taste? The perceptual transfer of product container haptic cues. *Journal of Consumer Research, 34*(6), 807–818. https://doi.org/10.1086/523286

Krishna, A., & Schwarz, N. (2014). Sensory marketing, embodiment, and grounded cognition: A review and introduction. *Journal of Consumer Psychology, 24*(2), 159–168. https://doi.org/10.1016/j.jcps.2013.12.006

Lam, S. K., Ahearne, M., Hu, Y., & Schillewaert, N. (2010). Resistance to brand switching when a radically new brand is introduced: A social identity theory perspective. *Journal of Marketing, 74*(6), 128–146. https://doi.org/10.1509/jmkg.74.6.128

Lam, S. K., Ahearne, M., Mullins, R., Hayati, B., & Schillewaert, N. (2013). Exploring the dynamics of antecedents to consumer–brand identification with a new brand. *Journal of the Academy of Marketing Science, 41*(2), 234–252. https://doi.org/10.1007/s11747-012-0301-x

Lam, S. K., Ahearne, M., & Schillewaert, N. (2012). A multinational examination of the symbolic-instrumental framework of consumer-brand identification. *Journal of International Business Studies, 43*(3), 306–331. https://doi.org/10.1057/jibs.2011.54

Lee, H. M., & Lee, C. K. (2012). Examining the relationship between place identity and multi-dimensional loyalty: A case of visitor to insa-dong cultural district. *Korean Journal of Hotel Administration, 21*(4), 69–85.

Leong, Q. L., & Karim, S. (2015). Global perspective in tourism development: Positioning Malaysia as a culinary destination. In Angelo A. Camillo (Ed.), *Handbook of research on global hospitality and tourism management* (pp. 406–439). IGI Global.

Lindstrom, M. (2009). *Zakupologia. Prawda i kłamstwa o tym dlaczego kupujemy.* Wydawnictwo Znak.

Lindstrom, M. (2005). Broad sensory branding. *Journal of Product & Brand Management, 14*(2), 84–87. https://doi.org/10.1108/10610420510592554

Markwell, K. (2001). An intimate rendezvous with nature'? Mediating the tourist-nature experience at three tourist sites in Borneo. *Tourist Studies, 1*(1), 39–57. https://doi.org/10.1177/146879760100100103

Mattila, A. S., & Wirtz, J. (2001). Congruency of scent and music as a driver of in-store evaluations and behavior. *Journal of Retailing, 77*(2), 273–289. https://doi.org/10.1016/S0022-4359(01)00042-2

Mayo, E. J., & Jarvis, L. P. (1981). *The psychology of leisure travel. Effective marketing and selling of travel services.* CBI Publishing Company, Inc.

Miller, D. W., & Stoica, M. (2004). Comparing the effects of a photograph versus artistic renditions of a beach scene in a direct response print ad for a Caribbean resort island: A mental imagery perspective. *Journal of Vacation Marketing, 10*(1), 11–21. https://doi.org/10.1177/135676670301000102

Mintz, S. W., & Du Bois, C. M. (2002). The anthropology of food and eating. *Annual Review of Anthropology, 31*(1), 99–119. https://doi.org/10.1146/annurev.anthro.32.032702.131011

Morgan, N., Pritchard, A., & Piggott, R. (2002). New Zealand, 100% pure. The creation of a powerful niche destination brand. *Journal of Brand Management, 9*(4), 335–354. 54. [Mismatch] https://doi.org/10.1057/palgrave.bm.2540082

Morgan, N., Pritchard, A., & Pride, R. (2006). *Destination branding-creating the unique destination proposition.* Routledge.

Pan, S., & Ryan, C. (2009). Tourism sense-making: The role of the senses and travel journalism. *Journal of Travel & Tourism Marketing, 26*(7), 625–639. https://doi.org/10.1080/10548400903276897

Pawaskar, P., & Goel, M. (2014). A concept model: Multisensory marketing and destination branding. *Procedia Economics and Finance, 11*, 255–267. https://doi.org/10.1016/S2212-5671(14)00194-4

Peck, J., & Childers, T. L. (2003). Individual differences in haptic information processing: The "need for touch" scale. *Journal of Consumer Research, 30*(3), 430–442. https://doi.org/10.1086/378619

Peck, J., & Shu, S. B. (2009). The effect of mere touch on perceived ownership. *Journal of Consumer Research, 36*(3), 434–447. https://doi.org/10.1086/598614

Porteous, J. D. (1985). Smellscape. *Progress in Physical Geography: Earth and Environment, 9*(3), 356–378. Smellscape."

Puccinelli, N. M., Goodstein, R. C., Grewal, D., Price, R., Raghubir, P., & Stewart, D. (2009). Customer experience management in retailing: Understanding the buying process. *Journal of Retailing, 85*(1), 15–30. https://doi.org/10.1016/j.jretai.2008.11.003

Quan, S., & Wang, N. (2004). Towards a structural model of the tourist experience: An illustration from food experiences in tourism. *Tourism Management, 25*(3), 297–305. https://doi.org/10.1016/S0261-5177(03)00130-4

Risitano, M. (2006). *The role of destination branding in the tourism stakeholders system. The Campi Flegrei case.* Department of Business Management Faculty of Economics-University of Naples Federico II.

Russell, C. A. (2002). Investing the effectiveness of product placements in television shows: The role of modality and plot connection congruence on brand memory and attitude. *Journal of Consumer Research, 29*(3), 306–318. https://doi.org/10.1086/344432

Ryu, K., & Jang, S. (2006). Intention to experience local cuisine in a travel destination: The modified theory of reasoned action. *Journal of Hospitality & Tourism Research, 30*(4), 507–516. https://doi.org/10.1177/1096348006287163

Sengel, T., Karagoz, A., Cetin, G., Dincer, F. I., Ertugral, S. M., & Balık, M. (2015). Tourists' approach to local food. *Procedia - Social and Behavioral Sciences, 195*, 429–437. https://doi.org/10.1016/j.sbspro.2015.06.485

Shabgou, M., & Daryani, S. M. (2014). Towards the sensory marketing: Stimulating the five senses (sight, hearing, smell, touch and taste) and its impact on consumer behavior. *Indian Journal of Fundamental and Applied Life Sciences, 4*(S1), 573–581.

Skinner, H. (2018). Who really creates the place brand? Considering the role of user generated content in creating and communicating a place identity. *Communication & Society, 31*(4), 9–25.

Son, A., & Pearce, P. (2005). Multi-Faceted image assessment. *Journal of Travel & Tourism Marketing, 18*(4), 21–35. https://doi.org/10.1300/J073v18n04_02

Spangenberg, E. R., Grohmann, B., & Sprott, D. E. (2005). It's beginning to smell (and sound) a lot like Christmas: The interactive effects of ambient scent and music in a retail setting. *Journal of Business Research, 58*(11), 1583–1589. https://doi.org/10.1016/j.jbusres.2004.09.005

Sparks, B., Bowen, J., & Klag, S. (2003). Restaurant and the tourist market. *International Journal of Contemporary Hospitality Management, 15*(1), 6–13. https://doi.org/10.1108/09596110310458936

Stevenson, R. J., Prescott, J., & Boakes, R. A. (1999). Confusing tastes and smells: How odours can influence the perception of sweet and sour tastes. *Chemical Senses, 24*(6), 627–635. https://doi.org/10.1093/chemse/24.6.627

Stockfelt, T. (1991). Sound as an existential necessity. *Journal of Sound and Vibration, 151*(3), 367–370. https://doi.org/10.1016/0022-460X(91)90533-P

Stringer, C. (1984). Human evolution and biological adaptation in the Pleistocene, 55–83. In R. Foley (Ed.), *Hominid evolution and community ecology: Prehistoric human adaptation in biological perspective*. London: Academic Press.

Telfer, D. J., & Wall, G. (2000). Strengthening backward economic linkages: Local food purchasing by three Indonesian hotels. *Tourism Geographies*, *2*(4), 421–447. https://doi.org/10.1080/146166800750035521

Tsai, C. L. (2013). Culinary tourism and night markets in Taiwan. *International Journal of Business and Information*, *8*(2), 247–266.

Tsaur, S., Yen, C., & Yan, Y. (2016). Destination brand identity: Scale development and validation. *Asia Pacific Journal of Tourism Research*, *21*(12), 1310–1314. https://doi.org/10.1080/10941665.2016.1156003

Urry, J. (1990). The consumption of tourism. *Sociology*, *24*(1), 23–35. https://doi.org/10.1177/0038038590024001004

Urry, J. (1995). A middle-class countryside. In T. Butler & M. Savage (Eds.), *Social change and the middle classes* (pp. 205–219). London: UCL Press.

Urry, J. (2002). *The tourist gaze: Leisure and travel in contemporary societies* (2nd ed.). Sage.

Viren, P. P., Murray, A. K., Brown, T., & Beckman, C. (2017). *North American Adventure Travelers: Seeking personal growth, new destinations, and immersive culture*. Adventure Technical Report, 1–33.

Worlu, R. E., Adekanbi, T. O., Ajagbe, M. A., & Isiavwe, D. T. (2015). Brand identity of tourist destination and the impact on patronage. *International Journal of Hospitality and Tourism Management*, *1*(3), 1–11.

Wright, R. (2006). *Consumer behavior*. Thomson Publishing.

Yorkston, E., & Menon, G. (2004). A sound idea: Phonetic effects of brand names on consumer judments. *Journal of Consumer Research*, *31*(1), 43–51. https://doi.org/10.1086/383422

Yuksel, A., Yuksel, F., & Bilim, Y. (2010). Destination attachment: Effects on customer satisfaction and cognitive, affective and conative loyalty. *Tourism Management*, *31*(2), 274–284. https://doi.org/10.1016/j.tourman.2009.03.007

Zukin, S. (2004). Dialogue on urban cultures: Globalization and culture in an urbanizing world. In *UN Habitat World Urban Forum, Barcelona* (pp. 13–17).

Part III

Symbolic sentiments

Feeling opulent: adding an affective dimension to symbolic consumption of themes

Namita Roy and Ulrike Gretzel

ABSTRACT

Themes direct the symbolic consumption of tourism. Most tourism research argues for symbolic association to represent cognitive meaning-making. Responding to the call for an affective turn in tourism studies, we argue for symbolic consumption of themes to be both affective and cognitive through the concept of 'feeling'. We draw from our five-year long (2014–2019) ethnomethodological study of a gastronomic themed trail and explore opulence as a feeling. We find affective symbols of opulence, including sensory engagements, materialities and discourses. They demonstrate opulence to be an affective and cognitive amalgamation that comprises feelings of exclusivity, eliteness, indulgence and enrichment. Opulence is embodied, felt, as well as knowingly conformed to, through the entanglement of meanings and affects, and as understood through the theoretical discourses on affective dimensions of symbolic consumption in tourism. Managerially, the marketing of gastronomic trails is understood as a luxurious pursuit.

摘要

主题引导着旅游的象征性消费。大多数旅游研究主张符号联想代表认知意义的产生。为了响应旅游研究情感转向的呼吁, 我们通过研究"感觉"的概念, 认为主题的符号消费应既具有情感性又具有认知性。我们利用对一个美食主题路线长达五年(2014–2019)民族志研究, 探索了富裕的感觉。我们发现了富裕的情感符号, 包括感官体验, 物质和话语。它们证明富裕是一种情感和认知的融合, 包括排他感、精英感、放纵感和丰富感。研究结果表明, 富裕是通过融汇意义和影响而被具象化、感知和有意地遵从。研究结果推进了符号消费在旅游情感维度的理论论述。从管理角度来看, 研究结果将美食路线作为一种奢华的追求进行了营销。

Introduction

Themed trails/routes include tourism destinations that are marketed under an overarching theme, which is interpreted through symbolic association (Lukas, 2007a). Themed routes reflect an alignment of destinations or services that result in experiences at different geographical scales (Broadway, 2017), including local (e.g. Westside

Wine Trail in Kelowna, Canada), regional (Great Ocean Road in Australia), national (Route 66 in USA) or international routes (e.g. Holy Grail Route in Europe). Themed trails use cues, motifs, signs and marketing paraphernalia to convey a thematic narrative open to symbolic consumption by the traveller (MacLeod, 2016) suggesting symbolic consumption to be key to the success of themed trails.

Symbolic consumption or meaningful association is integral to tourism experiences (Knobloch et al., 2017). Being able to 'subjectively' and 'meaningfully' connect with a place, is understood as one of the critical components of the tourist experience (Cutler et al., 2014; Gazley & Watling, 2015). This focus on meaning-making draws from a cultural turn where symbolic association is seen as a cognitive deliverance and people are considered to be interpreters of symbols embedded in the socio-material environment (Ekinci et al., 2013; Gazley & Watling, 2015). Following an 'emotional turn', several researchers have argued for prioritizing the 'felt', 'sensed' and 'lived' aspects of the tourist experience (Knobloch et al., 2017; Urry, 2016). However, much of this research considers feelings and emotions to be cognitively alert achievements or deliverances (Jepson & Sharpley, 2015) by arguing for their positioning in the neurological (Birenboim, 2016), physiological (Crouch & Desforges, 2003) and psychological realm (Buckley, 2016). While this line of research is helpful in locating the bodily or sensorial processes that trigger the consciousness of emotion, it struggles to explicate the unconscious, 'more-than-rational'(Anderson, 2006), pre-cognitive (Thrift, 2008), and indescribable experiences that are affectively sensed in the socio-material environment (Ahmed, 2013; Buda, 2015).

Following the call for an 'affective turn' in tourism and the importance of socio-material interactions in the symbolic consumption of themed routes, we argue for an affective dimension to symbolic consumption in tourism. Specifically, this research follows affect researchers Sara Ahmed (2013) and Sasha Newell (2018) by articulating 'feelings' or the 'felt experience' as a non-binary 'in betweenness' which exposits the relationship between affect and cognition. The research thus suggests that symbolic association is a more-than-cognitive affair and involves 'felt' and 'sensed' emotions. Using ethnomethodological principles and methods (including interviews and participant observation) to uncover socio-material arrangements that locate affect (Ahmed, 2013; Thrift, 2008), we demonstrate the role of feelings in shaping the symbolic consumption of opulence on a food and wine themed trail in the Hunter Valley, Australia. The research suggests that the theme is not only understood and interpreted cognitively but is also embodied affectively.

Opulence is an expression of grandeur and luxury suggesting a sense of power (Jacobsen 2012). Specific to the theme of gastronomy, associations of opulence and luxury are understudied (Wolf et al., 2016). While food and wine as products are often related to luxury and opulence through their production and consumption (Baer et al., 2018; Rokka, 2017), association of opulence with 'food and wine tourism' is not an obvious one. Bellini and Resnick (2018) suggest that opulence in food and wine tourism is related to feeling and sensing luxury as an experience. Through this research we demonstrate that opulence is sensed and experienced as feelings or an 'impression' of an emotion through the interplay of meanings and affects on the food and wine trail (Ahmed, 2013). Thus, this paper argues that tourists unconsciously and consciously seek and follow feelings of 'opulence' in the gastronomic theme.

Conceptual background

Literature on theming or themed routes builds on symbolic association as a mental process. It acknowledges the role of theming as a multi-sensory phenomenon (Lukas, 2007b), but 'sensing' itself is viewed as 'sense-making' and the senses as tools that help with it, emphasizing the role of cognitive interpretation (Baudrillard & Levin, 1981). Recent scholarship in tourism has started acknowledging feelings and emotions as integral to understanding consumption of tourist experiences (Haldrup & Larsen, 2006). Tourist experiences consist of sensory engagements, non-human materialities and discourses which are known to be affective in nature (Germann Molz, 2007). For example, Canniford et al. (2017) discuss affects triggered by smells in creating a sense of place. In a destination, non-human materialities such as architecture, landscapes, roads and animals create affects that instigate a sense of place (Jepson & Sharpley, 2015). For example, Reckwitz (2016) discusses the role of architecture in creating imaginings, interpretations as well as reflexive pre-cognitive practices through the materiality of buildings, lanes and roads. Discourses that produce imaginaries and past memories are also known to be affective (Thrift, 2008). Newell (2018) discusses discourses, texts, images and language as 'carrying affect'. This literature points towards things and discourses being affective symbols that are more-than-cognitively 'felt'.

In case of themed routes, marketing collateral, spatial elements and commodities shape tourist actions and experiences (Buda et al., 2014; Baerenholdt et al., 2017), suggesting a directive role of affect. For example, maps and signage that are important marketing paraphernalia on themed routes are known to assure comfort and competence in an unfamiliar environment (Rossetto, 2012). Landscapes and spatial elements such as roads, rivers, terrains also prompt an affective construction of space (MacLeod, 2016; Shaw & Williams, 2004). Thus, it can be assumed that travellers on themed routes unconsciously and consciously seek and follow such affective symbols that stimulate visceral imaginaries (Beardsworth & Bryman, 1999) in the themed environment (Caton & Santos, 2007; Cutler et al., 2014). Considering this affective nature of the themed environment, this paper studies opulence as a felt experience on a food and wine trail (Bellini & Resnick, 2018).

Opulence in tourism

Despite its importance in the field of marketing, opulence is one of the least researched topics in tourism (Correia et al., 2019). Literature suggests that associations of opulence with tourism experiences relate to 'consumer judgements and perceptions' of luxury (Yeoman & McMahon-Beattie, 2014), authenticity (Wang, 1999), social status (Veblen, 1899) and conspicuous and inconspicuous consumption (Eckhardt et al., 2015). Following a semiotic economic perspective (Thurlow & Jaworski, 2012), opulence is understood through individual subjectivity. Subjectivity is composed of acquired human competencies over time (Giddens, 1984). In the case of food and wine, discourses around production and consumption situations have resulted in their symbolic association with luxury, authenticity and status (Rokka, 2017).

While most studies on opulence or luxury postulate its dependence on social semiotics (Belk, 1987; Eckhardt et al., 2015; Yeoman & McMahon-Beattie, 2014), following an affective perspective suggests unearthing the emotional entanglements, feelings or impressions that constitute the meanings of opulence in socio-material interactions with the environment. Recent studies have highlighted the role of the socio-material context in creating symbolic associations of luxury (Baer et al., 2018); however, there is a lack of research defining how symbolic associations of luxury or opulence are felt and sensed. This is important in the context of gastronomic tourism, where opulence is experienced as a fleeting, fluid and sensorial atmosphere rather than a definitive social norm (Bellini & Resnick, 2018).

Acknowledging the affective nature of a themed route, we argue that symbolic association on the route goes beyond a mental process of interpretation. Symbolic association is 'felt' and 'sensed' before, while and after any meanings are derived, and it is this felt and sensed association with the themed landscape that is pursued by the travellers. The next section outlines the affective theoretical perspective that is fundamental to understanding these symbolic associations of opulence with a wine and food trail.

Affective dimensions of symbolic association

Following the cultural turn in geography, the world is understood as a sign system which is interpreted by social actors (Lew et al., 2008). Symbolic association is thus underpinned by theories of symbolic interactionism and social constructivism, whereby people make sense of things and their social environments through acquired learnings of signs and symbols (Aksan et al., 2009). Accordingly, symbolic association research in tourism discusses travellers as cognitive social actors who interpret motifs, cues and signs and relate to them through their personal experiences (Watling, 2015). Thinking about symbolic association as a processual act of the mind suggests non-recognition of the embodied, 'felt' and unconscious ways in which travellers perceive places (Baerenholdt et al., 2017).

The dominance of cognition is challenged by the recent affective discourse in tourism studies, which points towards symbolic association as being more-than-cognitive (Newell, 2018). Following the affective turn, attention has turned to the 'felt' aspects of an experience. The concepts of affect and emotion are paramount to the understanding of how an experience is 'felt' (Buda, 2015). However, these concepts are highly debated in the tourism literature and demonstrate two main perspectives towards positioning affect as external versus internal to social construction. Researchers who position affect as external to social construction differentiate between emotions and affects. Anderson and Harrison (2006) establish affect as non-cognitive, sensorial, pre-personal, unconscious shared intensities between bodies, while emotions are cognitively expressed feelings that are consciously experienced (Birenboim, 2016). These researchers describe meaning-making as a cognitive process where bodily interactions translate into cognition in a linear fashion, through affect, feeling, emotion and then cognition. Adopting these conceptualizations, much tourism literature distinguishes between affect and emotions and demarcates them as disparate fields of study that do not intermingle (Pile, 2010). Various tourism researchers also follow these distinctions when they describe emotions as affectively or sensorially acquired subjectivities (Germann Molz, 2017; Pocock, 2015), furthering a neurological or psychological conceptualization of emotion in the tourism literature (Buckley, 2016).

However, researchers who position affect as an integral part of social construction view meanings, emotions, feelings and affect as interdependent processes that play off each other, frequently being shared in socio-material interactions (Everingham & Motta, 2020; Holst, 2018; Saul & Waterton, 2018; Tolia-Kelly et al., 2016). For example, Molander and Hartmann (2018) argue for encounters that channel affect and emotion which reinforce and construct ideas and meanings simultaneously. These affective researchers disagree on emotions being conscious cognitive expressions and argue for the permeability of the body, and the non-binary, non-representational 'in-betweenness' that defines the relationship between affect and emotion (Everingham & Motta, 2020). In discussing the fluidity and non-hierarchical unfolding of emotions, Ahmed (2013) argues for emotions that creep up unknowingly, intermesh with ideas and personal subjectivities during affective encounters and may not even be decipherable, as we cannot assume we always know what we feel (Ahmed, 2013). Following the 'outside in' movement of emotions, Ahmed uses the term 'impression' instead of 'expression' to understand emotions. Thus, Ahmed (2013) argues against impersonalizing affect or personalizing emotions (Massumi, 1995). Following Ahmed (2013), emotions are always entangled with meanings, feelings and affect in an experience and hence do not need to be differentiated or distinguished.

Ahmed (2013)'s conceptualization of emotions and affect is helpful to understanding symbolic association on themed routes. Within existing scholarship on affect, symbolic association has been understood as a cognitive internal (to the body) process which is triggered by affect understood as external to the body (Buckley, 2016; Hemmings, 2005). However, similar to Ahmed (2013), several researchers argue that semiotic processes are always intertwined with meanings and feelings, which are sensed and made sense of simultaneously (Reckwitz, 2016). Newell (2018) argues that affective symbols create an affective sensation alongside conveying a meaning which is not necessarily understood but felt. Taking the example of a GIF image on the phone that shows a panda destroying an office, Newell argues how the panda as an affective symbol simultaneously conveys meanings and feelings of anger. Thus, symbolic association, like Ahmed's concept of emotion, is not reducible to a cognitive process but involves entanglement of meanings and feelings.

Drawing upon Ahmed (2013) and Newell (2018) who acknowledge the interplay between affect, emotion and cognition, this research conceptualizes symbolic association as both affective and cognitive in 'feelings'. Moving away from feelings as recognizable sensations that lead to emotions (Robinson & Picard, 2016), we conceptualize feelings as impressions of emotions, which mark the interplay between affect and cognition (Ahmed, 2013) and through which symbolic association is 'felt'.

Methodology and context

The study uses principles of ethnomethodology and employs ethnographic fieldwork methods. The study of affect requires a non-representational approach which can help locate affect in socio-material relations (Thrift, 2008). Ethnomethodology departs from other methodological orientations as instead of focusing on overarching social norms or internal motivations, it studies social norms and motivations as constructed in interactions or relations (Denzin & Lincoln, 2008). The interactionist orientation of ethnomethodology allows for a non-representational approach (Thrift, 2008). Ethnomethodology facilitates an interpretive, hermeneutic evaluation of processes and interactions where knowledge is abducted through multiple iterations (Denzin, 2017). An ethnomethodolgical orientation provides a diligent way to understand the processual origination of affect as it helps breaks down social phenomena into actions and interactions between entities, thereby locating the affective symbols and interactions (Newell, 2018). Further, as knowledge produced by ethnomethodology is always emplaced and situated (Denzin & Giardina, 2016), it is easier to unpack the ordering of socio-material interactions that situate feelings which are not only abducted from the experiences of participants but also sensed by the ethnographer.

Understanding emotions and feelings requires studying the socio-material arrangements revealed in the momentary teleology or onflow of events which would help account for people's feelings (Thrift, 2008). This is facilitated by ethnographic methods of activity narratives using 'interview to the double' (Nicolini, 2009) and 'emplaced participation' (Pink, 2015). The 'interview to the double' method suggests interviewing participants to recall details of activities and to list the minute interactions that led to decisions. Finding the why's and how's of each manoeuvre travellers made on the route facilitates learning about the feelings of opulence they perceived in each activity. Emplaced participation uses the researcher's own multi-sensory emplaced experiences to understand the interactions, thereby assisting in locating affect (Pink, 2015). Therefore, the findings include co-created, intermeshed voices of travellers along with the first researcher's voice through which feelings and affects are abductively located (Nicolini, 2009).

Research design

Adhering to non-representational approaches to uncover affect (Thrift, 2008), the research design particularly considered using the term 'travellers' and not 'tourists' (McCabe, 2005). We defined travellers as people who travelled on the trail for any reason. The use of the term travellers steers away from the representational understandings of the 'tourist' (McCabe, 2005) and helps identify travel as a part of different social practices that people embody and perform while on the trail (Sheller & Urry, 2000). This non-representational understanding of travelling helps unpack meanings and feelings associated with different practices and identities people perform while travelling on the themed route.

The information used for this research is part of an ethnographic study conducted over a period of five years (2014–2019) which included 12 research trips made to the research location over 11 months between June 2016 - May 2017. The research was carried out in two phases. In the first phase, 3 reconnaissance trips were made to understand the seasons between June 2016 and October 2016, identify possible interview locations and capture traveller profiles from discussions with various stakeholders, which also facilitated an emplaced understanding of the phenomena (Pink, 2015). In the second phase (9 research trips from November 2016 – May 2017), traveller interviews and participant observation were conducted in the high footfall period (weekends). As the focus of fieldwork was to identify socio-material interactions, teleology and activities and not individual behaviours, both phases of research allowed an understanding of different seasonal practices and interactions, thus complimenting each other. Interviewed travellers included domestic and international families, couples and friends of different age groups. The participants were asked to travel on the food and wine trail and were interviewed before and after the trip. Travellers were recruited through convenience sampling using strategies such as incentivization and flexible interviewing to not impede on travellers' themed trail experience (Denzin & Lincoln, 2011).

The information collected includes artefacts such as maps, brochures and magazines (for example destination websites, media discourses around food and wine, trail maps), interviews with 19 groups including 57 travellers, and over 140 pages of field notes gathered from participant observation. As the knowledge produced by using ethnomethodology is always situated and co-produced with the participants (Garfinkel, 1967), the information contained reflexive notes and emplaced observations of the researcher as part of the field notes. Principles of ethnomethodology guided interpretation as interviews and artefacts were coded for interactions happening on the route. Each activity or interaction was then further ordered by relating it to associated feelings and meanings. The results from the first level of ordering were then compared and contrasted, which resulted in key emergent associations. Enfolding these emergent feelings with extant literature helped analyse these key emotions. Amongst several associations analysed through this iterative process, only one association, i.e. 'opulence', is presented in this paper given its theoretical and practical importance as discussed above.

Researcher positionality

One key benefit of using ethnomethodology is that it records the emplaced feelings hermeneutically analysed by the researcher (Pink, 2015). In this case, the first author conducted the ethnography where she recorded interactions and her own feelings and analysed them along with the information gathered from the field. Thus, considering the abductive nature of this research and the performative role of the researcher in the ethnography, it is important to acknowledge the researcher's positionality in her own words.

My positionality as an outsider and a posthumanist researcher affected the interpretation of the findings. Being of Indian descent and belonging to a conservative Hindu family, my competencies of food and wine were dissimilar to the gastronomic context I witnessed. While wine in my culture is considered as alcohol and something to 'stay away from', food has religious subtexts. Going on a food and wine trail in rural

Australia enabled me to adorn the cap of an 'outsider' trying to study the practices of wine culture (Berger, 2015). However, after travelling on the trail for a few weeks, I could understand and reproduce practices that made me a wine drinker and an appreciator of wine. Through prolonged engagement with the field, I was able to notice interactions which incorporated diverse meanings and feelings for travellers, one of which was opulence.

Additionally, studying for my PhD, I was exposed to sociological concepts of posthumanism which played on my mind as I interpreted the information (Braidotti, 2006). Having been exposed to Deleuzian philosophy, I constantly looked for the relational context and positioning and framing of interactions, which almost every time pointed towards material elements that were crucial in generating affect (Bowden, 2011; Deleuze & Guattari, 1988). I could sense feelings being triggered through mere mention of terms on the map or the signage not only in me but also in my participants who wanted to 'get their map' to discuss their experience. The fact that they could talk about the experience only through 'their map' also suggested a sense of affect which enveloped personal meanings. Thus, the fieldwork combined with episodes of abductive research alerted me to the affective nature of gastronomic tourism.

Case context

This research studied the Around Hermitage Wine and Food Trail in the Hunter Valley (AHWFT), Australia as a context to understand the meanings and feelings that trigger movement on a themed route. AHWFT is one of eleven gastronomic trails that form part of the Hunter Valley region in Australia. Australia has been a leader in gastronomic tourism with tremendous tourism spend growth in gastronomy (winesaustralia. com, 2016). Hunter Valley being one of the main wine regions of the country recorded a total of 9 million visitors in 2015 with a total expenditure of over $2 billion by food and wine tourists (Tourism Research Australia, 2015). Following the increase in wine tourism, several wineries started diversifying their products to include cheeses, chocolates and olives, which have now become independent businesses in the region. Several high-end, expensive, fine-dining and café style restaurants have also opened following the increase in gastronomic tourism. Within the Hunter Valley's grand and historic narrative, the AHWFT is marketed as a luxurious, boutique region, where wines are expertly handcrafted by new generation winemakers. The AHWFT attends to wine and food tourism as an opulent experience by including spa businesses and boutique winery accommodation (Croce & Perri, 2010). Various businesses on the trail present wine classes, tours of vineyards and other experiences which exude a sense of luxury.

The AHWFT is conceptualized as a potentially affective environment due to the presence of sensory engagements, materialities and discourses. Sensory engagements on the trail include tasting and smelling food and wine, viewing landscapes, touching grapes and vines and hearing people (Mason & O'Mahony, 2007). The materialities on the trail include the terroir such as the soil, rain, vines, hills and other aspects of the earth which help with wine production (Croce & Perri, 2010). Further, object materialities such as wine glasses, labels, bottles, equipment, furniture and other 'things' also form important materialities on the trail. In case of the AHWFT, marketing material

Figure 1. Around Hermitage Wine and Food Trail Map, 2016 (reproduced with the permission of the Around Hermitage Association).

such as websites, brochures, signage and maps follow discourses of wine-making as a country practice and food and wine tourism as a luxurious pursuance which guides symbolic association. The map presented below (Figure 1), through the mention of destinations, illustrations of road curvature, icon-based depictions of attractions, classy colours and sleek design affectively expresses the feel of the route by giving a sense of what to expect.

Findings and discussion: Symbolic consumption of opulence

Travellers following the AHWFT felt a sense of opulence in the food and wine environment. Opulence relates to meanings of power and feelings of being powerful or dominant through expressions of grandeur and luxury (Jacobsen, 2012). Literature on gastronomy suggests that both wine and food are associated with luxury following their historical narratives and myths as reproduced in popular media and status discourses (Bellini & Resnick, 2018; Kivela & Crotts, 2006; Rokka, 2017). In the AHWFT context meanings and feelings of several sensory engagements, materialities and discourses come together to symbolize opulence. Opulence was sensed and felt on the trail through the coming together of both cognition and affect, which was witnessed in feelings, specifically feelings of exclusivity, eliteness, indulgence and enrichment. Each of these are discussed below.

Feeling 'exclusive'

On the AHWFT, opulence is felt as exclusivity. Marketing literature studies luxury as exclusivity whereby retailers and producers distinguish their products and services from other luxury goods to maintain superiority (Baer et al., 2018). Exclusivity helps marketers distinguish their products as conspicuous (Yeoman & McMahon-Beattie, 2014). Eckhardt et al. (2015) define conspicuous consumption as recognizable display of affluence or 'show off'. While literature on conspicuous consumption focusses on acquisition of luxury products, in this case conspicuous luxury was felt in the wine tourism experiences.

Meanings of exclusivity as a form of luxury and power guided travellers who encountered opulence while booking fine dining restaurants. Several travellers mentioned their enjoyment of fine dining at expensive and exclusive restaurants where they had to make a reservation beforehand. Joey and Christina, a mature age couple thinking of themselves as elite, considered specialty dining as a focal experience and structured their travel around their reservation. Rick and Amelia, professionals on a weekend break, also pre-booked the top-rated restaurant on the route as they knew that it was difficult to get reservations from the reviews on the website. Other exclusive activities included limousine rides, which were selected by several groups who were looking for ways to make the day special and 'feel rich'. Observations and general discussions revealed travellers opting for horse carriage rides to visit wineries in style. While selection of exclusive restaurants conveyed a sense of cognitive judgement of power infused with exclusivity, the feeling of exclusivity was achieved as meanings of exclusivity were reinforced through reading reviews during the booking of the table or through the affect felt by the presence of horse carriages (Newell, 2018). These findings highlight the importance of activities like sensorial interactions with the limousine or horse carriages and the act of eating in a 'fine dining' restaurant as key to meaning-making. Watson and Waterton (2019) argue that such 'encounters' are cognitive and affective. They suggest that affective forces registered in feelings are channelled in the encounter and interact with people's competencies and understandings. However, they argue for affective engagements as triggers to representational ideas about the encounter. What our findings suggest is that there is no specific chronology in the encounter. Feelings of exclusivity also emerged as people 'sought' affect from these encounters and relished it.

Travellers also felt special and exclusive during wine tasting sessions. Opulence was conveyed through the affective atmosphere of the cellar door space (Anderson, 2009). The cellar door spaces triggered an opulent atmosphere through offering views of the vineyards, art by local artists, seated/standing areas for tastings, and luxurious furnishings with modern and heritage details. For example, Monica, a female European backpacker in her early 20's, travelled on the trail and reflected on how she felt the luxuriousness of the cellar door at a winery:

Monica - so we liked it for the wine, we liked it better but for the atmosphere, Keith Tulloch wines and kitchen Cocoa Nib was very nice because you just relax on the couch, you're outside on the balcony and you can taste wine and suited servers just come to you, explain to you.

Monica refers to the material elements including the couch and the balcony that together create a luxurious ambience. She discusses the sense of opulence being conveyed through the relaxation afforded by the affective capacity of the couch. She specifically refers to the 'atmosphere' that she senses through the affective symbols of luxury such as the 'suited server', who positions her in a place of power suggesting her to be in command. This demonstrates how opulence was constructed from her understandings of power, which she 'felt' through a combination of affective symbols (Fisher, 2004). This finding underlines the importance of material arrangements in transmitting the meaning of power as an affect (Buda et al., 2014). The importance of material arrangements in the transmission of affect has been studied by various researchers (Anderson, 2009; Massumi, 2002; Thrift, 2008; Tolia-Kelly et al., 2016). However, what this finding further illustrates is the intermingling of affect and the meaning of power, which are felt simultaneously in specific material arrangements. Drawing from Ahmed (2013), the luxurious atmosphere is felt as the inbetweenness of affect and cognition and is sensed by the body.

Travellers also felt exclusive through service (Schmitt, 1999). Mary and friends (a group of four middle aged culinary educationists) discuss the classy and exclusive service that made them feel particularly 'welcomed'. Specifically, they discuss the wine tasting experience, the service not being pushy, and sharing local produce and information without expectations as affective symbols of generosity that made them feel special.

Emmie - yeah they were very welcoming.

Mary - like they could be uhh Monique's parents or Emma's parents. Like it was just so lovely

Emmie - they gave us a little ____

Mon - yeahh they gave us local produce as well

Mary - It was the whole experience wasn't it? It was an experience rather than just a taste.

Bart - They didn't force us to buy either

Emmie - Right they didn't really. They had the bits of paper out but yeah it was not about buying wine. It was about the information they had to offer.

Mary - More than happy and very generous too with their tasting serves.

The feeling of exclusivity in Mary's case is sensed in the combination of different affective symbols. In the quote above, the meanings of exclusivity intertwine with gestures and symbols of generosity passed on in the affect of the wine tasting experience. The feelings of exclusivity highlight the importance of 'alignment' of socio-material interactions in the wine tasting experience. This is in line with Saul and Waterton (2018), who point towards the need for an affective-cognitive alignment in tourist experiences. This is especially helpful in the case of themes, where such alignments can be manufactured and manipulated.

Another way travellers were made to feel special was through product positioning by the winemakers (Hollebeek & Brodie, 2009). The winemakers had restricted distribution systems and sold only at their own showroom. *'Mary - I think that they made the point in saying that they are exclusive that you can't buy them in restaurants, you only get them at the cellar door'.* Additionally, winemakers fuelled the feeling of urgency by promoting wines that were 'not to be missed'. Thus, travellers felt exclusive in thinking that they were being sold scarce premium wine and felt an affective sense of urgency to buy. This creation of a story around availability of wine creates a sense of exclusivity reinstating the feeling of opulence (Papacharissi, 2016). Stories have been used traditionally to create imaginaries (Salazar & Graburn, 2014) and help with interpretation, however, this finding demonstrates how stories could also trigger different affects.

Feeling 'elite' or 'upmarket'

Opulence was also signalled through the feelings of 'eliteness' while travelling on the route. Eliteness was communicated as a class distinction (Thurlow & Jaworski, 2012). Literature suggests that luxury marketing invokes aspirational emotional responses in the minds of the consumer (Baer et al., 2018). In the case of the AHWFT, promotional campaigns including text on websites positioned the AHWFT as a place that adheres to 'upmarket' tastes. The quote below displays the associations of country with food and wine that were observed on the website of the AHWFT.

You'll find some of the best scenery in the Hunter Valley, award-winning Hunter Valley wineries, fine-dining restaurants and cafes, and even meet the wine makers at family-owned cellar doors. Relax in luxury Hunter Valley accommodation with rooms to suit all tastes.

Specific vocabulary such as 'best', 'luxury', 'premium', 'award-winning', 'fine-dining' and 'tastes' create a sense of opulence to be consumed at the destination. These words combined in a narrative stimulate feelings of luxury by acting as affective symbols of imaginaries and reminders of related experiences. Other affective symbols such as images of expensive art combined with promotional information suggested the trail was a pursuit for the wealthy. Selting (2010) confirms that words and language are

Figure 2. Traveller Photograph (reproduced with the permission of the participant).

powerful affective symbols that intertwine with meanings. Travellers relate to the aspirational qualities of such affective symbols. Further, it is argued in gastronomic studies that most travellers who pursue the delicate and sophisticated tastes of food and wine are 'visible achievers' already wealthy and competent about taste (Hall & Mitchell, 2004). Thus, such discourses easily interact with an individual's competencies and imaginaries of taste to generate feelings of eliteness (Newell, 2018).

Travelling on a food and wine trail prompted links with being elite. Travellers visibly tried to 'fit in' by conforming with the notion of opulence. They embodied opulence in performances such as dressing up, fine dining and driving in expensive vehicles. Dressing up as a performance of opulence involved adorning expensive clothing and accessories. Christina was happy to share her photographs (Figure 2) where she is seen adorning an expensive dress and sunglasses. The field notes from participant observation also describe the need to fit in by the first author while travelling on the themed route.

'Observations of Clothes –

- *Men are wearing summer clothes, one was wearing a pink t-shirt from Ralph Lauren*
- *Women wear silky tops with stylish cuts, accessories such as dangling earrings, sun glasses from Prada, Gucci, one woman was carrying a bag from Hermes*
- *Shoes – sandals and nice looking shoes, even while cycling they are not wearing sports shoes.*
- *Men wearing shoes without socks – kinda relaxed look'*

I need to be part of this group in order to get some interviews, I need to gain their trust by showing them that I belong. (Fieldnotes, 22/11/2016)

This finding reflects two key ideas. First, it suggests an opulent affective atmosphere felt by the travellers. The relational positioning of 'expensive' clothes within the existing socio-material composition of opulence as discussed above, create an affective atmosphere which is embodied by the travellers (Steadman et al., 2020). Second, it highlights their need to conform to this felt atmosphere. Semiotically, clothes are known to create social distinctions by marking territories and demonstrating social norms and identities, thereby articulating their role as symbols (Belk, 1987). What the fieldnote illustrates is the use of clothes and accessories as affective symbols of eliteness that channel the affective atmosphere of opulence to which travellers like Christina feel the need to conform.

The goal of fitting in with the elite atmosphere became something that travellers actively pursued. They were attracted by and enjoyed having to dress up and be part of the upmarket culture. Many travellers like Joey and Christina followed the upmarket settings on the trail and travelled to wineries which helped them live their identities as elitists. In the quote below, Joey and Christina discuss their feelings of consuming an upmarket experience, marked by references to knowledge about fine wines, not going to the 'pub' and having access to high quality wines. They comprehend meanings of eliteness through the feelings of uniqueness the experience promotes, the gaining of new knowledge and the felt quality of wines. Thus, opulence is symbolized through the ways in which eliteness is felt as well as conformed to.

Joey: Another thing that really attracts us is – it's an up market, sort of a feeling, I suppose, when we were younger, and didn't know about fine wines and things, we'd go to a pub and you have a usual pub where you eat and drink, whereas this is a more up market, more elite

Christina: More elite, elegant, yeah, we like that

Joey: - this is – up market, this is high quality –

The reference to interactions and competencies that mark the emotional and cognitive reference to eliteness is particularly interesting. The comparison of the pub experience highlights the situatedness of the feeling of eliteness in the distinctive socio-material environment suggesting the importance of such alignments for channelling affect. Newell (2018) argues that different arrangements of signs or meanings and materials produce different affects which intertwine with semiotic processes.

Feeling 'indulgent'

Opulence was also communicated through feelings of indulgence (Yeoman & McMahon-Beattie, 2014). Indulgence was conveyed in the discourses of 'letting go' or 'not thinking about' expenditure. Indulgence was demonstrated as an opulent feeling as people consumed or bought expensive wines without thinking about money. Food and wine tourism has always been associated with self-indulgence (Hall & Mitchell, 2004). Whether it is related to gluttony (Andersson & Mossberg, 2017), the affect of alcohol on the body (Jayne et al., 2012) or the rules of holidaying (Kivela & Crotts, 2006), food and wine tourism allows people to relax and 'let go' in ways they would not grant themselves in everyday contexts.

Indulgence is also felt on the AHWFT as the affective atmosphere of being relaxed on a holiday is sensed as shared, 'Steve – it feels like everyone is just so relaxed, we are all doing the same thing.' Steve sees indulgence as part of 'letting go' or feeling relaxed which is transmitted through affect when everyone is 'doing the same thing'. This echoes the transferable nature of affect discussed by several researchers (Massumi, 2015; Seyfert, 2012). In this case, the above quote also demonstrates how sharing of affect by 'doing the same thing' allows for meanings and feelings to be intertwined (Ahmed, 2013) as travellers associate their experiences with opulence. Thus, opulence is sensed in the sharing of affect and is perceived as well as performed at the same time as travellers feel indulgent.

Feelings of indulgence also emerged as the meanings of holidaying were affectively connected to high expenditure:

> Joey: We come here to indulge ourselves, and if when you're at home (inaudible), you would say, and you want to go out to a restaurant, you'll probably think, oh well that's a bit expensive, and say ooh –
>
> Joey: ... you don't have that feeling here, you don't have that here
>
> Christina: Yeah, I want a bottle of wine – what? 18 dollars, 25 dollars, 40 dollars – I like it, we get it. Yeah, it is, and that's sort of the indulgent feeling now when we're coming here on a holiday, we just -
>
> Joey: It's the sort of place you come to, knowing that –
>
> Christina: That you're going to spend money. And it doesn't matter.

The quote demonstrates the meanings of expenditure and holidaying being ingrained into social competencies when Joey and Christina point out that 'you know that you are going to spend money'. Shove et al. (2012) argue for competencies as understandings of norms and practices that develop over time through repetition. Such competencies allow for travellers to draw meanings from activities and interactions. The quote shows that holidaying is intertwined with meanings of indulgence in the couple's competencies, making it easy for them to connect wine as an affective symbol of both eliteness and holidaying in their feeling of indulgence.

Feeling 'enriched'

Opulence was also communicated through feelings of being enriched by being in an authentic environment. Authenticity is most often understood as being in the eye of the beholder, suggesting a sense of moral superiority over others who are unable to understand or 'see' it (Zukin, 2009). Thus, following or seeking authenticity suggests a sense of opulence and power through which people identify themselves as superior. The findings on the AHWFT indicate that travellers feel enriched by practicing existential authenticity (Wang, 1999). Existential authenticity relates to a state of being that is achieved through personal experiences of the toured objects (Rickly-Boyd, 2012). On the AHWFT travellers felt enriched by gaining knowledge about the local terroir. They also felt enriched by traveling like a local, by following referrals from local networks to 'far off' wineries, visiting 'boutique-y' wineries, and buying locally made products (Hashimoto & Telfer, 2007). Such authenticity was felt through a combination of various beliefs, stories, conversations and interactions with affective symbols such as country roads and landscapes that created the sense of 'local' or 'authentic' and supported the quest (Tolia-Kelly et al., 2016).

Moreover, travellers felt enriched by learning about the country lifestyle that was authentic to the region. Local stories about the terroir fuelled feelings of gaining cultural capital in many travellers. The wine-makers' understandings of wine-making (tools and know-how), local terroir (vintage characteristics – heat, rains, soil etc.) helped travellers connect wine making to the authenticity of country, 'Emmie - he also made you appreciate the wines more because he explained in what way 2014 had a really good run and 2016 had a bit of rain, yeah all that history, how the seasons worked'. Emmie points out the affective elements of the story, such as the history, the rain and its impact on the quality of wine, as affective symbols that helped her connect with the terroir and make sense of the taste of the wine (Rantala et al., 2011). Views of countryside also channelled affect as Mary and Bart (who were on the trail to show the wine country to their friends) pointed out different elements from the terroir.

> Mary - of those little sights and everything and just pointing out a few things on the way and then before we knew it we were at Degen a little bit of a drive in but, you know, I even said, I think I said to Emmie on the way. Look at this you know you city people you go and buy a bottle of wine, there's your vineyard. That's where your wine - that's where it comes from. So was just trying to bring it all back, you know it's a whole thing it's a holistic thing.

In the quote above, Mary connects with winemaking as a country practice through the physical landscape of the vineyard, which allows her to 'show off' her knowledge to her friends. Mary feels a sense of superiority in connecting meanings of country life to its affective symbols which she proudly points out to her friends. This finding is in line with Zukin's (2009) argument on the interdependence of authenticity and superiority. The feelings of enrichment demonstrate that the meanings of authenticity and superiority are simultaneously associated with the affect of the physical landscape.

Travellers also felt enriched by following 'local knowledge' through referrals. In the quote below, Brad travelling on the trail with his partner combining work and leisure, mentions how he was happy to follow Glen as he formed part of the 'local network' and knew better. Brad discusses how he was made to 'feel welcome', suggesting a sense of exclusivity which he perceived by following local knowledge.

> Brad - We basically just went on with local knowledge Glen, he said there's another one here called which wasn't on the map. Hunter's Dream . so he said go here and they were fantastic… we felt welcome because Glenn's kind of sent us this way.

Brad's feeling of enrichment is also fuelled when he associates 'local knowledge' as learning about an exclusive winery. The quote conveys that the feeling of exclusive knowledge is sensed through the affect of the map, which marks the absence of the winery. Here, Brad's feeling of enrichment materializes from his connection of meanings of authenticity with exclusivity channelled in the affect of the map. This is in line with Ahmed's work (2013) on impressions of meanings being intertwined with affect in feelings.

Additionally, buying locally-made products helped travellers connect with the milieu of the wine country, making their experience more authentic. Feelings of enrichment were also reflected in the pursuance of boutique-y wines. Boutique-y was understood as a small independent winery which is regarded as authentic due to their limited supply and resourceful use of the terroir in winemaking. Travellers such as Danika and Melania were specifically looking for 'boutique-y' wineries to connect with the local milieu.

> Danika: … we decided we wanna do more boutique-y stuff, so they kinda guided us to other boutique-y areas which is where we got on to the hermitage road area.

> Melania: Well it makes it more whole I mean if I know, … it was really nice to go to Mistletoe for example today and talk to them and know that the wine we are drinking is not just off the shelf and it's not sold to everyone, you know, it's not mass produced and they don't buy the fruit and that it comes from that area. We're coming here to try the grapes from here, so it's interesting going to a vineyard when they're like actually we grow the grapes.

In the quote above, Melania demonstrates the symbolic association of boutique-y as authentic emerging through the performance of travelling to boutique-y wineries contrasted with 'buying from the shelf'. The act of not buying mass-produced wine or 'going to the winery' communicates a sense of superiority which sets travellers apart from people who 'buy from the shelf'. This sense of being able to taste the fruit at its source and buying something 'that is not sold to everyone' conveys feelings of being special that are channelled in the act of buying local, authentic wine. Further, both Mary and Melania mention the need to explore the 'whole' and learn about the entire process of winemaking. These findings stress the intertwining of meanings of authenticity with competencies of the travellers which are either showcased or enriched through socio-material affective encounters. Though much literature conceptualizes authenticity to be a cognitive capability (Kim & Bonn, 2016; Wang, 1999), this research points towards the role of affective symbols and interactions in forming and communicating emotional impressions of authenticity (Ahmed, 2004). The embodied performances suggest the channelling of meanings in affective encounters on the route (Buda et al., 2014; Tolia-Kelly et al., 2016). The findings demonstrate the meanings of authenticity and learning intertwined affectively in constructing the feelings of enrichment (Ahmed, 2013).

Conclusion

Exploring the symbolic consumption of a themed trail, this research demonstrated the role of affect and emotion in meaning-making. Much extant research distinguishes between emotion and affect, which results in situating symbolic association as a physiological (Germann Molz, 2017), psychological (Buckley, 2016; Robinson & Picard, 2016) or the neurological bodily competency (Birenboim, 2016). In contrast, following recent research expositing the intertwined nature of affect and emotion (Ahmed, 2013; Everingham & Motta, 2020; Newell, 2018; Saul & Waterton, 2018), this study articulated an affective dimension of symbolic association that is emergent in different socio-material arrangements. Through the ethnographic study of travellers on a gastronomic trail, this research argued that feelings are impressions of meaning and affect (Ahmed, 2013). It also pointed out the affective symbols and interactions that channelled symbolic associations of opulence in feelings of exclusivity, eliteness, indulgence and enrichment (Newell, 2018). Therefore, opulence was revealed to be a feeling that emerged from the socio-material entanglements of the theme of food and wine. What this research demonstrated was the simultaneity and achieved homogeneity of several heterogeneous affects, meanings and emotions that together constructed the feelings of opulence. This points towards non-linear and non-binary entanglements of affect, emotion and cognition that enable an experience, and fuel and construct individual competencies for future experiencing (Shove et al., 2012).

There are three key contributions of this research to the understanding of symbolic consumption, themes and opulence. First, using the construct of 'feelings' by drawing upon Ahmed and Newell's work, this research pointed towards an affective dimension to symbolic association. Buda (2015) presents feelings as 'felt geography' of the body that connects the body with internal and external bodily spaces. The research demonstrated how meanings and affects were intertwined as travellers, non-linearly, connected with impressions of opulence emerging from these feelings. It further revealed how travellers consciously and unconsciously connected affective symbols with emotional states, competencies, imagined futures and previous experiences, suggesting an interplay between affect and cognition. The findings showed how affects are semiotically transmitted through signs which permeate the thinking of people without their conscious awareness (Newell, 2018). Thus, this research progresses the discussion on emotion and affect to be an integral director of symbolic consumption in tourism.

Second, studying themed routes following an affective perspective presents further clarification on how themes in tourism are consumed and perceived. Considering the importance of theming in tourism for structuring alignments and partnerships (Ferreira & Hunter, 2017), studying theming from an affective perspective provides insights into its consumption and offers ideas for its development.

Third, this research discussed how opulence is felt on the gastronomic trail. Unearthing opulence through feelings, this discussion contributes to discourses of opulence or luxury in a gastronomic environment. The AHWFT travellers followed and sought opulence through affective and cognitive signalling transmitted in feelings of exclusivity, eliteness, indulgence and enrichment. This contributes towards understanding how wine and food tourism encapsulates opulence in an experience which is more 'felt' and 'sensed' rather than thought (Ahmed, 2013).

From a practical perspective, the paper demonstrates the role of emotions and affect in themed route marketing, planning and development. Feelings and impressions of opulence have the potential to be manipulated and directed by marketers to forward luxury gastronomic tourism (Bellini & Resnick, 2018). For example, introduction, continuity and management of affective symbols of luxury in service and landscape encounters could channel the feelings of opulence into a transactional exchange.

Trying to answer what role affect and emotions play on a themed trail, the research points towards an affective construction of movement following symbolic association. Future research could explore how travellers move following their need to seek and conform to opulence on the route.

Future research could also encompass the role of non-human entities in affective constructions of space. The findings pointed towards various elements of space such as furniture, vineyards and landscapes that helped create an affective atmosphere through which travellers felt opulent. Additionally, the research highlighted the relational arrangements of affective symbols such as wine, stories of the terroir, branded clothing and aesthetics that conveyed wealth and lifestyle. While individually these affective symbols could trigger different symbolisms, together they created the opulent feelings of the AHWFT. Future research could study the agency of non-human affective symbols and how specific socio-material arrangements could direct positive or negative affect.

Acknowledgements

We would like to thank Prof. Gordon Waitt and Dr. Venkat Yanamandram for their guidance during the research. This research is supported by an Australian Government Research Training Program (RTP) Scholarship.

Disclosure statement

No potential conflict of interest was reported by the authors.

References

Ahmed, S. (2004). Collective feelings: Or, the impressions left by others. *Theory, Culture & Society*, *21*(2), 25–42.
Ahmed, S. (2013). *The cultural politics of emotion*. Routledge.
Aksan, N., Kısac, B., Aydın, M., & Demirbuken, S. (2009). Symbolic interaction theory. *Procedia - Social and Behavioral Sciences*, *1*(1), 902–904. https://doi.org/10.1016/j.sbspro.2009.01.160

Anderson, B. (2006). Becoming and being hopeful: Towards a theory of affect. *Environment and Planning D: Society and Space, 24*(5), 733–752. https://doi.org/10.1068/d393t

Anderson, B. (2009). Affective atmospheres. *Emotion, Space and Society, 2*(2), 77–81. https://doi.org/10.1016/j.emospa.2009.08.005

Anderson, B., & Harrison, P. (2006). Questioning affect and emotion. *Area, 38*(3), 333–335. https://doi.org/10.1111/j.1475-4762.2006.00699.x

Andersson, T. D., & Mossberg, L. (2017). Travel for the sake of food. *Scandinavian Journal of Hospitality and Tourism, 17*(1), 44–58. https://doi.org/10.1080/15022250.2016.1261473

Australia, T. R. (2015). *Food and Wine Tourism in New South Wales: Executive Summary.* Sydney: Tourism Research Australia.

Baer, T., Coppin, G., Porcherot, C., Cayeux, I., Sander, D., & Delplanque, S. (2018). Dior, J'adore": The role of contextual information of luxury on emotional responses to perfumes. *Food Quality and Preference, 69*, 36–43. https://doi.org/10.1016/j.foodqual.2017.12.003

Baerenholdt, J. O., Haldrup, M., & Urry, J. (2017). *Performing tourist places.* Taylor & Francis.

Baudrillard, J., & Levin, C. (1981). *For a Critique of the Political Economy of the Sign.* (Vol. 262). Telos press St. Louis.

Beardsworth, A., & Bryman, A. (1999). Late modernity and the dynamics of quasification: the case of the themed restaurant. *The Sociological Review, 47*(2), 228–257.

Belk. (1987). Identity and the relevance of market, personal, and community objects. *Marketing and Semiotics: New Directions in the Study of Signs for Sale, 77*, 151.

Bellini, N., & Resnick, E. (2018). The luxury turn in wine tourism. In N. Bellini, C. Clergeau & O. Etcheverria (Eds.), *Gastronomy and local development* (pp. 262–267). Routledge.

Berger, R. (2015). Now I see it, now I don't: researcher's position and reflexivity in qualitative research. *Qualitative Research, 15*(2), 219–234. https://doi.org/10.1177/1468794112468475

Birenboim, A. (2016). New approaches to the study of tourist experiences in time and space. *Tourism Geographies, 18*(1), 9–17. https://doi.org/10.1080/14616688.2015.1122078

Bowden, S. (2011). *Priority of events: Deleuze's logic of sense: Deleuze's logic of sense.* Edinburgh University Press.

Braidotti, R. (2006). Posthuman, all too human: Towards a new process ontology. *Theory, Culture & Society, 23*(7-8), 197–208.

Broadway, M. J. (2017). Putting place on a Plate'along the West Cork food trail. *Tourism Geographies, 19*(3), 467–416. https://doi.org/10.1080/14616688.2016.1276615

Buckley, R. C. (2016). Qualitative analysis of emotions: Fear and thrill. *Frontiers in Psychology, 7*(, 1187 https://doi.org/10.3389/fpsyg.2016.01187

Buda, D. M. (2015). *Affective tourism: Dark routes in conflict.* Routledge.

Buda, D. M., d'Hauteserre, A.-M., & Johnston, L. (2014). Feeling and tourism studies. *Annals of Tourism Research, 46*, 102–114. https://doi.org/10.1016/j.annals.2014.03.005

Canniford, R., Riach, K., & Hill, T. (2017). Nosenography: How smell constitutes meaning, identity and temporal experience in spatial assemblages. *Marketing Theory, 18*(2), 234-248. https://doi.org/10.1177/1470593117732462

Caton, K., & Santos, C. A. (2007). Heritage tourism on route 66: Deconstructing Nostalgia. *Journal of Travel Research, 45*(4), 371–386. https://doi.org/10.1177/0047287507299572

Correia, A., Kozak, M., & Del Chiappa, G. (2019). Examining the meaning of luxury in tourism: a mixed-method approach. *Current Issues in Tourism, 23*(8), 952–970. https://doi.org/10.1080/13683500.2019.1574290

Croce, E., & Perri, G. (2010). *Food and wine tourism: Integrating food, travel and territory.* CABI.

Crouch, D., & Desforges, L. (2003). The sensuous in the tourist encounter: Introduction: The power of the body in tourist studies. *Tourist Studies, 3*(1), 5–22. https://doi.org/10.1177/1468797603040528

Cutler, S. Q., Carmichael, B., & Doherty, S. (2014). The Inca trail experience: Does the journey matter? *Annals of Tourism Research, 45*(0), 152–166.

Deleuze, G., & Guattari, F. (1988). *A thousand plateaus: Capitalism and schizophrenia.* Bloomsbury Publishing.

Denzin, N. K. (2017). Performance, hermeneutics, interpretation. In U. Flick (Ed.), *The SAGE handbook of qualitative data collection* (pp. 200). SAGE.

Denzin, N. K., & Giardina, M. D. (2016). Introduction. In N. K. Denzin & M. D. Giardina (Eds.), *Qualitative inquiry—Past, present, and future: A critical reader* (pp. 9–41). Routledge.

Denzin, N. K., & Lincoln, Y. S. (2008). *Strategies of qualitative inquiry.* Sage Publications.

Denzin, N. K., & Lincoln, Y. S. (2011). *The Sage handbook of qualitative research.* Sage.

Eckhardt, G. M., Belk, R. W., & Wilson, J. A. J. (2015). The rise of inconspicuous consumption. *Journal of Marketing Management, 31*(7-8), 807–826. https://doi.org/10.1080/0267257X.2014.989890

Ekinci, Y., Sirakaya-Turk, E., & Preciado, S. (2013). Symbolic consumption of tourism destination brands. *Journal of Business Research, 66*(6), 711–718. https://doi.org/10.1016/j.jbusres.2011.09.008

Everingham, P., & Motta, S. C. (2020). Decolonising the 'autonomy of affect' in volunteer tourism encounters. *Tourism Geographies,* 1–21. https://doi.org/10.1080/14616688.2020.1713879

Ferreira, S. L. A., & Hunter, C. A. (2017). Wine tourism development in South Africa: a geographical analysis. *Tourism Geographies, 19*(5), 676–698. https://doi.org/10.1080/14616688.2017.1298152

Fisher, T. H. (2004). What we touch, touches us: Materials, affects, and affordances. *Design Issues, 20*(4), 20–31. https://doi.org/10.1162/0747936042312066

Garfinkel, H. (1967). *Studies in ethnomethodology.* Prentice Hall.

Gazley, A., & Watling, L. (2015). Me, my tourist-self, and I: The symbolic consumption of travel. *Journal of Travel & Tourism Marketing, 32*(6), 639–655.

Germann Molz, J. (2007). Eating difference: The cosmopolitan mobilities of culinary tourism. *Space and Culture, 10*(1), 77–93. https://doi.org/10.1177/1206331206296383

Germann Molz, J. (2017). Learning to feel global: Exploring the emotional geographies of worldschooling. *Emotion, Space and Society, 23,* 16–25. https://doi.org/10.1016/j.emospa.2017.02.001

Giddens, A. (1984). *The constitution of society: Outline of the theory of structuration.* Univ of California Press.

Haldrup, M., & Larsen, J. (2006). Material cultures of tourism. *Leisure Studies, 25*(3), 275–289. https://doi.org/10.1080/02614360600661179

Hall, C. M., & Mitchell, R. (2004). *Consuming tourists: Food tourism consumer behaviour (Food tourism around the world* (pp. 72–92). Routledge.

Hashimoto, A., & Telfer, D. J. (2007). Geographical representations embedded within souvenirs in Niagara: The case of geographically displaced authenticity. *Tourism Geographies, 9*(2), 191–217. https://doi.org/10.1080/14616680701278547

Hemmings, C. (2005). Invoking Affect Au - Hemmings, Clare. *Cultural Studies, 19*(5), 548–567. https://doi.org/10.1080/09502380500365473

Hollebeek, L. D., & Brodie, R. J. (2009). Wine service marketing, value co-creation and involvement: research issues. *International Journal of Wine Business Research, 21*(4), 339–353. https://doi.org/10.1108/17511060911004914

Holst, T. (2018). *The affective negotiation of slum tourism: City walks in Delhi.* Routledge.

Jacobsen, H. (2012). *Luxury and power: The material world of the Stuart diplomat, 1660-1714.* Oxford University Press.

Jayne, M., Gibson, C., Waitt, G., & Valentine, G. (2012). Drunken mobilities: Backpackers, alcohol, 'doing place. *Tourist Studies, 12*(3), 211–231. https://doi.org/10.1177/1468797612461082

Jepson, D., & Sharpley, R. (2015). More than sense of place? Exploring the emotional dimension of rural tourism experiences. *Journal of Sustainable Tourism, 23*(8-9), 1157–1178. https://doi.org/10.1080/09669582.2014.953543

Kim, H., & Bonn, M. A. (2016). Authenticity: Do tourist perceptions of winery experiences affect behavioral intentions? *International Journal of Contemporary Hospitality Management, 28*(4), 839–859. https://doi.org/10.1108/IJCHM-05-2014-0212

Kivela, J., & Crotts, J. C. (2006). Tourism and Gastronomy: Gastronomy's Influence on How Tourists Experience a Destination. *Journal of Hospitality & Tourism Research, 30*(3), 354–377.

Knobloch, U., Robertson, K., & Aitken, R. (2017). Experience, emotion, and eudaimonia: A consideration of tourist experiences and well-being. *Journal of Travel Research*, 56(5), 651–662. https://doi.org/10.1177/0047287516650937

Lew, A. A., Hall, C. M., & Williams, A. M. (2008). *A companion to tourism*. John Wiley & Sons.

Lukas, S. A. (2007a). *The themed space: Locating culture, nation, and self*. Rowman & Littlefield.

Lukas, S. A. (2007b). Theming as a sensory phenomenon: discovering the senses on the Las Vegas strip. In S. A. Lukas (Ed.), *The themed space: Locating culture, nation, and self* (pp. 75–95). Rowman & Litfield.

MacLeod, N. (2016). The role of trails in the creation of tourist space. *Journal of Heritage Tourism*, 12(5), 1–8.

Mason, R., & O'Mahony, B. (2007). On the trail of food and wine: The tourist search for meaningful Experience. *Annals of Leisure Research*, 10(3-4), 498–517. https://doi.org/10.1080/11745398.2007.9686778

Massumi, B. (1995). The autonomy of affect. *Cultural Critique*, (31), 83–109. https://doi.org/10.2307/1354446

Massumi, B. (2002). *Parables for the virtual: Movement, affect, sensation*. Duke University Press.

Massumi, B. (2015). *Politics of affect*. John Wiley & Sons.

McCabe, S. (2005). Who is a tourist?':A critical review. *Tourist Studies*, 5(1), 85–106. https://doi.org/10.1177/1468797605062716

Molander, S., & Hartmann, B. J. (2018). Emotion and practice: Mothering, cooking, and teleoaffective episodes. *Marketing Theory*, 18(3), 371–390. https://doi.org/10.1177/1470593117753979

Newell, S. (2018). The affectiveness of symbols: Materiality, magicality, and the limits of the anti-semiotic turn. *Current Anthropology*, 59(1), 1–22. https://doi.org/10.1086/696071

Nicolini, D. (2009). Articulating practice through the interview to the double. *Management Learning*, 40(2), 195–212. https://doi.org/10.1177/1350507608101230

Papacharissi, Z. (2016). Affective publics and structures of storytelling: Sentiment, events and mediality. *Information, Communication & Society*, 19(3), 307–324.

Pile, S. (2010). Emotions and affect in recent human geography. *Transactions of the Institute of British Geographers*, 35(1), 5–20. https://doi.org/10.1111/j.1475-5661.2009.00368.x

Pink, S. (2015). *Doing sensory ethnography*. Sage.

Pocock, N. (2015). Emotional entanglements in tourism research. *Annals of Tourism Research*, 53, 31–45. https://doi.org/10.1016/j.annals.2015.04.005

Rantala, O., Valtonen, A., & Markuksela, V. (2011). Materializing tourist weather: ethnography on weather-wise wilderness guiding practices. *Journal of Material Culture*, 16(3), 285–300. https://doi.org/10.1177/1359183511413646

Reckwitz, A. (2016). Practices and their affects. In A. Hui, T. Schatzki, & E. Shove (Eds.), *The Nexus of Practices*. (pp. 126–137). Routledge.

Rickly-Boyd, J. M. (2012). Authenticity & aura: A Benjaminian approach to tourism. *Annals of Tourism Research*, 39(1), 269–289.

Robinson, M., & Picard, D. (2016). *Emotion in motion: Tourism, affect and transformation*. Routledge.

Rokka, J. (2017). Champagne: Marketplace icon AU - Rokka, Joonas. *Consumption Markets & Culture*, 20(3), 275–283.

Rossetto, T. (2012). Embodying the map: Tourism practices in Berlin. *Tourist Studies*, 12(1), 28–51. https://doi.org/10.1177/1468797612444192

Salazar, N. B., & Graburn, N. H. (2014). *Tourism imaginaries: Anthropological approaches*. Berghahn Books.

Saul, H., & Waterton, E. (2018). *Affective geographies of transformation, exploration and adventure: Rethinking frontiers*. Routledge.

Schmitt, B. (1999). Experiential marketing. *Journal of Marketing Management*, 15(1-3), 53–67. https://doi.org/10.1362/026725799784870496

Selting, M. (2010). Affectivity in conversational storytelling: An analysis of displays of anger or indignation in complaint stories. *Pragmatics. Quarterly Publication of the International Pragmatics Association (Ipra))*, 20(2), 229–277. https://doi.org/10.1075/prag.20.2.06sel

Seyfert, R. (2012). Beyond personal feelings and collective emotions: Toward a theory of social affect. *Theory, Culture & Society, 29*(6), 27–46.

Shaw, G., & Williams, A. M. (2004). *Landscapes of pleasure: The construction of new tourism spaces and places.* Sage.

Sheller, M., & Urry, J. (2000). The city and the car. *International Journal of Urban and Regional Research, 24*(4), 737–757. https://doi.org/10.1111/1468-2427.00276

Shove, E., Pantzar, M., & Watson, M. (2012). *The dynamics of social practice: Everyday life and how it changes.* Sage.

Steadman, C., Roberts, G., Medway, D., Millington, S., & Platt, L. (2020). (Re)Thinking place atmospheres in marketing theory. *Marketing Theory, 0*(0), 1470593120920344.

Thrift, N. (2008). *Non-representational theory: Space, politics, affect.* Routledge.

Thurlow, C., & Jaworski, A. (2012). Elite mobilities: The semiotic landscapes of luxury and privilege. *Social Semiotics, 22*(4), 487–516. https://doi.org/10.1080/10350330.2012.721592

Tolia-Kelly, D. P., Waterton, E., & Watson, S. (2016). *Heritage, affect and emotion: Politics, Practices and infrastructures.* Routledge.

Urry, J. (2016). The place of emotions within place. In J. Davidson, L. Bondi, & M. Smith (Eds.), *Emotional geographies* (pp. 91–98). Routledge.

Veblen, T. (1899). *1994 The theory of the leisure class.* Transaction Publishers.

Wang, N. (1999). Rethinking authenticity in tourism experience. *Annals of Tourism Research, 26*(2), 349–370. https://doi.org/10.1016/S0160-7383(98)00103-0

Watling, L. (2015). Me, my tourist-self, and I: The symbolic consumption of travel AU - Gazley, Aaron. *Journal of Travel & Tourism Marketing, 32*(6), 639–655.

Watson, S., & Waterton, E. (2019). The Spanish imaginary: A trilogy of frontiers. In H.Saul &, E. Waterton (Eds.), *Affective Geographies of Transformation, Exploration and Adventure: Rethinking Frontiers* (pp. 31–48). London: Routledge.

Wolf, H. L., Morrish, S. C., & Fountain, J. (2016). A conceptualization of the perceptions and motivators that drive luxury wine consumption. *International Journal of Wine Business Research, 28*(2), 120–133. https://doi.org/10.1108/IJWBR-09-2015-0038

Yeoman, I., & McMahon-Beattie, U. (2014). Exclusivity: The future of luxury. *Journal of Revenue and Pricing Management, 13*(1), 12–22. https://doi.org/10.1057/rpm.2013.29

Zukin, S. (2009). Changing landscapes of power: Opulence and the Urge For Authenticity. *International Journal of Urban and Regional Research, 33*(2), 543–553. https://doi.org/10.1111/j.1468-2427.2009.00867.x

Tourists' savoring of positive emotions and place attachment formation: a conceptual paper

Nanxi Yan and Elizabeth A. Halpenny

ABSTRACT

With increased interest in emotions and tourism, 'savoring', a process of attending to, enhancing, or prolonging positive emotions, should receive more scholarly attention. This article offers a conceptual look at the issues and perspectives related to the relationship between savoring and place attachment in the tourism context. Drawing from the positive psychology, tourism, and geography literature, we outline 12 propositions to suggest how tourists develop place attachment by savoring their vacation experiences and destinations, supported by the 'broaden-and-build' processes. By directing people's attention to their positive emotions and triggering a broaden-and-build experience, savoring has the potential to foster place attachment to a destination. In brief, we propose that savoring can influence the process of place attachment formation by influencing each phase of a tourism experience (i.e., pre-trip, on-site, post-trip). In particular, savoring, at pre-trip, can facilitate the development of favorable destination image to form place attachment. When on-site, or at post-trip phase, savoring can promote place attachment formation by helping individuals obtain higher level of positive affect and more memorable tourism experiences. The propositions are intended to guide and inspire future empirical examinations related to savoring positive emotions in the tourism context. Savoring's role in fostering place attachment has important potential practical outcomes including development and reinforcement of destination loyalty.

摘要

随着对情绪与旅游的研究兴趣的增加，"品味"作为一种关注、增强、或者延长正向情绪的过程，应该得到更多的学术关注。本文从概念上分析了旅游环境中品味与地方依恋之间的关系。通过借鉴积极心理学，旅游学，以及地理学相关理论成果，基于"拓展与建设"理论提出了游客如何通过品味其旅游经历和目的地来建立地方依恋的12个研究命题。品味是通过引导人们关注他们的正向情绪并引发他们经历"拓展与建设"从而促进建立对旅游目的地的地方依恋。简要来说，品味可以通过影响旅游过程的每个阶段（即旅行前、旅行中、旅行后）来影响地方依恋的形成过程。具体来说，旅行前的品味可以通过深化正面的目的地形象从而促进地方依恋的形成。旅行中及旅行后，品味能通过帮助人们获得更高程度的正向情绪和更难忘的旅游体验以进一步增强地方依恋。这些研究命题的提出旨在指导和启发旅游环境中的品味与正向情绪相关的

实证检验。品味在促进地方依恋形成中的作用具有重要的现实应
用意义, 包括培育与强化目的地忠诚度。

Introduction

Many tourism researchers have studied human–place relationships through an examination of place attachment, which concerns the depth and types of emotional attachments to one particular place. Current research on tourists' place attachment has emphasized the following two research agendas: (a) the structure or components of place attachment (e.g., Chen, Dwyer, & Firth, 2014; Kyle, Graefe, & Manning, 2005; Prayag, 2018; Ramkissoon, Graham Smith, & Weiler, 2013), and (b) place attachment's influences on various behavioral outcomes, which include revisit intention (Song, Kim, & Yim, 2017), visitation and other forms of loyalty (Plunkett, Fulthorp, & Paris, 2019; Prayag & Ryan, 2012), and pro-environmental behaviors (Halpenny, 2010; Qu, Xu, & Lyu, 2019). Effects of place attachment are particularly important to destination proponents who seek to leverage individuals' attachments to promote both visitation and stewardship of destinations.

Fewer studies have attempted to investigate how tourists develop place attachment with a destination (see Huang, Qu, & Montgomery, 2017; Hutson, Montgomery, & Caneday, 2010; Wilkins & de Urioste-Stone, 2018). This article aims to address this gap by contributing to theories designed to explain the process of visitors' development of place attachment, and in particular how attachment is inspired by the savoring of positive emotions arising from tourist experiences.

To achieve this goal, one main construct that should be well understood is positive emotion (Morgan, 2010). Positive emotion, or a pleasurable affective state, is an essential component of a tourism experience (Cutler & Carmichael, 2010; Goolaup, Solér, & Nunkoo, 2018; Hosany, Prayag, Deesilatham, Cauševic, & Odeh, 2015; Mitas, Yarnal, Adams, & Ram, 2012), which can influence the development of place attachment (Hosany, Prayag, Van Der Veen, Huang, & Deesilatham, 2017; Loureiro, 2014). The relationship between positive emotion and place attachment has received increased attention (Io, 2018). Savoring, the process of attending to or dealing with positive emotions (Bryant & Veroff, 2007), may be an important mechanism that tourists can employ to manage desired levels and duration of positive emotions. Savoring has been intensively examined in the area of positive psychology (e.g., its role in improving life satisfaction, Smith & Bryant, 2016). Although tourism is a context filled with positive emotions, savoring has not been extensively connected with tourism experiences. Reviewing extant studies conducted in positive psychology, tourism, and geography, this conceptual paper addressed this research gap by investigating why and how savoring can foster attachment to a destination, through regulating positive emotions.

The article has been arranged into two main sections. First, a literature review of the key concepts: place attachment, positive emotions, savoring, and their relationships are presented. Second, propositions that describe the possible relationships of how savoring can facilitate the process of developing place attachment in a tourism context are outlined. These propositions are presented to inspire and direct future empirical investigations.

Literature review

The construct of place attachment

Reviewing existing literature, a number of constructs have been used to describe people's relationship with place. From a social psychological perspective, these include place dependence (Stokols & Shumaker, 1981), place identity (Proshansky, Fabian, & Kaminoff, 1983), and place satisfaction (Stedman, 2002). Fundamentally, place attachment refers to the emotional ties between people and a setting (Brandenburg & Carroll, 1995; Low & Altman, 1992). In tourism and leisure research, a number of studies have tried to explain the sub-dimensions of place attachment. Depending on the varied emphases of scholars, the conceptions of place attachment have been grouped into three categories: personal, environmental, and/or social context of people–place interactions (Brown, Raymond, & Corcoran, 2015).

For tourists' experiencing of place, personal approaches to understanding place attachment may be most relevant here. For example, Williams, Patterson, Roggenbuck, and Watson (1992) conceptualized people's bonding with a place as place attachment with two dimensions: place identity (Proshansky et al., 1983) and place dependence (Stokols & Shumaker, 1981). Inspired in part by Williams et al. (1992) research, the structure or particularly the sub-components of place attachment have been researched frequently. The two-dimension model was criticized for overlooking the importance of social-cultural dimensions, as social interactions can enhance people' attachment with a setting as well (Hidalgo & Hernandez, 2001; Kyle & Chick, 2007). Thus, Hammitt, Backlund, and Bixler (2006) expanded Williams et al. (1992) construction of place attachment to a five-dimension model. They considered three social attachments to a place: place familiarity, place belongingness, and place rootedness as important sub-dimensions of place attachment, in addition to place identity and dependence.

Following that, Kyle et al. (2005) integrated these three aforementioned social attachment dimensions into social bonding. More specifically, Kyle et al. (2005) developed a three-factor construct of place attachment, which is composed of place identity, place dependence, and social bonding. In contrast, another research group underlines the importance of people's bonding with the natural environment (Raymond, Brown, & Weber, 2010). This can include people's emotional affinity towards environment (Kals, Schumacher, & Montada, 1999). For example, inspired by Jorgensen and Stedman (2001) research, Halpenny (2010) proposed a three-dimension model of place attachment: place identity, place dependence, and place affect, where the component of place affect concerns the emotions or feelings an individual has towards a particular place. Place attachment has also been conceptualized as encompassing personal, social, and environmental perspectives and representative of four dimensions: place dependence, place identity, place affect, and place social bonding (e.g., Ramkissoon et al., 2013).

Taken together, there exists no consensus in defining or measuring place attachment (Scannell & Gifford, 2010). One reason is that emotional relationships with physical settings (e.g., rural area, urban place, national parks) and people's experiences can be very diverse (Gursoy & Chi, 2018). However, even though these place dimensions can be dissimilar from each other, they overlap by suggesting that the two essentials of people's relationship with a place are: subjective interpretation of and emotional reaction to the physical setting (Hummon, 1992; Steele, 1996).

Developing place attachment with a destination

The preceding discussion suggests that the structure of place attachment has been frequently researched. However, the process of developing place attachment with a destination is a another complex process that has received much less attention (Huang et al., 2017; Prayag, 2018). A majority of studies have examined attachment to permanent residences, such as community and home (Lewicka, 2011), but developing attachment with a destination can be different from bonding with one's permanent neighborhood (Van Riper, Kyle, Wallen, Landon, & Raymond, 2018).

One main explanation is that the essence of staying at a destination can be significantly different from staying at home (e.g., the duration, motivation, experiences). For tourists, they usually stay at a destination for a finite amount of time, mainly with a motivation for fun or for exploring novelty (Dann, 1981), and spend the majority of time in recreational activities. Therefore, it is less likely for tourists to build attachment with a place due to reasons such as 'close ties with neighborhood' and 'generational rootedness' (Lewicka, 2011, p. 213).

The tourist gaze

In tourism literature, the tourist gaze (Urry, 1990; Urry & Larsen, 2011) can be used to understand how people relate to a destination. Tourists use their perceptions to selectively experience and define a place (Urry, 1990). Tourist gazes are socially constructed and shaped by personal experiences, memories, and expectations (Urry & Larsen, 2011). Tourists direct their attention to features in landscapes that are perceived as different from their everyday experiences or not ordinary for them. In recent years, the conceptualization has been expanded from emphasizing tourists' visual experiences solely to multi-sensory experiences (e.g., touching, tasting, and smelling; Williams & Lew, 2015). The tourist gaze navigates tourists' engagement with a place. It organizes the 'place, role, and effect of the other senses' (Urry & Larsen, 2011, p. 195). Hence, the tourist gaze concept entails that visitors develop relationships with a destination both reflexively and physically and through interpreting, contrasting, and evaluating what they have gazed upon.

Place attachment development

The tourist gaze concept mainly concerns subjective interpretations of a place, while, in recent years, the role played by emotion in developing place attachment has been incrementally emphasized. Drawing on attachment theory (Bowlby, 1969), Morgan (2010) proposed a theory to explicate the psychological process of developing place attachment. In this theory, Morgan (2010) emphasizes that emotion is a crucial component for developing place attachment, as over time people develop a pattern of emotional experiences with a place which in turn will evolve into place attachment. Fewer scholars have adopted this theory in tourism research, but one of them is Hosany et al. (2017), who attempted to explain the relationships among tourists' emotions, place attachment, satisfaction, and intention to recommend. However, they emphasized the outcome of place attachment rather than the process of developing attachment with a destination (Prayag, 2018).

Emotion and place attachment

In line with Morgan (2010), this conceptual paper suggests that emotion, which arises from appraisal processes through which people make evaluations on events, objects, or the environment based on their current goals (Lazarus, 1991; Smith & Ellsworth, 1985), is essential for developing a meaningful relationship with a destination (e.g., Morgan, 2010). Emotions link with cognitions such as evaluations and interpretations, to influence people's information processing and execution of behaviors (Bell & Wolfe, 2004). Meanwhile, emotion itself can shape tourists' visions and opinions of the world (Niedenthal, 2008) as well as how they behave, such as communicating through touching (Hertenstein, 2002). Hence, tourists' emotions can influence tourists' gaze, performances, and meaning-making towards a destination.

   In particular, positive emotions are essential for building attachment with a destination (Hosany et al., 2017; Io, 2018). Hosany et al. (2017) found that positive emotions, such as joy, love, and pleasure, can contribute to place identity and place dependence formation. Grounded in positive psychology, one of the theoretical frameworks that underpins the relationship between positive emotions and place attachment is Fredrickson's (1998, 2000) broaden-and-build theory.

The broaden-and-build theory of positive emotions (*Fredrickson, 1998, 2001*)

While negative emotions narrow one's thought-action repertoire, Fredrickson (1998, 2001) proposed that positive emotions can broaden people's scope of attention and thought-action repertoires (e.g., promoting people to pursue a wider range of thoughts and behaviors than usual), which can build a variety of personal resources and benefit individuals in the long run (e.g., resilience). Fredrickson and Branigan (2005) observed that participants who experienced positive emotions obtained broadened thinking and identified more things to do than they normally would do when compared with those who experienced negative emotions or who were ambivalent or neutral in their reactions. For example, joy increases an individual's urge to play and be playful (e.g., exploration, invention). Interest enables people to become more engaged, involved, and more exploratory (Izard, 1977). Contentment can involve a full awareness of experiences, which can contribute to forming a new sense of self and world view (Fredrickson, 2000). Thus, broadening mindset can facilitate positive meaning finding (e.g., the meaning of an event is reinterpreted in a more positive way, Samios, Abel, & Rodzik, 2013) and global cognitive focus (e.g., seeing the bigger picture of one's life, Hicks & King, 2007).

Positive emotions can also function as an internal signal to approach or continue actions (Carver & Scheier, 1990; Fredrickson, 1998; Watson, Wiese, Vaidya, & Tellegen, 1999). When experiencing positive emotions, people become more engaged with their environment and participate in more activities, feeling more motivated to explore novel objects, people, or situations (Fredrickson, 1998). From Fredrickson's (1998, 2001) perspective, the more positive emotions you encounter, the more benefits you get. In other words, it is likely that tourists who experience more positive emotions are more involved with their travel experiences (e.g., exploring new things, be more open-minded, interacting with more people), which fosters engagement and apprecia- tive actions essential to the development of place attachment.

Savoring

Although people may experience positive events, individuals hold various capacities to direct their attentions to their positive emotions (Bryant & Veroff, 2007; Wilson & Saklofske, 2018). Without attending to or appreciating positive emotions, people may not be able to obtain the numerous benefits that positive emotions can offer. One important mechanism that directs people's attention to positive emotions and helps them to stay in the broaden-and-build process is savoring (Tugade & Fredrickson, 2007). Savoring describes the ability for people to attend to, appreciate, and enhance positive emotions (Bryant & Veroff, 2007). When people savor, they attend to, regulate, and obtain more positive emotions (Fredrickson, 2004; Jose, Lim, & Bryant, 2012; Smith & Bryant, 2017; Smith, Harrison, Kurtz, & Bryant, 2014). Also, savoring can pro- long or intensify positive emotions by directing people's attention to sensory aspects of an experience that might be otherwise overlooked (Bryant, 2003).

Bryant and Veroff (2007) proposed that savoring has three critical conceptual com- ponents: (a) Savoring experience, which considers the 'the totality of a person's sensa- tions, perceptions, thoughts, behaviors, and emotions when mindfully attending to and appreciating a positive stimulus, outcomes, or event, along with the accompany- ing environmental or situational features of that encounter' (p. 13); (b) savoring pro- cess, which is a process that people attend to positive stimulus and transforms it into positive feelings that people attend to (Bryant & Veroff, 2007); and, (c) savoring strat- egies, when people savor, they engage in specific savoring strategies to attend to positive feelings.

Savoring strategies are concrete thoughts or behaviors that a person uses to attend to pleasurable feelings (Bryant & Veroff, 2007). Researchers have identified 11 savoring strategies that people use to attend to positive emotions (Bryant & Veroff, 2007; Quoidbach, Berry, Hansenne & Mikolajczak, 2010). People practice these strategies nat- urally (e.g., triggered by a specific positive event) or with intention. These savoring strategies are outlined in Table 1 with examples. The majority (8 out of 11) are cogni- tive strategies. Sharing with others, absorption, and behavioral expression are behav- iour-focused strategies. The effectiveness of these savoring strategies regarding cultivating, enhancing, or prolonging positive emotions has been assessed in multiple studies (Bryant & Veroff, 2007; Smith et al., 2014).

Table 1. Savoring strategies and examples.

Savoring strategies	Examples
Behavior-focused savoring strategies	
Sharing with others	Sharing positive experiences with other people; I expressed to others how much I valued the moment.
Absorption	Try not to think, but rather to get totally immersed in the moment.
Behavioral expression	Laughing, giggling, jumping up and down.
Cognitive savoring strategies	
Memory building	Actively storing image for future recall by taking mental photographs.
Self-congratulation	Telling yourself how proud you are or how impressed others must be.
Sensory-perceptual sharpening	Identifying pleasure by focusing on certain stimuli in the situation and blocking out others.
Comparing	Contrasting your own feelings with what others seem to be feeling.
Temporal awareness	Reminding oneself how transient and fleeting the moment is; wishing the moment can last forever.
Counting blessings	Reminding oneself how lucky one is; thinking about so many good things have happened to oneself.
Kill-joy thinking	Thinking about ways in which it could have been better;
Positive mental time travel	Vividly remembering or anticipating positive events.

Note. Adopted from Bryant and Veroff (2007) and Quoidbach et al.'s (2010) studies.

Research propositions

Savoring in the tourism context

Savoring can be particularly relevant to understanding tourism experiences. This is supported, in part, because tourism experiences can generate a great deal of positive emotions when compared with other life contexts (e.g., work). For tourists, the amount of positive emotions generated in the tourism context has been reported to be three times greater than positive emotions experienced during regular, non-vacation weekends (Mitas et al., 2012). Chen, Lehto, and Cai (2013) also observed that vacationers experienced more frequent positive affect than non-vacationers. Therefore, tourists have more opportunity to savor positive emotion.

In pleasurable tourism settings, savoring can serve as the mechanism for directing people's attention to positive emotions and encouraging them to engage in the broaden-and-build processes, which in turn can play a vital role in developing place attachment. When tourists savor their positive emotions, they become more flexible, creative, and open to the activities or environments they are experiencing. This in turn increases their interactions with destinations (e.g., more frequent visiting, trying different things, meeting more people) and facilitates the development of place attachment. Specifically, savoring may serve as either a mediator or a moderator between positive tourism experiences and place attachment.

In the case of mediation (Rucker, Preacher, Tormala, & Petty, 2011), tourism experiences generate positive emotions, which evoke certain savoring strategies (Jose et al., 2012), and in turn facilitate the development of place attachment (see Figure 1a). For example, peaceful natural tourism experiences may trigger visitors to practice a savoring strategy such as *absorption*, which may assist the process of building emotional connections with a destination.

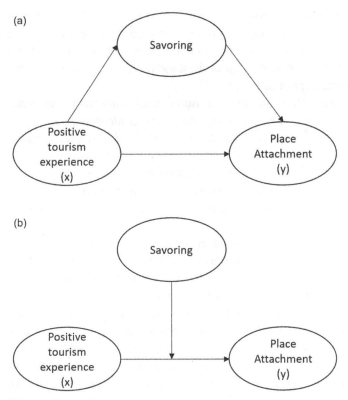

Figure 1. (a) Savoring can mediate the relationship between positive tourism experiences and place attachment. (b) Savoring can moderate the relationship between positive tourism experience and place attachment.

When considering savoring as a moderator, savoring strategies can enhance the strength of relations between tourism experiences and place attachment. Tourists intentionally practice savoring strategies when they encounter a positive experience, which can positively influence the development of place attachment (see Figure 1b). For instance, tourists who practice savoring strategies, such as *sharing with others*, may amplify the influence of positive tourist experience on the formation of place attachment compared to visitors who do not engage in these savoring strategies.

PROPOSITION 1: Compared with everyday life, the tourism context provides more opportunities for people to engage in savoring experiences.

PROPOSITION 2: Savoring facilitates tourists' development of place attachment with a destination, as a mediator or a moderator.

Savoring, tourism experience, and place attachment

A tourism experience can evolve over three phases (Borrie & Roggenbuck, 2001; Cutler & Carmichael, 2010): (a) the anticipatory phase (pre-trip), (b) the experiential phase (during-trip), and (c) the reflective phase (post-trip, Clawson, 1963; Craig-Smith & French, 1994; Wang, Park, & Fesenmaier, 2012). In particular, individuals' emotions and feelings will change over the course of a trip (Nawijn, 2011). For example, tourists experience more frequent positive emotions during their trip than compared with pre- or post-trip (de Bloom et al., 2010). Therefore, it would be beneficial to consider each phase of tourism experience when understanding how savoring can influence the process of place attachment formation.

Current research has proposed a number of antecedents to place attachment, which includes motivation (Halpenny, Kulczycki, & Moghimehfar, 2016; Xu & Zhang, 2016), destination image (Prayag & Ryan, 2012), destination attractiveness (Hu & Ritchie, 1993) and memorability (E. Sthapit, Björk, & Coudounaris, 2017; Tsai, 2016). Many other antecedents exist and are beyond the scope of this article to review, thus we choose to focus on two antecedents: destination image and memorable tourism experiences, and explore how savoring may be associated with them in the development of place attachment.

These relationships are elaborated in the following section. We use figures below to illustrate the process of how savoring can influence the relationship between positive tourism experiences and the antecedents of place attachment, by proposing that savoring can function either as a mediator (e.g., tourists are triggered to practice some savoring strategies by certain positive emotions, Figure 2) or a moderator (e.g., tourists intentionally practice savoring strategies, perhaps because the context affords ease of savoring or select individuals are more predisposed to engaging in savoring and thus they may savor more frequently or possess a greater repertoire of savoring techniques, Figure 3). Figure 2 and 3 depict relationships between factors proposed to influence place attachment including savoring, destination image, pre-vacation anticipation, during trip experience, post-trip recollection, and memorability of experience. These proposed relationships are outlined next.

Savoring at the pre, during, or post-trip phase and place attachment

PROPOSITION 3: At the pre-trip stage, savoring can positively influence the development of place attachment by shaping destination image.

Pre-trip phase

The first stage of tourism experiences is associated with anticipating the joy a tourism experience may bring. Once an individual has made the decision to travel, he or she enters the pre-trip or anticipation phase. At this stage, people start to increasingly direct their attentions to the future events. Gilbert and Wilson (2007) commented that individuals will anticipate a future event by simulations, which can be characterized as not representative (e.g., constructed from past memories), essentialized (e.g., imaging the essential features), and abbreviated. Engaging in simulations allows people to 'preview' the future events and 'pre-feel' the emotional consequences at present (Gilbert & Wilson, 2007).

In general, travelers' anticipation can be accompanied by positive affect (Gilbert & Abdullah, 2002; Nawijn, Marchand, Veenhoven, & Vingerhoets, 2010), such as excitement and enthusiasm (A. Sthapit, Choi, & Hwang, 2016). Also, people start to form expectations (Chen et al., 2014) or develop perceived destination images (Cheng & Qiang, 2018) toward the destination they are going to visit.

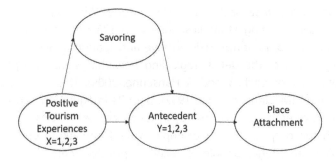

X1= pre-vacation anticipation, Y1= destination image
X2= during-trip experience, Y2= memorable tourism experiences
X3= post-trip recollection, Y3= memorable tourism experiences

Figure 2. The proposed theoretical relationship between savoring, positive tourism experiences, and place attachment (mediation).

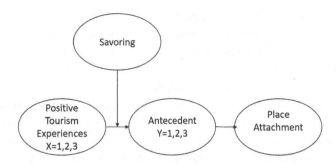

X1= pre-vacation anticipation, Y1= destination image
X2= during-trip experience, Y2= memorable tourism experiences
X3= post-trip recollection, Y3= memorable tourism experiences

Figure 3. The theoretical relationship between savoring, positive tourism experiences, and place attachment (moderation).

Destination image. Destination image is an important antecedent to tourists' place attachment (Prayag & Ryan, 2012; Yeh, Chen, & Liu, 2012). It is an image of a place, which is developed in the human mind in absence of the actual environment (Tuan, 1975). Destination image refers to a collection of beliefs, impressions, emotional thoughts, or knowledge that people held about a destination (Baloglu & Mangaloglu, 2001; Baloglu & McCleary, 1999). The construct of destination image (Pike & Ryan, 2004) can be captured by both cognitive (e.g., beliefs, knowledge) and affective components (e.g., feelings toward a destination).

First-time and repeat visitors may rely on different information or resources to form destination image. For example, when compared with repeat visitors, first-time visitors usually plan more in advance and place more value on information sources such as maps and transportation than repeat visitors (Li, Cheng, Kim, & Petrick, 2008). However, for both group of tourists, pre-visiting cognitive image can positively influence tourists' formation of place dependence, whereas their pre-visit affective image can impact tourists' construction of place identity (Cheng & Qiang, 2018).

Savoring at pre-visit phase and destination image. When anticipating, people can engage in cognitive savoring strategies, such as *positive mental time travel (MTT)*, to regulate (e.g., attend to, prolong) their positive anticipation. Practicing MTT involves a conscious imagination of the details regarding how things may happen in a specific time and location (Quoidbach, Wood, & Hansenne, 2009). This strategy, similar to vicarious consumption (MacInnis & Price, 1987), permits imagination and can enhance or evoke more positive emotions, which may in turn increase the positive affective image associated with the destination. For example, Yüksel and Akgül (2007) reported that postcards, which can trigger people to recollect positive memories or imaginings of the future, can induce positive emotions, such as relaxation, pleasantness, and excitement as well as positive affective destination image. Also, MTT requires a certain amount of knowledge to proceed, which can include features of the hotel and characteristics of the destination. This may drives people to do more information searching, which can in turn enhance the cognitive image of the destination (Baloglu & McCleary, 1999).

While anticipating, tourists may engage in a savoring strategy such as *sharing the good news or travel plans with their friends* also called *capitalizing*. It is suggested that by sharing the positive news with people, one will experience greater positive affect and increased positivity of the event itself (Langston, 1994). Moreover, Reis et al. (2010) observed that receiving enthusiastic feedbacks (see Gable & Reis, 2010) to the savoring strategy of *capitalizing* can enhance people's attention, appreciation, and enjoyment of the positive experience. In addition to enhancing affective image, tourist's cognitive image can be increased as well, especially when they receive more information or world-of-mouth recommendations from friends or relatives (Baloglu & McCleary, 1999; Simpson & Siguaw, 2008).

PROPOSITION 4: Savoring can facilitate the development of a more favorable affective image by maintaining or evoking more positive emotions.

PROPOSITION 5: Savoring can facilitate the process of developing a cognitive image by driving people to search more information.

PROPOSITION 6: Savoring can enhance people's affective or cognitive image of a destination.

PROPOSITION 7: At the during-trip stage, savoring can positively influence the development of place attachment by helping individuals obtain memorable tourism experiences.

During trip/experiential phase

People turn a space into a place through 'endowing it with value' (Tuan, 1977, p.6). When people are on site, they make sense of a place through their ongoing interactions with people and environment within the space (Kyle & Chick, 2007). Their interactions include constantly evaluating different physical aspects of the environment as well as social interactions that happen in the space (Morgan, 2010). However, interactions that occur between people and the environment are not sufficient enough to develop place attachment (Cresswell, 2004). For example, in his study of New Zealand residents and tourists, Hay (1998) pointed out that tourists developed a 'superficial sense of place' (p. 8) or obtained no rootedness or attachment to a place they visited, as they always paid too much attention to the aesthetic nature of a place. However, to help tourists develop bonding with a destination, quality in situ tourism experiences, or a memorable tourism experience is the raison d d'être (Kim, 2014; Loureiro, 2014; Pizam, 2010; Tsai, 2016; Zhang, Huang, Green, & Qiu, 2018).

Memorable tourism experiences. Memorable tourism experiences shape visitors' evaluations or attitudes towards a destination (Pizam, 2010; E. Sthapit & Coudounaris, 2018). Two factors are essential for obtaining memorable tourism experiences. Pine and Gilmore (1999) suggested that memory or memorableness can be one key indicator, as memories can positively impact individuals' attitude toward a destination (E. Sthapit et al., 2017). Another important indicator is arousal, which considers people's physiological response to a stimulus on the continuum from calmness to excitement (Lee & Oh, 2017). Arousal may facilitate the formation of positive memories (Loureiro, 2014) and impact people's attitudes (i.e., the halo effect, Bagozzi, 1996; Hosany et al., 2015). Both pleasant arousal and memory are two positive consequences of a memorable tourism experience as well.

Savoring during a trip. When visiting, tourists can engage in savoring strategies such as *absorption* and *sensory-perceptual sharpening*. These two strategies may differ as the former strategy is a state of mind, whereas engaging in sensory-perceptual sharpening can be one mode to achieve absorption. However, they share similarities in allowing people to feel fully involved in positive experiences and attend to aspects of positive experience to a greater depth or detail (Hong, Lishner, Han, & Huss, 2011). Feeling absorbed or immersed within a travel experience is fundamental for people to feel compelled to spend time reflecting about a trip (Knutson & Beck, 2004). Feeling absorbed in leisure activities can be linked to positive affect such as highly interested, enthusiastic, and excitement (Walker & Deng, 2003), which can in turn contribute to memorable tourism experiences (Servidio & Ruffolo, 2016).

People can savor by *capitalizing* or *sharing positive experiences with others*. For example, they can share positive experiences with travel partners or new friends. Tourists can also utilize real-time sharing to capitalize (e.g., Facebook, Twitters, messaging) with the advancement of technology (MacKay, Barbe, Van Winkle, & Halpenny, 2017; Wang et al., 2012). Capitalizing can help people to experience more positive affect than could be contributed by the event itself (Langston, 1994).

Behavioral expressions (e.g., jumping, laughing), which refer to using behaviors or performances to outwardly manifest inner feelings (Bryant & Veroff, 2007), can be practiced as well. People can engage in different behaviors to express their positive inner feelings. For example, people who put on a happy face obtain more positive reactions than people who portray a neutral mood (Kleinke, Peterson, & Rutledge, 1998). Engaging in different behavioral expressions, such as jumping up and down to congratulate the achievement of climbing to the top of mountain, can increase the positive emotions they are experiencing and in turn contribute to tourist' engaged visiting.

PROPOSITION 8: Savoring facilitates individual's attainment of memorable in-situ tourism experiences.

PROPOSITION 9: Savoring facilitates individual's more frequent experiencing of pleasant arousal emotions during their vacations.

PROPOSITION 10: At the post-trip stage, savoring facilitates the development of place attachment through enhancing memorable tourism experiences.

Post-trip phase

After tourists come home, they enter the post-trip stage. At this phase, individuals can still process their visiting experiences through reminiscing. Recollecting past experiences is not the 're-excitation of innumerable fixed, lifeless, and fragmentary traces. It is an imaginative reconstruction, or construction, built out of the relation of our attitude towards a whole active mass of organized past reactions or experiences' (Bartlett, 1932, p. 205). Therefore, recollection is an important moment for revisiting or reliving certain episodes of visiting experiences (Tung & Ritchie, 2011). This is also an important stage for enhancing memorable tourism experience, which can significantly influence place attachment (Jorgensen & Stedman, 2006; Loureiro, 2014; Tsai, 2016).

Savoring at post-trip. Similar to anticipation stage, tourists can engage in cognitive savoring strategies, such as positive MTT, to revisit several specific moments of their past trips in mind again. They can also engage in behavioral strategies, such as sharing positive visiting experiences with others. It is suggested that having a social exchange (e.g., a conversation) can help people to think more about their visiting experiences than remembering alone (Rimé, 2007). Also, sharing positive visiting experiences can produce higher positive affect (Kim & Fesenmaier, 2017). Thus, savoring past travel experiences can get people to experience different positive emotions including joy, interest, contentment, and love (Filep, Cao, Jiang, & DeLacy, 2013), which can increase the memorability of a destination (Hammitt et al., 2006; Manthiou, Kang, & Hyun, 2017).

PROPOSITION 11: Post-trip savoring helps tourists experience higher levels of positive affect after their vacation.

PROPOSITION 12: Post-trip savoring helps tourists have more memorable tourism experiences after their vacation.

Discussions and conclusions

In this conceptual paper, we reviewed the importance of positive emotions, particularly the theoretical framework of broaden-and-build, in developing place attachment. Based on these, we propose that enhancing positive emotions or savoring can assist the process of developing place attachment in the tourism context. We developed 12 propositions to describe the relationship among destination experiences, savoring, and attachment formation, which are submitted with the following assumptions: (a) Savoring is the mechanism triggering the broaden-and-build process of positive emotions, which expands people's thought-action repertoire that enables individuals to create more meanings from interactions with a destination, and (b) people possess savoring abilities, but they can be inspired to engage more extensively in savoring through assigned savoring strategies to regulate or attend to positive emotions (Smith et al., 2014).

Theoretical implications

One theoretical implication of this article is that it expands our understanding of positive emotions by discussing the theoretical process (i.e., the broaden-and-build process) underlying positive emotions. Although there are an increasing number of tourism studies that have identified the positive influences of positive emotions, not many of them have examined the theoretical backdrop underlying positive emotions (Lin, Chen, & Filieri, 2017), Thus, knowing the broaden-and-build framework provides tourism researchers with a new perspective on the significance of positive emotions, supplying more support for studying positive emotions and even cultivating positive emotions.

This present study is the first to incorporate the concept of savoring in the process of developing place attachment in a tourism context. We proposed that savoring plays an indirect role in the relationship between tourism experiences and place attachment. By directing people's attention to their positive emotions and triggering the broaden-and-build experience, savoring has the potential to facilitate the process of developing place attachment with a destination from the moment they make their decision to travel to several days after returning home (i.e., pre, during, post trips). We believe part of the value of this conceptual paper lies in stimulating more research on savoring through identifying and testing issues, variables, and possible relationships while studying tourists' experiences. More importantly, instead of investigating positive emotions by merely recording them (e.g., types of positive affect, the frequency of experience them), this paper invites tourism researchers to consider the process that fosters positive emotions and even the possibilities of manipulating positive emotions to achieve desired outcomes (e.g., satisfactory experience and destination loyalty).

Practical implications

Place attachment is vital for destination loyalty (Gursoy, Chen, & Chi, 2014), including visitation and positive recommendations (Prayag & Ryan, 2012). Knowing that savoring strategies have the potential for facilitating the building of memorable tourism experiences, forming destination images, and developing place attachment, tourism practitioners may prepare savoring opportunities or occasions to trigger savoring for their customers. For example, given that savoring can enhance positive expectations of place and increase overall experiences (Chun, 2009), hospitality and tourism managers can send flyers or brochures including short savoring tasks (e.g., some short videos with MTT interpretations) to visitors before their arrival. Also, tourism businesses or organizations can design some specific 'savoring spots' in their destinations to cultivate savoring opportunities for tourists to intentionally attend to their positive emotions and experiences. Some examples include posting message cues in several locations within a destination to gently suggest people to share experiences, take selfies, or practice meditation. Practitioners can also bring in new technologies (e.g., virtual reality headsets, Wi-Fi) to facilitate people's savoring (e.g., positive MTT).

Limitations and future research directions

Even though this conceptual paper advances tourism studies with extended discussion of the potential role of savoring in regulating positive tourist emotions and attachment formation, we acknowledge our article has several limitations. First, this conceptual paper focuses on positive emotions and regulating positive emotions given tourism experiences are predominantly pleasurable. However, people may experience negative emotions when traveling (e.g., encountering service failures, crime, or poor weather conditions). Future research should explore how tourists negotiate these incidents and in particular regulate their negative emotions and potential impacts on destination image, attachment, and related outcomes.

Second, we proposed that savoring strategies can help people to attend to or enhance positive emotions, and in turn facilitate the development of place attachment. However, due to limited research, we were not able to identify *a priori* how often or how long a tourist should engage in savoring strategies to reach an optimal result (Smith et al., 2014). Additionally, it is possible that people with different personalities, gender, and age may prefer to practice certain savoring strategies (Bryant & Veroff, 2007), and may want to avoid other strategies (e.g., introverts may be less likely to savor by capitalizing). Future researchers may want to systematically investigate each savoring strategy's appropriate application and duration as well as person-activity fit (Sheldon & Lyubomirsky, 2006).

These propositions are presented as a means to begin a conversation regarding the role played by savoring in developing place attachment in the tourism context; however we acknowledge that many other worthwhile related paths of inquiry will undoubtedly be unveiled as researchers continue to explore relationships among positive emotion, savoring, and destinations and our attachments to them.

References

Bagozzi, R. P. (1996). The role of arousal in the creation and control of the halo effect in attitude models. *Psychology and Marketing, 13*(3), 235–264. doi:10.1002/(SICI)1520-6793(199605)13:3<235::AID-MAR1>3.0.CO;2-D

Baloglu, S., & Mangaloglu, M. (2001). Tourism destination images of Turkey, Egypt, Greece, and Italy as perceived by US-based tour operators and travel agents. *Tourism Management, 22*(1), 1–9. doi:10.1016/S0261-5177(00)00030-3

Baloglu, S., & McCleary, K. W. (1999). A model of destination image formation. *Annals of Tourism Research, 26*(4), 868–897. doi:10.1016/S0160-7383(99)00030-4

Bartlett, F. C. (1932). Remembering: A study in experimental and social psychology. Cambridge: Cambridge University Press.

Bell, M. A., & Wolfe, C. D. (2004). Emotion and cognition: An intricately bound developmental process. *Child Development, 75*(2), 366. doi:10.1111/j.1467-8624.2004.00679.x

Borrie, W. T., & Roggenbuck, J. W. (2001). The dynamic, emergent, and multi-phasic nature of on-site wilderness experiences. *Journal of Leisure Research, 33*(2), 202–228. doi:10.1080/00222216.2001.11949938

Bowlby, J. (1969). Attachment and loss I (vol. I). Harmondsworth: Penguin Books.

Brandenburg, A. M., & Carroll, M. S. (1995). Your place or mine?: The effect of place creation on environmental values and landscape meanings. *Society & Natural Resources, 8*(5), 381–398. doi:10.1080/08941929509380931

Brown, G., Raymond, C. M., & Corcoran, J. (2015). Mapping and measuring place attachment. *Applied Geography, 57*, 42. doi:10.1016/j.apgeog.2014.12.011

Bryant, F. (2003). Savoring Beliefs Inventory (SBI): A scale for measuring beliefs about savouring. *Journal of Mental Health, 12*(2), 175–196. doi:10.1080/0963823031000103489

Bryant, F. B., & Veroff, J. (2007). *Savoring: A new model of positive experience.* Mahwah, NJ: Lawrence Erlbaum Associates Publishers.

Carver, C. S., & Scheier, M. F. (1990). Origins and functions of positive and negative affect: A control-process view. *Psychological Review, 97*(1), 19–35. doi:10.1037/0033-295X.97.1.19

Chen, N., Dwyer, L., & Firth, T. (2014). Conceptualization and measurement of dimensionality of place attachment. *Tourism Analysis, 19*(3), 323–338. doi:10.3727/108354214X14029467968529

Chen, Y., Lehto, X. Y., & Cai, L. (2013). Vacation and well-being: A study of Chinese tourists. *Annals of Tourism Research, 42*, 284–310. doi:10.1016/j.annals.2013.02.003

Cheng, P., & Qiang, W. (2018). Pre-visit destination image's effects on perceived travel service quality: The mediating effects of lace attachment. *2018 15th International Conference on Service Systems and Service Management (ICSSSM)* (pp. 1–5). doi:10.1109/ICSSSM.2018.8464966

Chi, C., Gursoy, D., & Chen, J. (2014). Theoretical examination of destination loyalty formation. *International Journal of Contemporary Hospitality management, 26*(5), 809–827. doi:10.1108/IJCHM-12-2013-0539

Chun, H. E. (2009). *Savoring future experiences: Antecedents and effects on evaluations of consumption experiences.* Dissertation.

Clawson, M. (1963). *Land and water for recreation; opportunities, problems, and policies.* Chicago: Rand McNally.

Craig-Smith, S. J., & French, C. (1994). *Learning to live with tourism.* South Melbourne: Pitman Publishing Pty Limited.

Cresswell, T. (2004). Defining place. In *Place: A short introduction* (pp. 127–136). Malden, MA: Blackwell Pub.

Cutler, Q., & Carmichael, B. (2010). The dimensions of the tourist experience. In M. Morgan, P. Lugosi, & B. Ritchie (Eds.), *The tourism and leisure experience: Consumer and managerial perspectives* (pp. 3–26). Bristol: Channel View Publications.

Dann, G. M. S. (1981). Tourist motivation an appraisal. *Annals of Tourism Research, 8*(2), 187–219. doi:10.1016/0160-7383(81)90082-7

de Bloom, J., Geurts, S. A E., Taris, T. W., Sonnentag, S., de Weerth, C., & Kompier, M. A. J. (2010). Effects of vacation from work on health and well-being: Lots of fun, quickly gone. *Work & Stress, 24*(2), 196–216. doi:10.1080/02678373.2010.493385

Filep, S., Cao, D., Jiang, M., & DeLacy, T. (2013). Savouring tourist experiences after a holiday. *Leisure/Loisir, 37*(3), 191–203. doi:10.1080/14927713.2013.842731

Fredrickson, B. L. (2001). The role of positive emotions in positive psychology. The broaden-and-build theory of positive emotions. *American Psychologist*, *56*(3), 218–226. doi:10.1037/0003-066X.56.3.218

Fredrickson, B. L. (2004). The broaden-and-build theory of positive emotions. *Philosophical Transactions of the Royal Society of London. Series B: Biological Sciences*, *359*(1449), 1367–1377. doi:10.1098/rstb.2004.1512

Fredrickson, B. L. (1998). What good are positive emotions?. *Review of General Psychology*, *2*(3), 300–319. doi:10.1037/1089-2680.2.3.300

Fredrickson, B. L. (2000). Cultivating positive emotions to optimize health and well-being. *Prevention & Treatment*, *3*(1). doi:10.1037/1522-3736.3.1.31a

Fredrickson, B. L., & Branigan, C. (2005). Positive emotions broaden the scope of attention and thought-action repertoires. *Cognition & Emotion*, *19*(3), 313–332. doi:10.1080/02699930441000238

Gable, S. L., & Reis, H. T. B. T.-A. (2010). Good news! Capitalizing on positive events in an interpersonal context. *Advances in Experimental Social Psychology*, *42*, 195–257. doi:10.1016/S0065-2601(10)42004-3

Gilbert, D. T., & Wilson, T. D. (2007). Prospection: Experiencing the future. *Science*, *317*(5843), 1351–1354. Retrieved from http://science.sciencemag.org/content/317/5843/1351.abstract

Gilbert, D., & Abdullah, J. (2002). A study of the impact of the expectation of a holiday on an individual's sense of well-being. *Journal of Vacation Marketing*, *8*(4), 352–361. doi:10.1177/135676670200800406

Goolaup, S., Solér, C., & Nunkoo, R. (2018). Developing a theory of surprise from travelers' extraordinary food experiences. *Journal of Travel Research*, *57*(2), 218–231. doi:10.1177/0047287517691154

Gursoy, D., Chen, J. S., & Chi, C. G. (2014). Theoretical examination of destination loyalty formation. *International Journal of Contemporary Hospitality Management*, *26*(5), 809–827. doi:10.1108/IJCHM-12-2013-0539

Gursoy, D., & Chi, C. G. (2018). The Routledge handbook of destination marketing. Abingdon: Routledge. Retrieved from http://public.eblib.com/choice/publicfullrecord.aspx?p=5371944

Halpenny, E. A. (2010). Pro-environmental behaviours and park visitors: The effect of place attachment. *Journal of Environmental Psychology*, *30*(4), 409–421. doi:10.1016/j.jenvp.2010.04.006

Halpenny, E. A., Kulczycki, C., & Moghimehfar, F. (2016). Factors effecting destination and event loyalty: Examining the sustainability of a recurrent small-scale running event at Banff National Park. *Journal of Sport & Tourism*, *20*(3-4), 233–262. doi:10.1080/14775085.2016.1218787

Hammitt, W. E., Backlund, E., & Bixler, R. (2006). Place bonding for recreation places: Conceptual and empirical development. *Leisure Studies*, *25*(1), 17–41. doi:10.1080/02614360500098100

Hay, R. (1998). Sense of place in developmental context. *Journal of Environmental Psychology*, *18*(1), 5–29. doi:10.1006/jevp.1997.0060

Hertenstein, M. J. (2002). Touch: Its communicative functions in infancy. *Human Development*, *45*(2), 70–94. doi:10.1159/000048154

Hicks, J. A., & King, L. A. (2007). Meaning in life and seeing the big picture: Positive affect and global focus. *Cognition and Emotion*, *21*, 1577–1584. doi:10.1080/02699930701347304

Hidalgo, M. C., & Hernandez, B. (2001). Place attachment: Conceptual and empirical questions. *Journal of Environmental Psychology*, *21*(3), 273–281. doi:10.1006/jevp.2001.0221

Hong, P. Y., Lishner, D. A., Han, K. H., & Huss, E. A. (2011). The positive impact of mindful eating on expectations of food liking. *Mindfulness*, *2*(2), 103–113. doi:10.1007/s12671-011-0048-3

Hosany, S., Prayag, G., Deesilatham, S., Causevic, S., & Odeh, K. (2015). Measuring tourists' emotional experiences: Further validation of the Destination Emotion Scale. *Journal of Travel Research*, *54*(4), 482–495. doi:10.1177/0047287514522878

Hosany, S., Prayag, G., Van Der Veen, R., Huang, S., & Deesilatham, S. (2017). Mediating effects of place attachment and satisfaction on the relationship between tourists' emotions and intention to recommend. *Journal of Travel Research*, *56*(8), 1079–1093. doi:10.1177/0047287516678088

Hu, Y., & Ritchie, J. R. B. (1993). Measuring destination attractiveness: A contextual approach. *Journal of Travel Research*, *32*(2), 25–34. doi:10.1177/004728759303200204

Huang, Y., Qu, H., & Montgomery, D. (2017). The meanings of destination: A Q method approach. *Journal of Travel Research*, *56*(6), 793–807. doi:10.1177/0047287516663652

Hummon, D. M. (1992). Community attachment. In I. Altman & S. M. Low (Eds.), *Place attachment* (pp. 253–278). Boston: Springer. doi:10.1007/978-1-4684-8753-4_12

Hutson, G., Montgomery, D., & Caneday, L. (2010). Perceptions of outdoor recreation professionals toward place meanings in natural environments: A Q-Method inquiry. *Journal of Leisure Research*, *42*(3), 417–442. doi:10.1080/00222216.2010.11950212

Io, M.-U. (2018). The relationships between positive emotions, place attachment, and place satisfaction in casino hotels. *International Journal of Hospitality & Tourism Administration*, *19*(2), 167–186. doi:10.1080/15256480.2017.1305315

Izard, C. E. (1977). *Human emotions*. New York: Plenum Press.

Jorgensen, B. S., & Stedman, R. C. (2001). Sense of place as an attitude: Lakeshore owners attitudes toward their properties. *Journal of Environmental Psychology*, *21*(3), 233–248. doi:10.1006/jevp.2001.0226

Jorgensen, B. S., & Stedman, R. C. (2006). A comparative analysis of predictors of sense of place dimensions: Attachment to, dependence on, and identification with lakeshore properties. *Journal of Environmental Management*, *79*(3), 316–327. doi:10.1016/j.jenvman.2005.08.003

Jose, P. E., Lim, B. T., & Bryant, F. B. (2012). Does savoring increase happiness? A daily diary study. *The Journal of Positive Psychology*, *7*(3), 176–187. doi:10.1080/17439760.2012.671345

Kals, E., Schumacher, D., & Montada, L. (1999). Emotional affinity toward nature as a motivational basis to protect nature. *Environment and Behavior*, *31*(2), 178–202. doi:10.1177/00139169921972056

Kim, J., & Fesenmaier, D. R. (2017). Sharing tourism experiences: The posttrip experience. *Journal of Travel Research*, *56*(1), 28–40. doi:10.1177/0047287515620491

Kim, J. H. (2014). The antecedents of memorable tourism experiences: The development of a scale to measure the destination attributes associated with memorable experiences. *Tourism Management*, *44*, 34. doi:10.1016/j.tourman.2014.02.007

Kleinke, C. L., Peterson, T. R., & Rutledge, T. R. (1998). Effects of self-generated facial expressions on mood. *Journal of Personality and Social Psychology*, *74*(1), 272–279. doi:10.1037/0022-3514.74.1.272

Knutson, B. J., & Beck, J. A. (2004). Identifying the dimensions of the experience construct. *Journal of Quality Assurance in Hospitality & Tourism*, *4*(3–4), 23–35. doi:10.1300/J162v04n03_03

Kyle, G., & Chick, G. (2007). The social construction of a sense of place. *Leisure Sciences*, *29*(3), 209–225. doi:10.1080/01490400701257922

Kyle, G., Graefe, A., & Manning, R. (2005). Testing the dimensionality of place attachment in recreational settings. *Environment and Behavior*, *37*(2), 153–177. doi:10.1177/0013916504269654

Langston, C. A. (1994). Capitalizing on and coping with daily-life events: Expressive responses to positive events. *Journal of Personality and Social Psychology*, *67*(6), 1112–1125. doi:10.1037/0022-3514.67.6.1112

Lazarus, R. (1991). *Emotion and adaptation*. New York: Oxford University Press.

Lee, S. A., & Oh, H. (2017). Sharing travel stories and behavioral outcomes: A case of travel. *Tourism Management*, *62*, 147–158. doi:10.1016/j.tourman.2017.04.005

Lewicka, M. (2011). Place attachment: How far have we come in the last 40 years?. *Journal of Environmental Psychology*, *31*(3), 207–230. doi:10.1016/j.jenvp.2010.10.001

Li, X., Cheng, C.-K., Kim, H., & Petrick, J. F. (2008). A systematic comparison of first-time and repeat visitors via a two-phase online survey. *Tourism Management*, *29*(2), 278–293. doi:10.1016/j.tourman.2007.03.010

Lin, Z., Chen, Y., & Filieri, R. (2017). Resident-tourist value co-creation: The role of residents' perceived tourism impacts and life satisfaction. *Tourism Management*, *61*, 436. doi:10.1016/j.tourman.2017.02.013

Loureiro, S. M. C. (2014). The role of the rural tourism experience economy in place attachment and behavioral intentions. *International Journal of Hospitality Management, 40*, 1–9. doi:10.1016/j.ijhm.2014.02.010

Low, S. M., & Altman, I. (1992). Place Attachment: A conceptual inquiry. In I. Altman & S. M. Low (Eds.), *Place attachment* (pp. 1–12). Boston: Springer. doi:10.1007/978-1-4684-8753-4_1

MacInnis, D. J., & Price, L. L. (1987). The role of imagery in information processing: Review and extensions. *Journal of Consumer Research, 13*(4), 473–491. doi:10.1086/209082

MacKay, K., Barbe, D., Van Winkle, C. M., & Halpenny, E. (2017). Social media activity in a festival context: Temporal and content analysis. *International Journal of Contemporary Hospitality Management, 29*(2), 669–689. doi:10.1108/IJCHM-10-2015-0618

Manthiou, A., Kang, J., & Hyun, S. S. (2017). An integration of cognitive appraisal theory and script theory in the luxury cruise sector: The bridging role of recollection and storytelling. *Journal of Travel & Tourism Marketing, 34*(8), 1071–1088. doi:10.1080/10548408.2016.1277575

Mitas, O., Yarnal, C., Adams, R., & Ram, N. (2012). Taking a "Peak" at leisure travelers' positive emotions. *Leisure Sciences, 34*(2), 115–135. doi:10.1080/01490400.2012.652503

Morgan, P. (2010). Towards a developmental theory of place attachment. *Journal of Environmental Psychology, 30*(1), 11–22. doi:10.1016/j.jenvp.2009.07.001

Nawijn, J. (2011). Determinants of daily happiness on vacation. *Journal of Travel Research, 50*(5), 559–566. doi:10.1177/0047287510379164

Nawijn, J., Marchand, M. A., Veenhoven, R., & Vingerhoets, A. J. (2010). Vacationers happier, but most not happier after a holiday. *Applied Research in Quality of Life, 5*(1), 35–47. doi:10.1007/s11482-009-9091-9

Niedenthal, P. (2008). Emotion concepts. In M. Lewis, J. M. Haviland-Jones, & L. Barrett (Eds.), *Hanbook of Emotions* (pp. 587–600). New York: Guildford Press.

Pike, S., & Ryan, C. (2004). Destination positioning analysis through a comparison of cognitive, affective, and conative perceptions. *Journal of Travel Research, 42*(4), 333–342. doi:10.1177/0047287504263029

Pine, B. J. I., & Gilmore, H. J. (1999). *Experience economy: Work is theatre & every business a stage.* (Harvard Business School Press editon), Boston: Harvard Business School Press Books. doi:10.1080/02642069700000028

Pizam, A. (2010). Creating memorable experiences. *International Journal of Hospitality Management, 29*(3), 343. doi:10.1016/j.ijhm.2010.04.003

Plunkett, D., Fulthorp, K., & Paris, C. M. (2019). Examining the relationship between place attachment and behavioral loyalty in an urban park setting. *Journal of Outdoor Recreation and Tourism, 25*, 36–44. doi:10.1016/j.jort.2018.11.006

Prayag, G. (2018). Destination attachment. In *The Routledge handbook of destination marketing.* New York: Routledge.

Prayag, G., & Ryan, C. (2012). Antecedents of tourists' loyalty to Mauritius: The role and influence of destination image, place attachment, personal involvement, and satisfaction. *Journal of Travel Research, 51*(3), 342–356. doi:10.1177/0047287511410321

Proshansky, H. M., Fabian, A. K., & Kaminoff, R. (1983). Place-identity: Physical world socialization of the self. *Journal of Environmental Psychology, 3*(1), 57–83. doi:10.1016/S0272-4944(83)80021-8

Qu, Y., Xu, F., & Lyu, X. (2019). Motivational place attachment dimensions and the pro-environmental behaviour intention of mass tourists: A moderated mediation model. *Current Issues in Tourism, 22*(2), 197–217. doi:10.1080/13683500.2017.1399988

Quoidbach, J., Berry, E. V., Hansenne, M., & Mikolajczak, M. (2010). Positive emotion regulation and well-being: Comparing the impact of eight savoring and dampening strategies. *Personality and Individual Differences, 49*(5), 368–373. doi:10.1016/j.paid.2010.03.048

Quoidbach, J., Wood, A. M., & Hansenne, M. (2009). Back to the future: The effect of daily practice of mental time travel into the future on happiness and anxiety. *The Journal of Positive Psychology, 4*(5), 349–355. doi:10.1080/17439760902992365

Ramkissoon, H., Graham Smith, L. D., & Weiler, B. (2013). Testing the dimensionality of place attachment and its relationships with place satisfaction and pro-environmental behaviours: A structural equation modelling approach. *Tourism Management, 36,* 552–566. doi:10.1016/j.tour-man.2012.09.003

Raymond, C. M., Brown, G., & Weber, D. (2010). The measurement of place attachment: Personal, community, and environmental connections. *Journal of Environmental Psychology, 30*(4), 422–434. doi:10.1016/j.jenvp.2010.08.002

Reis, H. T., Smith, S. M., Carmichael, C. L., Caprariello, P. A., Tsai, F.-F., Rodrigues, A., & Maniaci, M. R. (2010). Are you happy for me? How sharing positive events with others provides personal and interpersonal benefits. *Journal of Personality and Social Psychology, 99*(2), 311–329. doi:10.1037/a0018344

Rimé, B. (2007). The social sharing of emotion as an interface between individual and collective processes in the construction of emotional climates. *Journal of Social Issues, 63*(2), 307. doi:10.1111/j.1540-4560.2007.00510.x

Rucker, D. D., Preacher, K. J., Tormala, Z. L., & Petty, R. E. (2011). Mediation analysis in social psychology: Current practices and new recommendations. *Social and Personality Psychology Compass, 5*(6), 359–371. doi:10.1111/j.1751-9004.2011.00355.x

Samios, C., Abel, L. M., & Rodzik, A. K. (2013). The protective role of compassion satisfaction for therapists who work with sexual violence survivors: An application of the broaden-and-build theory of positive emotions. *Anxiety, Stress and Coping, 26,* 610–623 doi:10. 1080/10615806. 2013.784278

Scannell, L., & Gifford, R. (2010). Defining place attachment: A tripartite organizing framework. *Journal of Environmental Psychology, 30*(1), 1–10. doi:10.1016/j.jenvp.2009.09.006

Servidio, R., & Ruffolo, I. (2016). Exploring the relationship between emotions and memorable tourism experiences through narratives. *Tourism Management Perspectives, 20,* 151–160. doi: 10.1016/j.tmp.2016.07.010

Sheldon, K. M., & Lyubomirsky, S. (2006). Achieving sustainable gains in happiness: Change your actions, not your circumstances. *Journal of Happiness Studies, 7*(1), 55–86. Vol. doi:10.1007/s10902-005-0868-8

Simpson, P. M., & Siguaw, J. A. (2008). Destination word of mouth: The role of traveler type, residents, and identity salience. *Journal of Travel Research, 47*(2), 167–182. doi:10.1177/0047287508321198

Smith, C. A., & Ellsworth, P. C. (1985). Patterns of cognitive appraisal in emotion. *Journal of Personality and Social Psychology, 48*(4), 813–838. doi:10.1037/0022-3514.48.4.813

Smith, J. L., & Bryant, F. B. (2016). The Benefits of Savoring Life: Savoring as a moderator of the relationship between health and life satisfaction in older adults. *The International Journal of Aging and Human Development, 84*(1), 3–23. doi:10.1177/0091415016669146

Smith, J. L., & Bryant, F. B. (2017). Savoring and well-being: Mapping the cognitive-emotional terrain of the happy mind. In M. Robinson & M. Eid (Eds.), *The Happy Mind: Cognitive Contributions to Well-Being.* Cham: Springer. doi:10.1007/978-3-319-58763-9_8

Smith, J. L., Harrison, P. R., Kurtz, J. L., & Bryant, F. B. (2014). Nurturing the capacity to savor: Interventions to enhance the enjoyment of positive experiences. In *The Wiley Blackwell Handbook of Positive Psychological Interventions* (pp. 42–65). Malden: Wiley. doi:10.1002/9781118315927.ch3

Song, H. M., Kim, K. S., & Yim, B. H. (2017). The mediating effect of place attachment on the relationship between golf tourism destination image and revisit intention. *Asia Pacific Journal of Tourism Research, 22*(11), 1182–1193. doi:10.1080/10941665.2017.1377740

Stedman, R. C. (2002). Toward a social psychology of place: Predicting behavior from place-based cognitions, attitude. *Environment and Behavior, 34*(5), 561–581. doi:10.1177/0013916502034005001

Steele, F. (1996). *The sense of place.* Boston: CBI Publishing Company.

Sthapit, A., Choi, S.-A., & Hwang, Y. Y. (2016). Emotional happiness and psychological distance: How does happiness and psychological distance change during vacation?. *Journal of Distribution Science, 14*(7), 63–70. doi:10.15722/jds.14.7.201607.63

Sthapit, E., Björk, P., & Coudounaris, D. N. (2017). Emotions elicited by local food consumption, memories, place attachment and behavioural intentions. *Anatolia, 28*(3), 363–380. doi:10.1080/13032917.2017.1322111

Sthapit, E., & Coudounaris, D. N. (2018). Memorable tourism experiences: Antecedents and outcomes. *Scandinavian Journal of Hospitality and Tourism, 18*(1), 72–94. doi:10.1080/15022250.2017.1287003

Stokols, D., & Shumaker, S. A. (1981). People in places: A transactional view of settings. In J. Harvey (Ed.), *Cognition, Social Behavior, and the Environment*. Hillsdale, NJ: Lawrence Erlbaum Associates Publishers.

Tsai, C. T. S. (2016). Memorable tourist experiences and place attachment when consuming local food. *International Journal of Tourism Research, 18*(6), 536–548. doi:10.1002/jtr.2070

Tuan, Y.-F. (1975). Images and mental maps. *Annals of the Association of American Geographers, 65*(2), 205–212. doi:10.1111/j.1467-8306.1975.tb01031.x

Tuan, Y.-F. (1977). *Space and place the perspective of experience*. Minneapolis: University of Minnesota Press.

Tugade, M. M., & Fredrickson, B. L. (2007). Regulation of positive emotions: Emotion regulation strategies that promote resilience. *Journal of Happiness Studies, 8*(3), 311–333. doi:10.1007/s10902-006-9015-4

Tung, V. W. S., & Ritchie, J. R. B. (2011). Exploring the essence of memorable tourism experiences. *Annals of Tourism Research, 38*(4), 1367–1386. doi:10.1016/j.annals.2011.03.009

Urry, J. (1990). *The tourist gaze: Leisure and travel in contemporary societies*. London: Sage.

Urry, J., & Larsen, J. (2011). The Tourist Gaze 3.0, doi:10.4135/9781446251904

Van Riper, C., Kyle, G., Wallen, K., Landon, A., & Raymond, C. (2018). The antecedents of place attachment in the context of an Australian national park. *Journal of Environmental Psychology, 61*, 1–9. doi:10.1016/j.jenvp.2018.11.001

Walker, G. J., & Deng, J. (2003). Comparing leisure as a subjective experience with the Chinese experience of rùmí. *Leisure/Loisir, 28*(3-4), 245–276. doi:10.1080/14927713.2003.9651315

Wang, D., Park, S., & Fesenmaier, D. R. (2012). The role of smartphones in mediating the touristic experience. *Journal of Travel Research, 51*(4), 371–387. doi:10.1177/0047287511426341

Watson, D., Wiese, D., Vaidya, J., & Tellegen, A. (1999). The two general activation systems of affect: Structural evolutionary considerations, and psychobiological evidence. *Journal of Personality and Social Psychology, 76*(5), 820–838. doi:10.1037/0022-3514.76.5.820

Wilkins, E. J., & de Urioste-Stone, S. (2018). Place attachment, recreational activities, and travel intent under changing climate conditions. *Journal of Sustainable Tourism, 26*(5), 798–811. doi:10.1080/09669582.2017.1417416

Williams, D. R., Patterson, M. E., Roggenbuck, J. W., & Watson, A. E. (1992). Beyond the commodity metaphor: Examining emotional and symbolic attachment to place. *Leisure Sciences, 14*(1), 29–46. doi:10.1080/01490409209513155

Williams, S., & Lew, A. A. (2015). *Tourism geography: Critical understandings of place, space and experience*. London: Routledge.

Wilson, C. A., & Saklofske, D. H. (2018). The relationship between trait emotional intelligence, resiliency, and mental health in older adults: The mediating role of savouring. *Aging & Mental Health, 22*(5), 646–654. doi:10.1080/13607863.2017.1292207

Xu, Z., & Zhang, J. (2016). Antecedents and consequences of place attachment: A comparison of Chinese and Western urban tourists in Hangzhou. *Journal of Destination Marketing & Management, 5*(2), 86–96. doi:10.1016/j.jdmm.2015.11.003

Yeh, S. S., Chen, C., & Liu, Y. C. (2012). Nostalgic emotion, experiential value, destination image, and place attachment of cultural tourists. *Advances in Hospitality and Leisure, 8*, 167–187. Emerald Group Publishing Ltd. doi:10.1108/S1745-3542(2012)0000008013

Yüksel, A., & Akgül, O. (2007). Postcards as affective image makers: An idle agent in destination marketings. *Tourism Management, 28*(3), 714–725. doi:10.1016/j.tourman.2006.04.026

Zhang, H., Huang, Z., Green, B. C., & Qiu, S. (2018). Place attachment and attendees' experiences of homecoming event. *Journal of Sport and Tourism, 22*(3), 227–246. doi:10.1080/14775085.2018.1480404

Self-love emotion as a novel type of love for tourism destinations

Dimitra Margieta Lykoudi ⓘ, Georgia Zouni ⓘ and Markos Marios Tsogas ⓘ

ABSTRACT

Tourists nowadays do not travel only to experience a destination or visit attractions at different destinations, but also to find, explore, change and/or create their 'self' or fill their higher self needs. The present research constitutes a first attempt to explore the novel concept of self-love in tourism and examine which types of tourists develop this type of love. Two separate qualitative efforts were undertaken to gather primary data from tourists. The findings reveal that self-love is a higher self-need and a multi-item construct. Furthermore, results show that individuals from different cultures who are generally older, highly educated, of high monthly income, and mainly singles tend to develop self-love emotions at destinations and are repeat visitors to them. Hence, the present research opens up a new research area in affective attunements and certainly adds up to the discourse of an emotional birth of constructive values that is apparently rather absent in tourism literature. The proposed self-love framework could be useful for tourism providers in order to develop more meaningful, transformational or/and emotional experiences that better fulfil the self needs of tourists. Managerial targeted strategies are suggested for tourism experts in order to satisfy the self-lovers inner needs, as well as strengthen their loyalty programs, which could focus on intrinsic motives and sophisticated rewards that require ongoing (intellectual) interaction. Finally, new directions for further research have emerged.

摘要

现在的旅游者出行不仅仅为了体验目的地或参观不同目的地的景点,而是为了发现、探索、改变和/或创造他们的"自我身份"或满足更高的自我需求。本研究首次尝试探索旅游者自恋的新概念,并检验哪些类型的游客具有自恋的特征。本研究采取了两项不同的质性研究工作来收集游客的第一手数据。结果表明,自恋是一种更高层次的自我需要,并且是一个多项目的研究构念。此外,研究结果表明,那些来自不同文化背景、通常年龄较大、受教育程度高、月收入高,而且主要是单身的游客,往往会在目的地发展出自恋情感,并成为目的地的重游者。因此,本研究在情感融洽方面开辟了一个新的研究领域,当然也为旅游学术文献中明显缺失的创建建设性情感价值的话语提供了补充。本研究提出的自恋框架对旅游业者有帮助,以发展更有意义的、转变性的或/和情感性的体验,以更好地满足游客的自我需求。本研究也针对旅游专家提

出了经营目标策略, 以满足自恋爱好者的内在需求, 并加强他们的
忠诚计划, 这可以集中在内在动机和复杂的奖励, 需要持续的(智力
)互动。最后, 出现了进一步研究的新方向。

Introduction

Emotions and experiences are crucial concepts in consumer research, since they influence the behaviour of consumers regarding their choices (Goossens, 2000). Moreover, individuals tend to look for emotional conditions, cherish emotional stimuli or employ emotion when interacting with their social environment (Goossens, 2000).

In tourism, emotions have received a lot of attention since they formulate experiences, which usually entail satisfying and positive emotions (e.g. Mcintosh & Siggs, 2005). Emotions have a pervasive influence on tourists' reactions (Prayag et al., 2013) and play an essential role in tourism experience, as they influence travel behaviour at all the stages of travel journey (e.g., Gnoth, 1997). Despite the unprecedented recognition of the fundamental role of emotions in tourism such as place attachment, dependence and affect (e.g., Halpenny, 2010), there are few substantial empirical studies, which investigate tourists' associations and concepts related to emotions about the destinations they visit (e.g., Hosany & Prayag, 2013).

This study aspires to shed light on the understanding of the fuzzy world of emotions and specifically on the "self-love" type of destination love, by defining and operationalizing self-love, as well as exploring which tourist segments develop self-love regarding tourism destinations.

Literature review

Love

The most complex of all emotions is, probably, love (Loureiro & Kaufmann, 2012). Numerous sciences have studied the complex concept of love, such as sociology, psychology and lately marketing (brand love) and tourism (destination brand love).

In the tourism field, branding has been successfully applied in destinations (e.g., Boo et al., 2009) since brands are found in many categories of tourism goods/services and permeate almost all facets of tourism activities (Cai, 2002). However, the question remains as to *whether already accepted branding principles can be transferred to destinations* (Konecnik & Gartner, 2007, p. 401). Despite the great importance of love within tourism destinations (e.g., Hosany et al., 2015), it has only recently started to be investigated in today's tourism literature as destination brand love and thus as destination-specific emotion (e.g., Swanson, 2017; Aro et al., 2018; Christou, 2018).

However, there are no studies on love for destinations, as a universal concept. This study perceives destination love as a broader emotional concept than destination brand love. Destination brand love is only based on love for the specific destination(s) under investigation or/and already entrenched (brand) love conceptualizations, which constitute the only case in tourism research (e.g., Hosany et al., 2015; Lee & Hyun,

2016; Swanson, 2017; Aro et al., 2018; Christou, 2018). This study involves a universal approach of love for destinations (not destination-specific and not a single destination as a brand) as well as a multicultural and diverse sample. Participants of this study discussed destinations of their own choosing, which gives a universal approach in the research effort. This is in line with the procedure of previous studies in branding (e.g., Langner et al., 2016). Hence tourism experts need to delve into the understanding of tourists' destination love emotions not within a specific destination context but across the entire universe of destinations, in order to profoundly comprehend the concept. Finally, destinations must be strategically managed as the increasing importance of loved brands in marketing practice necessitates the theoretical development as well as the empirical measurement of love in the tourism context. This is the first attempt to investigate destination love adopting a universal approach.

Self-love as a type of love for destinations

The concept of 'self' should be seen as an integral part of tourism behavioural research, since its importance has been highlighted by many academics (e.g.,Gnoth, 1997). Tourism both sustains and is sustained by stories and moments that define tourist's self as well as impact upon tourist's senses of self (Crang, 2004). Some tourists develop and transform their 'self' by learning about other people and cultures, or by having challenging experiences (Wearing & Dean, 2003), while others conceive tourism as a resource to achieve self-realization, and thus self-confirmation (Rojek, 1993).

Two well-known influential psychological thinkers, Rogers (1961) and Maslow (1968) emphasized the importance of self-love. They stressed the importance of living up to one's ideals, even reaching self-actualization. Aristotle coined the terms 'self-love' and 'other-love' and the question whether people prefer their favourite other over the self has triggered philosophical and social-behavioural thinking over the years. In Aristotle's terms, people deep down love the self-more than their favourite others. However, humans can come to believe that they love their favourite others more than they love the self. Thus, it can be assumed that 'self- love' is evident in unidirectional kind of love, whereas 'other-love' is evident in bidirectional type of love.

Lew (2018) included 'love for self' in his global consciousness approaches and Cohen (1979) suggested five main modes of the tourist experience, one of which is the existential mode. The 'existential' tourist launches him/herself into a journey of self-discovery, self-fulfilment, self-enlightenment and self-actualization. During leisure time, a person is free from his/her everyday routine and responsibilities and he/she is therefore able to choose activities for his/her own enjoyment, personal development and re-skilling (Rojek, 1995). According to Kelly (1996, p. 45) *'this relative freedom makes possible the investment of self that leads to the fullest development of ourselves, the richest expression of who we want to become, and the deepest experience of fulfilment'.*

Travel behaviour, demographic and socio-economic attributes on self-love

Numerous academics across various disciplines have tried to investigate and give insights into the impact of culture - including the socio-demographic characteristics- and ethnicity on the emotion of love (Doherty et al., 1994). As love constitutes a subjective notion, it is found to be highly dependent on individual, socio-demographic and cultural factors (Hong, 1986; Christou, 2018). In their study, Jankowiak and Fischer (1992) provide strong evidence that romantic love is (nearly) universal across different cultures and ethnicities.

On the contrary, Stone (1988) highlights that romantic love is perceived differently across different cultures and societies. In relation to gender and love, no differences generally were found in the '80s research (e.g., Hendrick & Hendrick, 1986), as well as '90s (Doherty et al., 1994) but they have emerged in more recent years (e.g., Regan, 2016). Previous research demonstrates an obvious pattern with regard to the linkage between age and endorsement of an 'agapic' love style (e.g., Lin & Huddleston-Casas, 2005), showing that individuals who are emotionally mature and generally 'older' tend to develop love emotions (e.g., Lee, 1977).

Moreover, research proves that more educated individuals would potentially have psychological access to more advanced and committed relationships (Elder & Rockwell, 1979) in different contexts (e.g., Carland et al., 1995). On the contrary, no previous research can be found to correlate love or self-love development with higher income. It must be noted that income is related with higher educational level and age in tourism (Björk & Kauppinen-Räisänen, 2016).

Finally, to the extent of our knowledge no research has been carried out on love and emotions in relation to marital status in tourism context, and only scarce research has been found in psychology. However, a study in the field of psychology (Taormina & Gao, 2013) showed that satisfaction of the self-actualization needs had positive correlations with marital status.

A review on market segmentation literature recognises that all segmentation approaches can be classified as being either a priori, which use observed variables, or a posteriori that use unnoticed variables (e.g., Dolnicar, 2004). In particular, demographic and socio-economic attributes of travellers have been recognized over time as key determinants of travel behaviour by numerous tourism researchers (e.g., Wang et al., 2018). Moreover, travel behaviour is affected by numerous elements, one of which is previous experience (e.g. Dolnicar et al., 2015), as 'first-time visitors' and 'repeat visitors' have differences in their travel behaviour (Lau & McKercher, 2004). Furthermore, the behaviour of repeat visitors is more favourable for destinations and they constitute an attractive market segment as they can be accessed more easily than first-time visitors (e.g., Jiang et al., 2017). In this study, both a priori (demographics) and a posteriori (behavioural) variables were used for tourism market segmentation. In detail, demographic segmentation was used as an a priori approach for market segmentation of visitors (e.g., Juaneda & Sastre, 1999) who develop self-love emotions. Moreover, an a posteriori approach was also used and represented by repeat visitation (e.g., Gitelson & Crompton, 1984) in order to segment the visitors who develop self-love in destinations. The above discussion leads to the second objective of this study which is to identify the segments/types of tourists that develop this type of love, in terms of their socio-demographic variables and repeat visitation patterns.

Methodology

The study of self-love constitutes a smaller part of a broader study about love for destinations. Specifically, two separate survey attempts took place. The first study (Study 1) took place for five months in 2016. Afterwards, the second study (Study 2) took place for seven months in 2016 and 2017. A total number of 75 (Study 1) and 334 (Study 2) individuals, both national and international, eventually participated in the research. The sampling in both studies was mostly theoretically grounded and not statistically or purely personal oriented (Glaser & Strauss, 1967; Tan et al., 2013). Moreover, for further robustness of the theory building, a number of academics in Philosophy participated in both studies.

The prolonged period of the field research and the higher number of participants -compared to that of other similar studies- were deemed crucial in order to secure reliable conclusions to be drawn for a rather complex, personal and such an intricate inner issue, following Christou's (2018) procedure. The extended time of data collection in the research field meets ethnographic principles (Christou, 2018) and contributes to the avoidance of seasonality biases. Once some degree of information collection saturation was achieved, Study 2 ended (procedure by Mariampolski, 2006 and Christou, 2018), and a comparison with the existing literature was implemented (e.g., Tan et al., 2013).

The aim was to compare the emergent codes with existing ones-if any-, and to investigate the extent to which there are any similarities, differences, discrepancies as well as conflicts, in order to enhance the validity, credibility, transferability, and dependability of the codes emerged (Tan et al., 2013). In both studies, respondents used their own love prototype to actually determine whether their most favourite and/or ideal destinations for vacations were clearly loved or not. The items of self-love were elicited from tourists, by asking them to describe love for a destination, what they perceived and felt as well as how they acted, when they experienced love for destinations, following the research procedures of Batra et al. (2012). The studies have progressed from being exploratory towards being more focused.

The interviews of the first study, as well as the open-ended questions of the second study were in English and analysed employing grounded theory (Strauss & Corbin, 1994), in combination with McCracken's (1988) method, as suggested by Batra et al. (2012). The selection of the English language was based on the more recent studies which have shown no differences between language versions (e.g., Sanchez et al., 2000). Since coding took place, a combination of codes into broader concepts constituted a focal element of the methodology. The initial list of 23 codes/items was decreased to 13, which compose the construct of 'self-love'. Open Coding and axial coding techniques were employed to identify the discrete concepts or the building blocks of the data, following the methodology of Tan et al. (2013). Moreover, the open codes which seemed 'interconnected' were grouped together to generate tentative statements of relationships among phenomena (Daengbuppha et al., 2006). Rigor in data collection and coding was ensured via inter-coder reliability (Cohen's kappa and Fleiss kappa), ethical considerations (e.g., anonymity of the respondents) and relevance of outcomes.

Due to the exploratory nature of the study, a variety of qualitative approaches were employed to gather primary data, like studies of similar nature (e.g., Aro et al., 2018). This methodological procedure is appropriate when observing and interpreting reality in order to establish a theory that will clarify what was experienced (Newman et al., 1998), given the complex and ambiguous nature of the phenomenon to be investigated (e.g., Christou, 2018), as well as the fact that there is lack of the exploratory qualitative research normally conducted when developing a new topic area (Batra et al., 2012). The sampling procedure of this study followed analogous studies' sampling procedures, such as that of Batra et al. (2012) and Christou (2018). Finally, this study covers more broadly the need of a larger, multicultural and diverse sample composition since up until now, almost all studies on love in tourism have used smaller samples (e.g., Swanson, 2017, Aro et al., 2018; Christou, 2018) with less cultural diversity (e.g., Christou, 2018) or no cultural diversity (e.g., Lee & Hyun, 2016; Swanson, 2017; Aro et al., 2018).

Study 1

The first study combined two sampling techniques. The respondents were contacted both directly and randomly in Ancient Olympia, Greece, or via a snowball sampling procedure, following that of Batra et al. (2012) and Christou (2018), which was conducted internationally. Snowball procedure used in this survey was developed by following previous studies in love (Batra et al., 2012). The snowball sampling procedure initiated through personal contacts of the authors with the participants, who had not come into contact with the authors prior to the surveys (Batra et al., 2012). For achieving higher cultural diversity levels due to the multicultural nature of the research, the current study used an additional snowball collection method, by asking participants in the research field to suggest to their acquaintances back home to participate in the interviews via Skype.

In the research field, both national and international tourists were approached and chosen in public spots to be interviewed. The whole procedure ensured the input of a diverse spectrum of tourists, who have been exposed to various tourist destinations, tourism services and experiences. Moreover, this procedure helped the researchers to identify the main public spots where tourists relax and have free time and enabled the selection of individuals, who were able, available and willing to take part in the research and meet the objectives of the study (Christou, 2018).

Informal semi-structured interviews were employed as appropriate information collection tools, following the procedure of Batra et al. (2012) and Swanson (2017). Informal semi-structured interviews make people feel at ease, comfortable and allow them to develop themes naturally (Christou, 2018). Confidential taped semi-structured interviews were conducted by the researcher by using a voice recorder and lasted from 10 to 25 minutes, averaging 12-15 minutes.

Initially, in Study 1, respondents were asked about their general and behavioural travel patterns (e.g., activities they like to do during their trips, the main purpose of their trips, information sources for selecting destinations), based on EUROSTAT guidelines (2014). Participants discussed destinations of their own choosing. This is in line with the procedure of previous studies (e.g., Langner et al., 2016), where participants had to answer the surveys with respect to their (most) favourite or loved brands. This allowed some space to request additional information about participants' feelings for the destination(s), whether they love it/them, and if yes, what they really mean by loving a destination and the reasons for loving the destination(s) (following Langner et al., 2016).

Participants were also asked to articulate why each loved destination did qualify as perceived love, and they were encouraged to continue elaborating and reckoning more profoundly about it, when possible. Those questions aimed at revealing deeper meanings and facets of love for destinations, as perceived and articulated by each person. Interviews were transcribed and coded, by delving deeper into each issue (Hennink et al., 2011), in a database. Specifically, the identification of codes/items and subsequently of self-love dimension was achieved via a detailed and careful examination of the notes from the interview transcriptions, detecting similarities in tourists' responses as well as classifying common and specific self-love descriptions.

Study 2

In the second study, a semi-structured questionnaire was used, combined both qualitative (open-ended questions) and quantitative approaches in order to extend the results as well as the insights of the first study. The same procedure and data collection were used as in study 1 about destination love, and afterwards the love dimensions/types of study 1 were presented to the respondents who were asked to choose the two most important love dimensions for them and further elaborate. A main goal of the second study was to gather additional insights into the notion investigated. Following Batra et al. (2012) process, grouping initial codes/items into a more general concept was built on previous studies with respect to the relevance and similarity on the love prototype and constituted a main element of the studies' analysis, since the initial list of 23 self-love codes/items was reduced to 13 codes/items, which synthesise the self-love construct.

Results

Self-love items results

Inter-rater reliability, control and axis coding were conducted for analysing the results of both studies. Control coding was done to estimate whether the self-love items/codes were formulated in such a way that the items could "objectively" belong to the self-love construct. Initially, two independent raters and later seven independent raters evaluated the construct of self-love. Cohen's kappa coefficient κ (Cohen, 1960) was used to measure the agreement between two raters and found to constitute a

Table 1. Self-love articulation examples.

Respondent profile	Self-love items mentioned	Description of the loved destination
Male, Irish, 34, PhD, psychologist	self-definition, self-discovery	'Love for Athens is about finding myself there and **discovering facets of my personality, which contribute to my self-definition and spiritual awakening.**'
Male, German, 57, PhD, Philosopher	Self-actualization, Self-fulfilment and Inspiration	'Love is diving into knowledge, **achieving self-actualization and fulfilment** ... Greece is my **inspirational source of knowledge**'.
Male, USA, 63, PhD, Greek Ancient history expert	Self-balance, Self-investment, Self-fulfilment and Inspiration	'... by visiting this destination, **I feel inspired,** extremely happy. I learn a lot through my trips there and I have **sharpened my knowledge** about the Olympic Games spirit and Greek history. Olympia **lifts my spirit further and I am nurtured spiritually, I feel 'full' of knowledge,** excitement and harmony. **I achieve self-balance and self-fullness**'
Female, French, 46, master graduate, lawyer	self-appreciation, better version of me, understand the real values in life, self-investment, self-fulfilment	'Mozambique is the place which made me **reconsider my life values and priorities**. All the experiences I got from this place work as a **"thoughtful and mindful" compass** ... Mozambique changed completely my mind-set, which was **pushed forward, I learnt to live with less goodies and follow a simpler lifestyle** ... I have become a **more thoughtful and fulfilled person** ...'

Source: Authors.

substantial agreement between the raters (Cohen's kappa= .794), according to Landis and Koch (1977).

However, due to the high complexity of the notion under study and the exploratory nature of the research, seven independent raters further evaluated the items of self-love. In order to do that, Fleiss's Kappa measurement (Fleiss, 1971) was implemented, using the following calculation formula:

$$0 \leq x_{ij} \leq m \sum_{j=1}^{k} x_{ij} = m \sum_{i=1}^{n} \sum_{j=1}^{k} x_{ij} = mn$$

where n = number of subjects, k = number of evaluation categories and m = number of judges for each subject. For every subject $i = 1, 2, ..., n$ and evaluation categories $j = 1, 2, ..., k$, let x_{ij} = number of judges that assign category j to subject i.

In our coding, the 7 researchers agreed on 13 items out of 23, which gives a .779 rate of agreement (Fleiss kappa), that also constitutes a substantial agreement between the raters. All these 13 items were also included in the initial 15 items of the two raters. Therefore, 13 items of self-love construct were finally included, which are the following: *(1) self-actualization, (2) self-definition, (3) self-discovery, (4) self-fulfilment, (5) self-investment, (6) self-appreciation, (7) understanding the real values in life, (8) self-awareness, (9) self-confidence, (10) self-balance, (11) inspiration, (12) bringing out the best version of me, and (13) stimulating all my senses.* Table 1 provides self-love articulation examples.

Travel behaviour and socio-demographic results on self-love

Study 1 results. In the first study, 103 semi-structured interviews were conducted. From the total of 136 people who were initially contacted by the researcher, 103 of them agreed to participate in the research and 75 of them claimed that they do love a destination. The notion of self-love was evident amongst 12% of these participants. Several key findings emerge from the socio-demographic profile of those who articulate self-love: A percentage of 33,3% respondents were master graduates and 33,3% were PhD graduates as well. Furthermore, 77,8% were women and 22,2% were men of average age 40,7 years, and their average monthly income was 4.350 euros (SD = 1202,08). 66,7% were single, 22,2% married and 11,1% divorced. The majority of these respondents came from the USA (33,3%), followed by Portuguese (22,2%), Italians (11,1%), Indians (11,1%), Russians (11,1%) and Slovakians (11,1%). The main purpose of their trip was leisure (66,7%) or a combination of leisure and business (33,3%). The majority of them prefers to travel during the summer (33,3%) and autumn (22,2%). The striking majority travel independently (77,8%) and only 11,1% with organized groups or both (11,1%). They prefer to travel with a group of friends (55,6%) or alone (33,3%) and they get informed for destinations by relatives or friends (37,5%) as well as by conferences, studies and books (25,0%).

Finally, while the majority of the respondents (3 respondents) have visited the loved destination for the first time, it is of great importance to note that the remaining respondents that represent repeat visitors have visited the loved destination several times, namely 9, 15 or 20 (16,7% respectively).

Study 2 results. The total sample consisted of 334 participants and 75 participants of those (22,45%) articulated love for destinations as self-love. Of them, 38 were males and 37 females. The majority came from the USA (21,3%), followed by French (16%), Germans (9,3%), Greeks (8%), British (8%), Australians (6,7%), Dutch (5,3%) and Italians (4%). The average age of the participants who articulated love for destinations as self-love was 42,22 years (SD = 10.56) and the average monthly income was 5.517 euros (SD = 4.833). Moreover, the striking majority (52%) were master graduates, followed by university/college graduates (26,7%) and PhD graduates (20%). 47,3% were single, 36,5% married and 16,2% divorced.

The striking majority of self-lovers (86,5%) are repeat visitors and 13,5% of self-lovers are first time visitors of the destination, with a much lower percentage than in the first study. Again, it is of great importance to note that repeat visitors have visited the destination several times, specifically 10, 20 or 3 (10,8%, 9,5%, 8,1% respectively). Moreover, almost two out of three respondents have visited at least 5 times the destination.

Discussion

Self-love was emerged as a distinct type of love for destinations and a higher self-need, following Bransen's (2006), Rojek's (1993) as well as Wearing's and Dean's (2003) reasoning. Particularly, self-confirmation and/or transformation were found to (co) exist denoting the non-mutually exclusiveness of the concepts, and thus self-love concerns, among others, the quality of one's own flourishing, well-being and attunement (Bransen, 2006), confirmation (Rojek, 1993), and transformation (Wearing & Dean, 2003) to the normatively significant features of his/her life as well as it captivates oneself in virtue of the volitional necessity of his/her loving state of mind (Bransen, 2006).

Self-love was found to be a multi-item construct, as revealed by the respondents themselves, and was described by various items of 'self'. Specifically, the self-love construct was found to be composed by the following items:

1. *Self-actualization;* some individuals described their love for a destination as *self-actualization*, which is *'the tendency of the organism to move in the direction of maturation... . It moves in the direction of greater independence or self-responsibility'* (Rogers, 1961, p. 35). Pearce and Caltabiano (1983) claimed that positive experiences from travel reflect the attainment of self-actualization, among others. *'The pursuit of a (new) experience is based upon "self-actualization" through the (re)discovery of one's intellectual and physical aptitudes'* (Bouchet et al., 2004, p.130) as well as self-expression and socializing (Keller & Edelstein, 1993). Tourists want to achieve self-actualization out of their need for spare time and holidays (e.g., Gnoth, 1997). For example, cultural travel gives the chance to tourists to reach self-actualization, in order to achieve or attain one's potential (Holloway, 2004). Notably, one of the most important criteria that tourists use when choosing to visit again a destination is indeed self-actualization (Balakrishnan, 2009).

2. *Self-definition* was described as love for a destination by some participants. Self-definition is a concept that has been investigated mainly in the field of social psychology (e.g., Tesser & Paulhus, 1983; Epstein, 1990), but also in developmental psychology (e.g., Freund & Smith, 1999). The concept of self-definition is associated with a specific part of self-knowledge, which encompasses important elements for the definition of oneself or *'refers to that part of self-related knowledge that contains attributes crucial for the definition of oneself'* (Freund & Smith, 1999, p. 55). Self-definition does not constitute an 'objective' description of a person. On the contrary, it encompasses individuals' self-conceptions which are considered crucial for the definition of their own self (Freund & Smith, 1999).

3. *Self-discovery;* some tourists articulated their love for a destination as self-discovery. Indeed, tourism gives the opportunity to an individual to 'find his/herself" (Wearing & Dean, 2003). According to Fussell, *'a travel experience is bound up with personal discovery'* (as cited in Craik, 1986, p. 26). It is the discovery of self that is the goal of those tourists on their inner journey to enlightenment (Carr, 2017, p. 138).

4. *Self-fulfilment* was also described by participants as love for a destination. Self-fulfilment is regarded as a fundamental element of a good, happy human life and it is explained and evaluated in various ways (Gewirth, 1998). According to Gewirth (1998, p. 14) *'self-fulfilment consists in carrying to fruition one's deepest desires or one's worthiest capacities. It is a bringing of oneself to flourishing completion, an unfolding of what is strongest or best in oneself, so that it represents the successful culmination of one's aspirations or potentialities. In this way self-fulfilment betokens a life well lived, a life that is deeply satisfying, fruitful, and worthwhile'.* Self-fulfilment is considered as a broad conception, since it encompasses all other values of human life, and constitutes the ultimate purpose of human achievement for a good life (Gewirth, 1998).

According to Middleton and Clarke (2012), people who have a higher drive and will to participate in tourism will probably focus more on their attempt to reach personal fulfilment. Leisure travel and tourism are more and more associated with the fulfilment of tourists' self-development and inner-directed needs. This powerful association is what makes vacation travel to be considered as more of a necessity than a luxury. In the next decade, tourists' self-fulfilment aspirations will have an even more important effect on travel purchase decisions (Middleton & Clarke, 2012).

Even though some academics (Middleton & Clarke, 2012) consider that self-actualization is equal to self-fulfilment or self-development, it has to be stressed that self-fulfilment is different from self-actualization. It can be argued that in self-actualization, self is perceived as a set of determinate potentialities that await actualization, whereas self-fulfilment is more open to creativity since a person creates both his/her powers and his/her developed states or activities. This development is formed by the person's aspirations (Gewirth, 1998). Moreover, the process of actualization is automatic, like the natural process of growth. On the contrary, the process of fulfilment is marked by choices made by the self-fulfilling person, denoting individual's freedom to decide which potentialities he/she craves to develop based on his/her deepest aspirations (Gewirth, 1998). Furthermore, in self-actualization the aspect of the self that is due to be actualized dwells in diverse 'needs' based to a great extent on desires that emanate from adjustment problems experienced by individuals in diverse social relationships (Gewirth, 1998). In self-fulfilment, the aspect of self to be fulfilled stems from 'aspirations', denoting individuals' strongest desires for self-gratification.

5. *Self-investment;* some tourists perceived their love for a destination as self-investment. Tourism and travelling push an individual to surpass his/her own physical and psychological limits (Bouchet et al., 2004). Tourists through travelling can achieve their desire to meet different customs, cultures, people, and sceneries, acquire knowledge and live unique experiences that strengthen and justify one's investment in 'self-capital'. Tourists hold in themselves all these unique physical, sensual and cognitive experiences which contribute to their self-growth.

6. *Self-appreciation;* some other participants perceived their love for a destination as self-appreciation. Specifically, an individual's loved destination can make him/her appreciate and value him/herself more. Tourists can be affected, in any existential register, by every travelling experience they acquired at a specific destination. Moreover, these experiences can possibly make visitors appreciate or value themselves more. In a recent study, Walker and Moscardo (2014) identify self-appreciation as an important value in tourism and define it as the recognition of personal insight (p. 1186). Loved destinations incite some tourists to experience situations and things which make them value their self in a more positive way.

7. Some tourists claimed that their loved destination makes them *understand the real values in life*. They stated that their loved destination provides the means to modify their self-priorities and change their mind-set and lifestyle, in a meaningful and desired way, by focusing mainly on 'inner directedness' and not on consumerism and materialism. Such behaviours include acts that appear to be beyond the logic of commercialization .

8. *Self-awareness;* Some tourists claimed that self-awareness means being in love with a destination. *'For centuries travel has been associated with a broadening of awareness and self-development through knowledge and exposure to other cultures and human circumstances'* (Middleton & Clarke, 2012, p. 78). Brown and Ryan (2003, p. 823) define self-awareness simply as *'knowledge about the self'*, meaning that self-awareness is an internal awareness of one's cognitions and emotions. Other academics state that self-awareness constitutes awareness or knowledge of one's thoughts, emotions, and behaviours and it can be perceived as a state and thus, it can be situational (Fenigstein et al., 1975). Self-awareness is treated as similar to other concepts, such as self-consciousness and insight (e.g., Richards et al., 2010). In line with Morin's (2006) self-awareness view, this study has revealed that tourists' self-awareness occurs mainly when they focus not on the external environment of the destination, but on the internal milieu. Tourist's self-awareness stems from one's desire to make his/her holiday experience more meaningful by seeking for something that can refresh and recharge them. However, it should be stressed that the environmental and cultural context of destination encourages the tourist's self-awareness, as well. According to Tan et al. (2013), it is more possible for tourists who develop 'consciousness/awareness' to engage in 'creative experiences' rather than to take part in more general activities.

9. *Self-confidence;* some participants described their love for a destination as self-confidence, which constitutes an important concept that has been used in many cases to understand consumer behaviour. Consumer self-confidence is described as the extent to which a person *'feels capable and assured with respect to his or her marketplace decisions and behaviours'* (Bearden et al., 2001, p. 122). It *'reflects subjective evaluations of one's ability to generate positive experiences as a consumer in the marketplace'* (Adelman, 1987, as cited in Bearden et al., 2001, p. 122) and makes easier for the consumer to act in an efficient way in cases of complex decisions (Bearden et al., 2001). In this study, some tourists stated that their love for a destination is seen as 'self-confidence' and that love has encouraged and helped them to be more self-confident. For instance, tourists' social interactions in the loved destination encourage them to become more sociable in their everyday life or tourists feel more attractive and better looking when being in their loved destination.

10. *Self-balance;* Some tourists claimed that love for a destination is about developing principally tourists' mental balance and well-being which is achieved by the unique aesthetics, intellectual stimuli as well as hedonic pleasures experienced in the destination. To the extent of our knowledge no research has been carried out on love and emotions in relation to self-balance in psychology in general.

11. *11. Inspiration;* Love for destinations was perceived by some other tourists as inspiration. The uniqueness, goodness or beauty of the destination affects emotionally the inspired person. This may indicate a transcendent relationship. Watson et al. (1988) considered 'inspiration' as an item on their measure of positive affect.

12. Some other tourists stated that love for destinations is about *bringing out the best version of them* meaning that their loved destination contributes to reveal or

awake their best inner quality, behaviour, traits. It is their loved destination which triggers their best version. For example, when archaeologists visit a loved heritage destination, they live the real experience of their field at its birthplace. It is actually the amalgam of their interests, skills and place, which (the latter) triggers their best version.

13. *Stimulating all their senses;* According to Middleton and Clarke (2012, p. 78) *'vacations and their associations with rest and recreation (in a literal sense of being renewed in mental and physical ways), have always had a stimulating effect upon people's minds ... '.* Some tourists articulated that a loved destination awakes their senses through the tastes, sounds, smells, sights, interactions with all destination elements as well as its people. All these senses were also described to be intertwined. Moreover, even some ordinary routines back home (e.g., food) can trigger individuals' senses differently due to the setting of the loved place. Ultimately, the loved destination provides a combination of tastes, noises, aromas, sights that in other contexts could not impact tourists' senses, but in loved places, they stimulate and enrich them.

An additional objective of the present investigation was to build on cross-cultural love research by investigating potential demographic associations with self-love in tourism contexts and identifying homogeneous groups of tourists that can develop self-love among the heterogenous population. A number of self-love tourism segments emerged:

(a) *Nationality;* Firstly, the self-love notion was found to be universal across different cultures, in line with previous research on romantic love (Jankowiak & Fischer, 1992). However, other academics (e.g., Stone, 1988) found differences in how different cultural groups view love (Kim & Hatfield, 2004) and subjective well-being (Diener & Lucas, 2000).

(b) *Gender;* Even though a gender difference was found in the first study, no gender discrepancies were found in the second study. This demonstrates that attitudes and opinions largely cut uniformly across sex demographic characteristics. The results of the investigation, which show that men and women from different cultural and ethnic settings seem to have similar attitudes and behaviour towards self-love, are analogous to that of Doherty et al. (1994) study about love.

(c) *Age;* Age differences were found suggesting that there is an association between age and self-love. More specifically, individuals who are emotionally mature and generally 'older' tend to develop self-love emotions at destinations. These findings support previous research on love, such as Lee's (1977) explanation of the 'agapic' love and Butler et al. (1995) study on love and wellbeing (e.g., Steptoe et al., 2015) which stress the fact that human growth is associated with adult maturity and that higher motives (such as self-love) are stronger for older versus younger adults.

(d) *Education;* Education appears to be one of the demographic variables to distinguish the self-lovers. Self-lovers comprise the highly educated segments,

Table 2. Similarities and differences of the two studies.

Respondents' characteristics	Study 1	Study 2
Sex	women (77,8%)	both women and men (38 male and 37 female)
Age	middle age (average age 40,7 years)	middle age (average age 42,22 years)
Education	master graduates and PhD graduates (33,3% both categories)	master graduates (52%)
Marital status	Single (66,7%)	Single (47,3%),
Average Monthly income	4.350 euros	5.517 euros
Nationality	USA (33,3%) followed by mainly Europeans	USA (21,3%), followed by Europeans, as well as Australians
Repeat visitation	visited the loved destination several and many times, namely 9, 15, or 20	almost two out of three respondents have visited at least 5 times the destination

Source: Authors.

consistent with other researchers who postulate that a more educated individual would potentially have psychological access to more advanced and more committed relationships (Elder & Rockwell, 1979) in different contexts (e.g., Carland et al., 1995).

(e) *Income;* As expected, the question on the individual monthly level income caused the greatest reticence in the first survey. Thus, a total of 7 persons out of 9 did not answer, despite the open type question posed. However, 57 out of the 75 respondents answered the income question in the second study. The majority of self-lovers were of high monthly income. Even though no previous research can be found to correlate love or self-love development with higher income, it must be noted that income is related with higher educational level and age in tourism (e.g., Björk & Kauppinen-Räisänen, 2016)., a result found in the present study as well.

(f) *Marital Status;* Marital status also appears to be one of the demographic variables to distinguish the self-lovers. In both studies, self-love developers were mainly singles. To the extent of our knowledge no research has been carried out on love and emotions in relation to marital status in tourism context, and scarce in psychology in general. A study in psychology field (Taormina & Gao, 2013) showed that satisfaction of the self-actualization needs had positive correlations with marital status, a finding that is contradictory to our research.

(g) *Repeat visitation;* Self-lovers were proven to be repeat visitors of the loved destination in both studies, which shows that self-love development at a destination could be associated with loyalty. This amplifies the importance of first impressions and suggests to the destination managers that priority should be placed on providing emotional experiences in order to attract and satisfy tourists' higher inner needs more efficiently.

To sum up, there was a consensus of both studies for age, education, marital status, monthly income, nationality, and repeat visitation patterns. Only gender differed in these two studies, and further research should shed light on this. Table 2 summarizes the similarities and differences of studies.

Contribution and conclusion

Theoretical contribution

The key contribution of the present study is that it adds to the relatively small amount of tourism research that examines the concept of love for understanding human-place bonds and provides both theoretical and empirical evidence for the concept of self-love in tourism. In particular, this study is the first in tourism to perceive destination love as a universal and thus a broader concept than destination brand love. Up to now, all existing studies of love in tourism context are based on specific destinations (destination brand love) and/or already entrenched conceptualizations in love, denoting a narrow perspective in love tourism research with respect to the complexity, universality, and tourism-specific nature of love concept. This fragmented view has resulted in a substantial lack of tourism destination love types. This study contributes to this identified gap in the literature by adopting and providing a broader love research stance, which incorporates the complex, universal, and tourism-specific nature of love. Analogous to the view of Barker et al. (2015) on brand love, this study considers that love in a specific destination cannot be seen as the end game; instead destination love should be seen as universal, surpassing all manner of specific destinations and existing conceptualizations in other contexts. In this universal love context, the emergence of self-love as a type of destination love in tourism as well as the establishment of its conceptual framework are offered as the main contributions and yield new knowledge for academics and practitioners. Self-love as a specific love type was found to be evident in the tourism field as a stand-alone theoretical construct that has never been studied before.

Notably, the value of self- love in tourism research is profound for three main reasons:

1. First, it adds to the extremely under-searched and new notion of 'love' in the tourism field, and more specifically its 'self-love' type, to help in understanding further the human-place emotional attunement. This research establishes a supremely valuable condition of the self namely self-love which is a multi-item emotion and suggests the various higher self-need items. Self-love in tourism may be considered as a fundamental emotion towards self- growth, which enables people to experience existing or new aspects of their identities, their social relations, and/or their interaction with destination's integrated elements. This theoretical contribution can be considered as an expanded knowledge in emotions and affects in tourism. Specifically, the study's proposed framework could help researchers to delve into the constellation of tourists' emotions associated with their urge to enter or maintain a close relationship with a destination in order to fill their higher needs (e.g. Maslow, 1943) and to find, change or/and create their self (Crang, 2004). Hence the concept of self- love could be seen as an integral part of tourism behavioural research, since its importance has been highlighted by the findings of this study. Tourism destinations could, thus, be an ideal experiential arena in which human-place bonds become a fundamental source of self -love development. The contribution to the growing tourism literature on emotions is evident as it sheds light on the relationship between tourism and the self, but also to the extension of the literature regarding the implementation of the concept of self-love as a way of attracting and retaining tourists.

2. Second, self-love items help in construct building and lead to a much more comprehensive and integrated understanding of how tourists actually articulate and experience love at a tourism destination. Therefore, self-love could be considered as a higher human-place bond need. In detail, self-love was found to be a multi-item construct which defines the ultimate level of sense of self and compose self-love. All these self-love items were emerged as essential elements of human-place bonds. Results unravel tourists' mental prototypes, such as self-love, that constitute a great challenge in the tourism literature, since they are considered as tacit knowledge structures and thus, they cannot be easily described and verbalized. However, in tourism literature, the investigation of these concepts is rather missing. Therefore, the inclusion of these items in love theory could set the basis to fill a significant gap in tourism literature, since their importance in behavioural research has been proved to be major (e.g., Freund & Smith, 1999).

3. Moreover, this study reveals how tourists describe destination love as well as which type of tourists develop destination self-love by using both a priori and a posteriori variables for market segmentation. It provides empirical evidence for the profile of self-lovers at destinations. The findings signify the need to investigate the socio-demographic composition of the self-lovers in tourism destinations and their revisit patterns in order to shed light on the aspects of self-love development in tourism contexts. Analogous to romantic love research which indicates that cultural and socio-demographic variables affect how people define and experience love (Erber & Erber, 2017), in the present study, it was proven that socio-demographic and behavioural variables are associated with the development of self-love in destinations.

Managerial contribution

The crucial managerial question of this study is how destination managers can transform liked destinations into loved destinations where visitors create self-love emotions and keep that relationship over time. The main managerial implications can be summarised as follows:

1. Firstly, the proposed self-love framework could be useful for tourism providers in order to develop more meaningful, transformational or/and emotional experiences that better fulfil the self needs of tourists. In detail, tourism practitioners should research and analyse their destination in relation to the self-love characteristics and to *create personal higher needs connections for (potential and/or existing) tourists with the loved destination*, accordingly. This is more universal than creating just positive emotions, since it encompasses a sense of actualization and fulfilment as well as an intuitive feeling of soundness about the loved destination. This could be achieved by enhancing the loved destination with a sense of inspiration and self-discovery from its origin, history, culture, unique characteristics, in order the destination buyer to develop affinity about it. In both studies, loved destinations seemed to come from the heart and mind of self-lovers. They can additionally be built via the formation of engaging and tightly knit destination self-love communities on social media for tourists' connection and interaction, as well as destination presence at emotionally

meaningful events such as tourism exhibitions and travel festivals, which could be organized in the countries of self-lovers.

2. Moreover, the building of strong self-loved destination brands that symbolize or connect to what we refer to as self's deeper meanings and important values, could help in the creation of a self-love experience among different touchpoints within the travel customer journey in order to achieve positive outcomes. From this study, it is evident that respondents connect destination self-love emotions with intrinsic rather than extrinsic travel benefits. It could be suggested that if 'self-love' is to be created by destinations, then they should adjust their value proposition accordingly, in all stages of travel for the enhancement of the tourists' self-growth and inspiration. So, it is crucial for tourism managers to engage in 'self-love stories' in order to improve their destination product and service design as well as offerings.

3. Additionally, selective tourism marketing techniques are feasible only if self-lovers and socio-demographic variables are clearly indicated since this allows tourism experts to 'develop a better understanding of distinct tourist characteristics and for developing marketing strategies' (Park et al., 2002, p. 55). The highly subjective and individualistic nature of the tourist experience is gaining appreciation recently and this study stresses that tourism self-experience and love could not be 'stage-managed' by the service provider, but rather tourists aid in the production of their own experiences and emotions through their personal characteristics and the agendas they bring with them to the tourist encounters. The implementation of effective promotional and functional activities targeted at potential self-love developers requires a sound comprehension of these tourism segments. These results may also facilitate tourism professionals to carry out market research in order to identify the tourism segments that are more possible to develop self-love at their destination, which will make them able to gain better strategic marketing insights. Managerial targeted strategies can be adopted by destination managers in designing and planning their business focused on satisfying the self-lovers inner needs based on their individual characteristics. As an example, destinations could also create slogans that inspire individuals for their future visitation.

4. Finally, since self-lovers are found to be repeat visitors of the loved destination, repeat visitation could be further strengthened by securing high-quality self-emotional experience and loyalty programs, which could focus on intrinsic over extrinsic motives and sophisticated rewards that require ongoing interaction. Both to attract and enhance the volume of repeat self-love visitors, destination managers could focus on increasing the destination self-love and tourists' possible intellectual experiences at the destination. One possible method could be fostering tourists' higher needs by providing informative panels or an application presenting destination specific services/activities or learning experiences that would help them stimulate their mind and senses, contribute to their personal growth or increase visitors' interest and involvement.

The above discussion leads to a potential future research agenda that could lead to a deeper study of this unexplored notion. More studies are needed to further explore the items of self-love, since love is characterised as a difficult and disputable concept (e.g. Christou, 2018). Moreover, further research may examine the interaction of self-love items identified here. The items of the self-love concept could be complemented by further cross-cultural research, facilitating our understanding of the notion. In a nutshell, this investigation has only commenced to grasp the basics of this fascinating subject, but it provides the first exploration of self-love in tourism. After all, for Plato and Aristotle the ultimate goal of the polis (place) is to provide the means whereby persons could fulfil themselves!

ORCID

Dimitra Margieta Lykoudi ⓘD http://orcid.org/0000-0002-9046-2596
Georgia Zouni ⓘD http://orcid.org/0000-0002-3388-1591
Markos Marios Tsogas ⓘD http://orcid.org/0000-0002-3106-095X

References

Aro, K., Suomi, K., & Saraniemi, S. (2018). Antecedents and consequences of destination brand love—A case study from Finnish Lapland. *Tourism Management, 67*, 71–81. https://doi.org/10.1016/j.tourman.2018.01.003

Balakrishnan, M. S. (2009). Strategic branding of destinations. *European Journal of Marketing, 43*(5/6), 611–629. https://doi.org/10.1108/03090560910946954

Barker, R., Peacock, J., & Fetscherin, M. (2015). The power of brand love. *International Journal of Market Research, 57*(5), 669–672. https://doi.org/10.2501/IJMR-2015-056

Batra, R., Ahuvia, A., & Bagozzi, R. P. (2012). Brand love. *Journal of Marketing, 76*(2), 1–16. https://doi.org/10.1509/jm.09.0339

Bearden, W. O., Hardesty, D. M., & Rose, R. L. (2001). Consumer self-confidence: Refinements in conceptualization and measurement. *Journal of Consumer Research, 28*(1), 121–134. https://doi.org/10.1086/321951

Björk, P., & Kauppinen-Räisänen, H. (2016). Local food: a source for destination attraction. *International Journal of Contemporary Hospitality Management, 28*(1), 177–194. https://doi.org/10.1108/IJCHM-05-2014-0214

Boo, S., Busser, J., & Baloglu, S. (2009). A model of customer-based brand equity and its application to multiple destinations. *Tourism Management, 30*(2), 219–231. https://doi.org/10.1016/j.tourman.2008.06.003

Bouchet, P., Lebrun, A. M., & Auvergne, S. (2004). Sport tourism consumer experiences: a comprehensive model. *Journal of Sport & Tourism, 9*(2), 127–140. https://doi.org/10.1080/14775080410001732578

Bransen, J. (2006). Selfless self-love. *Ethical Theory and Moral Practice, 9*(1), 3–25. https://doi.org/10.1007/s10677-005-9001-7

Brown, K. W., & Ryan, R. M. (2003). The benefits of being present: Mindfulness and its role in psychological well-being. *Journal of Personality and Social Psychology, 84*(4), 822–848. https://doi.org/10.1037/0022-3514.84.4.822

Butler, R., Walker, W. R., Skowronski, J. J., & Shannon, L. (1995). Age and responses to the Love Attitudes Scale: consistency in structure, differences in scores. *International Journal of Aging & Human Development, 40*(4), 281–296. https://doi.org/10.2190/YAA7-3C7G-TVXT-VATB7558370

Cai, L. A. (2002). Cooperative branding for rural destinations. *Annals of Tourism Research, 29*(3), 720–742. https://doi.org/10.1016/S0160-7383(01)00080-9

Carland, Jr, J. W., Carland, J. A. C., & Carland, I. I. I., J. W. T. (1995). Self-actualization: The zenith of entrepreneurship. *Journal of Small Business Strategy, 6*(1), 53–66.

Carr, N. (2017). Re-thinking the relation between leisure and freedom. *Annals of Leisure Research, 20*(2), 137–151. https://doi.org/10.1080/11745398.2016.1206723

Christou, P. A. (2018). Exploring agape: Tourists on the island of love. *Tourism Management, 68*, 13–22. https://doi.org/10.1016/j.tourman.2018.02.015

Cohen, E. (1979). A phenomenology of tourist experiences. *Sociology, 13*(2), 179–201. https://doi.org/10.1177/003803857901300203

Cohen, J. (1960). A coefficient of agreement for nominal scales. *Educational and Psychological Measurement, 20*(1), 37–46. https://doi.org/10.1177/001316446002000104

Craik, J. (1986). *Resorting to tourism: Cultural policies for tourist development in Australia.* Allen and Unwin. https://doi.org/10.1177/1329878X9206400115

Crang, M. (2004). Cultural Geographies of Tourism. In A. A. Lew, C. M. Hall, & A. M. Williams (Eds.), *A companion to tourism* (pp. 74–84). John Wiley & Sons. https://doi.org/10.1002/9780470752272.ch6

Daengbuppha, J., Hemmington, N., & Wilkes, K. (2006). Using grounded theory to model visitor experiences at heritage sites: Methodological and practical issues. *Qualitative Market Research: An International Journal, 9*(4), 367–388. https://doi.org/10.1108/13522750610689096

Diener, E., & Lucas, R. E. (2000). Personality and subjective well-being across the life span. In V.J. Molfese and D.L. Molfese (Eds.), *Temperament and personality development across the life span* (pp. 221–244). Psychology Press.

Doherty, R. W., Hatfield, E., Thompson, K., & Choo, P. (1994). Cultural and Ethnic Influences on Love and Attachment. *Personal Relationships, 1*(4), 391–398. https://doi.org/10.1111/j.1475-6811.1994.tb00072.x

Dolnicar, S. (2004). Beyond "commonsense segmentation": A systematics of segmentation approaches in tourism. *Journal of Travel Research, 42*(3), 244–250. https://doi.org/10.1177/0047287503258830

Dolnicar, S., Coltman, T., & Sharma, R. (2015). Do satisfied tourists really intend to come back? Three concerns with empirical studies linking satisfaction to behavioral intentions. *Journal of Travel Research, 54*(2), 152–178. https://doi.org/10.1177/0047287513513167

Elder, G. H., Jr,., & Rockwell, R. C. (1979). The life-course and human development: An ecological perspective. *International Journal of Behavioral Development, 2*(1), 1–21. https://doi.org/10.1177/016502547900200101

Epstein, S. (1990). Cognitive-experiential self-theory. In A. Pervin (Ed.), *Handbook of personality: Theory and research* (pp. 165–192). Guilford Press. https://doi.org/10.1007/978-1-4419-8580-4_9

Erber, R., & Erber, M. (2017). *Intimate relationships: Issues, theories, and research.* Psychology Press.

Eurostat. (2014). *Methodological manual for tourism statistics* (version 3.1.EU). http://ec.europa.eu/eurostat/documents/3859598/6454997/KS-GQ-14-013-EN-N.pdf

Fenigstein, A., Scheier, M. F., & Buss, A. H. (1975). Public and private self-consciousness: Assessment and theory. *Journal of Consulting and Clinical Psychology, 43*(4), 522–527. https://doi.org/10.1037/h0076760

Fleiss, J. L. (1971). Measuring nominal scale agreement among many raters. *Psychological Bulletin, 76*(5), 378–382. https://doi.org/10.1037/h0031619

Freund, A. M., & Smith, J. (1999). Content and function of the self-definition in old and very old age. *The Journals of Gerontology Series B: Psychological Sciences and Social Sciences, 54B*(1), P55–67. https://doi.org/10.1093/geronb/54B.1.P55

Gewirth, A. (1998). *Self-fulfillment*. Princeton University Press.

Gitelson, R. J., & Crompton, J. L. (1984). Insights into the repeat vacation phenomenon. *Annals of Tourism Research, 11*(2), 199–217. https://doi.org/10.1016/0160-7383(84)90070-7

Glaser, B. G., & Strauss, A. L. (1967). *The discovery of grounded theory*. Aldine.

Gnoth, J. (1997). Tourism motivation and expectation formation. *Annals of Tourism Research, 24*(2), 283–304. https://doi.org/10.1016/S0160-7383(97)80002-3

Goossens, C. (2000). Tourism information and pleasure motivation. *Annals of Tourism Research, 27*(2), 301–321. https://doi.org/10.1016/S0160-7383(99)00067-5

Halpenny, E. A. (2010). Pro-environmental behaviours and park visitors: The effect of place attachment. *Journal of Environmental Psychology, 30*(4), 409–421. https://doi.org/10.1016/j.jenvp.2010.04.006

Hendrick, C., & Hendrick, S. (1986). A theory and method of love. *Journal of Personality and Social Psychology, 50*(2), 392–402. https://doi.org/10.1037/0022-3514.50.2.392

Hennink, M., Hutter, I., & Bailey, A. (2011). *Qualitative research methods*. SAGE Publications Limited.

Holloway, J. C. (2004). *Marketing for tourism*. Pearson education.

Hong, S.-M. (1986). Relationship between romantic love and length of time in love among Korean young adults. *Psychological Reports, 59*(2), 494–494. https://doi.org/10.2466/pr0.1986.59.2.494

Hosany, S., & Prayag, G. (2013). Patterns of tourists' emotional responses, satisfaction, and intention to recommend. *Journal of Business Research, 66*(6), 730–737. https://doi.org/10.1016/j.jbusres.2011.09.011

Hosany, S., Prayag, G., Deesilatham, S., Causevic, S., & Odeh, K. (2015). Measuring tourists' emotional experiences: Further validation of the destination emotion scale. *Journal of Travel Research, 54*(4), 482–495. https://doi.org/10.1177/0047287514522878

Jankowiak, W. R., & Fischer, E. F. (1992). A cross-cultural perspective on romantic love. *Ethnology, 31*(2), 149–155. https://doi.org/10.2307/3773618

Jiang, K., Potwarka, L., & Havitz, M. (2017, June). *Sub-dimensions of destination brand love and their influences on destination brand loyalty: A study of first-timers and repeat visitors* [Paper presentation]. In *2017 International Conference on Exploring Attractive Destinations*, Quebec, Canada.

Juaneda, C., & Sastre, F. (1999). Balearic Islands tourism: A case study in demographic segmentation. *Tourism Management, 20*(4), 549–552. https://doi.org/10.1016/S0261-5177(99)00006-0

Keller, M., & Edelstein, W. (1993). The development of the moral self from childhood to adolescence. In G. G. Noam & T. Wren (Eds.), *The moral self* (pp. 310–336). MIT Press.

Kelly, J. R. (1996). *Leisure* (3rd ed.). Allyn & Bacon.

Kim, J., & Hatfield, E. (2004). Love types and subjective well-being: A cross-cultural study. *Social Behavior and Personality: An International Journal, 32*(2), 173–182. https://doi.org/10.2224/sbp.2004.32.2.173

Konecnik, M., & Gartner, W. C. (2007). Customer-based brand equity for a destination. *Annals of Tourism Research, 34*(2), 400–421. https://doi.org/10.1016/j.annals.2006.10.005

Landis, J. R., & Koch, G. G. (1977). The measurement of observer agreement for categorical data. *Biometrics, 33*(1), 159–174. https://doi.org/10.2307/2529310

Langner, T., Bruns, D., Fischer, A., & Rossiter, J. (2016). Falling in love with brands: a dynamic analysis of the trajectories of brand love. *Marketing Letters, 27*(1), 15–26. https://doi.org/10.1007/s11002-014-9283-4

Lau, A., & McKercher, B. (2004). Exploration versus acquisition: A comparison of first-time and repeat visitors. *Journal of Travel Research, 42*(3), 279–285. https://doi.org/10.1177/0047287503257502

Lee, J. A. (1977). A typology of styles of loving. *Personality and Social Psychology Bulletin, 3*(2), 173–182. https://doi.org/10.1177/014616727700300204

Lee, K. H., & Hyun, S. S. (2016). The effects of perceived destination ability and destination brand love on tourists' loyalty to post-disaster tourism destinations: The case of Korean tourists to Japan. *Journal of Travel & Tourism Marketing*, *33*(5), 613–627. https://doi.org/10.1080/10548408.2016.1167349

Lew, A. A. (2018). Why travel?-travel, tourism, and global consciousness. *Tourism Geographies*, *20*(4), 742–749. https://doi.org/10.1080/14616688.2018.1490343

Lin, L. W., & Huddleston-Casas, C. A. (2005). Agape love in couple relationships. *Marriage & Family Review*, *37*(4), 29–48. https://doi.org/10.1300/J002v37n04_03

Loureiro, S. M. C., & Kaufmann, H. R. (2012). Explaining love of wine brands. *Journal of Promotion Management*, *18*(3), 329–343. https://doi.org/10.1080/10496491.2012.696460

Mariampolski, H. (2006). *Ethnography for marketers: A guide to consumer immersion*. Sage.

Maslow, A. H. (1943). A theory of human motivation. *Psychological Review*, *50*(4), 370–396. https://doi.org/10.1037/h0054346

Maslow, A. (1968). Some educational implications of the humanistic psychologies. *Harvard Educational Review*, *38*(4), 685–696. https://doi.org/10.17763/haer.38.4.j07288786v86w660

McCracken, G. (1988). *The long interview* (Vol. 13)Sage.

Mcintosh, A. J., & Siggs, A. (2005). An exploration of the experiential nature of boutique accommodation. *Journal of Travel Research*, *44*(1), 74–81. https://doi.org/10.1177/0047287505276593

Middleton, V. T., & Clarke, J. R. (2012). *Marketing in travel and tourism* (3rd ed.). Butterworth Heinemann, Routledge.

Morin, A. (2006). Levels of consciousness and self-awareness: A comparison and integration of various neurocognitive views. *Consciousness and Cognition*, *15*(2), 358–371. https://doi.org/10.1016/j.concog.2005.09.006

Newman, I., Benz, C. R., & Ridenour, C. S. (1998). *Qualitative-quantitative research methodology: Exploring the interactive continuum*. SIU Press.

Park, M., Yang, X., Lee, B., & Stokowski, P. A. (2002). Segmenting casino gamblers by involvement profiles: a Colorado example. *Tourism Management*, *23*(1), 55–65. https://doi.org/10.1016/S0261-5177(01)00063-2

Pearce, P. L., & Caltabiano, M. L. (1983). Inferring travel motivation from travellers' experiences. *Journal of Travel Research*, *22*(2), 16–20. https://doi.org/10.1177/004728758302200203

Prayag, G., Hosany, S., & Odeh, K. (2013). The role of tourists' emotional experiences and satisfaction in understanding behavioral intentions. *Journal of Destination Marketing & Management*, *2*(2), 118–127. https://doi.org/10.1016/j.jdmm.2013.05.001

Regan, P. C. (2016). Loving unconditionally: Demographic correlates of the Agapic love style. *Interpersona: An International Journal on Personal Relationships*, *10*(1), 28–35. https://doi.org/10.5964/ijpr.v10i1.199

Richards, K. C., Campenni, C., & Muse-Burke, J. L. (2010). Self-care and well-being in mental health professionals: The mediating effects of self-awareness and mindfulness. *Journal of Mental Health Counseling*, *32*(3), 247–264. https://doi.org/10.17744/mehc.32.3.0n31v88304423806

Rogers, C. R. (1961). *On becoming a person: A therapist's view of psychotherapy*. Houghton Mifflin.

Rojek, C. (1993). *Ways of escape: Modern transformations in leisure and travel*. Springer.

Rojek, C. (1995). *Decentring leisure: Rethinking leisure theory* (Vol. 35). Sage.

Sanchez, J. I., Alonso, A., & Spector, P. (2000, August). *Linguistic effects in translated organizational measures: A study of bilinguals*. Paper present at the annual Academy of Management meeting (4-9 August), Toronto.

Steptoe, A., Deaton, A., & Stone, A. A. (2015). Subjective wellbeing, health, and ageing. *The Lancet*, *385*(9968), 640–648. https://doi.org/10.1016/S0140-6736(13)61489-0

Stone, L. (1988). Passionate attachments in the West in historical perspective. In W. Gaylin & E. Person (Eds.), *Passionate attachments: Thinking about love* (pp. 15-27). The Free Press.

Strauss, A., & Corbin, J. (1994). Grounded theory methodology. *Handbook of Qualitative Research*, *17*, 273–285.

Swanson, K. (2017). Destination brand love: managerial implications and applications to tourism businesses. *Journal of Place Management and Development*, *10*(1), 88–97. https://doi.org/10.1108/JPMD-11-2016-0073

Tan, S. K., Kung, S. F., & Luh, D. B. (2013). A model of 'creative experience' in creative tourism. *Annals of Tourism Research, 41*, 153–174. https://doi.org/10.1016/j.annals.2012.12.002

Taormina, R. J., & Gao, J. H. (2013). Maslow and the motivation hierarchy: Measuring satisfaction of the needs. *The American Journal of Psychology, 126*(2), 155–177. https://doi.org/10.5406/amerjpsyc.126.2.0155

Tesser, A., & Paulhus, D. (1983). The definition of self: Private and public self-evaluation management strategies. *Journal of Personality and Social Psychology, 44*(4), 672–682. https://doi.org/10.1037/0022-3514.44.4.672

Walker, K., & Moscardo, G. (2014). Encouraging sustainability beyond the tourist experience: ecotourism, interpretation and values. *Journal of Sustainable Tourism, 22*(8), 1175–1196. https://doi.org/10.1080/09669582.2014.918134

Wang, Z., He, S. Y., & Leung, Y. (2018). Applying mobile phone data to travel behaviour research: A literature review. *Travel Behaviour and Society, 11*, 141–155. https://doi.org/10.1016/j.tbs.2017.02.005

Watson, D., Clark, L. A., & Tellegen, A. (1988). Development and validation of brief measures of positive and negative affect: the PANAS scales. *Journal of Personality and Social Psychology, 54*(6), 1063– 1070. https://doi.org/10.1037/0022-3514.54.6.1063

Wearing, S., & Deane, B. (2003). Seeking self: leisure and tourism on common ground. *World Leisure Journal, 45*(1), 4–12. https://doi.org/10.1080/04419057.2003.9674300

Part IV
Affective epistemologies

The 'MeBox' method and the emotional effects of chronic illness on travel

Uditha Ramanayake (iD), Cheryl Cockburn-Wootten (iD) and
Alison J. McIntosh (iD)

ABSTRACT

Within tourism studies, there has been a gap in attempting to understand chronic illness within the context of travel. Researchers examining affective tourism have noted that much of everyday life endeavours to create order through 'ontological security' for individuals. In creating this sense of order, positivity and emotional security are emphasised, while taboo issues such as death, pain and chronic illness are 'bracketed off'. Despite these attempts at bracketing, travel experiences can prompt individuals to reflect on their own mortality, existence and purpose, which in turn may reshape their travel experiences. For senior travellers, chronic illness may be part of their everyday reality, challenging the individual's sense of self, time and relationships with places, things and people. These topics can be challenging for data collection, because such experiences can be hidden, emotion-laden, difficult to articulate or difficult for others to observe. Researchers have noted the methodological challenges with the use of traditional data tools and have turned to creative visual methods to facilitate and gain deeper understandings of participants' experiences of chronic illnesses. We used one creative visual tool, the 'MeBox' method, to study the hidden aspects of chronic illness and to understand the embodied experience of chronic illness in the context of their travel. The 'MeBox' method was created to understand and communicate the participants' multifaceted experience of chronic illness. The 'MeBox' method contributes to tourism scholarship, particularly for sensitive topics, by facilitating the inclusion of participants' voices to capture their affective travel experiences. This method usefully represents the deeper emotionality of tourists' lived experience that may have otherwise remained invisible to others.

摘要

在旅游研究中, 在试图了解旅行背景下的慢性病方面存在着空白。检视情感旅游的研究人员发现, 日常生活中, 很多人都在努力通过"存在的安全"为个人创造秩序。在创造这种秩序感的过程中, 积极和情感安全感得到了强调, 而死亡、疼痛和慢性疾病等禁忌问题则被"划上了'句号"。尽管有这些尝试, 旅行经历可以促使个人反思自己的死亡、存在和目的, 这进一步可能重塑他们的旅行经历。对于年长的旅行者来说, 慢性病可能是他们日常生活的一部分, 挑战着个人对自我和时间的意识以及与地方、事物和人的关系。这些主题对于数据收集来说是具有挑战性的, 因为这样的经历可能是隐藏的、充满感情的、难以表达的或其他人难以观察到的。研究人员注意到使用传统数据工具在方法论上的挑战, 并转向创新性的视觉方法, 以促进和深化对参与者慢性病体验的理解。我们使用了一种创新性的视觉工具,"会员专属"(MeBox) 方法, 来研究慢性疾病的隐藏方面, 并在他们旅行的背景下理解慢性疾病的亲身体验。创建"会员专属"方法是为了了解和交流参与者对慢性疾病的多方面经验。"会员专属"方法有助于旅游学术研究, 特别是对敏感话题的研究, 它通过涵盖了参与者的声音来捕捉他们的情感旅行体验。这种方法有效地表达了游客生活体验中更深层次的情感, 否则其他人可能无法看到。

Introduction

Increasingly, tourism scholars have identified the role of emotions and affect in shaping an individual's travel experiences (Bosangit, Hibbert, & McCabe, 2015; Buda, d'Hauteserre, & Johnston, 2014; Hosany & Gilbert, 2010; Martini & Buda, 2018; McIntosh & Prentice, 1999). Researchers investigating affective tourism have noted that much of everyday life persists in projecting structure, order and stability in order to create 'ontological security', with death, chronic and terminal illness bracketed off or sidelined (Willson, McIntosh, Morgan, & Sanders, 2018). These topics, still underrepresented in tourism scholarship, present challenges, notably around careful consideration of the method used to ensure the participants' affective experiences are communicated to the researcher (Martini & Buda, 2018).

As previous scholars (e.g. Chiaranai, Chularee, & Srithongluang, 2018) have noted, death, pain and illness are intensely shaped by emotions and affect. Yet, this area of consideration is still 'not easily brought into representation' (Martini & Buda, 2018, p 4) in research, with significant challenges facing researchers, particularly around how to design appropriate methods that communicate the intensity of the participant's emotions and affect. Social networks and others in a person's life, for instance, can often struggle to understand the loss and pain that the person is experiencing. As Main (2014) notes, it becomes 'unshareable because of its resistance to language' (p. 33). Alternative methods are required in order to communicate these emotional and affect experiences. Creative visual methods have been particularly valuable in the health and rehabilitation area as they provide a 'bridge between the conscious and unconscious and therefore [are]helpful for working through complex, deep-seated or 'unspeakable' emotions such as grief' (Reynolds & Prior, 2003, p. 786). For the researcher, the challenge is how to help participants, who experience pain, grief, loss or illness, to communicate their lived experiences to others in their lives. Deeper consideration then is required around alternative possibilities for methodological tools, especially if the topic has the potential to cause emotional pain that can be deeply felt and long-lasting.

To contribute to this area of tourism scholarship, we draw on a phenomenological study that investigated the travel experiences of senior participants with chronic illness. In this paper, we aim to illustrate the 'MeBox' method and its potential contribution for overcoming the methodological challenges of studying emotion and affect. In the next section, we critically review the literature on the adoption of creative visual methods for understanding difficult to communicate topics. We then provide a detailed explanation of the 'MeBox' method and explain how we applied the tool to our phenomenological study. The latter sections of the paper critically reflect on the use of the method, particularly its use with sensitive participant experiences and/or topics in tourism. People respond differently to chronic illness and it shapes their travel accordingly (Hunter-Jones, 2005; Molzahn et al., 2012). When facing crisis situations, each culture has its own ways of reacting and many people are likely to go back to cultural systems based on their beliefs and expectations (Kagawa-Singer, 1998). In this study, we propose the 'MeBox' method as we hope, an alternative to traditional methods that can marginalize travellers with chronic illness (Liamputtong, 2007).

Literature review

While emotions can be considered as socially constructed, feelings are seen as the body's biological response to something. According to Massumi, emotion is 'a subjective content, the sociolinguistic fixing of the quality of an experience which from that point onward is defined as personal' (Massumi, 2002, p. 28). For Pile (2010), affect is a mood or an atmosphere which is not always perceived clearly and not easily representable. Emotions, feelings and the body are intertwined and, importantly for this study, individuals draw on their body, skin, senses and feelings in order to understand their experiences (Ahmed, 2004; Knights & Thanem, 2005; Martini & Buda, 2018; Philipose, 2007). Emotional and affective experiences have been defined as the 'embodied and mindful phenomena that partially shape, and are shaped by our interactions with the people, places and politics that make up our unique, personal geographies' (Davidson & Bondi, 2004, p. 373).

Living with chronic illnesses such as cardiovascular disease, diabetes, epilepsy, Parkinson's disease, arthritis and many others can lead to difficulties performing familiar tasks and living a 'normal' life (Townsend, Wyke, & Hunt, 2006). Chronic illnesses are defined as 'those conditions that last a year or more and require ongoing medical attention and/or limit activities of daily living' (Anderson & Horvath, 2004, p. 263; Chiaranai et al., 2018). Significantly, the symptoms of chronic illness may be mitigated to some extent, but the illness is not curable (Kralik, van Loon, & Visentin, 2006). Pain and chronic illness 'is not merely a biological phenomenon but ha[ve] significant social and psychological dimensions' (Tarr & Thomas, 2011, p. 143). Pain and the trauma of a significant 'disruption' such as long-term chronic illness become 'embodied and become core components of a person's experience of the world' (Philipose, 2007, p. 62). The pain associated with the illness becomes integral to the person's biography, understanding and relationships with others, places and things.

The senior age group differs from other age groups as the majority of seniors are retired, have completed their parental duties and are likely to have the time to reflect deeply about themselves (Jung, 1964). Senior citizens also tend to experience various losses more often than other age groups do (Kim, 2009). Facing a major illness can cause considerable emotional distress, for instance, and could lead to the senior individual losing their active social interactions, making them more vulnerable in their communities (Molzahn et al., 2012). Ageing is associated with a greater risk of experiencing long-term chronic illness (Hansson & Stroebe, 2007). Diabetes, cardiovascular disease and arthritis are among the most common chronic illnesses in elderly people (Chiaranai et al., 2018).

The reasons for the rapid increase in chronic illnesses are due to several factors such as an ageing population with increased life expectancy, as well as improvements in medical technology and lifelong conditions (Anderson & Horvath, 2004). Chronic illnesses are becoming more prevalent around the world. While many other disciplines are increasingly focused on the growing problem of chronic illnesses among elderly people (Baker & Wang, 2006; Chiaranai et al., 2018; Palinkas, Wingard, & Barrett-Connor, 1990), the experiences of people with chronic illness have not received adequate attention in tourism scholarship. Although a growing number of studies within the tourism literature have recently explored the tourism experiences of people with various disabilities (Alén, Domínguez, & Losada, 2012; Allan, 2015; Kazeminia, Chiappa, & Jafari, 2015; McIntosh & Harris, 2018; Tutuncu, 2017; Yau, McKercher, & Packer, 2004), the voices of elderly people with various chronic illnesses that affect their bodies, affects and emotions remain unheard in tourism scholarship.

Overall, for many seniors with chronic pain and illness, 'the ways in which we understand, experience, perform and talk about emotions are highly related to our sense of body' (Zembylas, 2007, p. 64). In tourism studies, there are currently limited research methods available to deepen our understandings and the meanings of the emotional experiences of people with chronic illnesses. Adopting methods that help individuals encapsulate their understandings and experiences is crucial for both researcher and participant. For the researcher, appropriate methodological tools can help us understand complex emotional issues within the individual's life, understanding, meaning and experiences (Papaloukas, Quincey, & Williamson, 2017). Taking a participatory and cocreative approach to the research design is essential. For the participant, this approach can facilitate empowerment, feelings of control over the illness and 'wholeness … [to assist the] process of adjustment and coping with disability and chronic illness' (Rozario, 1997, p. 432).

The majority of tourism management research has focused on traditional tools that emphasize words as the dominant communication mode, obtaining feedback about travel experiences through written surveys, in-depth interviews, or focus groups and mystery shoppers (Pullman & Robson, 2007). These approaches 'have limitations [as they] conform to societal rules and constraints [and] fail to capture the nuances and subtlety of human behaviour' (Westwood, 2007, p. 294). Within health and emotionally sensitive topics, object elicitation can overcome rehearsed 'established narratives' about the individual's condition to elicit critical insightful reflections from being actively involved in the data process (Willig, 2017, p. 213). Affective and emotional experiences are not always expressed in words; thus, they are challenging for researchers to examine. However, the inclusion of nonlinguistic aspects in research allows access to richer, hidden levels of experiences of people living with chronic illnesses (Bagnoli, 2009; Gibbons, 2013).

Visual methods have been widely acknowledged for their therapeutic value in cocreative knowledge production and translation (Fraser & Al Sayah, 2011). Traditional qualitative tourism methods such as interviews rely on language, yet our living experiences involve multiple visual and sensory dimensions, and those experiences cannot always easily be expressed in words (Gibbons, 2013). Indeed, pain is a constantly known sensory experience for those with long-term illness, experience that is not easily translated through written or verbal communication (Philipose, 2007). Creative visual participatory methods are, however, familiar tools in other disciplines such as sociology, health, therapy, rehabilitation, refugee studies, indigenous studies, anthropology and education (Baker & Wang, 2006; Harrison, 2002; Reynolds, 1997; Rozario, 1997).

Studies that employ creative visual methods aim to achieve meaningful social change outcomes for both researcher and participants (Cockburn-Wootten, McIntosh, Smith, & Jefferies, 2018). Art, objects and activities have frequently been used during the research process to help scholars gain an understanding of their participants' experiences and, importantly, to help develop the individual's self-esteem to 'resist mastery by her illness' (Reynolds, 1997, p. 355). Refugee and indigenous studies, for instance, use art, objects, creative and participatory methods to overcome difficulties in understanding diverse experiences of trauma and 'othering' and empower participants through involvement and critical reflection to gain control or reframe their lives (Guruge et al., 2015; Lenette & Boddy, 2013).

Art and objects used within the research process are seen as effective prompts for enabling the tacit emotional and cultural meanings to become explicit. They are used to 'engage participants who would otherwise be marginalized or disregarded, and enable[s] reflexivity amongst participants and between the researcher and participants' (Zurba & Berkes, 2014, p. 822). Furthermore, people in their 60 s and above can have great difficulty in remembering and finding words to describe their past experiences (Craik, 1994). In addition, some elderly people can experience fatigue and hearing or visual problems that can impact the interview process (Hall, Longhurst, & Higginson, 2009). It is, therefore, important to look beyond using traditional methods when exploring the embodied experiences of senior people living and travelling with chronic illnesses.

The 'MeBox' method in practice

This study employed phenomenology and, hence, adopted qualitative research methods to collect data. This approach was chosen due to the distinct strengths of phenomenology in aiding the researcher to interpret the nature of the participants' lived experiences (Willson, McIntosh, & Zahra, 2013). The phenomenology paradigm, with its primary focus on the individual, body, reflection and lived experiences, offers researchers important opportunities to deepen their understandings of the body, emotions and affect (Knights & Thanem, 2005). A qualitative approach is appropriate when attempting to draw on inductive indexical understandings and, thus, to better represent the experiences of the participants (Riches & Dawson, 1996). This perspective has been used effectively by previous scholars to explore the lived experiences of sensitive populations (Lowe, 2005; Richardson & Balaswamy, 2001).

To achieve this inductive approach, we used the 'MeBox' method to explore the travel experiences of 12 senior citizens. Community communication channels were used to invite potential individuals to participate in the study. For example, information was circulated through acquaintances, community notice boards, not-for-profit organizations such as Age Concern New Zealand, meetup groups, and local churches and interested individuals were invited to contact us directly for more details about the study. The study focused on a sample of research participants aged 65 years and over. The data were collected from New Zealand senior citizens who mainly resided within the North Island region of New Zealand. The recruitment processes helped us to begin the journey towards building a strong rapport with our participants throughout the research process. Before the actual data collection, the first author conducted an initial meeting with participants to clarify expectations around the research process and to discuss confidentiality and ethical aspects of the research.

The first author conducted the data collection. As he had gained relevant experience through volunteering for various community not-for-profit organisations for elderly people, he ensured that contact information for emotional support services was always available to the participants. The data for this study were collected using the 'MeBox' method as part of an interview process. Gibbons (2010) created this method and used it in a visual anthropology project to understand and communicate the participants' multifaceted experience of chronic illness. The method helped the researcher to study the hidden aspects of chronic illness and to understand the embodied experience of chronic illness (FitzPatrick, Elphingston-Jolly, Friend, & Payne, 2019). According to Gibbons (2010), 'a 'MeBox' is usually created by gathering together important items that represent different aspects of the person, including hobbies, memories, important milestones, and family history, etc.' (p. 34). In our study the data-gathering locations ranged from the participant's own home to university library rooms to less crowded cafes.

The complexity and multiplicity of lived experiences are not always expressed in words (Bagnoli, 2009; Gibbons, 2013). Therefore, we wanted to include nonlinguistic aspects in our data collection process. The inclusion of the 'MeBox' method within the interview process allowed us to access the hidden levels of the participants' lived emotional experiences. Gibbons used only the 'MeBox' method to collect data in her study (Gibbons, 2010). However, in our study, we employed the 'MeBox' method to complement in-depth interviews with participants. Therefore, we had to adapt the 'MeBox' method into our research process. The standard 'MeBox' method involved three sessions: first, an introductory meeting; second, a session in which participants started to create the 'MeBox'; and third, a final session in which the 'MeBox' was completed from participant-provided objects.

However, in this study, an initial preliminary conversation was held with participants. This was followed by the first in-depth interview and then the second interview, where we employed the 'MeBox' method. These steps are discussed further below. A preliminary conversation enabled the first author to explain the research process and, more specifically, the 'MeBox' method to the participants. This initial conversation informed the participants about all aspects of the study and helped them make their participation decision (Smythe & Murray, 2000). The first interview was held approximately 2 to 3 weeks after the preliminary conversation, with the participants deciding an interview date, time, and place that was convenient for them. The first author asked the participants directed open-ended questions, in line with Giorgi (1997). The questions were broad and open-ended so that the participants had sufficient opportunity to express their viewpoint extensively. These open-ended questions encouraged participants to discuss different aspects of life which then provided a base for the 'MeBox' interview (FitzPatrick et al., 2019). At the end of the first interview, the researcher explained the next stage of the interview process, the 'MeBox' sessions.

The initial stage of creating the 'MeBox' occurred during the second interview. This interview took place approximately 2 to 3 weeks after the first interview. Having time between the first and second interviews gave participants enough time to emotionally prepare for the interview and decide which objects for reflecting on their experiences to select. The participants selected certain objects that were personally important relative to the study (FitzPatrick et al., 2019). At the beginning of the second interview, the first author set out a range of gift boxes so that participants could choose one to be their 'MeBox'. The second interview was conducted in two parts. In the first half, researcher-provided objects were used in the process of completing the 'MeBox'. These artefacts were designed to help the participants to create their 'MeBox' and represent their lived experiences. Initially, the objects provided by the researcher acted as visual stimuli to elicit data (FitzPatrick et al., 2019). The researcher-provided objects eased the participants into the method, as the researcher offered some everyday objects such as a candle, flower, diary, etc. that participants could use to describe their lived experiences (FitzPatrick et al., 2019). In the second half of the interview, the participant completed the 'MeBox' using participant-provided objects.

While the interviewer had his own ideas of what the objects he provided meant, the participants were free to choose or reject any of the objects offered and free also to assign their own meaning to any object they chose. For example, one of the objects the researcher's list offered was a partly burnt candle. For him, this object represented later life and reflections on mortality. However, many participants saw it as the light of God in their life. The interviewer left the room or interview area while the participants chose their 'MeBox' objects. Participants were asked to look at the interviewer-provided objects and pick out any they believed related to their experiences. By leaving the interpretation of the objects relatively open, participants were able to select and add objects to their 'MeBox' that reflected their experiences. The participants were then invited to pick the object that they felt most comfortable talking about first.

The second half of the interview started with the researcher inviting participants to talk about the objects that they had brought and also to add any further missing objects to their 'MeBox' that they felt would reflect their experiences. This interview took approximately 90–120 minutes with each participant. The interview continued until it reached a natural conclusion where information was no longer new (Becker, 1992). The 'MeBox' objects facilitated the researcher's exploration of the participant's experiences. The interviewer took photos of the 'MeBox' objects individually and as a group. Photographing 'MeBox' objects allowed the researcher to visually represent the study's findings on the 'MeBox' process and to provide images for the researcher to create hypertextual self-scape images of participants' lived experiences (Elphingston-Jolly, 2012; FitzPatrick, Elphingston-Jolly, Friend, & Payne; Gibbons, 2010). According to Gibbons (2013), the hypertextual self-scape image has the potential to enable the viewer to gain a level of access to the lived experience (p. 28).

Gibbons' aim in creating this method was to understand and communicate the participant's multifaceted experiences. However, Gibbons (2013) has argued that photographs can miss some sensory information; in her research, participants said they believed that the snapshot put forward a false reality, as their illness is not visible in the photographs. Moreover, Gibbons pointed out that even the 2D photographs of the objects could miss the multisensory narratives. Therefore, she turned those images into hypertextual self-scape images as a way to add more information that was still missing in the photographs (Gibbons, 2013). In representing these lived emotional experiences, we, therefore, added in art forms to create hypertextual self-scape images (Gibbons, 2013). After creating these images, we sent them to our participants. We asked for their comments and for any changes they wanted in their hypertextual self-scape (Gibbons, 2013). (Gibbons, 2013). According to Gibbons (2013), it is important that participants identify themselves and their lived experiences before hypertextual self-scape images goes public.

Results

As mentioned previously, a key challenge for participants with a chronic illness is the difficulty in communicating and describing to researchers their lived experiences and how these shape their lives (Main, 2014). Art, music and creative methods can provide a bridge between the body, emotions and social life (Letherby & Davidson, 2015). The results presented below illustrate how the 'MeBox' objects overcame communication challenges to reflecting on interpretations, connections and relationships of senior participants travelling with a chronic illness. It helped them think with, and through, affects feelings, emotions, a sense of self, and in some cases reconstructed an understanding of the senior participant's life. We have illustrated this process through one of our research participants, Jane. This example provides a rich and insightful understanding not only of how the 'MeBox' method was able to communicate unseen emotional experiences of chronic illness and travel, but also how researchers can use the 'MeBox' method to study and analyse emotion/affect (Wood & Kenyon, 2018). The latter half of this paper provides a critical reflection on the method's contributions to the role of emotion/affect in tourism research. The objects chosen by Jane during the 'MeBox' session represent her lived emotional experiences.

Jane's 'MeBox'

Jane is a New Zealand senior citizen who had recently faced eye cancer; she describes herself as a 'people person'.

Figure 1. Jane's 'MeBox'.
"Source: Authors"

Figure 2. Jane's Bible.
"Source: Used with permission"

Jane chose the box shown in Figure 1 as her 'MeBox' from the collection of boxes which we provided at the beginning of the interview. This section describes the objects which Jane included in her 'MeBox'.

Jane wanted to put this bible Figure 2 at the centre of her 'MeBox' because the bible represents her travel guide through life. Jane said that after facing eye cancer, her belief in God had become the centre of her life and provided stability. The bible was her go-to book for comfort, strength and assurance during those tough times.

Figure 3. Jane's Broken Pot.
"Source: Authors"

The broken pot Figure 3 reminded Jane that her life is cracked and she is a broken vessel full of imperfections. For example, she explained:

> Life has broken me in places. I lost my eye, so I am not perfect anymore. That grounds me to the reality of who I am, that I am a flawed human being. I said to God, how can I live with one eye? I know people do, but I do not want to be one of those people.

The broken area of the pot reflects her attitude towards life: 'How my broken spots or my rough edges may affect the relationships with other people'. Through this broken pot, she expressed how she felt valued in the tourism context:

> And again, I think of hotel rooms. We are all staying overseas where people have suddenly realized I have not been able to see as well as I could, have opened a door or done some similar seemingly small act of kindness. When I am thumping with my card and trying to get it on the slot on the door and cannot see. It is sort of, it is okay, you're broken, but you're all right. Moreover, I can feel very valued and a very moving moment.

She further explained her emotions before and after getting her prosthetic eye. 'The people, if you do accidentally bump into them or they bump into you, most people are so lovely, and they stop. They are just like, I am sorry. Are you okay?' Moreover, once she got her prosthetic eye, she mentioned that she almost missed feeling special, as she commented that when she had a bandage around her head, it was obvious that something was wrong, so others treated her in the nicest way. In her words, 'And when you get your prosthetic, and you just blend back into humanity, you kind of, I do not feel quite so special anymore. I'm just normal'. In the same way when looking from one angle, we do not see that this pot is broken; it looks complete. Metaphorically, this completeness/incompleteness is the same for Jane, as other people may not initially be able to see her prosthetic eye.

> Because of my age, I am not sure what people see first, whether they see my age first - that I am an older lady - or whether they see my prosthetic eye. Moreover, I suspect they see me as an older lady first. Moreover, many people do not know that I am wearing a prosthetic eye. So, I think their reaction to me when I travel is seeing me first as an older woman travelling.

This quote demonstrates how Jane perceives the depth of her inclusion in the travel experience. Further, this example suggests how much more difficult it is to understand the multiplicity of the experiences of those living with chronic illness, notably in the context of travel. The broken pot, for instance, revealed some of Jane's emotional experiences of travel that related to her body. Also, the broken pot shows when Jane's illness became visible to other people and her. At those times, Jane's pain and chronic illness acted as a bridge that connected her with others and sometimes made her feel included, yet on occasions distanced her from others. For Jane, her cancer and its repercussions meant that she needed time to heal and come to terms with her changed identity.

Figure 4. Jane's Toy Car.
"Source: Authors"

This toy car Figure 4 reminded Jane of her recent travel experience in Chicago. The noise and vibrancy of the city affected her, probably even more so because she comes from a rural farming background. Jane said she felt that

We are all different. We are all going in our different directions at times, and we're all in a hurry to get there sometimes. And we're focused on often where we're going as an individual. And at times, it can create quite a mayhem, and we can get caught up in it and miss, in the hustle and bustle, we can miss the sacredness, I suppose, of our life's journey. But that does not mean that our life's journey is all peace and quiet. Life is also exciting because it brings changes, it brings challenges, and that is part of living. So that probably balances the quiet retreat side with the energy that comes from living and being amongst others.

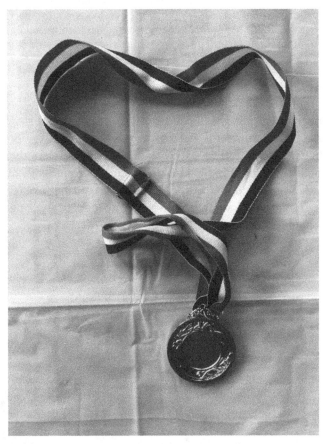

Figure 5. Jane's Medal.
"Source: Authors"

According to Jane, this medal Figure 5 represents running a race for God and the importance of continuing to run, being part of that race, not stopping and falling out. In her words, 'that reminds me I am on a race and to continue faithfully to the end. So, there is a prize, I suppose you'd call it, in the end, and that's what I'm working for'.

The objects chosen by Jane represented a variety of different aspects of her illness and travel experiences. These examples show us that the 'MeBox' method provides researchers with opportunities to represent a participant's experiences in ways that

Figure 6. Jane's Hypertextual self-scape image.
"Sousrce: Authors"

differ from traditional research methods. The 'MeBox' images were able to add the initial layer of emotional experiences of travelling with a chronic illness. The researcher then created a hypertextual self-scape image by digitally altering the images, with the aim of providing more information about the sensory experiences of travelling with a chronic illness (Gibbons, 2010, 2013).

As Gibbons (2013) states:

> 'through our actions and symbols on the body, we communicate about ourselves beyond what we say... therefore, making hidden illness visible is more than creating pictures and images; it is about recreating the missing information and returning it to the discourse about chronic illness. (p. 19)

The 'MeBox' and hypertextual self-scape image creation enable unseen information and experiences to be represented and communicated to the viewer. These helped the participants to externalize their emotions and chronic illness more fully for the researchers (Gibbons, 2013). Jane's 'MeBox' images illustrate her lived experiences with illness. Through the major loss of one eye, Jane's life had taken a social, material and existential turn that forced her on to a new course. Jane believes that if she had not had these experiences, despite their pain and negativity, she would have been a different person, but perhaps not a better person. The 'MeBox' methodology shows that through the use of objects and hypertextual self-scape images, researchers can communicate more information about people's emotions than can be conveyed through words alone (Gibbons, 2013). The images shown above were created using the information gathered during the interview sessions, which included listening to the audio recordings of the interviews, and by looking at the photographs of the 'MeBox' objects and reviewing the sessions (Gibbons, 2013).

The hypertextual self-scape image above Figure 6 represents and brings together Jane's story in a more complex way than the individual items in the 'MeBox' can do. The collated image shows a broken pot, a bible, a toy car, a flower and a medal. The hypertextual self-scape image which shows a broken pot, a bible, a toy car, a flower and a medal brings together three elements from Jane's life experience and, especially, her experience of losing her eye to eye cancer. The pot represents that fact that she saw herself as 'broken and 'imperfect' after her surgery. In her words, 'knowing that coming out of it, I would be even less perfect than what I am. Not that I was perfect before, but even more broken'. The bible represents the comfort she gained from her strengthened belief in God.

In the collated image, the toy car represents Jane's travels after facing cancer. These broadened her perspective on life and kept her in touch with life in all its different forms and shapes. Cancer made Jane reflect, appreciate life and take advantage of exciting experiences whenever they came her way, as she stated, 'If you get the opportunity to travel with your daughter to Adelaide or Chicago, go for it'. Further, travelling with a serious condition made her realize that life is exciting because it brings changes, it brings challenges, and that that is all part of living. Jane's comments suggest that her chronic illness had strengthened her. For example, when she said: 'I think they [her travels] brought out in me qualities that needed to be brought forward to strengthen my faith, to find what I could do as a person'.

Overall, Jane's life is akin to a broken vessel. Depending on which angle you view the pot from, she can be interpreted differently or her illness can be hidden. Overall, however, she confirms that she is still usable and functions. Her broken pot is filled with travel memories, her increased belief in God and the belief that she can still flower. In this image, the centre of the flower represents the medal, which Jane says she is winning now. She did not lie down under the experience of having cancer; instead she faced it successfully and won a medal, something which she had never achieved before in her life.

Critical reflection on the 'MeBox' method

The results of the study highlight how participants differentiated the 'Mebox' method from general interviews. During our research, many participants stated that they enjoyed the 'MeBox' process and the opportunity to talk. For example, Jane explained:

> I don't mind the direct questions. I sometimes need to stop and think and then go home, driving home think, gosh, did I answer that right, or did I get lost halfway through my answer? Which I could be willing to, but because I am a visual person, I really like having physical objects that I can put out there and talk about. I found that perhaps more helpful than the direct questions. Objects feel more personal to me because I can touch them, hold them and see them. Words for me are good, I like words but visually, I'm much stronger visually.

The introduction of a visual element is, therefore, helpful for the process of idea generation, as it allows participants to move beyond the verbal mode of thinking and to think about wider dimensions of experience (Bagnoli, 2009). All of our participants were over 65 and some had difficulties in remembering their experiences in the initial meeting. For example, Lily said, 'And now I've forgotten, sorry, what the other situation was, there was one other situation. Can I tell you later if I remember?' However, it is interesting to note that, in general, participants did not have difficulty remembering during the 'MeBox' session. For example, as one participant explained:

> It helps me to remember the things that I value, the experiences that I have and the joy that they have brought me at the time or the sadness that they have brought me, which is part of, I suppose, the weaving of life.

Further, the meaning of objects was not discussed with the participants in advance, so each was free to assign their own meanings to any object.

Additionally, some participants felt that the 'MeBox' interview experience was therapeutic. Generally, older people agree to participate in research to increase their human contact (Hall et al., 2009). Moreover, after an emotional experience, there tends to be a natural desire to share those feelings with others (Wood & Kenyon, 2018). It is important to note that the elderly participants were also able to benefit from participating in this research by having someone to listen to them and to have someone with whom to share their experiences (Hall et al., 2009). Such a research experience can be part of a healing process and can help to develop new understandings of past events. As one participant explained:

I would classify it as therapeutic because I think it's therapeutic in the sense that it's good to remember. And whether those memories are good or bad, I think as time goes on, you can look back and reflect on them and think, it can be therapeutic to do so.

Participants identified that the 'MeBox' process helped them with recognition, provided context, memory cues and allowed one-to-one time to share their experiences. The objects became effective memory prompts for the participants to recall and analyze their experiences. They enjoyed having someone to share their stories about travelling with chronic illness. The visual and tactical nature of the objects provided mindful, in-the-moment reflections for them during the process. The participants were also involved as active meaning makers in the research process rather than passive respondents to researcher questions. Furthermore, this study's results also suggested that this method is ideal for use with small samples, as it requires time and commitment from both participants and researchers.

Discussion

The participant's experiences suggest how much more difficult it is to understand the multiplicity of experiences of living with chronic illness, notably in the context of travel. Participants with chronic illness and researchers or tourism professionals may hold very different interpretations about the condition, including its limitations and opportunities. The same way found to be true with other studies, for example, Gibbons (2013), which stated that 'when standing in front of a person who has a healthy appearance and is smiling, the symbols of health on the body can trigger the thought that this person is not ill' (Gibbons, 2013, p. 17). In another example from King (2018), a participant stated:

> ... on most days, I am able to wake up and go to sleep after a normal day - my interactions with those around me have been normal, and everybody has treated and thought of me as 'normal'. For the most part, I have always felt it a benefit to have an invisible illness. (p. 403)

These examples suggest that in circumstances impacted by long-term pain, ill-health and other physical issues, the body's skin effectively becomes the boundary between what is internally experienced and what is externally seen (Gibbons, 2013).

Therefore, in taking this perspective in the tourism context, this paper has illustrated the potential opportunities of the 'MeBox' method for researchers. The method allows participants to reflect and engage with the process in order to communicate the real emotional and bodily experiences of travelling with chronic illness. It was clear that participants felt their chronic illness often affected relationships with other people, who would see them as a person who lives with a malfunctioning body. Instead, participants described how the travel journey helped them to reconsider their self-identity. This reassessment was illustrated by Jane, as she moved during the 'MeBox' process from seeing herself as 'a flawed human being' to accepting that '[l]ife is also exciting because it brings changes, it brings challenges, and that is part of living'. Similarly, other studies in disciplines such as medicine, for example, have identified that visual and creative methods have helped people with a chronic illness to resist their illness and focus on other things in their lives (King, 2018).

Many people with a chronic illness try to bracket or hide their illness from others, framing it as not a distinguishing feature of their lives (King, 2018). For example, in King's study (2018), one participant with chronic illness stated: 'I spend most of my time focusing on everything else in life, trying to keep any time devoted to my illness away from the eyes of the world' (p. 402). Many research participants endeavour to project and perform as a 'normal' and 'healthy' person. This self-portrayal provides a challenge for service providers in the tourism sector when catering to this segment, due to the imbalance between what is visible·externally and the real lived affective experience of chronic illness (Gibbons, 2013). However, the results of our study highlighted that the 'MeBox' method had the potential to capture these hidden aspects of living with chronic illness that participants experience and enable them to reflect on, and share, emotions that are not easy to communicate through words alone (Gibbons, 2013).

In doing so, many participants enjoyed the interview experience and, in comparison to general interviews, participants liked the 'MeBox' research method. For example, Gibbons (2013) pointed out that for a person with chronic illness a simple question such as '"What do you do?" can cause an inside conversation of "What do I tell them?," "Do I really want to start this discussion?" and "Do I have to put my life out there to be judged?"' (p. 18). In these scenarios, traditional talk-based tools would miss this internal reflection and opportunities for critical reflection. Instead, a creative and visual technique such as the 'MeBox' method can help researchers and participants elicit deeper understandings and insights that might not be accessible through other data collection methods (Banks, 2007; Pink, Kürti, & Afonso, 2004; Rakic & Chambers, 2009). Selecting and touching the objects helped the participants to remember and describe them, notably as skin 'brings to its surface a remembered past' (Prosser, 2001, p. 52). This method helped participants to think in different ways and overcome silences. Indeed, participants in our study stated that the 'MeBox' method gave them the opportunity to revisit the experience and easily express themselves. The researcher-provided objects eased participants into the method and helped them to create their own 'MeBox' to start the data generation process.

The participants' comments emphasise the potential empowerment and therapeutic value of the 'MeBox' research method and its ability for reflection and sharing of experiences that were especially meaningful to them. Research into the potential therapeutic benefits of using similar visual methods in tourism studies remains limited and requires further investigation. For example, researchers can differ in terms of how they approach, conceptualise and respond to the experiences to their participants, especially participants who face chronic illness. There is also the potential for the research to cause emotional pain to participants (Hadjistavropoulos & Smythe, 2001; Rydzik, Pritchard, Morgan, & Sedgley, 2012), as there are specific challenges when investigating sensitive topics in tourism, particularly participant experiences that warrant deeper consideration.

When exploring sensitive topics, researchers cannot predict how their data collection will unfold (Hadjistavropoulos & Smythe, 2001). Therefore, as researchers, we need to reflect on our understandings, strengths and weaknesses. As Bourne and Robson (2015) have stated, researchers 'may need to consider how to handle, or draw boundaries within, interviews where they feel the participant is seeking a degree of therapeutic support they are unable or insufficiently skilled to provide' (p. 114). Tourism researchers need to consider these aspects when studying how individuals with chronic illnesses experience various tourist environments: specifically, how to ethically design research that represents people's experiences in an inclusive and humane way. A perspective that acknowledges humane, affective, emotional and existential lived experience is likely to have a positive impact on people's lives. Therefore, in comparison to the natural sciences research model, the 'MeBox' direction was highly influenced by the research participants in this study. However, the researcher also played a significant role in the 'MeBox' process. For example, the researcher also offered objects for participants to use when creating their 'MeBox'. These objects acted as visual stimuli to elicit data and eased the participants into the method.

The 'MeBox' and hypertextual self-scape image added a new layer of narrative by representing the sensory experiences of the participants. When examining participants' experiences, researchers can struggle to understand the embodied understandings of the travel, while participants may be unable to articulate and verbally describe their lived experiences. As Wood and Moss (2015) note when investigating emotional memory and experiences in their work on festivals and events, 'some people have predominantly visual images with no verbal content, others have inner speech with no visual imagery' (p. 48). Creative, visual and object elucidation tools such as the 'MeBox' method overcome this impasse in understanding and the domination of verbal techniques. Further, when using this method, it is important to understand the cultural contexts of the participants. We also think this method is ideal for research that uses small samples, as it requires a significant amount of time and commitment on the part both participants and researchers.

Conclusion

This paper has illustrated how the 'MeBox' method can function as a tool for examining the emotional experiences of people living with chronic illness in the context of their travel experiences. Chronic long-term illnesses prompt individuals to feel different, judged by others and alienated from their usual surroundings. Emotions and, in particular, bodily sensations such as pain, encourage individuals to reflect, question their existence and reevaluate their relations with others and the environment. For many tourists with chronic illnesses, this process produces feelings of 'inbetweenness' or a liminal space (Buda et al., 2014; Tung & Brent Ritchie, 2011). The 'MeBox' method offers an effective method for participants, in this case, Jane, to communicate their experiences, reflect on their lives and feel a sense of empowerment over their illness. The meanings of the participants' chronic illness and tourism experiences were different for each individual. For example, the results revealed that some participants experienced feelings of inclusion and some felt excluded as tourists. However, most of them experienced feelings of insecurity and vulnerability, given their condition. Therefore, tourism researchers could explore the factors that create an unwelcome feeling for people with chronic illness; doing so will lead us to obtain a deeper understanding of this segment's affective behaviour as they seek inclusion and to be viewed as 'normal' in the tourism environment (Baker, Holland, & Kaufman-Scarborough, 2007). We also think that people will involve differently in this 'MeBox' process in relation to the sensitive topic, and interpretation of the objects based on their culture, gender and age etc. Many tourism researchers are still doubtful about using visual methodologies, mainly because of the general acceptance of conventional methods and the hardships of publishing research outputs which have used visual methods (Rakić & Chambers, 2010). Other scholars have identified that these tools require time and commitment from both participants and researchers (Rydzik, Pritchard, Morgan, & Sedgley, 2013). However, our exploratory research shows how this method can be used as a tool, particularly around sensitive topics or where there is a need to involve participants with greater needs to generate sufficient inclusion of participants' voices and capture their affective travel experiences. Furthermore, this method is a very useful way to represent the emotionality of tourists' lived experience that may otherwise remain invisible to others but which is nonetheless significant for understanding the subjective and affective nature of travel.

Acknowledgements

The authors wish to acknowledge the research participants for their contribusion, Dr Mary FitzPatrick who looked over an early draft of the paper, and the anonymous reviewers for their constructive comments on the manuscript.

Disclosure statement

No potential conflict of interest was reported by the author(s).

ORCID

Uditha Ramanayake http://orcid.org/0000-0001-8146-893X
Cheryl Cockburn-Wootten http://orcid.org/0000-0002-3339-630X
Alison J. McIntosh http://orcid.org/0000-0003-1593-700X

References

Ahmed, S. (2004). Collective feelings: Or, the impressions left by others. *Theory, Culture & Society, 21*(2), 25–42. doi:10.1177/0263276404042133

Alén, E., Domínguez, T., & Losada, N. (2012). New opportunities for the tourism market: Senior tourism and accessible tourism. In M. Kasimoğlu (Ed.), *Visions for global tourism industry: Creating and sustaining competitive strategies* (pp. 139–166). London, England: IntechOpen.

Allan, M. (2015). Accessible tourism in Jordan: Travel constrains and motivations. *European Journal of Tourism Research, 10*, 109–119.

Anderson, G., & Horvath, J. (2004). The growing burden of chronic disease in America. *Public Health Reports, 119*(3), 263–270. doi:10.1016/j.phr.2004.04.005

Bagnoli, A. (2009). Beyond the standard interview: The use of graphic elicitation and arts-based methods. *Qualitative Research, 9*(5), 547–570. doi:10.1177/1468794109343625

Baker, S. M., Holland, J., & Kaufman-Scarborough, C. (2007). How consumers with disabilities perceive "welcome" in retail servicescapes: A critical incident study. *Journal of Services Marketing, 21*(3), 160–173. doi:10.1108/08876040710746525

Baker, T. A., & Wang, C. C. (2006). Photovoice: Use of a participatory action research method to explore the chronic pain experience in older adults. *Qualitative Health Research, 16*(10), 1405–1413. doi:10.1177/1049732306294118

Banks, M. (2007). Using visual data in qualitative research. Retrieved from http://methods.sagepub.com/book/using-visual-data-in-qualitative-research doi:10.4135/9780857020260

Becker, C. S. (1992). *Living and relating: An introduction to phenomenology.* Newbury Park, CA: Sage Publications.

Bosangit, C., Hibbert, S., & McCabe, S. (2015). If I was going to die I should at least be having fun": Travel blogs, meaning and tourist experience. *Annals of Tourism Research, 55*, 1–14. doi: 10.1016/j.annals.2015.08.001

Bourne, A. H., & Robson, M. A. (2015). Participants' reflections on being interviewed about risk and sexual behaviour: Implications for collection of qualitative data on sensitive topics. *International Journal of Social Research Methodology, 18*(1), 105–116. doi:10.1080/13645579.2013.860747

Buda, D. M., d'Hauteserre, A.-M., & Johnston, L. (2014). Feeling and tourism studies. *Annals of Tourism Research, 46*, 102–114. doi:10.1016/j.annals.2014.03.005

Chiaranai, C., Chularee, S., & Srithongluang, S. (2018). Older people living with chronic illness. *Geriatric Nursing, 39*(5), 513–520. doi:10.1016/j.gerinurse.2018.02.004

Cockburn-Wootten, C., McIntosh, A. J., Smith, K., & Jefferies, S. (2018). Communicating across tourism silos for inclusive sustainable partnerships. *Journal of Sustainable Tourism, 26*(9), 1483–1498. doi:10.1080/09669582.2018.1476519

Craik, F. I. M. (1994). Memory changes in normal aging. *Current Directions in Psychological Science, 3*(5), 155–158. doi:10.1111/1467-8721.ep10770653

Davidson, J., & Bondi, L. I. Z. (2004). Spatialising affect; affecting space: An introduction. *Gender, Place & Culture, 11*(3), 373–374. doi:10.1080/0966369042000258686

Elphingston-Jolly, B. L. (2012). *Women's use of possessions to cope with abusive relationships.* (Unpublished master's dissertation). University of Waikato, Hamilton, New Zealand.

FitzPatrick, M., Elphingston-Jolly, B., Friend, L., & Payne, P. (2019). Possessions and self in the identity work of survivors of domestic violence. *Journal of Consumer Psychology, 29*(2), 167–186. doi:10.1002/jcpy.1080

Fraser, K. D., & Al Sayah, F. (2011). Arts-based methods in health research: A systematic review of the literature. *Arts & Health, 3*(2), 110–145. doi:10.1080/17533015.2011.561357

Gibbons, R. (2010). *A table of metaphors: The visual representation of chronic illness.* (Unpublished master's dissertation). Massey University, Albany, New Zealand. Retrieved from http://hdl.handle.net/10179/1520

Gibbons, R. (2013). Hypertextual self-scapes: Crossing the barriers of the skin. In N. K. Denizen (Ed.), *40th anniversary of studies in symbolic interaction* (pp. 15–42). Bingley, England: Emerald.

Giorgi, A. (1997). The theory, practice, and evaluation of the phenomenological method as a qualitative research procedure. *Journal of Phenomenological Psychology, 28*(2), 235–260. doi: 10.1163/156916297X00103

Guruge, S., Hynie, M., Shakya, Y., Akbari, A., Htoo, S., & Abiyo, S. (2015). Refugee youth and migration: Using arts-informed research to understand changes in their roles and responsibilities. *Qualitative Social Research, 16*(3) doi:10.17169/fqs-16.3.2278

Hadjistavropoulos, T., & Smythe, W. E. (2001). Elements of risk in qualitative research. *Ethics & Behavior, 11*(2), 163–174. doi:10.1207/S15327019EB1102_4

Hall, S., Longhurst, S., & Higginson, I. J. (2009). Challenges to conducting research with older people living in nursing homes. *BMC Geriatrics, 9*(1), 38–38. doi:10.1186/1471-2318-9-38

Hansson, R. O., & Stroebe, M. S. (2007). *Bereavement in late life: Coping, adaptation, and developmental influences.* Washington, DC: American Psychological Association.

Harrison, B. (2002). Seeing health and illness worlds – using visual methodologies in a sociology of health and illness: A methodological review. *Sociology of Health &Amp; Illness, 24*(6), 856–872. doi:10.1111/1467-9566.00322

Hosany, S., & Gilbert, D. (2010). Measuring tourists' emotional experiences toward hedonic holiday destinations. *Journal of Travel Research, 49*(4), 513–526. doi:10.1177/0047287509349267

Hunter-Jones, P. (2005). Cancer and tourism. *Annals of Tourism Research 32*(1), 70–92. doi:10.1016/j.annals.2004.03.013

Jung, C. G. (1964). Approaching the unconscious. In *Man and his symbols* (pp. 18–103). New York, NY: Anchor Press.

Kagawa-Singer, M. (1998). The cultural context of death rituals and mourning practices. *Oncology Nursing Forum, 25*(10), 1752–1756.

Kazeminia, A., Chiappa, G. D., & Jafari, J. (2015). Seniors' travel constraints and their coping strategies. *Journal of Travel Research, 54*(1), 80–93. doi:10.1177/0047287513506290

Kim, S. H. (2009). The influence of finding meaning and worldview of accepting death on anger among bereaved older spouses. *Aging & Mental Health, 13*(1), 38–45. doi:10.1080/13607860802154457

King, J. (2018). Living with a chronic illness. *Medicine, 46*(7), 402–404. doi:10.1016/j.mpmed.2018.04.007

Knights, D., & Thanem, T. (2005). Embodying emotional labour. In Brandth B., Morgan D., Kvande E. (Eds.), *Gender, Bodies and Work*, (pp. 31–43). London: Routledge.

Kralik, D., van Loon, A., & Visentin, K. (2006). Resilience in the chronic illness experience. *Educational Action Research, 14*(2), 187–201. doi:10.1080/09650790600718035

Lenette, C., & Boddy, J. (2013). Visual ethnography and refugee women: Nuanced understandings of lived experiences. *Qualitative Research Journal, 13*(1), 72–89. doi:10.1108/14439881311314621

Letherby, G., & Davidson, D. (2015). Embodied storytelling: Loss and bereavement, creative practices, and support. *Illness. Crisis & Loss, 23*(4), 343–360. doi:10.1177/1054137315590745

Liamputtong, P. (2007). *Researching the vulnerable: A guide to sensitive research methods.* London, England: Sage.

Lowe, M. E. (2005). *The lived experience of untimely spousal bereavement.* (Unpublished master's dissertation). University of Saskachewan, Saskatoon, Canada.

Main, S. (2014). Picturing pain: Using creative methods to communicate the experience of chronic pain. *Pain News, 12*(1), 32–35.

Martini, A., & Buda, D. M. (2018). Dark tourism and affect: Framing places of death and disaster. *Current Issues in Tourism*, 1–14. doi:10.1080/13683500.2018.1518972

Massumi, B. (2002). *Parables for the virtual: Movement, affect, sensation.* Durham, NC: Duke University Press.

McIntosh, A. J., & Harris, C. (2018). Representations of hospitality at The Special Needs Hotel. *International Journal of Hospitality Management, 75*, 153–159. doi:10.1016/j.ijhm.2018.05.021

McIntosh, A. J., & Prentice, R. C. (1999). Affirming authenticity: Consuming cultural heritage. *Annals of Tourism Research, 26*(3), 589–612. doi:10.1016/S0160-7383(99)00010-9

Molzahn, A., Sheilds, L., Bruce, A., Stajduhar, K., Makaroff, K. S., Beuthin, R., & Shermak, S. (2012). People living with serious illness: Stories of spirituality. *Journal of Clinical Nursing, 21*(15-16), 2347–2356. doi:10.1111/j.1365-2702.2012.04196.x

Palinkas, L. A., Wingard, D. L., & Barrett-Connor, E. (1990). Chronic illness and depressive symptoms in the elderly: A population-based study. *Journal of Clinical Epidemiology, 43*(11), 1131–1141. doi:10.1016/0895-4356(90)90014-G

Papaloukas, P., Quincey, K., & Williamson, I. R. (2017). Venturing into the visual voice: Combining photos and interviews in phenomenological inquiry around marginalisation and chronic illness. *Qualitative Research in Psychology, 14*(4), 415–441. doi:10.1080/14780887.2017.1329364

Philipose, L. (2007). The politics of pain and the end of empire. *International Feminist Journal of Politics, 9*(1), 60–81. doi:10.1080/14616740601066390

Pile, S. (2010). Emotions and affect in recent human geography. *Transactions of the Institute of British Geographers, 35*(1), 5–20. doi:10.1111/j.1475-5661.2009.00368.x

Pink, S., Kürti, L., & Afonso, A. I. (2004). *Working images: Visual research and representation in ethnography*. London, England: Routledge.

Prosser, J. (2001). Skin memories. In S. Ahmed and J. Stacie (Eds.). *Thinking through the skin* (pp. 52–68). London, England: Routledge.

Pullman, M. E., & Robson, S. K. A. (2007). Visual methods: Using photographs to capture customers' experience with design. *Cornell Hotel and Restaurant Administration Quarterly, 48*(2), 121–144. doi:10.1177/0010880407300410

Rakic, T., & Chambers, D. (2009). Researcher with a movie camera: Visual ethnography in the field. *Current Issues in Tourism, 12*(3), 255–270. doi:10.1080/13683500802401972

Rakić, T., & Chambers, D. (2010). Innovative techniques in tourism research: An exploration of visual methods and academic filmmaking. *International Journal of Tourism Research, 12*(4), 379–389. doi:10.1002/jtr.761

Reynolds, F. (1997). Coping with chronic illlness and disability through creative needlecraft. *British Journal of Occupational Therapy, 60*(8), 352–356. doi:10.1177/030802269706000806

Reynolds, F., & Prior, S. (2003). A lifestyle coat-hanger': A phenomenological study of the meanings of artwork for women coping with chronic illness and disability. *Disability and Rehabilitation, 25*(14), 785–794. doi:10.1080/0963828031000093486

Richardson, V. E., & Balaswamy, S. (2001). Coping with bereavement among elderly widowers. *OMEGA - Journal of Death and Dying, 43*(2), 129–144. doi:10.2190/Y2Q6-BB75-ENM7-BBYR

Riches, G., & Dawson, P. (1996). Making stories and taking stories: Methodological reflections on researching grief and marital. *British Journal of Guidance & Counselling, 24*(3), 357–365. doi:10.1080/03069889608253020

Rozario, L. D. (1997). Spirituality in the lives of people with disability and chronic illness: A creative paradigm of wholeness and reconstitution. *Disability and Rehabilitation, 19*(10), 427–434. doi:10.3109/09638289709166568

Rydzik, A., Pritchard, A., Morgan, N., & Sedgley, D. (2012). Mobility, migration and hospitality employment: Voices of Central and Eastern European women. *Hospitality & Society, 2*(2), 137–157. doi:10.1386/hosp.2.2.137_1

Rydzik, A., Pritchard, A., Morgan, N., & Sedgley, D. (2013). The potential of arts-based transformative research. *Annals of Tourism Research, 40*, 283–305. doi:10.1016/j.annals.2012.09.006

Smythe, W. E., & Murray, M. J. (2000). Owning the story: Ethical considerations in narrative research. *Ethics & Behavior, 10*(4), 311–336. doi:10.1207/S15327019EB1004_1

Tarr, J., & Thomas, H. (2011). Mapping embodiment: Methodologies for representing pain and injury. *Qualitative Research, 11*(2), 141–157. doi:10.1177/1468794110394067

Townsend, A., Wyke, S., & Hunt, K. (2006). Self-managing and managing self: Practical and moral dilemmas in accounts of living with chronic illness. *Chronic Illness, 2*(3), 185–194. doi:10.1177/17423953060020031301

Tung, V., & Brent Ritchie, J. R. (2011). Exploring the essence of memorable tourism experiences. *Annals of Tourism Research, 38*(4), 1367–1386. doi:10.1016/j.annals.2011.03.009

Tutuncu, O. (2017). Investigating the accessibility factors affecting hotel satisfaction of people with physical disabilities. *International Journal of Hospitality Management*, *65*, 29–36. doi:10.1016/j.ijhm.2017.06.002

Westwood, S. (2007). What lies beneath? Using creative, projective and participatory techniques. In I. Ateljevic, A. Pritchard, & N. Morgan (Eds.), *The critical turn in tourism studies: Innovative methodologies* (pp. 293–316). Oxford, England: Elsevier

Willig, C. (2017). Reflections on the use of object elicitation. *Qualitative Psychology*, *4*(3), 211–222. doi:10.1037/qup0000054

Willson, G. B., McIntosh, A. J., Morgan, A., & Sanders, D. (2018). Terminal illness and tourism: Aa review of current literature and directions for future research. *Tourism Recreation Research*, *43*(2), 268–272. doi:10.1080/02508281.2018.1443053

Willson, G. B., McIntosh, A. J., & Zahra, A. L. (2013). Tourism and spirituality: A phenomenological analysis. *Annals of Tourism Research*, *42*, 150–168. doi:10.1016/j.annals.2013.01.016

Wood, E., & Kenyon, A. J. (2018). Remembering together: The importance of shared emotional memory in event experiences. *Event Management*, *22*(2), 163–181. doi:10.3727/152599518X15173355843325

Wood, E., & Moss, J. (2015). Capturing emotions: Experience sampling at live music events. *Arts and the Market*, *5*(1), 45–72. doi:10.1108/AM-02-2013-0002

Yau, M. K-S., McKercher, B., & Packer, T. L. (2004). Traveling with a disability. *Annals of Tourism Research*, *31*(4), 946–960. doi:10.1016/j.annals.2004.03.007

Zembylas, M. (2007). Theory and methodology in researching emotions in education. *International Journal of Research & Method in Education*, *30*(1), 57–72. doi:10.1080/17437270701207785

Zurba, M., & Berkes, F. (2014). Caring for country through participatory art: Creating a boundary object for communicating Indigenous knowledge and values. *Local Environment*, *19*(8), 821–836. doi:10.1080/13549839.2013.792051

Attuning to the affective in literary tourism: Emotional states in *Aberystwyth, Mon Amour.*

Jon Anderson (iD) and Kieron Smith (iD)

ABSTRACT

On a literary walking tour, many emotional 'states' are experienced by participants. These states have multiple causes, products and consequences, influenced in part by the socio-spatial identities of participants, their own imagined versions of the novel, and the material and cultural geographies of the tour itself. The Literary Atlas project sought to examine these emotional states by conducting literary walking tours based on English-language novels set in Wales. It attuned to the emotional states experienced by participants, in particular on a tour based around the locations cited in Malcolm Pryce's Aberystwyth Mon Amour. It did so to examine the ways in which these states cohere and collide to actively constitute the ongoing composition of the real-and-imagined worlds produced through this emergent literary geography. Attuning to the affects of the literary tour suggest that the strengths and persistence of these emotional attachments – to individual's own identities, imaginings and material places – come to define not only their place in the world, but also their world itself. As such, the ability of the participants to retain their cohesiveness as a group – however temporarily – in the face of difference and disagreement says much for their willingness to contextualise their own imaginings, and ultimately tolerate others', in a world of relational multiplicity.

摘要

在文学旅游地漫步之旅中, 许多情感"状态"是由参与者体验的。这些状态有多种原因、产物和结果, 部分受到参与者的社会空间身份、他们自己想象的小说版本以及旅游本身的物质和文化地理的影响。文学地图集项目试图通过以威尔士为背景的英语小说为基础的文学漫步旅行来研究这些情感状态。它与参与者所经历的情感状态相协调, 尤其是在马尔科姆·普莱斯(Malcolm Pryce)的《阿伯里斯特威斯的爱情》(Aberystwyth Mon Amour)中所提到的地点进行徒步时。它这样做是为了研究这些状态是如何相互融合和碰撞的, 从而积极地构成通过这种新兴文学地理产生的现实和想象世界的持续构成。与文学之旅的影响相协调表明, 这些情感依恋的力量和持久性——对个人身份、想象和物质空间的依恋——不仅决定了他们在世界上的位置, 也决定了他们的世界本身。因此, 参与者在面对差异和分歧时保持团队凝聚力的能力(无论这种凝聚力多么短暂), 在一个关系多元化的世界里, 很大程度上说明了他们愿意将自己的想象融入情境, 并最终容忍他人的想象。

Introduction

This paper attunes to the emotional states experienced on literary tours. Following Anderson (2015), the paper interprets an emotional state as a temporary condition that joins us and defines our relations with the world. As Anderson has argued, the notion of the state is at once an experiential condition; it is physically sensed, affectively felt, psychologically considered, and cognitively reflected upon. However, the state is not simply human in a physical sense; it is also crucially defined by geographical place. The state is influenced by the environment that the individual experiences and contributes to, as well as the cultural customs and ideologies of that location. The notion of the state is of particular interest when considering tourism, and in this case, literary tourism. Tourism and its associated mobility involves the individual moving from one set of socio-spatial relations to another, and integral to this process is the individual adapting, orientating, and finding themselves within these new networks (see Oberg, 1960; Pizam, 1999; Robinson, 1999; Ward, Bochner, and Furnham 2001). This paper suggests that literary tourism offers a unique perspective to attune to the relational states associated with this mobility as it does not simply involve individuals moving from one set of socio-spatial relations to another, but rather involves individuals bringing three often separate worlds of experience into direct contact with one another, namely: their own socio-spatial identity; the version of the novel they have creatively imagined; and the geographies of the literary tour. By drawing on one example of the literary tour enacted by the *Literary Atlas* project – a walking tour based on the novel *Aberystwyth, Mon Amour* – it illustrates how the affective states associated with each aspect of the individuals' lived experiences are brought into coincidence with another. It explores how this coincidence can lead to a strong sense of resonance but also in some cases a sense of rupture between real-and-imagined literary geographies. These affective states have the consequence of contextualising and giving definition to the participants and the practice itself.

In order to attune to the emotional states of literary tourism the paper employs a relational approach. Over recent years, relational approaches have offered new insights into the range of disciplines that constitute the arts, humanities, and social sciences. From studies of tourism, geography, and literature, relational thinking has changed how the world is understood and produced through practice. As Anderson and Saunders (2016) have summarised, relational approaches employ the orthodox, individualised categories of the modern – accepting that 'things', 'objects' or 'components' have significance in the western imagination – but argue that their meaning and definition are derived from their positioning within broader sets of cultural, temporal, and spatial networks. Relational thinking therefore does not consider 'things', 'objects' or 'components' to be 'a priori' in the world, but rather considers their meaning and definition to be continually ephemeral, (re)composing, and emergent (see also Whatmore, 1999, p31-2). This paper seeks to apply relational thinking to the practice and critique of the literary tour. As we will see, literary tourism is often suggested as a practice that offers insight in to the real or imagined places of literature (e.g. author's birthplaces, or fictionalized versions of real life places, e.g. Thomas Hardy's Wessex), using brochures, guides and cartography to offer metaphorical 'keys' or 'passwords' to understand the definitive truth behind the places of writing or setting. Relational approaches counter this passive 'reading' of literary tourism, and offer in its stead a creative, agential, co-production of literary places through practice. Literary tours, in this view, are not pass*words* to open up definitive and singular readings of any literary geography, but rather pass*ports* which invite the reader on a journey into an emergent world that they contribute to. This contribution is made through the coming together of the three worlds of experience that the literary tour explicitly calls forth. Namely, the socio-spatial identity of the participant; a version of the novel created through their own creative imagining; and the geographies of the literary tour. The following sections outline necessarily brief introductions to relationality and how they have influenced geography, literary studies, and tourism.

Relating to the spaces of literary tourism

Relationality has long been significant to the ways in which social science scholars understand and approach the world (see Doel 1999; Murdoch 2006). According to Jones (2009, p. 487), a relational approach insists that the world is constituted as "an open-ended, mobile, networked, and actor-centred geographic becoming". In this ongoing *constituting* of the world (contrasted to a fixed modern *constitution*, seminally critiqued by Latour, 1993), components are defined by their 'type of connection' to other components, rather than being designated by any isolated properties or discrete capacities. In this view, the fixed independent chunks of the modern constitution no longer hold sway, these now give way to an *inter* dependent epistemology where *things* are always acting and being acted upon by every*thing* else.

The relational approach has consequences for how human geographers understand the world. Drawing on representational approaches to culture, geographers continue to emphasise how all places are 'relative and symbolic' (Aitcheson, 1999) due to their production through ideological discourse and material construction. In relational thinking, however, representational approaches are allied to theories of practice which sensitise scholars to the ways in which worlds are brought forth not simply through cognitive meaning and considered reflection, but also through impulsive and affective activities. As a consequence, the 'conversations' that come to construct place are no longer held solely by dominant 'voices' within any culture, but by a range of actors articulating and responding to a range of 'voices' (including non-verbal practices, bodily communications, physical interventions, creative imaginings, etc.) which co-produce places into being (see Anderson & Harrison, 2010). As a consequence of these contributions, multiple actors and voices no longer produce geographies that are solidified and singular, but rather dynamic and multiple (see Massey 2005, for a full review).

The relational approach can be identified not only in approaches to human geography, but also with respect to the other disciplines relevant to this paper: literary studies and tourism. In terms of literary studies, scholars have challenged the perceived stability and homogeneity of literature and the characters and places within them. Texts are no longer framed as fixed and singular, but have a variety of interpretations based on a rich amalgam of authorial intent and audience (re)interpretation. The reception of literature, its spaces, characters and plot, is widely recognized as being far from fixed or absolute, but rather as 'phenomenal' in nature – specific novels are configured as individually "contextualised and always emerging geographical even-t[s]" (Hones, 2008, p. 1301). Books are therefore rendered into being not simply by iso-lated authorial intent, but through the "complex production of meaning and effect [...] from the dynamic interaction" between a reader, their imagination, pre-existing knowledge, and the work of the author (Drucker 2008, cited in Barnes 2013, p. 166). In this approach, the reader is no longer positioned as a passive consumer of authorial purpose, but rather enjoys the agency to produce their/our own reading of any fiction (following Barthes, 1977; see also Cameron, 2012; Ljungberg, 2003; Piatti and Hurni, 2009). As a result, it is now understood that even when you and I open the same cov-ers of a novel, we will both read (or to be specific, we will both co-produce with the author) a completely different book.

The relational approach also has consequences for the understanding and prac-tice of tourism. Representational and modern approaches to tourism could be sim-plistically characterized though the creation of fixed, commoditized place 'packages' which can be 'serially reproduced' by locals or tour companies (Richards and Wilson, 2006) for the consumption by an unthinking or inactive mass culture. In this view, "the tour brochure directs expectations, influences perceptions, and thereby provides a preconceived landscape for the tourist to `discover'" (Weightman 1987, p. 230, also cited in Pritchard and Morgan, 2001, p. 167). However, the rela-tional approach suggests that this framing offers only a partial view of the ways in which places are produced and consumed. From a relational perspective, the prac-tice of tourism cannot go out to discover a singular, authentic place revealed through insider knowledge, local guides, or expert insight, because such a defini-tive, discrete place does not exist. Rather tourism is a practice of co-constituting place in the moment, and understanding this practice requires sensitivity to the unique, emergent experiences which cannot be wholly programmed or predicted, and are co-produced by the coming together of discrete components which all have a degree of agency over the process and outcome.

The practice of 'creative tourism' (see Richards, 2011) seeks to actively cater for those who wish this form of relational engagement in their tourism experience. For those seeking to be part of bespoke, one-off encounters, creative tourism parallels the growth of what Pine & Gilmore identify as the 'experience-' and 'creative- economy' (Pine & Gilmore, 1999), where tourism elides the differences between cultural heritage, skill-building, and performance, through providing the opportunity for individuals to actively contribute to experiential and affective encounters in spatially-relevant set-tings. Literary tourism is a good example of both increased sensitivity to the relational, and the rise of creative tourism itself. Conventionally, literary tourism has focused on quasi-educational visits to real places (including birthplaces of writers, their homes, and significant cultural sites in their lives), as well as places associated with fictional works (see Herbert, 1996; 2001; Robinson & Andersen, 2002; Watson, 2006[1]). However, as many scholars have noted, the relations between 'real' places and 'fictional' places are not sharp or well-defined (see Soja, 1996; Reijnders, 2010; Anderson, 2004; Hones, 2014; Jiang and Xu, 2016) and due to the nature of positionality with respect to both place- and literary- co-production, relational approaches enable these complex coming togethers to be traced and understood in new and innovative ways (see below).

Relational approaches have thus taken hold in the array of disciplines that are the focus of this paper. In order to understand actor-centred understandings of a relational world, human geography, literary studies, and tourism have sought to increasingly attune to the affective. Affect and emotions have been widely integrated into social sciences study in recent years (see, for example, Game and Metcalfe, 1996; Davidson & Bondi, 2005), and much of this integration has borne the hallmarks of the modern constitution. For example, the Platonic distinction between body and mind has been widely retained, with affect precisely categorised as the biophysical process of sensing (i.e. the moment of feeling), and emotion defined as the subsequent cognitive representation of this corporeal process (see for example, Thien, 2005; Anderson & Harrison, 2006; 2010). In this framing, affect is interpreted as a sensation felt through the body, and emotion as the capturing of affect through linguistic representation (e.g. through the label of 'love', 'empathy', 'hate', or 'compulsion') (see Wetherell, 2012). However, it is possible to adopt relational approaches to the affective which identify 'sensibilities' emanating not from isolated bodies (or indeed minds), but through the interdependent coming together of a range of forces and processes (see also Anderson, 2009). The notion of the relational state is one example of this, referring to an experiential condition which is at once physically sensed, affectively felt, psychologically considered, and cognitively reflected upon. Indeed, the state is not simply human in a physical, limited, sense; it is also crucially defined by the geographical place in which that human is situated. The state is influenced by the environment that the individual experiences and contributes to, as well as the cultural customs and ideologies in which they find themselves. Indeed, this process of locating oneself within a set of socio-spatial relations is central to the process of developing and refining self-hood; it is these relational states that frame our socio-spatial identities, it is relational states that are the means through which individuals are joined to and define their relations with the world.

When worlds collide ...

The importance of the relational state to socio-spatial identity is such that a number of studies have used the notion to track and trace how humans register changes in their social and geographical setting (see, for example, Barry, 2016). Anderson (2015) acknowledges, for example, how disorientation can be experienced as individuals exchange one set of socio-spatial relations for another (see also Reisinger and Turner, 2003; Hottola, 2004). In the case of literary tourism however, a different set of relations are brought into being. This paper argues that three aspects of lived experience are directly brought into coincidence with each other through the practice of literary tourism, namely; an individual's socio-spatial identity; their version of the novel created through imaginative reading; and, the geographies of the literary tour. Traditionally, the socio-spatial identity of an individual is produced through a range of physical and mental interactions (including, for example, daily physical exchanges, one-off significant experiences, and fantastical imaginings), which form the co-constitutive bond between a person and a place (see, for example, Casey, 2001; Sack, 1997). From a relational perspective, these bonds are registered in the individual as an affective 'state', for example one may feel a sense of 'belonging' or 'home' when in familiar places with appreciated customs, or strangeness when either in locations with alien cultural 'traces' (Anderson, 2015) or when familiar places are under threat from the same (see Tuan, 1977). This socio-spatial identity is actively employed in the second aspect of lived experiences that is of concern to us here, the relational reading of a novel. As we have seen above, a reader's contribution to any text is vital in realising its potential (see Ljungberg 2003, p.174). The reader is therefore a key contributor to the creation of story, as Larsen points out:

> "It is sometimes said that the reader meets the author halfway to the page, but I would say it is more like .0001% author, 99.999% reader's architecture of imagination... the trick, of course, [lies with the author] knowing what details to include [to spark this construction process]" (2018, p.168).

If the reader's imagination does the 'heavy lifting' in relation to building literary worlds, it does so triggered by the linguistic prompts offered by the author, and filtered by a reader's socio-spatial identity. The author's invitation to build collaborative worlds will only be taken up if the reader's identity and imagination is captured by them, and the author's words will be streamed through the reader's own sense of geography, morality, and politics, to begin building the architecture of that world. The socio-spatial identity of the reader, and that reader's 'architecture of imagination' is then brought into coincidence with the 'real' world through the literary tour. As seen above, the literary tour brings individuals into encounters with 'real' settings used in novels, and "promotes an interactive relationship between readers, authors, and places" (Gentile & Brown, 2011, p. 25). If we take the relational approach to literary tourism seriously then new questions are posed by the coincidence of these three worlds of lived experience. As Anderson and Saunders suggest, the relational approach requires us to engage in the process of:

> "identifying the causes, products, and consequences of these many-to-many relations [and] explore... how these different agents come to cast their spell over the ongoing composition of literature and place. [We must ask how] literary geographies... issue from the lived to the imagined world, and the imagined to the lived world, and how they circulate and transform one another[?]" (2015, p. 117).

This paper explores these 'causes, products, and consequences of the many to many relations' using the example of a literary tour based on the novel *Aberystwyth, Mon Amour* (Pryce, 2001). Through so doing, it attunes to the affective states that 'circulate and transform one another' as the lived worlds of experience coincide to create its relational literary geographies.

Relational methodology

The literary tour based on the novel, *Aberystwyth, Mon Amour* was operationalised by the *Literary Atlas* project. *Literary Atlas* was developed through an Arts and Humanities Research Council grant, supported by Literature Wales, and run by the authors alongside scholars from Cardiff and Swansea University. Its primary purpose was to create an online cultural resource based on English language novels set in Wales (www.literaryatlas.wales). Drawing on the broader project which mapped over 570 novels (http://www.literaryatlas.wales/en/library/), it focused on 12 specific novels and under-took a range of innovative cartographies to depict their literary geographies not only on the *Literary Atlas* website but also in a series of exhibitions (http://www.literaryat-las.wales/en/art/exhibitions/). A specific part of this project involved running creative forms of literary tourism based on these 12 novels. Members of the public were recruited from direct invitations to reading clubs and creative writing groups, as well as open calls to public libraries. Participants had to be over 18, and reflecting the con-stituency of the majority of reading and writing groups involved, in practice the aver-age age was over 40. Each event involved both locals based in close proximity to the setting of the novel, as well as those travelling up to 150 miles to participate. In the case of the *Aberystwyth, Mon Amour* tour, fifteen people participated. Nine were female, six male; ages ranged from six in the 25-40 age bracket, five between 41 and 59; and four over 60; eleven were local to the community (for a minimum of ten years), and four had travelled from South Wales to Aberystwyth for the first time for the event. All tours were conducted in English, although some of the participants were fluent in Welsh. Unlike other tours conducted by Literary Atlas, the issue of Welsh language did not arise in the context of *Aberystwyth, Mon Amour*. As a conse-quence, this paper will not directly engage with the significant issue of Cymraeg and English co-existing in many places and plots in Welsh writing in English.

Each tour operationalised by Literary Atlas was explicitly set up as 'creative' in nature (following Richards, 2011); attendance was premised on having read the book which was the focus of the tour, but beyond this, there were no 'experts' formally designated, and the itinerary was loosely improvised around key geographical references and associ-ated passages from the novel. This itinerary was open to change, depending on practi-cality of movement, time involved, and collective will. Most tours were based on foot, and operated in the talking whilst walking tradition (see Anderson, 2004; Pink, 2007, and more broadly, Sheller & Urry, 2006, Binnie, Edensor, Holloway, Millington, & Young, 2007; de Certeau, 1984). In practice, this meant using the embodied art of walking to move through, "particular co-ingredient environments for recollection" (afer Anderson, 2004: 259). In the case of the literary tour, these 'environments' were the imagined novel and the spatial cultures of Aberystwyth itself, and cues from both the book, the participants, and the place were used to prompt ideas and feelings that had become part of individuals' 'architecture of imagination'. In short, physiological engagement with the 'real' world was used to bring the participant's socio-spatial identities and imagined worlds of *Aberystwyth, Mon Amour* 'into conversation'.

Participants carried micro- and smart-phones in order to record all encounters. Individuals were invited to take photos and make notes to simply record their interac-tions, post to social media, or as a memento for later discussion; and these were later shared with the *Literary Atlas* team Audio recordings were also taken by the *Literary Atlas* team (three were in attendance on this tour) using professional standard record-ing equipment with three-way external microphones. All recordings were later tran-scribed and thematically analysed. All participants on the tour were actively encouraged to engage in dialogue and share their impulses and reactions with each other – in short, share their relational states – prompted by the coming together of their identities, their books, and the places of the literary tour.

Walking into the worlds of *Aberystwyth, Mon Amour*

This paper is based on one illustrative example of these tours: the literary geographies of *Aberystwyth, Mon Amour* (2001). This novel was the first in a six-part series involving the fictional detective Louie Knight, authored by Malcolm Pryce. As the title suggests, the book was set in the relatively remote, mid-Wales seaside town of Aberystwyth, and juxtaposes very British notions of seaside holidays – lost innocence, saucy post-cards, and donkey rides – with characters and plots grafted from American crime thrillers in the genre typified by Raymond Chandler. In Pryce's words, "the concept [of the series] is basically a private eye from the American 1930s tradition, in Aberystwyth" (Pryce, in interview). This simple fish out of water premise combined with Pryce's deep-rooted affection for the area to produce an invitation to readers to engage with what he describes as his "love poem to the town" (in interview)[2].

The tour started at a key geographical location in the town of Aberystwyth itself, the Royal Pier. According to guidebooks (e.g. Lewis, 1967), the pier was built in 1865 and was originally 242 metres long; following construction it became the centrepiece of the town that marketed itself as 'the Biarritz of Wales'. Due perhaps to the town's relative inaccessibility, hopes of international glamour and wealth were not realised, and for Pryce, the pier symbolises the thwarted ambitions of those who inhabit his version of the town (Figures 1 and 2). As the following fantastical excerpt, read by the tour participants on the Aberystwyth prom, suggests:

> "The mangled ironwork of Aberystwyth Pier points out across the waters of Cardigan Bay like a skeletal finger. In happier times it had been a brightly painted boulevard of kiosks and sideshows where the ladies and gentlemen of the day came to enjoy the restorative properties of the seaside air. Parasols were twirled, moustaches waxed and ships bound for Shanghai, Honolulu, Papeete and 'Frisco' could be embarked from the end of the jetty. But the intervening years had seen a sad, slow fall from grace. The ships had all been turned into garden sheds and the Pier now lay stunted and truncated like a bridge to the Promised Land that had run out of funds" (2001, p. 13).

Figure 1. Royal Pier, Aberystwyth (Source: Literary Atlas).

Figure 2. Amusement Arcade, Royal Pier (Source: Literary Atlas).

Beyond the parodic musings of Pryce, in the present the Pier hosts a number of bars and cafes, but is dominated by an amusement arcade. Participants on the tour went in to the arcade to experience its atmosphere first hand:

M (Male) 1[3]: Help yourself to the 2ps.

F (Female) 1: Oh, this is my idea of hell! [laughs]

For those on the tour, the experience of the physically real amusement arcade resonated strongly with the world that Pryce invited his readers into imagining; as the following excerpt goes some way to illustrate:

"Inside it was bedlam: a flashing labyrinth of fruit machines at which boys, who should have been in school, stood chewing like cows in the late-afternoon sun and examining the reels with the concentration of chess players. Sullen girls slouched next to them with heavy kohl-rimmed eyes like handmaidens from Egyptian tombs" (Pryce, 2001, p. 14).

Although in the moment of the tour, ruminant teenagers had yet to emerge, the maze of machines had direct parallels with the novel; the characters Pryce depicted inhabiting this space played to the cultural expectations of the tour participants, reinforcing their suspicions that although this wasn't quite a den of iniquity, it was nevertheless a space that was more designed for holiday-makers, students, or youths seeking an escape from inclement weather or similar adolescence, rather than a place where they were supposed to feel at home. The tour participants could imagine that it was precisely the kind of place that 'Calamity' Jane, Louie Knight's teenage sidekick would inhabit, as a tour conversation suggested:

M1: I quite like this idea of Louis's meeting his ... you know, his youthful sidekick here ... Louis is this hard-boiled tough detective figure, who wouldn't really fit in in this type of place ....

F1: Yeah, meeting his sidekick here basically.

F2: Yeah, … in this rundown arcade [laughs] you know.

F1: Run down? It's state-of-the-art! [laughter]

F3: Maybe so, I don't know!

[over the music and sound of arcade machines]

F2: He'd have to bellow at her, he wouldn't be able to just chat!

In the novel, the reader is invited to imagine the actual meeting between Louie and Calamity in the Pier arcade. Pryce sketched the meeting as follows:

" … At the far end of the room, next to a window looking out to a forlorn ocean, there was a player who differed from the rest. Dressed in school uniform, she looked about fifteen or sixteen years old, and had a turned-up nose, a mass of freckles, spiky blonde hair and a chocolate-rimmed mouth.

…

'Wouldn't it be better to put some money in?' [Louie Knight asked the girl]

She answered mechanically without removing her gaze from the screen.

'No point. This machine isn't going to come up for another fifty games. Lady over there in the blue scarf is going to win this one'.

… The lady in the blue scarf shouted, 'House!'

I looked at the kid with renewed respect. 'Pretty good! What's your name?'

'Calamity Jane, what's yours?'

'Louie Knight.'

'What can I do for you, Louie?'" (Pryce, 2001, p. 14/15).

In the moment of the tour, there was considerable emotional and cognitive assonance between the 'real' place of the pier, and the relational space of the imagined pier that participants had conjured through their reading of the novel. Regardless of whether tour participants were experiencing Aberystwyth – and the Pier – for the first time, or whether they were long-standing inhabitants of the town, their cultural expectations of seaside amusement arcades, the version they conjured through their reading of the novel, and their experience on the tour, elided together to reinforce the compatibility of these different aspects of this relational literary geography. For these tour participants, the relationships between these different aspects were 'plausible', to use the phrase adopted by the author Phillip Pullman to describe the 'trick' he aims to pull off when aligning fictional and real places (2018). Although Louie and Calamity were an unlikely crime fighting duo, and Aberystwyth an unlikely place for Pryce to situate a criminal underworld (for more see below), the pier created a plausible platform on which these characters could meet and begin their professional relationship. Due to the polarising culture of the pier, Calamity appeared completely at home here, mastering the knowledge of the slot machines and out-tomboying the male teenagers with her smart quips and self-assurance. Yet whilst Calamity exhibited a topophilia and sense of belonging in this setting (see Tuan, 1974), Louie – despite his seniority and experience - exhibited a relational topophobia, or out of placeness, in this site. For those on the tour, the place of the pier compounded the idea that one character possessed a sense of streetwise nous and youthful naiveté that would usefully combine with the other's cynical logic and scepticism. Indeed, the juxtaposition between the two characters – itself reflecting genre tropes of odd couple detective 'buddies' – had the effect of reassuring participants that this strange territory was nevertheless oddly familiar, and this unlikely duo could form a sense of family which could hold them together as they began to track down the mafioso-druids running the town.

Exit Pier right

The tour exited the Pier and walked a few yards south along the Prom.

F1: Which building is that one there, then?

M1: That's the Old College, that was the university building.

F1: Oh, it's the old one, is it, yeah?

F2: These [buildings] are looking very grim and disrepaired, aren't they?

F3: Yeah, but it is a fantastic location isn't it? The views from these buildings are... phenomenal.

F2: On a day like this [warm Autumn sun], it's just gorgeous.

For Pryce, the Old College sited Barnaby and Merlin's pink-smoke belching Rock Factory. In it, the child genius Dai Brainbox perfected the art of inserting words into sticks of candy (commonly signaturing the holiday destination for tourists and visitors) and changing them as the candy is sucked away (Figure 3). As Pryce, through the character of Meirion, Aberystwyth's crime reporter, narrates:

"You know, so it starts off saying Blackpool and then after a few mouthfuls it says Zanzibar or something. It's one of the last great challenges of the rock-maker's art.

Figure 3. The Old College/Rock Factory (Source: Literary Atlas).

And he cracked it. Just like that. Sat down with a pen and paper and a set of log tables and worked it out. So then the management make him head of R&D and within a week - and the kid is still in school, don't forget, hasn't even done his O levels - within a week he'd found a way of computer type-setting the letters. Saved a fortune: twenty old-timers were thrown out of work the same afternoon" (2001, p. 39).

On the tour, the place of the Old College/Rock Factory prompts and provokes the participants to share their own knowledge about the building, and the other locations it springs to mind.

> F1: It's became one of the old university buildings, and it was built in a time when show was everything, you know?

> F2: It reminds me of the banks, the old banks in Cardiff Bay, you know, in Mount Stuart Square in the docks. Those type of stately buildings that were built when there was obviously money around

> F1: It was built as a hotel when the railway came but it just never, you know, fulfilled its ambition, there just weren't enough people coming and so then it went over to the university.

Into this discussion about the broader diaspora of buildings and histories that the place of the Old College/Rock Factory suggested, the following passage from a later novel in the series *Don't Cry for Me Aberystwyth* was introduced:

> "It was a lovely building, but architecturally it was the equivalent of a kid in a fancy-dress costumier's who tries on everything at the same time. It had Rhineland castle and gothic turrets, battlements and mosaics, statues and garrets. It would have been absurd but for the warm yellow stone from which it was constructed. It soothed the incongruity and lent it a strange beauty. You could forgive a lot of architectural sins with stone like that" (2007, p. 105).

This passage – although morphing the real building into a Rock Factory – was nevertheless engaged with by those on the tour as a form of guide book, prompting reflection and a fresh gaze on the actual architecture of the building itself.

> F1: At first glance I thought, oh look, a big grand 19th century building. But actually, you know, what he's saying … he's kind of … it's kind of a criticism of the of the architects that would have designed this, you know, trying to build something grandiose but ending up mashing lots of different designs into one. But I really wouldn't have thought about that by just looking at it, you know, without reading the passage in front of it, does that make sense?

> M1: Yes, yes it does.

> F2: It's brought it to our attention, you know, we're looking for the detail.

> M1: [The design] it's harking back to gothic … it's fantasy, isn't it? Fantasy [laughs].

> F3: It is a bit of a … yeah, maybe a bit of a folly, yeah.

> F2: Yeah, folly, yeah, like Castell Coch [just north of Cardiff], perhaps.

> F3: Yes, yes, it's a mixture of styles.

For those on this literary tour, the 'real' world of Aberystwyth and the fictional world sketched by Pryce had again resonantly coincided at the Old College/Rock Factory. So much so, that the novel itself has functioned as a something more than an invitation into building an imagined world, but as a parodic form of 'documentary' source (Brosseau, 1994, p. 333). Here the tour participants consumed the meeting between fiction and materiality 'unproblematically' (see Sharp, 2000, p.327, see also Hones, 2008), the architectural history of the building as depicted by Pryce had functioned akin to a "valuable storehouse of vivid depictions of landscapes and life" (Meinig 1983, p. 316, also cited in Sharp, 2000, p.327), which was interpreted as (more or less) authentic and 'real'. In this way, this meeting of fiction and reality, starting at the Pier, and now extended to the Old College, had created a coming together that was more powerful and affective than either world in isolation. In Pocock's words, a different 'truth' was emerging:

> "the truth of fiction [merged with reality offered] a truth beyond mere facts. Fictive reality [was beginning to] transcend or contain more truth than the physical or everyday reality" (Pocock 1981, p.11, cited in Sharp, 2000, p. 328).

As a result of engaging with the literary geographies of *Aberystwyth, Mon Amour* in practice, it was making less sense for the tour participants to retain the 'big dichotomy' (after Soja, 1996) of 'imaginative space' on one hand and 'real space' on the other, and rather entertain a relational "complex of multiple imaginations and realities" that were conjoined through their activities (after Reijnders, 2010, p. 41). The participants continued their journey into what for them was becoming a 'real-and-imagined' world (Soja, 1996) as they walked to the end of the Old College/Rock Factory (Figures 4 and 5).

F1: Does anyone know who that actually is, 'cause I …

F2: It's Archimedes.

F1: Well, he's pondering something and if he's not working out how many grains of sand there are in the world, it's taken him a long time because he's grown a beard, hasn't he?

M1: Are you googling now who it is?

F2: I am [laughter].

[quoting] "At the same time, the south range was rebuilt as a science block so that was after it was made into the university. Rebuilt as a science block in a more plain, gothic style, with a circular tower at its end bearing a mosaic triptych by CF Voysey showing

Figure 4. Archimedes on The Old College/Rock Factory (Source: Literary Atlas).

Figure 5. Old College/Rock Factory gargoyles (Source: Literary Atlas).

Archimedes being presented with models of modern technology, a steam locomotive and a steam ship with its sails also set. Two gargoyles above a door show science defeating error and light overcoming darkness".

F1: Oh … [laughter].

F2: So, it's … yeah.

F1: I fancy going finding those gargoyles.

Entering into the real-and-imagined world that was being created through the practice of the literary tour, the participants actively sought to create connections between the novel and the material geographies around them, using their imagination to build links to other places as well as extend their knowledge of this world through their own insights, remembered fragments, and through internet encyclopaedia. This knowledge was communicated and shared, with an element of enthusiasm and wit, which appeared to mimic the tongue-in-cheek atmosphere prompted by Pryce in his novel.

M1: Can you imagine this building as a rock foundry, with 'criminal' links?

F1: No! [laughter].

F2: You'd have to make a lot of money out of rock, wouldn't you, to be able to afford it.

F3: Ah, but this was special rock, isn't it? Dai Brainbox's special rock, and they're probably supplying every rock emporium in the country!

M2: There was one of those things when I lived here, I loved that juxtaposition [of crime in this quiet, friendly town] because, you know, the biggest headline in the Cambrian News was 'someone left their shed open' … you know! [laughter].

F3: I know, I know!

M2: And you're thinking yeah, and they're supposed to be this kind of underworld... come on! Of all the places in the world, this is the least likely place to have that! So the clear kind of obvious [juxtaposition] ... is actually why it kind of works [laughs]

F3: Mm. My favourite local news headline was 'Cat flap Slightly Damaged' [laughter] That's how exciting our news gets [laughs].

F4: My favourite is, 'Father of Ten Shot, Mistaken for Rabbit.'

F1: Oh no... [laughs], oh God.

The discussion prompted by engagement with the Old College/Rock Factory led the tour participants into reflecting on the personality of the town that Pryce had captured in his choice of words for the novel. For some on the tour the unlikely juxtapositions in the novel (of Calamity and Louie; of Rock Factory in a university building; of mafioso druids in a quiet seaside town) were certainly outlandish, yet they were so unlikely that they allowed themselves to be charmed into believing their plausibility. For some, it was nature of the town itself that allowed the acceptance of this flight of fancy:

M1: I thought when I first started reading it, I read the back and I thought, how the heck is that [gumshoe thriller] going to work in Aberystwyth? It's like a sort of detective thing from the 40s, what ... ?! but [in the end] the dialogue and everything just caught my imagination.

M1: Yeah ... it shouldn't work...

M2: And it wouldn't... it wouldn't work anywhere else I don't think [laughs].

Other authors have remarked upon the capacity of Aberystwyth to spark the imagination, as the novelists Niall Griffiths and then Fflur Dafydd state:

"There's a strange draw to the place; get off the train and you can't go any further. Stand on the promenade and the next landmass is Ireland and, after that, America. Mountains pile up behind you and you feel that you can't go back into their bulwark mass but the sea, there, in front of you, is a blue world of possibility. And between that and the giant rocks is this small, intriguing town, its lanes and alleys and doorways a jumbled alphabet waiting to be re-assembled" (Griffiths, 2008, p.11–12).

"with the world turned on its head at this strange angle, you know you're in Aberystwyth" (Dafydd, 2008, p.62)

The relational space created by the tour allowed many of its participants to be lured further into the real-and-imagined world of *Aberystwyth, Mon Amour*, fuelled by their own identities, their imaginative reading, and the material geography of the town itself. However, despite the attraction of these imaginative musings on a recreational sunny day – along with the capacity for 'group think' on such an inherently collaborative event (see Cline, 1990) – others on the tour remained reluctant to forgive the creative interpretations of the town which they found in the novel.

F1: There seems to be a bit of a split here - we didn't really like the book, our reading group really hated it. I just found it really wrong.

F2: Really, I've read every single book in the series!

F1: Mm, I'm amazed, I'm absolutely amazed.

"Let's be clear about it then: Aberystwyth ... was no Babylon" (Pryce, 2001, p. 1)

Despite affective and cognitive assonance between many of the locations in the novel and Aberystwyth itself, some of the local tour participants explained how the more creative interpretations that the author prompted them to imagine simply didn't resonate with their experience and knowledge of the town. These invitations ranged from geographical inaccuracies - as the following two examples illustrate:

Example 1

F1: There were some beautiful descriptions, like when he goes over ...

F2: Yes, going over to Borth, over the old road, yes.

F1: The only problem there, he said that the fields were dotted with cows. Now, I would argue with that. I think the fields are dotted with sheep [laughter].

Example 2

F3: The museum ... It's not where it is and it doesn't have a whatever the flying fortress or whatever the airplane was ... the bomber was parked outside ...

F4: Oh yes, that's right. That's a bit weird isn't it, having a bomber ... did we ever have a bomber?

F3: Was it ... a Lancaster, wasn't it? A Lancaster bomber parked outside ... you think, what? [laughs].

... to the author stretching poetic interpretation too far in encouraging a particular criminal view of the town:

F3: I always felt like Aberystwyth is a little bit like an island.

F4: Yes, you're isolated here, yeah.

F3: Yes, you know, it made it much more of a community.

F2: We used to say the 'Aberystwyth bubble'.

F3: Yes, so much so that that I almost couldn't read the book anymore 'cause it [the criminal depiction] is just so wrong.

F4: Yeah, it really put me off.

F3: I mean, poor Aberystwyth, it's a terrible advertisement really. It seems to be the crime centre of Wales!

Unlike the world suggested by Malcolm Pryce, for these local, middle class tour participants Aberystwyth *was* a form of 'Babylon' (see above), from their positionality and based on their experiences of the town, they found it impossible to fully imagine their place rife with criminality, albeit of an absurd variety[4]. At a superficial level, this could appear to be an arcane position to take, with the refusal to contemplate the presence of cattle in the countryside a small and somewhat pedantic 'hill to die on'. However, this view nevertheless represents the affective power not simply of an individual's connection to place, but also its fragility. These participants' connection to the cultural and physical landscape of the town – what they termed the Aberystwyth 'bubble' – was so defining *of* them and valuable *to* them that they were unwilling and unable to risk its puncturing; as was suggested on the tour:

F3: It's your imagination, isn't it, you've got to create that. And if you've already got [another version of] it there, it's harder for you to create it, isn't it, in a different way?

F4: If it doesn't fit, it's not going to go ...

F3: I think if you're more acquainted and familiar with a place, then you have a stronger image of that place in your head and it's much harder to revise, you know? And I think that is ... that is partly what it's about, you know? It contradicts that ... you know, the experience you have of a place.

For these individuals therefore, *Aberystwyth, Mon Amour* and the tour through its literary geographies wasn't simply a neutral passport to an imaginary world (although they were able to understand that it could simply be this), it was also a form of existential threat to their place in the world. They not only wished for this fragile set of person-place relations to remain undisturbed, they were also compelled to articulate their affinity and loyalty to the place under the 'threat' that the novel and tour posed. In a similar way that tour participants had themselves experienced at the Old College/ Rock Factory, these individuals were concerned that the book may be taken by some to be a 'documentary' resource, and lead to a significant misinterpretation of the town that they were a part of. With this in their minds, Pryce's invitation to collaborate on an alternative imagining of Aberystwyth was problematic:

F4: Dylan Thomas wrote about Laugharne, but he [gave] the village another name, so he could do what he liked. If you're going to call it Aberystwyth, I think you do ... should have a bit of respect for the location, really. But that's my personal view.

F5: I'm just so torn by it because yeah, parts that I really dislike because like you say, I found them very unfair to the town. There were some parts that I really like. I knew it was going to be very surreal, it wasn't serious, as such, and although I kind of forgave that, I'm very much torn. ... I'm just very divided.

For these participants the coming together of their worlds of lived experience – their socio-spatial identity, their imagined world of the novel, and the material geographies of Aberystwyth – led not to complementarity and resonance, but conflict and rupture. In real time they experienced how this coming together had the potential to cause a 'tear' in their understanding of the world, and their own place within it. Encountering other participants' willingness to engage in interpretative flights of fancy did little to ameliorate their feelings, and indeed compounded them. They felt required to re-assert these identities and retain their bearings before these literary geographies threatened to 'divide' their worlds in two.

Conclusion: Attuning to the affective

This paper has attuned to the emotional states experienced on literary tours. Adopting a relational approach to literary tourism, it has sought to explore 'how the real and imagined come together and move apart' (Anderson & Saunders, 2016) through the practice of a walking tour based on the locations of *Aberystwyth, Mon Amour*. It has demonstrated how three worlds of lived experience – participants' socio-spatial identity, individuals' creative imagining of the novel, and the geographies of material places – coincide together in an emergent practice which has consequences not only for our understanding of literary tourism, but also for the capacity of its affects to context-ualise and define person-place relations more broadly.

The paper has shown how the 'many to many relations' that coincide to produce a literary tour affects its participants. Following Cameron (2012, p. 581) it emphasises how "stories do not simply represent ... they affect, they move", and encountering stories in the material places in which they are set act to compound these affects. Through prompting local knowledges and encouraging the articulation of co-ingredi-ent affiliations to different locations, alliances can be formed between a participant's creative imaginings of a novel and the material geographies of a place. When personal imaginings are shared with others whose own identities and interpretations comple-ment their own, then the literary tour can act to alter the affective and cognitive map of these participants, eroding the apparent distinctions between these different worlds so much so that they emerge together; where the real, or the imagined, are no longer fixed and immovable entities, but rather now categories that we 'fondly imagine' to be not only mutually informing, but also mutable to their core (Pullman, 2018, p.12).

The ability of the literary tour to affect the emotional 'maps' of participants is such that, following Battista et al (2005, p. 439), the creative imaginings of each reader and their own socio-spatial identities can be 'wobbled' out of their fixed and separate planes. This may produce a resonant coincidence of real-and-imagined experience, but it may also threaten rupture. Where there is a lack of congruence between the three worlds of experience within any participant – or indeed between participants on a tour – it is possible for individuals to sense the novel-as-passport as a threat, seeking to counter its affects in case they risk de-stabilising their place in the world.

In this way, the emergent geographies of the literary tour are not always coherent and agreed, the potential for dissolution and disagreement are inherent within their composition. Attuning to the affects of the literary tour suggest that the strengths and persistence of these emotional attachments – to individual's own identities, imaginings and material places – are not lightweight and trivial sutures, but come to define not only their place in the world, but also their world itself. As such, the ability of the par-ticipants to retain their cohesiveness as a group – however temporarily – in the face of difference and disagreement says much for their willingness to contextualise their own imaginings, and ultimately tolerate others', in a world of relational multiplicity.

These issues raise the potential for exploring the affective potential of literary tour-ism further, as well as the emphasising the need to trace the literary geographies brought into being through this practice. Attuning to the affective in literary tourism requires a sensitivity to the ways in which different aspects of lived experience are called forth and interact to create that literary geography. What other personal links, insights, and lenses are used to co-produce the real-and-imagined places of the tour, how are these shared and communicated, and how are they received by other tour participants? What other forms of local knowledge, borne of particular experiences, coincide with broader cultural assumptions and literary knowledges (e.g. expertise in genre, other novels set in proximate locations, or author positionalities and interests) to transform the complex assemblies that come to define the literary tour? In sum, and to use Hones' terms (2014: 67), this paper suggests it is necessary to trace further the 'intra-textual' geographies of literary tours (i.e. how different 'real-and-imagined' places within the covers of the book are connected by participants), their 'inter-textual' geographies (in other words, the ways these relational spaces cohere or contradict similar locations in other published novels), as well as their 'extra-textual' affects, i.e. how the encounters on the literary tour can not only play "a major role in how that place is experienced" by participants, but also potentially have "literal, physical impact on a place" through their successful iteration. Exploring these issues further can offer insights into the role of literary geography in enhancing interest in reading, local histories, and walking, as well as providing parameters through which locations can be successfully marketed for creative tourism practices.

Notes

1. With respect to the geographical area focused on in this paper, Literature Wales have undertaken this type of quasi-educational literary tour in the past, including, for example, 'The Wild West' tour of Aberystwyth, including the work of Cynan Jones, Niall Griffiths and Samantha Wynne Rhydderch (see Literature Wales, 2013). It is also important to note that Literature Wales were a 'project partner' in the Literary Atlas project.
2. Although during the tour Pryce's own connection with Aberystwyth was discussed, his actual places of writing were not. The author's (fantastical?) admission that "the first draft of [Aberystwyth, Mon Amour] was finished on board a cargo ship off the coast of Guyana" (2001: 247) was therefore not drawn into the assembly of locations, ideas, and states of this tour's literary geographies.
3. In each transcribed excerpt, each participant response is coded from 1, to note the range of difference voices contributing.
4. From the broader Literary Atlas project, it is clear that not all inhabitants, readers and writers of Aberstwyth shared this particular idyllic view of the town (see for example, http://www.literaryatlas.wales/en/novels/sheepshagger/)

Disclosure statement

No potential conflict of interest was reported by the authors.

ORCID

Jon Anderson https://orcid.org/0000-0002-6052-5154
Kieron Smith https://orcid.org/0000-0003-4471-8615

References

Aitcheson, C. (1999). New cultural geographies: The spatiality of leisure, gender and sexuality. *Leisure Studies*, *18*, 19–39.

Anderson, B. & Harrison, P. (eds.). (2010). *Taking-place: Non-representational theories and geography*. Farnham: Ashgate.

Anderson, J. (2004). Talking whilst walking: A geographical archaeology of knowledge. *Area*, *36*(3), 254–261. doi:10.1111/j.0004-0894.2004.00222.x

Anderson, J. (2009). Transient convergence and relational sensibility: Beyond the modern constitution of nature. *Emotion, Space, & Society*, *2*, 120–127. doi:10.1016/j.emospa.2009.10.001

Anderson, J. (2015). Exploring the consequences of mobility: Reclaiming jet lag as the state of travel disorientation. *Mobilities*, *10*(1), 1–16. doi:10.1080/17450101.2013.806392

Anderson, J. (2015). *Understanding cultural geography: Places and traces*. London & New York: Routledge.

Anderson, J., & Saunders, A. (2016). Relational literary geographies: Co-producing page and place. *Theme Editorial. Literary Geographies*, *1*(2), 115–119.

Barnes, A. (2013). Geo/graphic design: The liminal space of the page.' *Geographical Review*, *103*(2), 164–176. doi:10.1111/gere.12006

Barry, K. (2016). Transiting with the environment: An exploration of tourist re-orientations as collaborative practice. *Journal of Consumer Culture*, *16*(2), 374–393. doi:10.1177/1469540516635406

Barthes, R. (1977). *Mythologies*. London: Paladin.

Battista, K., LaBelle, B., Penner, B., Pile, S., & Rendell, J. (2005). Exploring 'an area of outstanding unnatural beauty': A treasure hunt around King's Cross, London. *Cultural Geographies*, *12*(4), 429–462. doi:10.1191/1474474005eu345oa

Binnie, J., Edensor, T., Holloway, J., Millington, S., & Young, C. (2007). Mundane mobilities, banal travels. *Social & Cultural Geography*, *8*(2), 165–174. doi:10.1080/14649360701360048

Brosseau, M. (1994). Geography's literature. *Progress in Human Geography*, *18*(3), 333–353. doi:10.1177/030913259401800304

Cameron, E. (2012). New geographies of story and storytelling. *Progress in Human Geography*, *36*(5), 573–592. doi:10.1177/0309132511435000

Casey, E. (2001). Between geography and philosophy: What does it mean to be in the place-world? *Annals of the Association of American Geographers*, *91*(4), 683–693. doi:10.1111/0004-5608.00266

Cline, R. (1990). Detecting Groupthink: Methods for observing the illusion of unanimity. *Communication Quarterly*, *38*(2), 112–126. doi:10.1080/01463379009369748

Dafydd, F. (2008). Making waves. In J. Barnie, M. Lloyd Jones, C. Dafydd, G. Morgan, F. Dafydd, Green, A. Aber (Eds.), *Essays on Aberystwyth* (pp. 55–64). Llandysul: Gomer Press.

Davidson, J., & Bondi, L. (2005). Smith, M. (eds.) *Emotional geographies*. Ashgate: Aldershot.

de Certeau, M. (1984). *The practice of everyday life*. Berkeley: University of California Press.

Doel, M. (1999). *Poststructuralist geographies: The diabolical art of spatial science*. Lanham, MD: Rowman & Littlefield.

Drucker, J. (2008). The virtual codex from page space to E-space. In S. Schreibman, & R. Siemans (Eds.), *A companion to digital literary studies* (pp. 333–342). Oxford: Blackwell.

Game, A., & Metcalfe, A. (1996). *Passionate sociology*. London: Sage.

Gentile, R., & Brown, L. (2011). A life as a work of art: Literary tourists' motivations and experiences at Il Vittoriale Delgi Italiani. *European Journal of Tourism, Hospitality and Recreation*, *6*(2), 25–47.

Griffiths, N. (2008). *Real Aberystwyth*. Bridgend: Seren.

Herbert, D. (1996). Artistic and literary places in France as tourist attractions. *Tourism Management*, *17*(2), 77–85. doi:10.1016/0261-5177(95)00110-7

Herbert, D. (2001). Literary places, tourism and the heritage experience. *Annals of Tourism Research*, *28*(2), 312–333. doi:10.1016/S0160-7383(00)00048-7

Hones, S. (2008). Text as it happens: Literary geography. *Geography Compass*, *2*(5), 1301–1317. doi:10.1111/j.1749-8198.2008.00143.x

Hones, S. (2014). *Literary geographies. Narrative space in let the great world spin*. New York: Palgrave Macmillan.

Hottola, P. (2004). Culture confusion. Intercultural adaptation in tourism. *Annals of Tourism Research*, *31*(2), 447–466. doi:10.1016/j.annals.2004.01.003

Jiang, L., & Xu, H. (2016). Reading, tourism, and geography consumption in literary places. *Tourism Geographies*, *18*(5), 483–502. doi:10.1080/14616688.2016.1217033

Jones, M. (2009). Phase space: Geography, relational thinking, and beyond. *Progress in Human Geography*, *33*(4), 487–506. doi:10.1177/0309132508101599

Larsen, R. (2018). Connecting contours. In H. Lewis-Jones (Ed.), *The writer's map*. Thames Hudson: London.

Latour, B. (1993). *We have never been modern*. Cambridge: Harvard University Press.

Lewis, G. (1967). *A bibliography of Cardiganshire* (pp. 1600–1968). Aberystwyth: Ceredigion Library.

Ljungberg, C. (2003). Constructing new 'Realities'': The performative function of maps in contemporary fiction. In B. Maeder (Ed.), *Representing realities: Essays on American literature, art and culture. Gunter Narr, Series SPELL* 16 (pp. 159–176).

Massey, D. (2005). *For space*. London: Sage.

Meinig, D. (1983). Geography as an art. *Transactions of the Institute of British Geographers*, *8*(3), 314–328. doi:10.2307/622047

Murdoch, J. (2006). *Post-structural Geography: A guide to relational space*. Thousand Oaks, CA: Sage.

Oberg, K. (1960). Cultural shock: Adjustment to new cultural environments. *Practical Anthropology*, *7*, 177–182. doi:10.1177/009182966000700405

Piatti, B., & Hurni, L. (2009). Mapping the ontologically unreal - Counterfactual spaces in literature and cartography. *The Cartographic Journal*, *46*(4), 333–342. doi:10.1179/000870409X12554350947386

Pine, J., & Gilmore, J. (1999). *The experience economy*. Boston: Harvard Business School Press.

Pink, S. (2007). Walking with video. *Visual Studies*, *22*(3), 240–252. doi:10.1080/14725860701657142

Pizam, A. (1999). Cross-cultural tourist behavior. In A. Pizam, Y. Mansfeld (Eds.), *Consumer behavior in travel and tourism* (pp. 393–412). New York: Haworth Hospitality Press.

Pocock, D. (1981). Introduction: Imaginative literature and the geographer. In D. Pocock (Ed.), *Humanistic geography and literature: Essays in the experience of place* (pp. 9–19). London: Croom Helm.

Pritchard, A., & Morgan, N. (2001). Culture, identity and tourism representation: Marketing Cymru or Wales? *Tourism Management*, *22*(2), 167–179. doi:10.1016/S0261-5177(00)00047-9

Pryce, M. (2001). *Aberystwyth, Mon Amour*. Bloomsbury: London.

Pullman, P. (2018). A plausible possible. In H. Lewis-Jones (Ed.), *The writer's map* (pp. 8–13). London: Thames Hudson.

Reijnders, S. (2010). Places of the imagination: An ethnography of the TV detective tour. *Cultural Geographies*, *17*(1), 37–52. doi:10.1177/1474474009349998

Reisinger, Y., & Turner, L. (2003). *Cross-cultural behaviour in tourism: Concepts and analysis*. Oxford: Butterworth-Heinemann.

Richards, G. (2011). Creativity and tourism. The state of the art. *Annals of Tourism Research*, *38*(4), 1225–1253. doi:10.1016/j.annals.2011.07.008

Richards, G., & Wilson, J. (2006). Developing creativity in tourist experiences: A solution to the serial reproduction of culture? *Tourism Management*, *27*(6), 1209–1413. doi:10.1016/j.tourman.2005.06.002

Robinson, M. (1999). Cultural conflicts in tourism: Inevitability and inequality. In M. Robinson, P. Boniface (Eds.), *Tourism and cultural conflicts* (pp. 1–32). Wallingford: CAB International.

Robinson, M., & Andersen, H. (eds.). (2002). *Literature and tourism: Essays in the reading and writing of tourism*. London: Thomson.

Sack, R. (1997). *Homo geographicus*. Baltimore: John Hopkins University.

Sharp, J. (2000). Towards a critical analysis of fictive geographies. *Area*, *32*(3), 327–334. doi:10.1111/j.1475-4762.2000.tb00145.x

Sheller, M., & Urry, J. (2006). The new mobilities paradigm. *Environment and Planning A: Economy and Space*, *38*(2), 207–226. doi:10.1068/a37268

Soja, E. (1996). *Thirdspace*. Blackwell: Malden.

Tuan, Y.-F. (1974). *Topophilia: A study of environmental perception, attitudes, and values*. Englewood Cliffs: Prentice Hall.

Tuan, Y.-F. (1977). *Space and place: The perspective of experience*. Minneapolis, MN: University of Minnesota Press.

Ward, C., Bochner, S., & Furnham, A. (2001). *The psychology of culture shock* (2nd ed). London: Routledge.

Watson, N. J. (2006). *The Literary tourist: Readers and places in romantic and Victorian Britain*. Basingstoke: Palgrave Macmillan.

Weightman, B. A. (1987). Third world tour landscapes. *Annals of Tourism Research*, *14*(2), 227–239. doi:10.1016/0160-7383(87)90086-7

Wetherell, M. (2012). *Affect and emotion: A new social science understanding*. London: Sage Publications.

Whatmore, S. (1999). Culture-Nature. In P. Cloke, M. Crang, & M. Goodwin (Eds.), *Introducing human geographies* (pp. 4–11). London: Arnold.

Affective entanglements with travelling mittens

Outi Kugapi 🆔 and Emily Höckert

ABSTRACT

Researchers have, most commonly, been studying souvenirs from two different streams: one that discusses the impact of souvenirs on the producers and another that focuses more on tourists as consumers of the souvenirs. Recently, the studies have also concentrated on the stories given with souvenirs, connectiveness to places and on the effectiveness of their memorability. However, research about the embodied experiences of and, most importantly, with souvenirs has been overlooked even in craft tourism, which can be seen fundamentally different way of experiencing tourism destinations as it invites people to involve the body in the actions, touch and move together. Therefore, in order to grasp the embodied encounters with souvenirs, we use an autoethnographic narrative of self-knitted green and white mittens to gain understanding about our experiences with the non-human actors, to research how emotions and affect are produced through craft tourism and the souvenirs, and how care as an affect is present in different situations and. By drawing inspiration from previous discussions on relational ethics, non-representational theory and affect in Tourism Studies, the narrative of the mittens explores the intensive entanglements in meanings and matter between handicrafts, places and humans. There, the ability to care is not limited to the social lives of humans. The self-made souvenirs emerge in unpredictable ways around everyday actions and create multiple affects, with movement, vitality and encounters on their own, becoming part of a life-long journey filled with memories of certain moments. Furthermore, our findings encourage future tourism research to go beyond representation when exploring the intensive entanglements between people, souvenirs and places.

摘要

最常见的是，研究人员从两种不同的理路研究纪念品：一种是讨论纪念品对生产者的影响，另一种更为关注纪念品对作为消费者的游客的影响。最近，研究还集中在人们赋予纪念品以故事，纪念品与地方的连接以及纪念品纪念性的效果。然而，即使在手工艺旅游中，关于纪念品本身的亲身体验，以及最重要的是，购买纪念品的亲身体验研究也被忽视了，这是一种完全不同的体验旅游目的地的方式，它使得人们卷入到制造和购买纪念品的行动中，一起触摸，一起移动。因此，为了把握旅游者对纪念品的亲身体验,我们使用一个旅游者自织绿色和白色手套的自我民族志叙事，获得对非人类行动者体验的理解，研究情绪和情感是如何通过手工艺旅游和纪念品生产出来的,以及关怀作为一种情感如何存在于不同情景中的。通过借鉴以往旅游研究中关系伦理、非表征理论和情感研究的讨论,手套叙事探索了手工艺品、地方和人之间在意义和物质上的紧密纠缠。在那里,关怀的能力并不局限于人类的社会生活。自制纪念品以不可预测的方式出现在日常活动中,通过纪念品的携带、纪念品本身所体现出来的活力以及人们与纪念品的相遇故事,创造了多重影响,成为终生旅程的一部分,充满了特定时刻的记忆。此外,我们的研究结果鼓励未来旅游研究探索人、纪念品和地方之间的紧密联系时要超越纪念品的表征。

Introduction

I hear the bus coming and realise that I must leave the church. My backpack bounces up and down as I run towards the bus stop in the snow. I feel like Rocky Balboa when I climb up the stairs of the bus. I try to catch my breath before telling the driver that I would like to buy a ticket to Kiruna. The feeling of success vanishes when I hit the front seat; my mittens are missing. This cannot be true. Oh my, I must have dropped Outi's precious mittens – which I have been hugging in my hands for more than two years now.

This is the story of two green and white mittens that have touched us, taken care of us and made our hearts beat faster. The research journey began in 2016 with an urge to understand why this souvenir, a pair of hand-knitted mittens, had become so meaningful and important to us (see Thrift, 2008). This journey has allowed us – two tourism researchers and enthusiastic crafters – to shift our identities between those of tourists, friends, researchers and collaborators, who knit and purl and sometimes unravel stitches and, most importantly, to explore the potential of living with mittens like these (see Hokkanen, 2017; Mackenzie & Kerr, 2013b; Reed-Danahay, 1997). In our storyline, we approach handicrafts as souvenirs that entangle people and places and enrich both physical and mental travelling.

Researchers have studied souvenirs for decades. As Kim and Littrell (2001) argue, the stream of research has been divided into two directions: one that discusses the impact of souvenirs on the producers and another that focuses more on tourists as consumers of the souvenirs. Generally, souvenirs can be seen as artefacts and memories of holidays and events (Edelheim, 2015; Graburn, 2005), as pieces of a place that travel back home with tourists (see Peters, 2011). In recent research on souvenirs in tourism, the focus has been more on the stories given with souvenirs (Edelheim, 2015), connectiveness to places and experiences (Cave & Buda, 2018) and on the effectiveness of their memorability (Sthapit & Björk, 2019). Moreover, Kimberley Peters' (2011) research on 'banal tourism items' and Susan Stewart's (2005) discussion of postcards as souvenirs open up the different meanings that tourists give to these things, and how they affect the people who receive them.

We accept here Stewart's (2005, p. 133) suggestion that experience of the object can be saturated with meanings that can never be fully revealed to us. Nevertheless, our wish has been to gain more understanding about our relationships with these kinds of travelling objects by researching them via craft tourism, which can be seen as a fundamentally different way of experiencing tourism destinations: it invites people to involve the body in the actions (see Thrift, 2008, p. 116), touch and move together. In craft tourism, tourists can be involved in making their own souvenirs and this pair of green and white mittens is one good example of this. Hence, the purpose of this article is to explore the role of embodied encounters with souvenirs and this way to gain understanding about our experiences with the non-human actors.

Our research has been guided by Nigel Thrift's (2005, 2008) non-representational theory in particular. Thrift has encouraged us to look beyond the representation of hand-made souvenirs and their meanings and to dig deeper into the materiality and seek the multidimensional attachments of handicrafts. Non-representational theory or, perhaps more correctly, more-than-representational theory seeks to better cope with our multisensory worlds (see Barron, 2019; Lorimer, 2005, p. 83), stressing the importance of the affective capacities of our bodies. Drawing inspiration from discussions on affect, moods, passions and intensities (Anderson, 2006), we hope to gain further understanding of why and how souvenirs become much more than just objects and, in this case, clothing that keeps us warm. We wonder what emotions and affect produced through craft tourism and handicrafts – which are inherently embedded in the idea of embodied encounters and touching – might do, and how care as an affect is present in different situations. Therefore, we understand affect here both as concrete, embodied encounter and as abstract intensity of being and feeling (Barron, 2019; Thrift, 2008, pp. 175–176; Vannini, 2015a, p. 8; see also d'Hauteserre, 2015).

In tourism research, a growing stream of studies has called for more holistic understandings of embodiment (Jokinen & Veijola, 1997; Veijola & Jokinen, 2008), feelings (Buda et al., 2014), emotions and affects (Buda, 2015; Cuthill, 2007; d'Hauteserre, 2015; Tucker & Shelton, 2018) that enrich and surpass our visual senses and representations. Anne-Marie d'Hauteserre's (2015) longitudinal research underlines the role of all the different agents producing the affect vibes generated in tourism spaces (Haraway, 2003). Likewise, researches by Gordon Waitt et al. (2014) and Buda (2015) offer examples and analysis of affective and emotional relationships that are triggered in the touch between both human and non-human bodies. However, while the affect theory has previously been applied to exploring encounters among human and non-human animals (Tucker & Shelton, 2018; Veijola et al., 2014), dark tourism routes (Buda, 2015) and affects that shape the ambiences of tourist places (Cuthill, 2007; d'Hauteserre, 2015; Noy, 2008), there is less guidance available to understanding the affective life of objects, such as gifts and souvenirs (Cave & Buda, 2018; Haldrup & Larsen, 2006; Hokkanen, 2017; Lund et al., 2018; Ren, 2011) .

The article proceeds by unfolding meaningful, affective events over the past four years. The narrative starts in 2016 when Outi travelled to Kiruna, Sweden, where she bought the yarn as a souvenir for herself. The story continues with reflections on knitting, gift giving and a discussion of how care as an affect is present in often surprising situations. Needless to say, there are plenty of non-human actors that entangle us with places and to other members of the Earth. Lastly, we conclude with how the mittens have emerged in unpredictable ways around our actions and different events and how they have created multiple affects, with movement, vitality and encounters of their own.

Autoethnographic narrative

This narrative of the green and white mittens is written using the autoethnographic approach. We have sought guidance from previous autoethnographic studies on affect and emotions, for instance, in the context of family voluntourism (Germann Molz, 2017) and family holidays (Noy, 2008), adventure guiding (Mackenzie & Kerr, 2013a, 2013b), site-specific dancing (Barbour & Hitchmough, 2014) and conducting fieldwork (Hokkanen, 2017). In addition, we follow Stewart's (2005, pp. 135–136) thought of how, by giving the souvenir a narrative, it offers deeper meanings, attaches the object to the origin and creates an experience for the possessor. Most significantly, we have followed Philip Vannini's (2015b) writings on non-representational research methodologies that encourage us to focus on relationships that are not quite graspable. Engaging with non-representational research means replacing the idea of representation with striving to give life to non-humans and being on the move. It encourages us to 'hear the world and make sure that it can speak back' (Thrift, 2008, pp. 18–20). Vannini's (2015b) ethnographic field journey to an off-grid cabin in the Arctic tundra in Canada has encouraged us to focus on the partiality, immediacy, proximity, fluidity and reflexivity in our writings.

Autoethnographic data were collected over two and a half years, between summer 2016 and winter 2019, and written in field notes, email exchanges, personal journals, knitting notes and photographs. We have chosen to re-tell the story by remaining loyal to chronological emergence, 'aha' moments and 'eureka' experiences (see Edelheim, 2015; van Manen, 1990, p. 26) and the recognition and interpretation of different entanglements, emotions and affects (see Haldrup & Larsen, 2006). This is in line with the focus of non-representational research on events that shape our relationships and reveal old and new potentialities for collective 'being, doing and thinking' (Anderson & Harrison, 2010, p. 19 as cited in Vannini, 2015a, p. 7). So, instead of observing handicrafts and tourism from a distance, we use the autoethnographic approach and hold on to the knitting needles and become part of the phenomenon we wish to understand (see Maydell, 2010). We agree with Vannini (2015b), Manning and Adams (2015) and Spry (2001) that autoethnography and 'thick description' allow us to see our experiences both as the process and outcome of the research (Ellis et al., 2010; Ellis & Bochner, 2000) and the search for the unconscious thoughts that can affect our ability to see and experience things (Thrift, 2008). In other words, autoethnography allows us to research the embodiment and affective touch of the mittens – how our bodies understand the meanings of the mittens before the words even enter our minds (Törmä, 2015, p. 14). Our hope is that our style of writing will create all kinds of affect, ranging from joy to irritation, just as souvenirs may do.

Origins of the yarns – Outi

I knit outside of a Sámi church in Jukkasjärvi in northern Sweden. I have already been in the Kiruna region for three days, participating in a Nordic Knitting Symposium – Nordiskt Sticksymposium – to collect data for my PhD project (the Danish organisation, Gavstrik, organises the Nordic Knitting Symposium yearly). Almost 150 enthusiastic handcrafters have gathered here to learn new methods in workshops, to buy materials for future crafts, to visit local shops and, not least, to enjoy the midnight sun. Today we took a bus to the village of Jukkasjärvi, where we are spread around the church yard, most of us knitting and enjoying the sunshine. A guide arrives to tell us more about the church and we take our belongings with us, walking slowly indoors. A cold breeze welcomes us and invites us to hide on the benches; it is nice to sit down away from the warm sun for a while. After a moving speech about the history of the church and the stories of the paintings and bodies buried under the floor, a Sámi man walks in and starts singing us *yoiks* (a traditional Sámi way of singing) that he has written himself (Figure 1). Chills go through me. Memories of the events during the last three days come to mind: how welcoming the atmosphere has been even though I am new to this group of people, how a lecture hall full of knitters has affected me and how emotionally empowering this trip has been (see Brennan, 2014; d'Hauteserre, 2015; Törmä, 2015). I feel that I finally belong somewhere: in this place with other knitting enthusiasts.

During this trip I have had the chance to visit an exhibition of the work of Erika Nordvall Falck, called *Samiska Marknadsvantar - Fancy Mittens,* in the Kiruna Town hall, where I took a picture of a pair of beautiful green and white 'kaffebönor' (coffee bean) mittens, that reminded me of my friend, Emily, and her research on tourism in coffee-growing communities (Höckert, 2018a). The picture will become a part of my narrative from the holiday (Edelheim, 2015; Noy, 2008; Stewart, 2005). In the town hall, I have also had the chance to watch other artisans showing off their skills. Most importantly, I have been able to take part in workshops where I have learned new ways of knitting and making jewellery from different materials. These workshops have particularly affected me due to the nature of embodied actions that has happened in them; the touch of the material, learning new techniques for cutting fabric and concentrating on the lectures, to name just a few. The affect needs embodiment, as both Thrift (2008, p. 116) and Buda (2015) argue. I have also bought yarn that is produced by a Sámi company named Stoorstålka, which advertises itself as doing designs 'by Sámis, for Sámi people and equally cool souls' as a physical souvenir. The yarn has attracted me with its colours and origins, and it will certainly give me a connection to this place (see Peters, 2011; Timothy, 2005). All the souvenirs from this trip, both mental and physical ones, are allowing me to be in this world, to experience and to feel objects through my body (see Thrift, 2008, p. 239). The feeling of belonging somewhere and the embodied, emotional experiences will surely make the memories of this journey last a long time (see Sirgy et al., 2011).

By reflecting on the experiences of the day more carefully and writing notes in my travel journal (see Noy, 2008), I can see that I have been participating in many different forms of craft tourism. In craft tourism, places and experiences are understood via embodiment and physical emotions (see Haldrup & Larsen, 2006). Accordingly, actions are interpreted through the bodies, which respond well to Risatti's (2007, p. 179) explanation of craft's relationship to the body: ' ... craft objects are by their very nature intended to be physiologically functional, they are objects made for the body and bodily actions ... '. On occasions like these, tourism is usually defined as creative tourism, which has been discussed in tourism studies (see Richards, 2011) Richards & Wilson, 2006;. Creative tourism can refer to something special, like bungee jumping (Richards, 2011), but on this occasion I would rather refer to this trip as craft tourism, as there are embodied actions, emotions and affects which offer a fruitful basis to discuss what the essential elements in tourism are (see, e.g., Aho, 2001; Ritchie & Zins, 1978). Nevertheless, in both definitions tourists actively involve themselves in tourist services – and interacting with places and others – instead of merely watching and

Figure 1. Knitting in the Jukkasjärvi church. Source: Outi's personal file.

interpreting the culture via a guide, something for which cultural tourism has been criticised (Richards & Wilson, 2006). In other words, in craft tourism, tourists can do souvenir shopping, visit museums and galleries, see artisans working and touch material elements in workshops (see Pitkänen, 2005; Richards & Wilson, 2006) and feel the crafts through their bodies.

Knitting the mittens – Outi

Autumn has turned to October and it is raining outside. I go through my yarn box and discover the multi-coloured skeins of Stoorstålka yarn: they have been hiding from me for some months already. Only by looking at the yarn, do I remember the days I spent in Kiruna and Jukkasjärvi, the kaffebönor-pattern, my emotions and embodied feelings and the beautiful scenery in Swedish Lapland (see Peters, 2011). I also remember how being together with all the knitting enthusiasts filled the journey with joy (see Brennan, 2014). The narrative of the souvenir starts taking shape in my head (Stewart, 2005). I take the green and white skeins of yarn out of the box and visualise the mittens made in the kaffebönor pattern for Emily. Our friendship had begun six months earlier, when we started to prepare a grant application for a project on indigenous tourism in the Arctic. If I use the yarn that I bought from Kiruna, I could knit together human and non-human actors (see Thrift, 2005, p. 233) and the pattern, the colours and the origin of the thread would hold a story behind them – the mittens would be a hand-made souvenir from this time of working with the project and becoming close friends. Moreover, they would add one more level to our friendship and possibly new connections and ways of thinking for both of us (Thrift, 2008).

I make a cosy place on my sofa, wrap a warm woollen blanket around myself and cast on the first rows of the mittens. There are many unfinished objects in my project bag (knitters call them 'UFOs'), but I just want to knit these for Emily. The pattern looks so cute and is haunting me so that I cannot do anything else. I can thank my grandma for the ability to knit, she had a real talent with knitting needles. Knitted objects used to be taken for granted, but the image is (luckily) changing and knitting is nowadays seen something of a chance to emancipate both men and women, and a part of popular culture (Turney, 2009, pp. 2, 9; del Vecchio, 2006; see also STT Info, 2019). There are many workshops, seminars, knitting festivals and craft fairs that people can attend, where they can mobilise themselves and be together with others. In recent research by the Finnish craft organisation, Taitoliitto (2018), knitting is gradually gaining more interest. Making crafts and knitting are nowadays seen as ways to bring positive effects to our lives. This can be seen as moving towards a more relaxing mental and physical space where we can relieve stress, ease the chaos in our minds and regain focus – not only for knitting, but also for life itself (Rauhala, 2019, pp. 205–206; see also Pöllänen, 2015). Knitting also gives multiple meanings to life. Although these are personal and changing all the time, the meaningfulness is the most important reason to do crafts (Kouhia, 2016). It is easy to agree with these studies, as knitting not only makes me calm and brings balance to my otherwise quite hectic lifestyle, but also gives meaning to my life itself (see Pöllänen, 2015; Rauhala, 2019, p. 206).

After a few hours on the sofa, the first rounds of fair isle pattern with a beautiful 3 D-effect are ready: the mitten starts to take the shape of a material object. I stroke the pattern with my hands, feeling the warmth of the wool and admiring the pattern at the same time. It seems unclear when and, more exactly how, a pair of mittens actually materialises. How can I make sure that I will pass these embodied experiences on to Emily so that this pair of mittens does not hold only a symbolic value for her, as Hitchcock and Teague (2000) argue? I want to reveal the experiences behind the object (Stewart, 2005, p. 133), transform 'the mental into the material within the context of tourism' (Noy, 2008) as the whole process of knitting these mittens has brought more possibilities for thinking and understanding – both of myself and of souvenirs (2008, p. 175; Stewart, 2005; Thrift, 2005). By giving Emily something that she can use when she travels here to Lapland, by telling the story behind the mittens and by sharing the embodied experiences I had with them, I can only hope that the mittens can create similar affects in her as they have done for me (see Barbour & Hitchmough, 2014; Barron, 2019; Stewart, 2005; Thrift, 2008).

Mittens as happy objects – Emily

I wake up to a blinking phone, which delivers birthday wishes from my family back home. Inhaling the divine smell of the coffee, I climb down the steep wooden stairs. We have gathered at Keropirtti, a log-house on the outskirts of the Pyhä fell in Finnish Lapland, for a research seminar and to write our project application on culturally sensitive tourism. This is a sacred place that allows us researchers to slow down our thinking and let our ideas become entangled (see, e.g., Rantala et al., 2018; Veijola et al., 2014). Indeed, I am so excited about being here that I could have easily forgotten my birthday. However, by the kitchen door I realise that my colleagues would not have allowed me to forget. They have lit candles on the breakfast table; a big strawberry cake is waiting for me; there is a greeting card and even a present wrapped in colourful paper. I lift the card, which is a quite typical tourist postcard in Finnish Lapland. Under the text 'Life is Good' there are two smiling men with missing teeth, wearing Sámi clothing. I appreciate the ironic banality of the card, which insists that there are multiple layers that must be acknowledged (see Morton, 2010, p. 17). I wave the card and state that it looks like our forthcoming project on cultural sensitivity is timely.

I remove the ribbons, thinking how fortunate I am to have a job and friends like these. I am carefully taking off the tapes, peeking inside the wrappings and seeing something green. Indeed, this the first encounter between the green and white mittens and me (Figure 2). I hug the mittens to my chest with tears of joy. I look at Outi to confirm that she has made these by herself, and she nods with a smile. I had often seen Outi knitting during seminars and meetings and admired the beautiful things she made. While she knits, the yarns travel through safe and caring hands and she follows the discussions with a peaceful and focused aura around her. Indeed, over the past few years I have seen more and more people knitting in conferences and lecture halls, which creates a cosy and calming ambience and, in Tucker and Shelton (2018, p. 67) words, 'a hopeful mood, or affect'. I have also heard Outi describing knitting as her 'yoga' (see also Turney, 2009, p. 216), which has encouraged me to relax and meditate with knitting).

I pour myself a big cup of coffee and cut a piece of my breakfast birthday cake. The mittens circulate around the heavy log table and it seems like everybody wishes to try them on and feel their smooth surface (see Waitt et al., 2014). We pose questions for Outi and she shares with us memories from her trip to Kiruna, the story of the patterns and details about the bright green and snow-white yarn bought on the same journey. While the story of 'my mittens' – my souvenir from this trip – begins here, Outi's memories reveal how the mittens have already been living a long, adventurous life without me. It is all these stories that make the mittens more meaningful and precious: that the pattern, the colours and the origin of the thread hold a story behind them. It is the narrative and our relationship with Outi that enables me to

Figure 2. The green and white mittens. Source: Outi's personal file.

have my personal relationship with the mittens, because without it these mittens would be only a piece of wool (Stewart, 2005, p.137). It is valuable to become attuned and sensitised towards the multiple ways that these kinds of non-human-actors mobilise, spread and entangle stories and create new affects beyond tourist destinations (van der Duim et al., 2017; see also Cave & Buda, 2018; Tsing, 2015).

Sitting at the end of the table with my new mittens and the peculiar greeting card, I feel I am holding some very happy objects. I have previously been reading the world-famous Japanese tidying expert Marie Kondo's (2014) book, where she encourages and motivates people to stick with things that 'spark joy' in our homes and lives. While Kondo's advice is based on feeling, the phenomenology of happiness can help us to explore and evaluate more specifically how our bodies turn and relate to those things that we find joyful and delightful; that is, how those objects affect us (Ahmed, 2010a, p. 23). Sara Ahmed's *The Promise of Happiness* (2010b, p. 21) suggests that happiness puts us in intimate contact and proximity with objects. Then – and this seems central to hand-made handicrafts – when happiness creates its objects and such objects are passed around, they accumulate positive affective value as a social good (Ahmed, 2010b; Rauhala, 2019). In Ahmed's critical analysis on how objects become happy, affect is treated as something 'sticky'; that is, in here 'affect is what sticks, or what sustains or preserves the connection between ideas, values and objects' (Ahmed, 2010a, p. 230). In this case, we can ask whether handicrafts like these become affective, joyful, happy and sticky due to the multiple meanings we give to them and stories that they carry with them (see also Edelheim, 2015)?

When I put the mittens on, I get an intense sensation of receiving a hug. Not a passionate one, but a hug that calms me and makes me feel safe. I think of non-representational theorists who encourage us to open research and theorising to more joy, action and imagination (Thrift, 2008, pp. 18–20). Hence, instead of treating the green and white mittens merely as happy objects with symbolic qualities, non-representational theory encourages us to give life, to boost aliveness, to the supposedly inanimate, to non-human actors. From the perspective of non-representational writers, these mittens are active, and it is through their doings, qualities, movements and force that they exert their life (Vannini, 2018, pp. 5–7). What become interesting here are the relations and entanglements between this pair of active mittens and our bodies with their affective capacities (see Vannini, 2018, p. 5). It sounds like what Donna Haraway (2016) describes as nurturing (unlikely) kinships between bodies, materialities, things and ideas.

Mittens that care – Outi

The same evening, at the log-house, we continue to discuss the mittens' journey to this point. Just to make the journey more concrete and visible, I turn one of the mittens inside out. The fair isle pattern, looked at from the wrong side with its overlapping yarns, can be understood as a place which holds knowledge about the destination, culture, pattern, memories and relationality and, at the same time, it allows us to dig deeper into the affects, embodied actions and the stories they whisper into our ears (Buda, 2015; Cave & Buda, 2018; Thrift, 2005, 2008). Haldrup and Larsen (2006) discuss the fact that, understanding the collaboration between embodied actions and material objects is a crucial element of tourism activities; tourists do not only see things, we always act at the same time, we have our bodies with us. Moreover, our bodies interact with those of others – the guide, other tourists, locals – and there is a need to adapt to the movements of others (Risatti, 2007, p. 198; see also Veijola & Jokinen, 1994). Thrift (2008, p. 176) explains that emotions and affect usually come from the outside, like settings for different events. However, in craft tourism, and especially in those cases when crafts are done as a touristic activity, the affects emerge in relation to the handicrafts. It is as if the handicrafts can trigger affects of care, while we care for them (Puig de la Bellacasa, 2017).

In this way, craft tourism could be seen as travelling to experience how humans and non-humans take care of each other in tourist destinations (Höckert, 2018b) and bringing home ideas, inspiration, skills and things (like mittens and other hand-made souvenirs) that enhance caring relations, even at home (cf. Peters, 2011). Maybe craft tourism could also be understood as a phenomenon in which care is always present; not only tourists caring for each other, but also the host caring for guests, and – most importantly – locals caring for the human and non-human members of their community (see d'Hauteserre, 2015; Kenning, 2015). Many art-related projects have been criticised for lacking continuity, but if the knowledge and enthusiasm come directly from the community, the engagement in the activities is higher (Kenning, 2015). Maybe tourists participating in craft activities can help locals to understand the value of the cultural heritage of their own community, as discussed in Markwick (2001) and Miettinen (2007). This leads back to Sara Ahmed's (2010b) ideas about accumulating positive thinking via happy objects.

The next day, I feel joy when I see Emily wearing the mittens, just as I did when I saw tears of happiness in her eyes when she opened the present. At this point I can confess to Emily that I had been a little bit scared to give the mittens to her. I was worried about whether she would appreciate my mittens as much as I do (Turney,

2009, pp. 27–28) and feel the care that the mittens share (Puig de la Bellacasa, 2017, p. 70). Now, when I am watching her wearing the mittens, I understand that the caring agency toward the mittens has moved from me to her. I can no longer touch and feel the warmth of the mittens, but I can only hope that the narrative of the mittens, that consists of warmth, love and friendship, filling the mental and physical needs of both the receiver and giver, will travel with them (see Stewart, 2005, pp. 136–137) and show and practise care without using words (Pöllänen, 2015).

On careful touch – Emily

'Have any of you seen my mitten?' I shout. 'You know, the green and white mittens that Outi made...' I add, with anxiety in my voice.

It feels as if I have already looked for it everywhere. I dive into the box where we keep the woollen things, while squeezing the right-hand mitten towards my chest. I comfort my bare left hand with the lonely mitten. I slip my feet into a pair of too-big shoes without tying the shoelaces. I rush with clumsy steps through the snow, hoping that I will find the mitten from the car (see Tucker & Shelton, 2018). I gaze along the path, trying to see if I have dropped it somewhere in the snow. However, in that case a thick layer of new snow would already have covered it.

The mitten has overnighted under the passenger seat. Walking back to the house with lighter steps, I think of the latest occasion when one of our neighbours acknowledged their spreading positive mood. I had proudly told them about where the yarn had come from, about the pattern and about who was a real knitting-wizard. Moreover, I implicitly tried to slip in some information about the richness and vitality of Sámi handicrafts, which are constantly being revitalised and modernised (see Stewart, 2005). There have also been many times when the mittens have accompanied me to the neighbouring forest. On these occasions, I have thought about whether the mittens may feel more at home among all the different shades of green. I have also remembered my visit to the wonderful Museum of Anthropology in Vancouver, where a woman discussed the difference between First Nations' handicrafts that are in use and those that are in the museums – how those hanging in the museums seem so lifeless, as if they had lost their vitality (see Rantala et al., 2020). This made me realise that, by trying to protect the mittens by not using them, by not allowing them to travel, I would reduce their vitality. As if not touching them would deny or reduce their ability to care.

I have often experienced feeling as if it were impossible to describe how special these mittens are. As if others saw them as just another pair of replaceable gloves, or as 'ornamentation', as Thrift (2008, p. 239) says. After being frustrated a few times about the non-stickiness (Ahmed, 2010a) of their happy story, I had come to realise and embrace the difficulty of representing or sharing an affect in a concise, pre-determined form (see Hokkanen, 2017; Thrift, 2008). Because isn't it so with affect – just as with care, beauty, love and kindness – that it keeps escaping words? It is an experience, a feeling, like a thought without having a thought (Morton, 2010; see also Hokkanen, 2017; Höckert, 2018b; Zylinska, 2014), the unsaid or the barely sayable (see McCormack, 2002 as cited in Vannini, 2015a, p. 9), something that we are destined to fail to capture (Vannini, 2018, p. 7). Or as Felicity Coleman (2005; see also Grit, 2014, p. 124) puts it so well, while affect is a knowable product of an encounter, 'it is also as indefinite as the experience of a sunset, transformation or a ghost'.

Coleman (2005) describes affect as 'the change or variation that occurs when bodies collide or come to contact'. Non-representational scholars, as Vannini (2015a, p. 9) describes, can examine affect as the body's capacity to be moved and affected – and the body's capacity to move and affect. Puig de la Bellacasa (2017, p. 95) seems to agree about how the affective engagements of caring invoke involved, embodied, embedded relations (see also Waitt et al., 2014). Hence, could it be that transmitting the meaningful story of the mittens, enabling others to think and know through these mittens, falls short without having experienced a personal 'touch'? This is what Stewart (2005) suggests; we need physical encounters. It seems like touching and being touched is the best example of ontological and epistemic relationality where the boundaries between the self and the other have been blurred (Waitt et al., 2014, pp. 95–96). Drawing on Sara Ahmed and Jackie Stacey's (2001) ideas in *Thinking through the Skin*, Puig de la Bellacasa (2017, p. 96) argues that asking what it means to touch and to be touched, or to move and to be moved, deepens our 'awareness of the embodied character of perception, affect and thinking'. She suggests that by thinking with touch, we can inspire our sense of connectedness and problematise dualistic divisions between subjects and objects, self and other, affects and facts and those who care and those who are being cared for (Puig de la Bellacasa, 2017, p. 97).

Towards new patterns – Outi

- 'Hi there. Sorry for calling this late, but I have bad news. You'd better sit down.'
- 'Ok … What is it?'
- 'I lost the mittens. Both of them. I must have left them in a church in Jukkasjärvi. I had to run to the bus and could not turn back to go looking for them. I am so sorry! I was visiting that beautiful church there, at the end of the road. The one with colourful paintings of Sámi culture. Next to the Museum and Café Sámi. I think you have also been there, haven't you?'

I hear Emily's voice on the phone and my face breaks into a big smile. My mind travels to a beautiful summer day two and a half years ago when I spent a day in that same church. In a few seconds, I am no longer seated at the kitchen table but sitting and knitting on the church bench. Could it be that the mittens had returned home? I hear Emily asking whether she should try to contact the church to see whether someone could send the mittens to her. Then she apologises once more. Despite her challenge of coping without mittens in minus 30-degree Celsius temperatures in the Arctic (see also Vannini, 2015a, p. 113), I note that we could see this as a sign. Perhaps the mittens have inspired us enough, made us think beyond the representation. Now it is time for them to move on, to take care of someone else and whisper their stories to others. That particular church in Jukkasjärvi is a great place to leave them, because around that area most of the people recognise the coffee-bean pattern and will

Figure 3. The book about fancy mittens. Source: Outi's personal file.

respect them. I want to believe that if the mittens wanted to leave now, this was the perfect place to get separated from the owner[1].

This narrative of the mittens has allowed us to explore the intensive entanglements in meanings and matter between handicrafts, places and humans, and we have wished to join the ongoing discussions about relational ethics in tourism research where agency, relationality and ability to care are not limited to the social lives of humans (Grimwood, 2015; Rantala et al., 2020; Ren et al., 2017; Veijola et al., 2014). Although the yarns of these green and white mittens are knitted and knotted in tidy ways, they have kept entangling as we have allowed their response-ability. They have travelled to places and been present at different events, like the Nordic Tourism Symposium in Alta, Norway, where we stood proudly in front of a crowd of tourism researchers telling about the caring, travelling mittens while wearing Icelandic sweaters (known as 'lopapeysias' – another good example of craft tourism), as a token of thankfulness for all the inspiration we have received from our Icelandic colleagues' research on more-than-human-actors in tourism (see Jóhannesson & Lund, 2017a, 2017b; Lund, 2005; Lund et al., 2018).

As the mittens share their stories with others, they keep creating new affects in our daily lives (see Barron, 2019). The mittens have opened up a discussion about the role of embodied experiences in craft tourism, the stories behind the hand-made souvenirs and the care embedded in material objects. Moreover, this journey we have taken together has shaped our personal lives – we no longer take pieces of material for granted, and we have become more curious about the stories of the knitted objects. Every mitten, sock or jumper that we knit holds a story behind it. Sometimes the journey is taken together, sometimes the paths will be parted. But eventually, the material objects do become part of a life-long journey filled with memories of certain moments.

***

Just before writing the last lines of this article, Erika Nordvall Falck (2018) book *Fancy Mittens - Markkinavanthuita* arrives by mail (Figure 3). I quickly scan the pages, admiring the beautiful photos of the mittens and reading some of the stories of fancy mittens. When I turn to the last pages of the book, I see the pattern of those coffee-beans I made for Emily. I laugh with disbelief; this cannot really be true: the pattern is here given the same name as Emily's daughter! As if it were Emily's daughter's pattern. It seems that the pattern is really haunting us, and this story of the mittens has truly been full of surprises (see Mackenzie & Kerr, 2013b). I send a text message to Emily about the mittens' name and she instantly replies: 'This is a sign: you shall knit new mittens for my entire family'.

Note

1. While it may sound like the disappearance of the mittens is only a staged happening, we can assure readers that it happened for real. The mittens were way too precious to be sacrificed for science.

Acknowledgements

We are grateful to the reviewers of Tourism Geographies whose constructive and inspiring comments helped us rewrite and improve our story. Wholehearted thanks to the entire ARCTISEN-team and the Northern Periphery and Arctic -programme. Special thanks to our dear colleagues Monika Lüthje and Heli Ilola for all the inspiring talks, and the research community at the Multidimensional Tourism Institute at the University of Lapland. Moreover, thanks to University of Lapland for supporting Outi's travel to Kiruna, Sweden. We also want to express our gratitude to all of you who have given us encouraging feedback in conferences. Sincere thanks to Emily's previous colleagues at the Linnaeus University for discussions around non-representational theory, and to ILA-group at the University of Lapland for careful co-exploration of intra-living in the Anthropocene. Finally, thanks to the yarns that keep tying us together.

Disclosure statement

No potential conflict of interest was reported by the author(s).

ORCID

Outi Kugapi 🆔 http://orcid.org/0000-0003-2347-7963

References

Ahmed, S. (2010a). Happy Objects. In M. Gregg & G. J. Seigworth (Eds.), *The affect theory reader* (pp. 29–51). Duke University Press.

Ahmed, S. (2010b). *The promise of happiness*. Duke University Press.

Ahmed, S., & Stacey, J. (2001). *Thinking through the skin (transformations); thinking through feminism*. Routledge.

Aho, S. K. (2001). Towards a general theory of touristic experiences: Modelling experience process in tourism. *Tourism Review, 56*(3–4), 33–37. https://doi.org/10.1108/eb058368

Anderson, L. (2006). Analytic Autoethnography. *Journal of Contemporary Ethnography, 35*(4), 373––395. https://doi.org/10.1177/0891241605280449

Barbour, K., & Hitchmough, A. (2014). Experiencing affect through site-specific dance. *Emotion, Space and Society, 12*, 63–72. https://doi.org/10.1016/j.emospa.2013.11.004

Barron, A. (2019). More-than-representational approaches to the life-course. *Social & Cultural Geography*, 1–24. https://doi.org/10.1080/14649365.2019.1610486

Brennan, T. (2014). *The transmission of affect*. Cornell University Press.

Buda, D. (2015). *Affective tourism: Dark routes in conflict*. Routledge.

Buda, D., d'Hauteserre, A., & Johnston, L. (2014). Feeling and tourism studies. *Annals of Tourism Research, 46*, 102–114. https://doi.org/10.1016/j.annals.2014.03.005

Cave, J., & Buda, D. (2018). Souvenirs in dark tourism: Emotions and symbols. In *The Palgrave handbook of dark tourism studies* (pp. 707–726). Palgrave Macmillan.

Coleman, F. (2005). Affect. In A. Parr (Ed.), *The Deleuze dictionary* (pp. 11–14). Columbia University Press.

Cuthill, V. (2007). Sensing and forming hospitalities and socialities of tourist places: Eating and drinking out in Harrogate and Whitehaven. In J. Germann Molz and S. Gibson, (Eds.), *Mobilizing hospitality. The ethics of social relations in a mobile world* (pp. 83–100). Ashgate Publishing.

d'Hauteserre, A.-M. (2015). Affect theory and the attractivity of destinations. *Annals of Tourism Research, 55*, 77–89. https://doi.org/10.1016/j.annals.2015.09.001

del Vecchio, M. (2006). *Knitting with balls: A hands-on guide to knitting for the modern man*. DK Publishing.

Edelheim, J. R. (2015). *Tourist attractions: From object to narrative*. Channel View Publications.

Ellis, C., Adams, T., & Bochner, A. (2010). Autoethnography: An overview. *Forum Qualitative Sozialforschung/Forum: Qualitative Social Research, 12*(1), 1–18. http://www.qualitative-research.net/index.php/fqs/article/view/1589/3095

Ellis, C., & Bochner, A. P. (2000). Autoethnography, personal narrative, reflexivity: Researcher as subject. In N. K. Denzin, & Y. S. Lincoln (Eds.), *Handbook of qualitative research* (pp. 733–769). Sage.

Germann Molz, J. (2017). Giving back, doing good, feeling global: The affective flows of family voluntourism. *Journal of Contemporary Ethnography, 46*(3), 334–360. https://doi.org/10.1177/0891241615610382

Graburn, N. H. H. (2005). Foreword. In M. Hitchcock & K. Teague (Eds.), *Souvenirs: The material culture of tourism* (pp. xii–xvii). Ashgate Publishing.

Grimwood, B. S. R. (2015). Advancing tourism's moral morphology: Relational metaphors for just and sustainable Arctic tourism. *Tourist Studies*, *15*(1), 3–26. https://doi.org/10.1177/1468797614550960

Grit, A. (2014). Messing around with Serendipities. In S. Veijola, J. Germann Molz, O. Pyyhtinen, E. Höckert, & A. Grit (Eds.), *Disruptive tourism and its untidy guests. Alternative ontologies for future hospitalities* (pp. 122–141). Palgrave MacMillan.

Haldrup, M., & Larsen, J. (2006). Material cultures of tourism. *Leisure Studies*, *25*(3), 275–289. https://doi.org/10.1080/02614360600661179

Haraway, D. (2003). *The companion species manifesto: Dogs, people and significant otherness.* Prickly Paradigm Press.

Haraway, D. (2016). *Staying with the trouble: Making Kin in the Chthulucene.* Duke University Press.

Hitchcock, M., & Teague, K. (2000). *Souvenirs: The material culture of tourism.* Ashgate Publishing.

Höckert, E. (2018a). *Negotiating hospitality: Ethics of tourism development in the Nicaraguan Highlands.* Routledge.

Höckert, E. (2018b, August 20–24). *Thinking with Care [Keynote]. Critical Tourism Studies North America (CTS-NA) II: Critical connectivities and caring communities across borders.* Thompson Rivers University.

Hokkanen, S. (2017). Analyzing personal embodied experiences: Autoethnography, feelings, and fieldwork. *The International Journal of Translation and Interpreting Research*, *9*(1), 24–35. https://doi.org/ https://doi.org/10.12807/ti.109201.2017.a03

Jóhannesson, G. T., & Lund, K. A. (2017a). Aurora Borealis: Choreographies of darkness and light. *Annals of Tourism Research*, *63*, 183–190. https://doi.org/10.1016/j.annals.2017.02.001

Jóhannesson, G. T., & Lund, K. A. (2017b). Creative connections? Tourists, entrepreneurs and destination dynamics. *Scandinavian Journal of Hospitality and Tourism*, *18*(sup1), S60–S74. https://doi.org/10.1080/15022250.2017.1340549

Jokinen, E., & Veijola, S. (1997). The disoriented tourist. The figuration of the tourist in contemporary cultural critique. In C. Rojek & J. Urry (Eds.), *Touring cultures. Transformations of travel and theory* (pp. 23–51). Routledge.

Kenning, G. (2015). "Fiddling with threads": Craft-based textile activities and positive well-being. *Textile*, *13*(1), 50–65. https://doi.org/ https://doi.org/10.2752/175183515x14235680035304

Kim, S., & Littrell, M. A. (2001). Souvenir buying intentions for self versus others. *Annals of Tourism Research*, *28*(3), 638–657. https://doi.org/10.1016/S0160-7383(00)00064-5

Kondo, M. (2014). *The life-changing magic of tidying up: The Japanese art of decluttering and organizing.* Ten Speed Press.

Kouhia, A. (2016). *Unraveling the meanings of textile hobby crafts* [Doctoral Dissertation]. Digital Repository of the University of Helsinki. http://urn.fi/URN

Lorimer, H. (2005). Cultural geography: The busyness of being 'more-than-representational'. *Progress in Human Geography*, *29*(1), 83–94. https://doi.org/10.1191/0309132505ph531pr

Lund, K. A. (2005). Seeing in motion and the touching eye: Walking over Scotland's mountains. *Etnofoor*, *18*(1), 27–42. http://www.jstor.org/stable/25758084

Lund, A. K., Kjartansdóttir, K., & Loftsdóttir, K. (2018). Puffin love": Performing and creating Arctic landscapes in Iceland through souvenirs. *Tourist Studies*, *18*(2), 142–158. https://doi.org/10.1177/1468797617722353

Mackenzie, S. H., & Kerr, J. H. (2013a). Can't we all just get along? Emotions and the team guiding experience in adventure tourism. *Journal of Destination Marketing & Management*, *2*(2), 85–93. https://doi.org/10.1016/j.jdmm.2013.03.003

Mackenzie, S. H., & Kerr, J. H. (2013b). Stress and emotions at work: An adventure tourism guide's experiences. *Tourism Management*, *36*, 3–14. https://doi.org/10.1016/j.tourman.2012.10.018

Manning, J., & Adams, T. E. (2015). Popular culture studies and autoethnography: An essay on method. *The Popular Culture Studies Journal*, *3*(1–2), 187––222. http://commons.lib.niu.edu/handle/10843/14754

Markwick, M. C. (2001). Tourism and the development of handicraft production in the Maltese islands. *Tourism Geographies, 3*(1), 29–51. https://doi.org/10.1080/14616680010008694

Maydell, E. (2010). Methodological and analytical dilemmas in autoethnographic research. *Journal of Research Practice, 6*(1), M5. http://jrp.icaap.org/index.php/jrp/article/view/223/216

Miettinen, S. (2007). *Designing the creative tourism experience: A service design process with Namibian craftspeople* [Doctoral dissertation]. University of Art and Design Helsinki.

Morton, T. (2010). *The ecological thought.* Harvard University Press.

Nordvall Falck, E. (2018). *Fancy mittens.* Lumio.

Noy, C. (2008). The poetics of tourist experience: An autoethnography of a family trip to Eilat. *Journal of Tourism and Cultural Change, 5*(3), 141–157. https://doi.org/10.2167/jtcc085.0

Peters, K. (2011). Negotiating the 'place' and 'placement' of banal tourist souvenirs in the home. *Tourism Geographies, 13*(2), 234–256. https://doi.org/10.1080/14616688.2011.569570

Pitkänen, A. (2005). Matkailu käsityöllisen hyvinvointitoiminnan mahdollisuutena [Tourism as a possibility for creative wellness]. In M. Kälviäinen (Ed.), *Käsityö – yrittäjyys – hyvinvointi. Uusia liiketoimintapolkuja. [Crafts – entrepreneurship – wellness. New ways for business].* KTM Publications. http://ktm.elinar.fi/ktm_jur/ktmjur.nsf/All/7387C9AE067D33D0C2256FF1003FCDCB/$file/jul9-touko_2005_netti.pdf

Pöllänen, S. H. (2015). Crafts as leisure-based coping: Craft makers' descriptions of their stress-reducing activity. *Occupational Therapy in Mental Health, 31*(2), 83–100. https://doi.org/10.1080/0164212X.2015.1024377

Puig de la Bellacasa, M. (2017). *Matters of care. Speculative ethics in more than human worlds.* University of Minnesota Press.

Rantala, O., Salmela, T., Valtonen, A., & Höckert, E. (2020). Envisioning tourism and proximity after the anthropocene. *Sustainability, 12*(10), 3948. https://doi.org/10.3390/su12103948

Rantala, O., Höckert, E., Garcia-Rosell, J. C., & Haanpää, M. (2018). A message from conference organisers. In *TEFI10 Conference,* Pyhä, Finland. https://www.ulapland.fi/loader.aspx?id=b9f0bf31-d107-46b1-b9c0-9b7b9cc6a638

Rauhala, A. (2019). *Neulonnan taito [The skill of knitting]* [Doctoral dissertation]. University of Helsinki]. http://urn.fi/URN

Reed-Danahay, D. E. (1997). Introduction. In D. E. Reed-Danahay (Ed.), *Auto/ethnography: Rewriting the self and the social* (pp. 1–17). Berg Publishers.

Ren, C. (2011). Non-human agency, radical ontology and tourism realities. *Annals of Tourism Research, 38*(3), 858–881. https://doi.org/10.1016/j.annals.2010.12.007

Ren, C., van der Duim, R., & Jóhannesson, G. T. (2017). *Co-creating tourism research: Towards collaborative ways of knowing.* Routledge.

Richards, G. (2011). Creativity and tourism. The state of art. *Annals of Tourism Research, 38*(4), 1225–1253. https://doi.org/10.1016/j.annals.2011.07.008

Richards, G., & Wilson, J. (2006). Developing creativity in tourist experiences: A solution to the serial reproduction of culture? *Tourism Management, 27*(6), 1209–1223. https://doi.org/10.1016/j.tourman.2005.06.002

Risatti, H. A. (2007). *A theory of craft: Function and aesthetic expression.* University of North Carolina Press.

Ritchie, J. R. B., & Zins, J. R. M. (1978). Culture as determinant of the attractiveness of a tourism region. *Annals of Tourism Research, 5*(2), 252–267. https://doi.org/10.1016/0160-7383(78)90223-2

Sirgy, M. J., Kruger, P. S., Lee, D.-J., & Yu, G. B. (2011). How does a travel trip affect tourists' life satisfaction? *Journal of Travel Research, 50*(3), 261–275. https://doi.org/10.1177/0047287510362784

Spry, T. (2001). Performing autoethnography: An embodied methodological praxis. *Qualitative Inquiry, 7*(6), 706–732. https://doi.org/10.1177/107780040100700605

Stewart, S. (2005). *On longing. Narratives of the miniature, the gigantic, the souvenir, the collection.* Duke University Press. 9th printing in paperback, original version 1993.

Sthapit, E., & Björk, P. (2019). Relative contributions of souvenirs on memorability of a trip experience and revisit intention: A study of visitors to Rovaniemi, Finland. *Scandinavian Journal of Hospitality and Tourism, 19*(1), 1–26. https://doi.org/10.1080/15022250.2017.1354717

STT Info. (2019). *Nyt tulee äijäneulonta - Novitan YouTube-videolla jäyhät miehet tarttuvat puikkoihin*. [Here comes manly knitting – In Novita Youtube video men take knitting needles to their hands]. https://www.sttinfo.fi/tiedote/nyt-tulee-aijaneulonta—novitan-youtube-videolla-jayhat-miehet-tarttuvat-puikkoihin?publisherId=66964509&releaseId=69852117

Taitoliitto. (2018). *Käsitöiden harrastaminen Suomessa 2018*. [Handicrafts as a hobby in Finland 2018]. https://www.taito.fi/wp-content/uploads/sites/5/2018/11/K%C3%A4sit%C3%B6iden-harrastaminen-Suomessa-kyselyyhteenveto_taitofi.pdf

Thrift, N. (2005). *Beyond mediation: Three new material registers and their consequences*. In D. Miller (Ed.). Materiality. Duke.

Thrift, N. (2008). *Non-representational theory. Space, politics, affect*. Routledge.

Timothy, D. J. (2005). *Shopping tourism, retailing, and leisure*. Channel View.

Törmä, T. (2015). *Oma ruumis ja kerronnan kaari: Merkityksen muodostuminen Maurice Merleau-Pontyn ruumiinfenomenologisen ja Paul Ricoeurin narratiivisen imaginaatiokäsityksen mukaan*. [The body and storytelling: Constructing the meaning with Merleay-Ponty's phenomenological perception and Paul Ricoueur's narrative imagination]. Suomalainen Teologinen Kirjallisuusseura.

Tsing, A. L. (2015). *The mushroom at the end of the world: On the possibility of life in capitalist ruins*. Princetown University Press.

Tucker, H., & Shelton, E. J. (2018). Tourism, mood and affect: Narratives of loss and hope. *Annals of Tourism Research, 70*, 66–75. https://doi.org/10.1016/j.annals.2018.03.001

Turney, J. (2009). *The culture of knitting*. Berg.

van der Duim, R., Ren, C., & Jóhannesson, G. T. (2017). ANT: A decade of interfering with tourism. *Annals of Tourism Research, 64*, 139–149. https://doi.org/10.1016/j.annals.2017.03.006

van Manen, M. (1990). *Researching lived experience: Human science for an action sensitive pedagogy*. State University of New York Press.

Vannini, P. (2015a). Non-representational research methodologies. An introduction. In P. Vannini (Ed.), *Non-representational research methodologies. Re-envisioning research* (pp. 1–18). Routledge.

Vannini, P. (2015b). Enlivening ethnography through the irrealis mood. In search of a more-than-representational style. In P. Vannini (ed.), *Non-representational research methodologies. Re-envisioning research* (pp. 112–129). Routledge.

Vannini, P. (2018). *Doing public ethnography: How to create and disseminate ethnographic and qualitative research to wide audiences*. Routledge.

Veijola, S., Germann Molz, J., Pyyhtinen, O., Höckert, E., & Grit, A. (2014). *Disruptive tourism and its untidy guests. Alternative ontologies for future hospitalities*. Palgrave MacMillan.

Veijola, S., & Jokinen, E. (1994). The body in tourism. *Theory, Culture & Society, 11*(3), 125–151. https://doi.org/10.1177/026327694011003006

Veijola, S., & Jokinen, E. (2008). Towards a hostessing society? Mobile arrangements of gender and labour. *Nora - Nordic Journal of Feminist and Gender Research, 16*(3), 166–181. https://doi.org/10.1080/08038740802279901

Waitt, G., Figueroa, R. M., & Nagle, T. (2014). Paying for proximity: Touching the moral economy of ecological voluntourism. In M. Mostafanezhad & K. Hannam (Eds.), *Moral encounters in tourism* (pp. 167–181). Ashgate Publishing.

Zylinska, J. (2014). *Minimal ethics for the anthropocene*. Open Humanities Press.

Conclusion: Affective railway journeys in an age of extremes

Matilde Córdoba Azcárate

The ideas shaping this book on tourism, affect and emotion started in a train journey. In this conclusion, I come back to its main contributions also from a train journey and the embodied affects and emotions that drove it and that, in turn, it generated too. My observations resonate deeply with the main message of this book – the urgency to place affects and emotions as well as their politics at the center stage of tourism research, planning and practice. As Germann Molz and Buda assert in the book's introduction, "tourism geographies register as emotional and affectual geographies" and as such, tourism scholars and practitioners should aim to comprehend them. In this short conclusion, I also take the opportunity to reflect on tourism, emotions and affects in the contexts of abjection and ruination marked by the pandemic, war, ecological crisis and renewed patterns of urban touristification. These are contexts largely enabled and routinely shaped by infrastructures, affects and imagination that have tourism at their core.

In what follows, I start like Germann Molz and Buda, from an autobiographical note. I do so with the intention to bring the reader's body and emotions into the story as well as importantly to offer, from the personal, a window into larger contemporary social processes that might resonate with other histories and stories. As Hartman (2008, p. 7) puts it, the personal journey is a privileged avenue "to tell a story capable of engaging and countering the violence of abstraction" that so often permeates academic writing.

***

After almost ten years of living abroad, I rode the train again in Europe in August 2022. This time it was not for duty but for pleasure, on a small backpacking trip with my family. We were not the only ones on the move. We added to the thousands of travelers that European cities have received this summer after international travel restrictions eased in late June. For my children, used to the car-centric culture of San Diego, California, where we live, this was their first train travel experience. Despite service disruptions, early mornings, summer agglomerations, the heat and sometimes, the absence of seats, they were mesmerized with the experience. For me, who grew up riding public transportation, used to train commutes, the summer railway journey felt this time, equally appealing.

Traveling by train my body felt relatively at ease. These are two sensations, being on the move and being comfortable, or feeling contented, that I had long learned to disassociate. The railway journey was free from the various individual decisions, the emotional labor and solitude one experiences when traveling by car. It lacked the amplified and torturing security procedures, hypervigilance and anxiety-driven protocols that plane travel means today. Thankfully, it also lacked that uncomfortable feeling of not being in total control of the travel experience, your body or belongings. Furthermore, traveling by train I did not feel as environmentally guilty for being on the move. I knew train travel is a more sustainable means of transportation than the car and the plane, and this understanding lifted part of my anthro-travelers' guilt (Taranath, 2019).

I experienced what many transportation scholars, historians and mobilities scholars have already shared about train travel. That the railway journey, even with the structural class inequalities and old privileges it materializes, is also generative of a unique form of being in interconnectedness and relatedness to place and people that no other means of transportation can so democratically generate (Bisell, 2010; Spalding & Fraser, 2012; Schivelbusch, 2014; Urry, 2007). I had not felt these interconnectedness and relatedness, this overall well-being, in a while whilst being on the move. For a few days, I let myself savor them. In letting go, I was able to witness my kids developing a sense of rootedness and of place-attachment to the landscapes that informed their parents' family histories – landscapes and histories foreign to them due to transoceanic migration. That attachment continues to flourish today, miles away, through shared memories, mementos, conversations, photographs and the re-reading of travel diaries.

Just a few weeks back from that train trip, at home in San Diego, I sit re-reading Germann Molz and Buda's introduction to this book. Smiling but with certain sadness, definitively a pinch of nostalgia for summer days and life in the cities where I grew up. I cannot avoid but feeling intimately connected to the authors' train travel experience. I feel as if I could have been riding that train with both of them, back then, pre-pandemic, kids free, my body entangled with all the same vibes and sounds and movements that they describe. Suffocated and frustrated at times with conversation, the random passing of snacks down the aisle, the videogame music, the chit chat on the phones among passengers. Then a release, rocked by the train's rattle and captivated by the landscape outside once some bodies disembark and silence ascends. So much of what they describe as the *atmosphere* of their train travel experience was still the same this first summer post-pandemic – if we might call it that way.

And yet, our train experiences are over three years apart. In the midst, a global pandemic, Russia's war in Ukraine, a deadly scorching sustained extreme heat wave in Europe, a large migratory and humanitarian crisis and cities all around the world turning back to summer tourist masses "just like before". These are some of the elements characterizing the affective geographies of today's travel: geographies of ruination and abjection (Navarro, 2012) informed by new emotions and affects, certain disorientation and what seemed to be a heavy awareness, a recognition or mutual understanding that things as we knew them were definitively changing.

Permeating these emotions there was a striking placidity, almost joyful, stemming from a common disposition that seemed to claim "let's do it now before we cannot do it ever again" – because of the war, because of climate change, because of COVID-19 or a new virus – that filtered conversations inside the trains. This disposition has been described in social media and recently among researchers with the word "revenge travel", a form to retaliate at COVID-19 and COVID-19-related travel restrictions, by making up for the time lost and booking trips and traveling just for the love of it (Wang & Xia, 2021). In the summer of 2022, however, this description felt not entirely accurate.

A deep awareness of contemporary socio-political, economic and ecological events seemed to punctuate, to regularly rupture this joy and to morph it into something else that was not properly a revenge or a practice that had to do just with tourism. This something else was not speaking to the intransitive worlds of one's affections but rather to the political capacity of those affects (Stewart, 2007). It was a mixture of feelings grounded and informing a much larger political atmosphere of solidarity, anger, distress and despair.

Among these events punctuating yet sustaining the shared joy, there was, on the one hand, the urgent, not always verbalized, solidarity with Ukrainian refugees. This was a solidarity emerging from a war context. It was present in all train stations, most with designated spots informing about the gratuity of tickets, free food and clothing and with volunteers picking up refugees and/or collecting aid items on the spot. On the other hand, there was also a generalized indignation with the rising prices of tickets and amenities as well as with shrinking services and shortages of personnel. These practices seemed to scream: corporate control is here to stay at the cost of suffering workers, your pockets and your own bodies – extenuated, thirsty, enraged. Refugees, strikes and upset consumers, yet consumers after all, seemed to mark the contours of this new affective geography regulating summer travel and its atmospheres. There was also still relative apprehension with COVID-19. This uneasiness was augmented through the dissonance between ubiquitous printed posters urging passengers to wear masks and the information people gathered online about changing policies, the aleatory enforcement by authorities and fellow passengers and awkward looks and silent changes of seats and carriages when detecting a passenger with a persistent cough or runny nose. At a more embodied level, in most train stations it transpired the absolute certainty that the trains that one was about to ride were not ready to handle the summer excessive heat and that the journey ahead would be indeed a sweaty, sticky one.

These factors anchored the travel experience in and within an emotional and affectual geography that transcended the individual tourist experience but that was deeply informed by traveling itself and the infrastructures that make travel possible. Furthermore, they crafted what felt as a shared, embodied form of apprehension regarding a future which announced itself to be blatantly apocalyptic.

In the train, an apocalyptic future was already present through the windows showing brush fires and huge patches of dry, yellowed landscapes due to the absence of rainfall. It was present in the chit chat of passengers and their red-faced and sweaty bodies trying to generate some air under impossible conditions. In the persistent coughs of some, it was audible in passenger's radio or phone conversations where the rising temperatures, an unanticipated change of route, the price of the ticket or a new Russian bombardment were heatedly discussed. And, if it was not the heat itself, loud announcements in some of the stations and trains' megaphone systems made even the more absent-minded passenger instantly physically present.

Train announcements advised passengers not to board trains unless they were carrying water with them. They showed us how to recognize the effects of heat exhaustion in our own bodies and urged us to help other passengers that showed signs of it by clearly indicating what to do and how to help them out of the train. The messages automatically transported me to those science fiction scenarios where despite all warnings that the world is about to end, that things are about to change, life for some keeps going as usual.

The way in which these, at points, ominous train window views, conversations, messages and body dispositions were combined with welcoming aboard messages and the announcement of the next train stops corroborated an already here future of melting roads, rails and runways. It was at times overwhelming, certainly conducive to what experts have described as climate anxiety or eco-anxiety (Panu, 2022). The news reported accordingly. In June and July, the World Health Organization reported that almost five thousand people died from heat-related causes in Spain, Portugal, Germany and Britain (with almost two thousand alone in the Iberian Peninsula). In July, runways heated up so much that they started to lift at London Luton Airport. All across Europe trains were heavily delayed or canceled because the heat had distorted rails and companies and governments had to impose speed controls to prevent permanent damages. In August, train travelers in Spain were engulfed by wildfire, some jumping out of windows to escape and generating an intense political debate over the way the train company and the government issued warnings and communicated actions to each other and to passengers.[1] Deadly, extreme situations and talk of collapse.

And yet, despite the too proximate war, heat waves and transportation meltdowns, tourists kept flocking to European destinations, over-crowding cities once more. According to the Washington Post this has been "the busiest summer travel season in a generation".[2] Cruises, flights, more cruises and more flights. Despair. Agglomerations. And also, new urban measures: pre-book entries and increased fees, turnstiles and quotas to enter cities such as Venice or highly touristified spaces such as the houses of Gaudí in Barcelona and the Sainte-Chapelle in Paris. With these measures, there were also a lot of warnings to exercise one's emotions before, during and after the travel, mostly, to educate travelers to be mindful of themselves, of others and of residents. "Take a breath and lower your expectations" read USA Today in early June 2022,[3] "practice gratitude", "take breaks" and a lot of messages in social media, news and printed boards and pamphlets encouraging people to "check in with their bodies" – to avoid anxiety and overwhelm, heat strokes or panic attacks. These were all signs and examples of Berlant's (2011) cruel optimism at work in an age of extremes and new catastrophic futures articulated through the naturalization of dystopian structures of feeling (Urry, 2007).

During the trip and now some time after, I wondered how do different people attune to this simultaneous and intensely related reality of post-COVID-19 travel, war, climate apocalypse and tourists' unsustainable crowds. The railway journey in between the largely tourist cities of London, Paris and Barcelona made clear for the most common traveler that tourism and tourists mobilities were such a big player in heating up places – metaphorically and literally. Train travel, with its pauses and rhythms, with its breakdowns, heightened this shared awareness. Many travelers we spoke with this summer told us that they chose to travel by train because it was more environmentally sustainable, because they cared – about the planet, about the future. They also complained about excessive prices and the absence of coordinated public responses when services broke down. Only those with relative economic and cultural capital, with access to technologies such as smart phones, were fast to re-act and find alternative journey plans, the rest remained anxiously waiting for things to get fixed.

What will happen if train travel becomes only available to the privileged ones? This is already visible in the corporate privatization of railways and trains in the UK, for example, where prices of tickets have skyrocketed. Is privatization the only way forward to make (train) travel possible for human bodies under conditions of extreme heat? After this summer railway journey, I wonder to what extent is the heat, the war, the masses and the uncomfortable bodily sensations it creates, being weaponized against public infrastructures and the commons. I wonder up to what point the affects these geographies inform are politically used to legitimize interventions that favor only a few, for the sake of the whole. How do we go toward the future like this? What kind of cities and what kind of urban fabrics are needed to sustain our desires to travel for pleasure under such affective geographies? Shouldn't we withhold from traveling at all? What affects, emotions and feelings would withholding *en masse* need and entail? And, if we choose to keep going as usual, for how long would existing infrastructures hold up with current environmental conditions, more crowds, more precarious labor? Would these heated, failing infrastructures and the uneven political responses they are prompting induce a loss of affection, solidarity and connection? How effective can emotions of joy, revenge, fear and hope that inform our contemporary travel experiences be to mobilize citizens to political action? These among others are some areas of potential future research that might be useful in order to comprehend the workings of the emotional and affectual geographies that traveling and tourism so adamantly contribute to generate.

Notes

1. www.wired.com/story/europe-transport-heat-wave-solutions/ Accessible at: https://www.wired.com/story/europe-transport-heat-wave-solutions; and Kirby, P. (2022, August). Spanish fires: Passengers injured fleeing train in Bejís. *BBC News*, (17 August 2022). https://www.bbc.com/news/world-europe-62574732
2. Elliot, C. (2022, August). Pro tips for finding a little space on vacation. *The Washington Post*, (10 August 2022). Accessible at: https://www.washingtonpost.com/travel/2022/08/10/pro-tips-finding-little-space-vacation/
3. Elliot, C. (2022, June). Coping strategies for crazy 2022 travel season: take a breath and lower your expectations. *USA Today*, (17 June 2022). https://www.usatoday.com/story/ travel/advice/2022/06/17/summer-travel-2022-how-to-cope-stress/7633167001/

References

Berlant, L. (2011). *Cruel optimism*. Durham: Duke University Press.

Bissell, D. (2010). Passenger mobilities: Affective atmospheres and the sociality of public transport. *Environment and Planning D: Society and Space, 28*(2): 270–289.

Hartman, S. (2007). *Lose your mother: A journey along the Atlantic slave route*. Durham: Duke University Press.

Navarro, Y. (2012). *The make-believe space: Affective geography in a postwar polity*. Durham: Duke University Press.

Panu, P. (2020). Anxiety and the ecological crisis: An analysis of eco-anxiety and climate anxiety. *Sustainability, 12*(19): 7836.

Schivelsbusch, W. (2014). *The railway journey. The industrialization of time and space in the nineteenth century*. Oakland: University of California Press.

Spalding, S. and Fraser, B. (2012). *Trains, literature, and culture: Reading/writing the rails*. Maryland: Lexington Books.

Stewart, K. (2007). *Ordinary affects*. Durham: Duke University Press.

Taranath, A. (2019). *Beyond guilt trips: Mindful travel in an unequal world*. Minnesota: Between the Lines.

Urry, J. (2007). *Mobilities* London: Polity Press.

Wang, J. and Xia, L. (2021). Revenge travel: Nostalgia and desire for leisure travel post COVID-19. *Journal of Travel & Tourism Marketing, 38*(9): 935–955.

Index